Information Systems for Business

AN EXPERIENTIAL APPROACH

Edition 3.0

France Bélanger
Virginia Tech

Craig Van Slyke
Louisiana Tech University

Robert E. Crossler
Washington State University

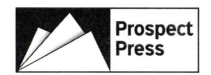

Founded in 2014, Prospect Press serves the academic discipline of Information Systems by publishing essential and innovative textbooks across the curriculum including introductory, emerging, and upper-level courses. Prospect Press offers reasonable prices by selling directly to students. Prospect Press provides tight relationships among authors, publisher, and adopters that many larger publishers are unable to offer. Based in Burlington, Vermont, Prospect Press distributes titles worldwide. We welcome new authors to send proposals or inquiries to Beth.golub@prospectpressvt.com.

Editor: Beth Lang Golub
Production Management: Scribe Inc.
Cover Design: Annie Clark

eTextbook:
Edition 3.0
ISBN: 978-1-943153-46-6
Available from Redshelf and VitalSource

Printed Paperback:
Edition 3.0
ISBN: 978-1-943153-47-3
Available from Redshelf

For more information, visit
https://prospectpressvt.com/titles/belanger-information-systems-for-business/

To all the students who have inspired us
FB, CVS, and REC

To my parents, who never stopped believing in me,
and to Pierre, the rock of my life
FB

To Tracy, who brought life to my existence,
and to Maggie, Dallas, and Fred for all the joy their antics bring
CVS

To Crystal and my children, who bring such joy and purpose to my life.
Thanks for encouraging me through the process of creating this edition of the text.
REC

About the Authors

Dr. France Bélanger, *Virginia Tech* France Bélanger is the R. B. Pamplin Professor and Tom and Daisy Byrd Senior Faculty Fellow in the College of Business at Virginia Tech. Dr. Bélanger has been teaching information systems (IS) for more than 25 years in the United States, as well as in Canada, Ethiopia, Portugal, and New Zealand. She has published several books and articles on IS education-related topics, including a highly cited book on distance learning. She has won several international awards, including the 2008 IEEE Education Society Research Award. Dr. Bélanger is a proponent of learner-centered approaches to IS education and has developed a number of tools and materials to facilitate such learning. She led numerous workshops related to education, learner-centered teaching, and mentoring. She currently teaches information systems classes to undergraduate, graduate, and executive students, in addition to teaching IS research seminars to PhD students.

Dr. Craig Van Slyke, *Louisiana Tech University* Craig Van Slyke is the Mike McCallister Eminent Scholar Chair in Computer Information Systems at Louisiana Tech University. Prior to joining Louisiana Tech, he was dean and professor of computer information systems at the W. A. Franke College of Business at Northern Arizona University. Dr. Van Slyke has more than 20 years of university teaching experience, primarily in the area of information systems. He has published extensively on information systems education and has coauthored four IS textbooks. Dr. Van Slyke is on the editorial review board of the *Journal of IS Education* and has held leadership positions in Southern Association for Information Systems and Association for Information Systems Special Interest Group on Education. In addition, he has applied the principles of learner-centered education to a variety of courses, including the Introduction to IS course for undergraduates and the Core IT course for MBA students.

Dr. Robert E. Crossler, *Washington State University* Robert E. Crossler is an assistant professor of information systems at Washington State University. Dr. Crossler has more than 10 years of university teaching experience, primarily in the area of information systems. He has published on information systems education and facilitated innovative teaching workshops. In addition, he has applied the principles of learner-centered education to a variety of courses, including the Computer Concepts course for freshman, the Introduction to IS course for juniors and seniors, the Core IT course for MBA students, database courses at the undergraduate and master's levels, and information security courses at the undergraduate level.

Contents

Appendices

Note that the following appendices are included in the e-textbook only. The appendices are also posted at the title's website at https://prospectpressvt.com/titles/belanger-information-systems-for-business/student-resources-3e/. Users of the printed textbook can freely access the appendices at the website.

Appendix A: Computer Hardware

Appendix B: Computer Software

Appendix C: Access Fundamentals

Appendix D: Advanced Access

Appendix E: Advanced Database Concepts

Appendix F: Excel Fundamentals

Appendix G: Advanced Excel

Appendix H: Networking Basics

Appendix I: Security and Privacy

Appendix J: Funding Information Technology

Appendix K: Managing IS Projects

Preface

Mission/Purpose

An interesting paradox often exists in introductory information systems courses. Information systems touch almost every aspect of students' lives, yet students are often detached and uninterested in the introductory course. Often they do not see the point of taking such a class, unless they are information systems majors. This book is meant to generate an interest in information systems for everyone by taking a learner-centered approach, providing experiential learning activities and reflection questions throughout the book. In addition to being effective in terms of learning outcomes, learner-centered education is also more satisfying for the learner. The focus of a learner-centered class is on a learner-teacher partnership with shared responsibility for learning. The method not only introduces important concepts but also deepens the learning through active application of the concepts and reflection upon what has been learned. The learner-centered approach fits well with the characteristics of millennial-generation students, who are team oriented, value continuous learning, and seek frequent feedback.

The purpose of the book is to engage students while helping them become intelligent consumers of information. The book puts information center stage to allow the relevance of information systems to be put into context, thus increasing student interest. Our goal is to help students understand that they will be using information throughout their personal and professional lives. Information systems not only produce information but also help us make better use of information. By focusing on information rather than systems, students are grounded in the end goal and are better able to understand why knowledge of information systems is important. This translates into greater engagement; students are more engaged when they understand the relevance of what they are learning.

Target Audiences and Approach

The book is primarily directed at students who are taking the Introduction to IS course as juniors or seniors, or even first-time non-IS master's students. Students who are not IS/IT majors often fail to see the value in the course, especially if the course is traditionally structured and focused on conceptual knowledge. Our approach to this text is based on our experience in reaching these students. Allow us to describe two experiences that have helped shape our approach.

I (Van Slyke) was asked to teach a junior-level Introduction to IS course in a large-section format (200+ students per section). The first semester was somewhat of a disaster. It was the first time I had ever received evaluations below the mean. For the next semester, two changes were made. One change was to add a third exam. The more meaningful change was to have an activity in every class meeting. Instead of a 75-minute lecture, each meeting had an activity approximately halfway through the class. The activities typically lasted 5 or 10 minutes. After the activity, I led a discussion based on the activity. For example, during the class on supply chain management, students were asked to get into groups of two or three and come up with three ways in which supply chain management (SCM) systems and enterprise resource planning (ERP) systems are similar and three ways in which they differ. During the activity, my fellow instructor and I (the course was team taught, although I was primarily responsible for the lectures) would wander around the auditorium answering student questions. We knew we had a winner when we saw many students flipping back through their notes on ERP, which had been covered a few weeks earlier. After the activity, I would ask students to share their findings. The findings were insightful and showed a solid grasp of the basic concepts of *both* SCM and ERP systems. The results of the more active, learner-centered class sessions were remarkable. Not only did students perform better on the exams, but our evaluations went up almost a full point on a five-point scale. A nice side benefit was that class sessions were much more enjoyable for the students and the instructors.

On a different level, I (Bélanger) was asked to take over and improve our Introduction to Information Systems master's course targeted at master of accountancy (and a few MBA) students. For years, the students had been complaining about the course, which is a requirement for completion of their degree. When I first taught the class, I quickly realized that the students did not want to be there and did not care about the content. I did bring in cases, as I had used the case approach in most of my master's classes. I quickly realized that the case discussion went well but that the remainder of the "lecture" material was pretty much lost on them. In redesigning the class for the second semester, I decided to include "practice" slides for every subtopic, resulting in shorter lectures and "practice" elements throughput. The most obvious impact was that students really wanted to know why certain things happened when they acted on some technology-related issue, be it developing a privacy policy, testing their computer's security, or finding information about an emerging technology. The resulting discussions were animated, and the students came to class, even though I made attendance nonmandatory! The most blatant example of the impact of practice on student interest is the first exercise of the semester (Chapter 1), where students have to spend five or six hours without using any information technology and then blog about it. I am always surprised every time to see the depth of their realization about the importance of IT in their lives . . . and in their future careers. It starts the semester on a very different foot than what I had experienced with the traditional lecture (and case) approach.

These experiences led us to embrace a learner-centered, active approach in all our classes (both graduate and undergraduate). Such an approach seems to be especially effective for today's students. They seem to appreciate being an active participant, rather than a passive vessel, in the learning process.

Key Features of the Book

The book is designed to support an active, learner-centered approach, with the guiding model of "praxis," or putting learning into practice. Students learn best when they actively apply their learning rather than simply learn to parrot facts and concepts. The book facilitates a learning cycle of "learn-do-reflect," which closely follows the ideas of experiential learning.

To ensure continued relevance, the book will be updated on a frequent basis, since information technologies and the use of information in business will continue to evolve. An important feature of the book is that it is concise but complemented with substantial additional (optional) material in the Appendices. The conciseness of the book helps students who today are used to receiving information in small chunks; they live in a world of Facebook wall postings, tweets, and text messages. Forty- and fifty-page chapters, filled with details, are incongruent with their world. As a result, we offer tightly focused, concise chapters that provide the necessary information without being bogged down in unnecessary detail. Students will actually fill in many of the details themselves through the active learning exercises and online materials. Our goal is to help students understand how to utilize information systems rather than just regurgitate facts. As such, the chapters are not meant to give every detail on every topic but rather to provide broad guidelines for students to explore the topics of interest.

The activities and content of the text embrace a constructivist perspective to learning. We try to connect the new information to what most students will already know, either from general life experience or from material covered earlier in the course. For example, the SCM/ERP activity described above connected the new SCM concepts to the ERP concepts covered earlier in the course.

In the text, we implement the concepts of experiential learning in the following ways:

- *Concise, focused chapters:* Textbooks often try to cover all possible aspects of a topic. While this is appropriate for many courses, in the introductory course, we believe it is better to focus on key information. Because of this, our chapters are concise and focused.

- *Focusing stories:* Each chapter opens with a focusing story accompanied by focusing questions that ask students to reflect on the story. This approach helps students ground the content in a concrete example. It also demonstrates the relevance of the material, which increases student engagement. The topics are specifically chosen to be relevant and understandable to most students.

- *Designed for active learning:* For each major topic, we provide activities that are designed to help students deepen their learning through application.

- *Reinforcing end-of-chapter materials:* Each chapter provides additional learning activities and reflection and review questions that help students synthesize the various concepts in the chapter. There are three types of reinforcing elements. Review questions are straightforward questions designed to help students check their declarative knowledge of the material. Reflection questions require deeper thinking. Many of these questions require synthesis of multiple concepts. Additional learning activities are active-learning exercises that reinforce the material in the chapter through application and synthesis.

- *Detailed instructor's manual:* An important element of this book is the instructor's manual, which provides guidance to instructors on how to use the book in various settings and on how to apply the learning-centered approach to the material provided in the chapter. The instructor's manual provides detailed teaching notes and suggestions regarding the duration of each section and learning activity.

- *Online resources for active learning:* Links to tutorial videos are available on the book's website (https://prospectpressvt.com/titles/belanger-information-systems-for-business/).

- *Cases:* Recommended cases from sources such as the Ivey Business School or the Harvard Business School are provided for some of the chapters so that instructors can also use this book in a case-based class.

Supplemental Materials

In addition to the instructor's manual, supplemental materials include test banks and slide decks. These resources are specifically designed to support the active-learning approach. In addition, there are test questions that are constructed to assess deeper levels of learning beyond simple declarative knowledge. The instructor's material is available at https://prospectpressvt.com/titles/belanger-information-systems-for-business/.

Changes in Edition 3.0

We are excited to provide this new edition, which has been created to provide up-to-date, relevant material in this ever-changing world of information systems.

Substantive detailed changes (beyond text editing) are identified below. Overall, we updated all statistics and links in every chapter, changed numerous business example boxes to include more current and relevant examples, and updated or changed most of the focusing stories and stats example boxes. We also created new focusing stories for some of the chapters and appendices. Several major topics were added, including mobile privacy, two-factor authentication, blockchain, ransomware, and bitcoins. Some outdated material was removed. We also updated the hands-on software activities and examples to the most recent versions of the relevant software. All URLs were verified and updated as needed. Finally, we created several new learning activities to provide instructors with more opportunities to apply the learner-centered approach in their classes.

Substantive Detailed Changes

- *Chapter 2:* The business example about Southwest Airlines was replaced with a more current discussion about Uber.

- *Chapter 4:* Learning activities and examples throughout the chapter were updated to more timely and student-relatable contexts.

- *Chapter 5:* The "Storing Data" section was updated to include a discussion of data lakes. The "Retrieving and Disseminating Data" section was updated to include data analytics.

- *Chapter 7:* Web 2.0 and 3.0 are now discussed together in this chapter. Learning activities were added to help students understand the modern Internet. Other outdated learning activities were removed or updated. Internet of Things was moved closer to the section on the Internet and the discussion of unified communications was removed.

- *Chapter 8:* This chapter was revised to provide a better discussion of how risk management is related to information security. A discussion about passwords and two-factor authentication has been added to the text. The malware section was updated to include polymorphic viruses and ransomware (and bitcoins). Other malware information that isn't as prevalent currently was removed. Discussion was added on biometrics for mobile devices and web and credit card security. Other text was updated with current examples to stay up-to-date with changing issues and trends in the world of security.

- *Chapter 9:* The focusing story was replaced to discuss students' perceptions that they can be anonymous online. Learning Activity 9.1 (Finding Mindy) was replaced with a new activity regarding smartphone privacy. Other examples and stories were replaced with more current stories and situations in which privacy has played a central role recently.

- *Chapter 11:* Business Example Box 11.1 was replaced with a discussion of Quicken Loans Rocket Mortgage.
- *Chapter 12:* The focusing story was updated to include new information regarding how Wal-Mart manages their supply chain. Learning Activity 12.3, which discusses blockchain and supply-chain management, was added.
- *Chapter 13:* Stats Box 13.2 was changed to focus on mobile phone ownership. The first additional learning activity was changed to focus on Alibaba.

Overview of the Content and Organization

The book is organized around three main sections of content. Section I provides introductory material, Section II focuses on topics related to managing information, and Section III discusses various uses of information. Section IV comprises a set of appendices that provide hands-on coverage of Microsoft Office tools and other topics that may be used to support and extend the main chapters.

Each chapter starts with a focusing story and includes learning activities for each major topic. The chapters all end with a summary of the chapter, review questions, reflection questions, additional learning activities, references, further readings (if applicable), and a glossary.

A brief summary of the chapters follows.

Section I: Introduction
Chapter 1: The Value of Information
Chapter 1 sets the stage for the rest of the book by discussing information and its role in business. The focus here is on understanding what information is and how it is used both personally and by businesses. We classify information use into three areas: communication, process support, and decision making. This provides the framework that is used throughout the book. We also discuss the wisdom hierarchy (data, information, knowledge, wisdom), which provides further grounding for students.

Chapter 2: Introduction to Information Systems
This chapter gives a high-level view of information systems. A brief overview of key systems concepts is also provided. This overview gives students the foundation knowledge necessary to better understand information systems. In addition, the chapter provides an overview of information and information systems as strategic resources. The chapter also builds a case for the importance of understanding information systems even if one is not an information systems professional.

Chapter 3: Evaluating Information
With the tremendous amount of information available today, it is especially important to be able to evaluate information. This chapter provides an overview of information quality and presents a methodology for evaluating information. Also, it discusses how to deal with information overload, information quality, and source credibility.

Chapter 4: Gaining Strategic Value from Information

The material in this chapter expands the concepts introduced in Chapter 1 to explore the strategic value of information. The chapter provides an overview of the key frameworks and concepts related to the role of information and information systems in the creation and maintenance of competitive advantage. The chapter includes popular frameworks that can be used to identify strategic initiatives and others that can be used to evaluate such initiatives. It also includes a discussion of whether competitive advantage can be sustained or not.

Section II: Managing Information
Chapter 5: Storing and Organizing Information

Databases are the core of information systems. Many business students have considerable experience with using information systems, but few have any understanding of the databases that sit at the core of these systems. This chapter serves two purposes. First, it introduces and provides a high-level overview of relational databases, database management systems, and data warehousing. The intent is to provide foundational knowledge that is useful for users rather than the in-depth knowledge necessary for IS professionals. Second, the chapter discusses how to retrieve information from databases and online resources. (Note that more detail regarding databases and database management systems is available in Section IV: Appendices.)

Chapter 6: Analyzing Information for Business Decision Making

Making good decisions requires information, but that is not enough. You must also be able to analyze information. In this chapter, we want to help you understand the basics of business-oriented decisions and the process by which they are made. In Chapter 14, you will learn about systems specifically designed to support decision making. Here the focus is on understanding more about the decision-making process and tools that can help you retrieve and analyze information as part of that process.

Chapter 7: Transmitting Information

This chapter covers basic networking concepts, including the Internet and Web. To demonstrate the relevance of the topics covered, the chapter opens with a discussion of cloud computing. The chapter concludes with considerations and tools for collaboration, which have become very important to business with their increasingly globally distributed workforce.

Chapter 8: Securing Information

This chapter provides an overview of information security concepts and issues and the technologies used to handle information security. This includes discussions of personal information security, security threats, security technologies, and approaches.

Chapter 9: Protecting the Confidentiality and Privacy of Information

This chapter gives an overview of information privacy and the technologies and techniques used to help protect information privacy. The ethics of privacy are also discussed. Issues are discussed from both the individual and organizational perspectives.

Section III: Using Information

Chapter 10: Developing Information Systems

In this chapter, we provide a high-level view of the information systems development process. We focus on the perspective of an end user who may be involved in the development process. We achieve this by helping students understand the goals, processes, and roles involved with systems development.

Chapter 11: Information-Based Business Processes

This chapter discusses how information supports business processes. The concept of a process is introduced, along with some familiar examples. Emphasis is placed on how information and its flow are critical to the successful completion of processes. In addition, the idea of redesigning processes to make use of information technology is discussed.

Chapter 12: Enterprise Information Systems

This chapter includes a general overview of enterprise information systems. ERP, supply chain management systems, and customer relationship management (CRM) systems are discussed. The chapter makes the point that virtually all business professionals interact with one or more of these systems. Examples of how each type of system is applied are also included.

Chapter 13: Information for Electronic Business

Because of its importance to individuals and businesses, we devote an entire chapter to e-business. Common e-business models are discussed. A brief discussion of e-government is also included.

Chapter 14: Information and Knowledge for Business Decision Making

Making good decisions requires good information and good decision-making processes, skills, and tools. This chapter ties together various elements of the book by showing how information is central to the decision-making process. The chapter provides students with an understanding of what is necessary for good decision making and introduces a decision-making methodology. Because ultimately an organization's only sustainable competitive advantage lies how its employees apply knowledge to business problems, in this chapter we discuss the concept of knowledge and various approaches to knowledge management.

Acknowledgments

Writing a book is always a major undertaking, and we are fortunate to have received the help of many individuals. First, we want to thank Richard Egan from the New Jersey Institute of Technology and Paul Witman from California Lutheran University for their help on identifying areas of improvement in the substantial changes made to this manuscript. We wish to thank Beth Lang Golub at Prospect Press and the publishing team at Scribe Inc. Also, thank you to the following individuals who responded to the User Survey to provide feedback for Edition 3.0:

Linda Jo Calloway, Pace University

Richard Egan, New Jersey Institute of Technology

Bob Gregory, Bellevue University

Beverly Kahn, Suffolk University

Joseph Pugh, Immaculata University

Radney Redd, Florida Southern College

Ali Vedadi, Mississippi State University

Paul Witman, Cal Lutheran University

We also are grateful to the following individuals for their insightful suggestions and ideas for prior editions of this text:

Mandy Yan Dang, Northern Arizona University

C. Matt Graham, University of Maine

Brian Hall, Champlain College

Mike Pangburn, University of Oregon

Dan Phelps, Carnegie Mellon University Qatar

David Reavis, Texas A&M Texarkana

Radney Redd, Florida Southern College

Gavin Yulei Zhang, Northern Arizona Universit

SECTION I

Introduction

CHAPTER 1

The Value of Information

Learning Objectives

By reading and completing the activities in this chapter, you will be able to

- Compare and contrast data, information, and knowledge
- Explain the concepts of connectedness and usefulness as they relate to information
- Name the skills required for information literacy
- Discuss the importance of information literacy in a business career
- Name and describe the three main uses of information in businesses
- Compare and contrast information systems careers and information analysis careers

Chapter Outline

Focusing Story: How Information Cost Me (a Lot of) Money
Learning Activity 1.1: The Rapid Growth of Information
Learning Activity 1.2: A Day in My Technology-Free Life
Data, Information, Knowledge, and Wisdom
Information Literacy
Learning Activity 1.3: How I Use Information
Uses of Information
Learning Activity 1.4: How Businesses Use Information
Information and Your Career
Chapter Summary
Review Questions
Reflection Questions
Additional Learning Activities
References
Glossary

This book is about information systems. Although it seems obvious, it is worth noting that there are two parts to "information systems": information and systems. All too often, people tend to get caught up in the "systems" part (the technology) and do not pay enough attention to the "information" part. But the information is really the critical part. If the information is not valuable, there is not much need for the system. Because of this, we begin the book by focusing on the value of information.

However, it is also important to understand that knowing about technology can help you better deal with information. Information technology helps us organize, locate, and use information. So while we start the book by focusing on information, much of the book helps you understand the technologies and systems that can help you deal with information.

FOCUSING STORY

How Information Cost Me (a Lot of) Money

Here's a personal story that illustrates the value of good information or, more accurately, the consequences of *not* having the right information. After running my own business for several years, I decided that it was time to try something different. One of my clients wanted to expand their use of computers to a new department and needed someone with my capabilities. Since they were one of my long-term clients, I knew the company and its employees quite well. The company and its needs were a good match for me, so I discussed the possibilities with the president of the company. He was very enthusiastic about my coming to work for him. At the end of our discussion, he asked me my salary requirements. I knew what salary I needed to meet my living expenses and I gave him a figure. He immediately agreed; I instantly knew I'd make a mistake, one that would cost me quite a bit of money. My mistake was in not gathering information on the market salaries for that particular type of job. Had I been armed with this simple bit of information, I could have increased my salary by at least 20%. That's quite a bit of money to leave on the table! The thing to remember about this little tale is that better information usually results in better outcomes.

While this might seem like a simple example, it illustrates how being "information deficient" can have serious consequences. The decisions that business professionals face every day often have significant impacts. Making good decisions requires having good information. With the rapid pace of today's business world, being successful in a business career requires being able to understand what information is required and being able to efficiently and effectively gather, evaluate, and analyze that information. Because of this, the theme of this book is information. We will help you understand information and the systems businesses use to deal with the vast quantity of information they generate and use. Our goal is for you to build the knowledge and skills you'll need to be successful in your career.

FOCUSING QUESTIONS

1. What were the consequences of not having competitive salary information?
2. Suppose I did have information on competitive salaries but that information was inaccurate. What are the possible consequences of having poor-quality information?

LEARNING ACTIVITY 1.1

The Rapid Growth of Information

Did you know that the amount of data and information around us is constantly increasing? Think about information that you have access to that you did not have five or even two years ago. As you do, watch this video then consider the questions that follow:

https://www.youtube.com/watch?v=uqZiIO0YI7Y

1. How does the rate of change in information affect us?
2. Do you think the data in this video is current? Why?
3. What does this mean to you as finish school and embark on a career?

LEARNING ACTIVITY 1.2

A Day in My Technology-Free Life

Most of us interact with information technology (IT) throughout the day, although we may not always be aware of it. Some uses of IT are relatively obvious, such as using email or surfing the Web. Others are not readily apparent, such as texting a friend or using a debit card. Your assignment is to go one half day (six hours when you are awake) without using any information technology and then write a short paper reflecting on the experience. Here are a few of the things you *won't* be able to use:

Facebook, email, or the Web (Don't even turn on your computer!)

Text messaging

Debit or credit cards (unless the merchant uses an old-fashioned imprint machine)

Smartphone applications (apps)

And many, many others

You need to time this so that you will not have any issues with completing assignments from this or other classes. Also, if there is an emergency that requires your use of IT, disregard this assignment and deal with the emergency. It may also be a good idea to inform those with whom you communicate regularly, such as family and close friends, that you are going without information technology. This may prevent them from thinking it is an emergency when you are not answering text messages.

At the end of the half day, prepare a one- to two-page reflection paper that addresses the following questions:

1. What did you learn from your experience?
2. What technology was the most difficult to live without?
3. What kinds of tasks were the most difficult to complete without technology?

Data, Information, Knowledge, and Wisdom

Consider the following question. Is 62 good or bad? Of course, this is a meaningless question, but why is this so? The number 62 is an item of **data** (or datum), but it lacks any real meaning. Let's combine 62 with some other bits of data. Maybe 62 is the score you received on an exam. Perhaps it is the score you need to receive on your final exam to retain an A in a class. When we combine the original data with other related data, we now have **information** that helps us interpret whether 62 is good or bad. Once we have the meaningful information, we need to interpret it in order to determine what actions should be taken. (In our example, you might decide to spend more time studying for the final exam in a class that you need a much higher score in.) When we apply information to some decision or action, we have **knowledge**. **Wisdom** involves using knowledge for the greater good. Because of this, wisdom is deeper and more uniquely human. It requires a sense of good and bad, right and wrong, ethical and unethical.

One way to think about this is to consider how data, information, and knowledge form a hierarchy. Data are raw symbols (unconnected facts), information is data that have been processed so that they are useful, and knowledge is when information is applied to some decision or action. Russell Ackoff (1989) popularized this concept, although the root of the idea goes back to part of T. S. Elliot's poem "The Rock":

Where is the Life we have lost in living?

Where is the wisdom we have lost in knowledge?

Where is the knowledge we have lost in information?

There are two reasons we bring up this hierarchy. First, it gives us a way to think about different kinds of systems and how they have evolved. Data processing is relatively straightforward. Handling information is messier. You need the capability to do ad hoc (e.g., specific, customized) queries to allow different views and combinations of data. Managing knowledge is messier still.

The hierarchy also parallels how businesses have applied **information technology**. In the early days, the focus was on processing data for relatively straightforward tasks, such as tracking payrolls or bookkeeping. This evolved into **information**

systems, which enabled users to connect and process data to help with management decision making. More recently, there has been movement toward being able to manage knowledge. Although it is hard to imagine, it is possible that we may see a day when technology helps us manage wisdom. This is debatable, since many consider wisdom to be uniquely human.

A second, and perhaps more important, reason to understand the hierarchy is that it helps frame two important concepts: connectedness and usefulness. The shift from data to information requires connecting data elements. Combining bits of data gives the data some context and meaning. This meaning may or may not be useful, though. To be useful, information is interpreted and applied (in other words, is used), leading to knowledge.

One last thought on the hierarchy is that when we reach the knowledge level, we often realize that we need more data and information. This creates a sort of cycle, as illustrated in Figure 1.1.

While it is useful to understand the relationships among data, information, and knowledge, it is more important to know how to deal with the tremendous amount of information available today. In other words, it is important to be information literate, which is the topic of the next section.

Information Literacy

What does it mean to be information literate? While there are a number of definitions of **information literacy,** it boils down to the ability to efficiently and effectively determine what information is needed and then access, evaluate, use, and manage that information in an ethical manner.

It may be hard to believe, but not that long ago, we had access to a much more limited amount of information. Then along came the Web, and today we're faced with a tremendous amount of information every day. While it is great to have access to almost unlimited information, this comes at a price; we must learn how to deal with

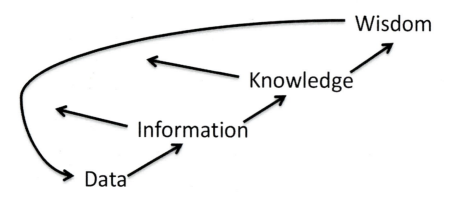

Figure 1.1 Data, Information, Knowledge, Wisdom Hierarchy

this information. Think about it this way: If you do not have any money, understanding investments and money management is not very important. But once you start to make a good living, you need to pay a lot more attention to these matters. It's great to have money, but the price is that you have to pay more attention to using it effectively. We are faced with a similar situation with respect to information; we're information rich, which has many advantages but requires more skill and effort if we want to use that information effectively.

Let's look at an example. In the "old days" (before the Web), if you wanted to buy a car, you might look at a couple of magazines for reviews and then go to two or three dealers to check their prices. You would also need to get quotes on your trade-in. This was all very time consuming and inefficient, and the information you gathered was incomplete. Today, the situation is very different. You can access multiple automobile reviews, get a good estimate of the value of your current car, and see the pricing of dozens of dealers—all without leaving home. There's a catch, though—you have to know what you're doing. You have to know what information you need, where to get that information, and whether that information is trustworthy. Then, since you will have so much information, you need to be able to manage and use it effectively. In other words, you need to be information literate.

Understanding how to deal with information may well have serious benefits as you move through your business career. There are many who believe that information literacy is *the* critical skill for the future. Ilene Rockman (2004), a leading authority on information literacy, put it well:

Individuals who are knowledgeable about finding, evaluating, analyzing, integrating, managing, and conveying information to others efficiently and effectively are held in high esteem. These are the students, workers, and citizens who are most successful at solving problems, providing solutions, and producing new ideas and directions for the future.

LEARNING ACTIVITY 1.3

How I Use Information

You might be surprised at the variety of different ways in which you use information every day. Take a few minutes to identify five ways in which you use information. For example, when deciding what to buy for lunch, you might use information about the restaurant's offerings, such as the descriptions and prices of the items. Try to come up with a range of decisions from simple to more complex. Then, for each one, rate the impact of having bad information as being a large, moderate, or small impact. After you have done this, compare your lists with another student. For each item, discuss why you rated the impact of bad information the way you did.

Uses of Information

All businesses, regardless of their size, use information for three main purposes: communication, process support, and decision making. When properly applied, information technology enhances all of these.

The *Merriam-Webster Dictionary* defines communication as "a process by which information is exchanged between individuals through a common system of symbols, signs, or behavior." This definition clearly shows that one use of information is to communicate. Organizations must exchange information for a variety of reasons, including sharing ideas, coordinating actions, and transmitting information to stakeholders. Chapters 8 to 10 deal with technologies that help with business communication.

Businesses also use information to support processes. A **business process** is a set of coordinated activities that lead to a specific goal or outcome. (Chapter 11 goes into much more depth regarding business processes.) Many business processes are quite complex and involve various parts of a business. For example, a customer order process might look something like Figure 1.2. (Note that this is a greatly simplified view.)

Information is used at each stage in the process. We need to know what products were ordered, whom the customer is, where to ship the order, how much the products cost, and so on. This information must be communicated and properly processed throughout the process. Without information, the process simply cannot be completed. **Information systems** can help streamline and improve the quality of business processes.

Businesses (and individuals) also use information for **decision making**. Decision making involves choosing among alternatives. Making this choice requires information about the alternatives (as well as other information). Put simply, you can't make decisions without information. For most of you, this is the main way in which you will use information. Because of this, quite a bit of this book is related to using information for decision making, including Chapters 6, 7, and 13.

Two other aspects of business information use are worth mentioning. First, some businesses actually use information as a product. For example, Google is a company that you are probably familiar with. Although they provide services such as a search engine and email, they are really in the business of information. They offer their products for free as a means to gather information. This helps them achieve their mission to "organize the world's information and make it universally accessible and useful."* While all businesses use information for communication, process support, and decision making, only some businesses use information as a product. Second, information can be used to gain strategic value; this is the topic of Chapter 4.

---

* https://www.google.com/intl/en/about/.

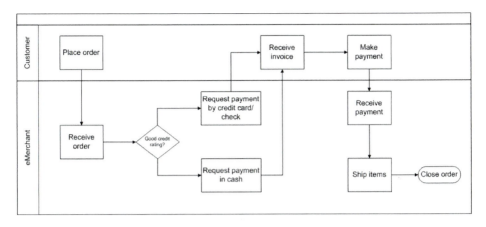

Figure 1.2 Order Process
Source: Adapted from http://www.readbag.com/media-visual-paradigm-media-documents-bpva20ug-pdf-bpva-user-guide-ch6.

LEARNING ACTIVITY 1.4

How Businesses Use Information

As we've discussed, businesses use information in several ways. Team with another student and think about a business (one you've worked for, one you frequent, or one assigned by your instructor). Identify three decisions and three processes related to the business. Identify key pieces of information required to support each decision or process. Write these down and be prepared to share them with the class.

Knowing how to successfully deal with the incredible and growing amount of information available to us is a key life and professional skill. Businesses use information in several important ways, including for communication, to support processes, and for decision making. Some businesses also use information as a product. They gather and perhaps analyze information and then sell that information to other businesses that use it for a variety of purposes. Understanding information and how it is used and having good information literacy skills will help you be more successful professionally and personally.

Information and Your Career

Information systems and technologies are key elements of business. Because of this, knowledge of the systems and technologies you will learn about in this book can help you in your future career.

BUSINESS EXAMPLE BOX 1.1

Promising Information Careers

Careers related to information systems and information analysis are in high demand. They also tend to pay well. The table below shows a few examples.

	Median Salary ($)	Growth (%)
Information Systems Careers		
Computer systems analyst	87,220	9
Information systems manager	135,800	12
Computer support specialists	52,160	10
Software developer	102,280	24
Database administrator	84,950	11
Information Analysis Careers		
Financial analyst	81,760	11
Auditor	68,150	10
Information security analysis	92,600	28

Notes: Median salaries are from 2016; growth projections are from 2016 to 2026.

Source: Bureau of Labor Statistics, U.S. Department of Labor, Occupational Outlook Handbook, October 2017, http://www.bls.gov/ooh/.

Individuals in information systems careers design, build, support, or manage information systems. These are the jobs that typically require a major in information systems or a related field. People in information analysis careers use these systems to retrieve, report on, and analyze the information contained in the systems. The results of the analyses are passed along to information consumers, who use the results to carry out transactions and make decisions. Information systems and information analysis offer a surprising variety of interesting, rewarding careers, as illustrated in Tables 1.1 and 1.2. Information-consuming careers include almost any business career, so we do not provide a table of examples for those.

Table 1.1 Information Analysis Careers

Business intelligence professional	Uses various reporting and statistical tools to help organizations gain value from their informational assets
Data analyst	Collects, processes, and analyzes data using various data management and statistical analysis tools
Data scientist	Develops and implements systems and processes to gain knowledge and insights from data
Compensation analyst	Analyzes information related to the costs of paying employees
Economic analyst	Develops economic models that help organizations predict economic conditions and outcomes
Financial analyst	Provides guidance in how to best utilize financial assets
Forensic accountant	Analyzes accounting and financial information to determine whether an activity is illegal or fraudulent
IT auditor	Ensures that an organization's information systems are operating properly and producing accurate information
Marketing analyst	Analyzes information related to the marketing activities of an organization

Table 1.2 Information Systems Careers

Business process analyst	Analyzes business processes in order to find ways to improve efficiency and/or effectiveness (which often involves applying information systems)
Chief information officer	Oversees all information and information systems–related activities of an organization
Database administrator	Manages systems that store and organize data used in information systems
Information security specialist	Ensures that the information contained in information systems is properly protected
Information system trainer	Designs or delivers educational programs that help users utilize information systems
IT project manager	Organizes and controls projects related to information systems
Software developer	Writes the computer programs that make up part of an information system
System analyst	Works with users to understand and document system requirements
System architect	Develops high-level designs of information systems, including the overall structure and essential design features

Chapter Summary

The overall goal of this chapter is to help you understand why information is valuable in business and your personal life. Understanding the value of information is important to understanding the importance of the various information systems presented in this book. Here are the main points discussed in the chapter:

- Data are raw symbols or unconnected facts.
- Information is processed data that is useful.
- Knowledge is information that is applied to a decision or action.
- Information literacy is an important professional and personal skill.
- Being information literate requires being able to efficiently and effectively determine information needs and then acquire, evaluate, use, and manage that information ethically.
- Businesses use information for communication, process support, and decision making.
- Information-related knowledge is important to virtually all careers.
- There are many careers that involve designing, building, supporting, managing, and analyzing information.

Review Questions

1. Contrast data, information, and knowledge.
2. Apply the data, information, and knowledge (DIK) hierarchy to the evolution of how information technology has been applied in businesses.
3. Describe the concepts of connectedness and usefulness as they relate to the DIK hierarchy.
4. Describe how the DIK hierarchy can be thought of as a cycle.
5. What are the key abilities related to information literacy?
6. Why is it important to be information literate?
7. Name three general ways in which businesses use information.
8. Name and briefly describe three information systems careers.
9. Name and briefly describe three information analysis careers.

Reflection Questions

1. What is the most important thing you learned in this chapter? Why do you think it's important?
2. Why is it important for business professionals to be information literate?

3. How does better information help businesses?

4. What impact do you think improving your information literacy skills will have on your career?

5. When did bad information or incomplete information lead to bad outcomes in your life? If you were facing that situation again, what would you do differently?

Additional Learning Activities

1.A1. Think about a common situation that a business professional (such as one in marketing, accounting, or finance) might face. For example, a finance professional might be analyzing an investment opportunity. Identify five pieces of information that would be useful in that situation. For each, discuss how bad or incomplete information might lead to negative outcomes.

1.A2. Share your findings from #1 with two other students who are in different majors. Compare your answers. How are the answers similar? How are they different?

1.A3. Consider one of the following major decisions: (a) where to go to grad school, (b) what car to buy, (c) which apartment to move to, (d) which job offer to accept. Identify five important pieces of information that you would need to make a good decision.

   a. For each, discuss why you think that information is important. Focus on consequences.

   b. Where would you find the information you need?

   c. How will you know whether or not to trust the information you gather?

1.A4. Consider the order process shown in Figure 1.2. For each stage in the process, what information is needed? What might be the consequences of bad information at that stage?

1.A5. Use a job-hunting website (e.g., Monster.com, Career.com, or your school's career website) to find job postings for two of the information systems and two of the information analysis careers discussed in the chapter. Be prepared to share your results.

References

Ackoff, R. L. 1989. "From Data to Wisdom." *Journal of Applied Systems Analysis* 16: 3–9.

Rockman, I. F. 2004. *Integrating Information Literacy into the Higher Education Curriculum: Practical Models for Transformation.* San Francisco: Jossey-Bass.

Glossary

Business process: Set of coordinated activities that lead to a specific goal or outcome.

Data: Raw symbols (unconnected facts).

Decision making: Process of choosing among alternative courses of action.

Information: Data that has been processed so that it is useful.

Information literacy: The ability to know when information is needed, and to be able to locate, evaluate, and effectively use that information.

Information system (IS): A combination of technology, data, people, and processes that is directed toward the collection, manipulation, storage, organization, retrieval, and communication of information.

Information technology (IT): The hardware, software, and media used to store, organize, retrieve, and communicate information.

Knowledge: Information that is applied to a decision or action.

Wisdom: The use of knowledge for the greater good.

CHAPTER 2

Introduction to Information Systems

Learning Objectives

By reading and completing the activities in this chapter, you will be able to

- Describe the major functions of an information system
- Explain why it is important for business professionals to understand information systems
- Explain key concepts related to systems
- Describe the information processing cycle
- Describe the critical elements of an information system
- Explain how information systems help managers deal with information
- Give examples of business rules
- Discuss how information systems facilitate organizational change
- Compare and contrast common information systems

Chapter Outline

Focusing Story: Registering for Classes in 1981
Learning Activity 2.1: Identifying My Information Systems
Why All Business Professionals Need to Be Information Systems Managers
Learning Activity 2.2: Components of a System
Overview of Systems
Learning Activity 2.3: Components of a Business Information System
Foundations of Information Systems
How Information Systems Help Us Deal with Information
Learning Activity 2.4: Information Systems and Change

FOCUSING STORY

Registering for Classes in 1981

When you registered for this class, you probably did so over the Web. Registration was very different in the 1980s. Let us describe how one of us registered for classes in 1981.

First, you get a copy of the printed schedule of classes. After spending quite a bit of time studying the course offerings, you finally come up with an ideal schedule. But wait . . . the chances of getting all your "first choice" classes are pretty slim (some things haven't changed!). So you come up with some backup plans—alternative courses and sections that are less than ideal but will still work. Fortunately, you have a good registration appointment time this semester. A little before your appointment time, you head to the student union and join the very long line for registration. While you're waiting in line, you keep an eye on the bank of television screens that are scrolling through the classes and their statuses. You're constantly checking to see if any of your ideal classes have closed out. When this happens, you start turning to your backup plans. You finally make it into the registration room, which is just a big multipurpose room filled with computer terminals and people. As you stand in line, you keep a sharp eye on the screens displaying the most up-to-date class statuses. These screens are showing the transparencies of the entire class schedule. As you watch, a person with a transparency marker walks around, crossing off classes that have recently filled. Of course, if one of your classes closes, you turn to your backup, backup plan. You finally make your way to one of the computer terminals, which is operated by trained university staff. The staff person takes your desired schedule, enters the code numbers into the system, and in a minute or two you find out if you're successfully registered. If one of your classes happens to close between the time you checked out the transparencies and the time your data actually got entered, you're sent to the "problem table," where someone works with you to finally get a schedule. Once your schedule is successfully entered, you stand in another line, waiting for your printed schedule and tuition bill. Congratulations, after a couple of hours (if you're lucky), you're registered!

FOCUSING QUESTIONS

Compare the scenario above to your course registration process.

1. Name four ways the current process is better for students.

2. Name four ways the current process is better for universities.

LEARNING ACTIVITY 2.1

Identifying My Information Systems

An **information system (IS)** is a combination of technology, data, people, and processes that is directed toward the collection, manipulation, storage, organization, retrieval, and communication of information. The system you use to register for classes is an example of an information system. Identify three information systems that you use frequently. What do you accomplish by using these systems? How would your life be affected if these systems did not exist?

Why All Business Professionals Need to Be Information Systems Managers

Information systems, such as the registration system in the focusing story, are an ingrained part of our daily lives. Each of us interacts with many information systems throughout the day. In fact, information systems are so prevalent that we often do not even notice them. Most of you probably use these systems as consumers. You check your course grades online, buy a song on the Web, and use your credit card to pay for a purchase. However, in the future, most of you will use information systems as part of your profession. Because of this, it is useful to start to think like an information systems manager.

Today, everyone in business needs to be an information systems manager to some extent. Let's be blunt about this; regardless of your major or your career path, you're going to be using information systems. Learning how to effectively use these systems can help you be more effective and successful in your career. Sales representatives who know how to use customer relationship management systems well, accountants who know the ins and outs of a company's enterprise system, and finance managers who know how to use a spreadsheet to analyze different investment scenarios will all be more successful than those who lack knowledge of these systems. To utilize these (and other) systems, it is helpful to know something about how they work. In this chapter, we lay the foundation by helping you understand concepts that are the basis of all information systems.

One reason it is useful to think like an IS manager is that information systems are increasingly ingrained in our business and professional lives. As you may have learned in the previous chapter, it is pretty hard to get through the day without interacting with an information system. How much of a pain would it be if you could not use these systems? To top it off, information systems are likely to become even more pervasive. So it is going to become even more important to understand and know how to use information systems. A big part of career success is knowing how to use important tools of the trade. Just as a carpenter needs to be skilled in using a hammer and saw, a businessperson needs to be skilled in using information systems. Our goal throughout this chapter and the entire book is to help you gain the knowledge you will need to make the best use of information systems in your career.

LEARNING ACTIVITY 2.2

Components of a System

Part 1: Consider one of the following systems:

- Video game system
- Personal computer
- Home entertainment system

Sketch the different components (pieces) of the system. (For example, a television might be a component of a home entertainment system.) Draw lines to indicate which components interact.

Part 2: Repeat Part 1 using your school's course registration system (or another system assigned by your instructor).

Overview of Systems

A **system** is a set of interacting components working together to form a complex, integrated whole in order to achieve some goal by taking inputs and processing them to produce outputs. Figure 2.1 shows a simple system and its key elements. Let's break down this definition to understand the key ideas related to systems.

- A system is made up of different pieces, called components. Components can take many different forms, ranging from human organs to computer software.
- These components work together; they are interrelated.
- A system has some purpose or goal.
- The goal is achieved by taking inputs and processing them to produce outputs.

There are a few systems-related concepts that are not apparent from the definition. First, a system is separated from its environment by the system's boundary. Most systems are **open systems,** which means that they interact with their environments (closed systems, in contrast, do not). For example, your body reacts to hot weather (an element of the environment) by sweating. This is also an example of **feedback**. Your body senses

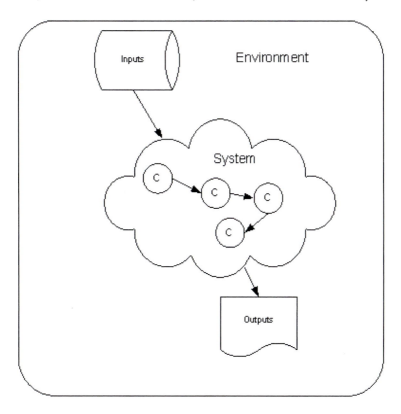

Figure 2.1 A System and Its Environment (*Note:* Components are labeled *C.*)

its temperature rising, so the brain sends a signal to your sweat glands to activate. It is also important to note that systems are often made up of **subsystems**. A subsystem is a system that is part of a larger system. Your respiratory system is an example; it is a complete system in its own right but is also part of the larger system of your body. Finally, **equifinality** is the idea that in an open system there are many different potential paths to the final outcome. In other words, there are different ways to end up in the same place.

One way to think about systems is to consider the components as a set of transformation processes. In this view, systems follow an input-process-output sequence. Consider a manufacturing system. Raw materials are the inputs, which are processed by various machines to produce the final product (the output). Of course, this is a greatly simplified view of a manufacturing system. Information systems work similarly. They take data as the raw material and transform it in various ways to produce usable information.

This brings us to our final general systems concept, feedback and **control**—a set of functions intended to ensure the proper operation of a system. Systems often have a feedback loop, where information from the environment is sensed by the system, which may change its behavior based on the feedback. Feedback is closely linked to the concept of system control. Many systems include a control element. Think about a thermostat, which is a subsystem of a heating and air conditioning system. The thermostat receives data (the current temperature) as feedback from its environment. When the temperature reaches a certain level, the thermostat sends a signal to the air conditioner or heater to begin operation (the control). Then, when the temperature reaches the desired level, the thermostat signals the air conditioner or heater to turn off.

Now that you have a basic understanding of systems in general, let's turn our attention to information systems. In the next section, we cover some important concepts regarding systems designed to deal with information.

LEARNING ACTIVITY 2.3

Components of a Business Information System

Pick one of the business information systems below (or another system assigned by your instructor). Identify at least five components of the system. Briefly describe the purpose of each component.

- Online ordering system (for example, ordering something from Amazon.com)
- Membership tracking system for a health club
- Hotel reservation system

Foundations of Information Systems

Earlier we defined an information system as a combination of technology (hardware, software, and communication media), data, people, and processes that is directed toward the collection, manipulation, storage, organization, retrieval, and communication of information. Later in the chapter, we discuss the six elements in more detail. The goal of this section is to help you understand some fundamental ideas related to information systems. Keeping these in mind will help you better understand the material in the rest of this book.

Before going further, it is important to realize that an information system does *not* require a computer. Information systems existed for hundreds of years before the invention of the electronic computer. In this book, we are primarily concerned with *computerized* information systems, which, of course, *do* require computers. Throughout this book, when we say "information systems," we are referring to computerized systems. Noncomputerized systems will be called "manual information systems."

One final note before we get into the details: people are the most important component of any information system. We will discuss the role of people in an information system in more detail later. However, we want to make sure that you understand that people are critical to the success of any information system.

Information systems include the following operations, as shown in Figure 2.2. This is sometimes called the information processing cycle. (*Note:* Some versions of this cycle do not include control as a separate operation.)

1. *Input:* Collection of data and their conversion into a form that allows processing.
2. *Processing:* Manipulation and transformation of data.
3. *Storage:* Holding place for data so that they can be retrieved at a later time.
4. *Output:* Transformation of processed data into a form that can be understood by its eventual user.
5. *Control:* Enforcement of correct processing procedures.

These operations are carried out by the various components of the information system. For example, the screen on your laptop computer may perform output operations. As is the case with any system, these components interact with one another in an organized manner. For instance, when you drag your mouse to select some text, the mouse provides input to the system, which processes the input and highlights the

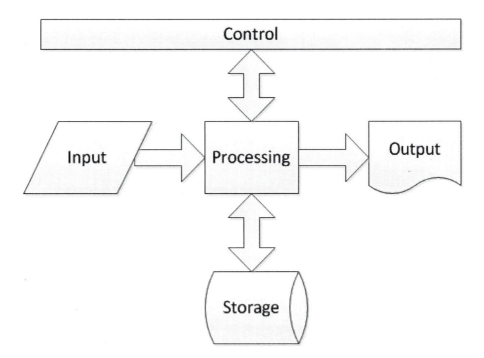

Figure 2.2 Information Processing Cycle

text on your screen (an output device). Your computer's central processing unit (CPU) carries out much of the processing and control activities, while your hard drive performs storage activities.

Information systems have six critical elements, as shown in Figure 2.3:

- *Data:* Raw facts, text, numbers, images, and the like that serve as the inputs for producing information.
- *Hardware:* Physical devices such as the processor, storage media, and peripheral devices (such as printers and displays).
- *Software:* Set of instructions that govern the operation of an information system.
- *Communication media:* Set of devices and protocols (rules) that enable computers to communicate with each other.
- *Procedures:* Instructions for the proper use of the information system.
- *People:* Individuals who use the information system.

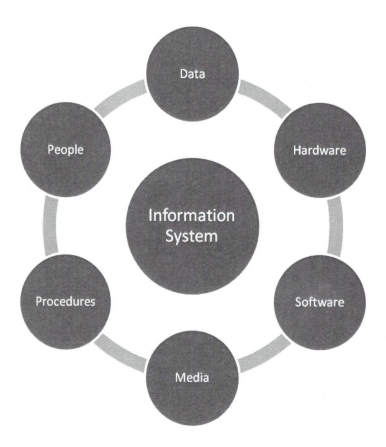

Figure 2.3 Elements of an Information System

You might be a little surprised to see people included in this list—even though we included them in our earlier definition—but they are critical to any information system. People are necessary to use and interpret the output of the information system. Even in information systems that seem like they are totally automated, people still need to monitor the system to make sure it is working correctly. Of course, people also build and maintain the system. Procedures for using the system are also necessary. Basically, the procedures tell the users how to properly utilize the system to support their tasks.

Before moving on, let's talk a little more about hardware and software. (There is more detail about this in Appendices A and B.) Software provides the instructions that govern the operation of a computerized system. Broadly speaking, there are two types of software: systems software and application software. Systems software includes operating systems, such as Windows and Linux, and utilities such as antivirus and data-compression software. This is a little confusing, because when you install an operating system, numerous utility programs are often installed at the same time. For our purposes, it is enough to just think of system software as a "necessary evil." Most people would not buy a computer just to run the system software, but you have to have the system software in order for the computer to operate.

People buy computers to run application software, which lets you do what you really want to do with the computer. Examples include word processors, spreadsheets, accounting packages, games, and media players. One of the exciting aspects of today's information systems landscape is the dizzying array of applications that are available. As more and more applications are developed, our computers become more and more useful (and more fun!).

Some applications are installed directly on your computer, tablet, or other device. Others are "in the cloud," which means that they are accessed through a network, usually the Internet, rather than being stored on your computer. Cloud applications have many advantages, including being able to be accessed from virtually anywhere that has network access. One disadvantage to that, however, is that they typically require network access to operate, although some cloud applications allow limited offline operation. In Chapter 7 we discuss cloud computing in more depth.

There are also different types of hardware involved in an information system. In addition to the computers involved, there are storage devices (such as hard disks), printers, keyboards, and communication devices. You can learn more about hardware in Appendix A.

To understand how the elements of an information system fit together, let's consider a simplified view of an information system for hotel reservations. (To keep this discussion from being too long, we are omitting some details of the system.) The goal of this system is to allow reservation agents at a hotel to reserve rooms for guests. Let's look at the specific roles involved in this information system.

- *Data:* The data serve as the facts that are manipulated by the system to produce information that is used by the reservation agent and hotel management.

- ○ A list of rooms, their status (available or reserved), prices, payments, customer information, and name of reservation clerk
- *Hardware:* The hardware performs computations, stores the data and software used by the system, displays information, and provides the platform for users to interact with this system.
  - ○ A reservation agent's personal computer, a computer that has the software for the system, hard drives that have the database that stores the data for the system, and printers for reports
- *Software:* The software controls the operation of the computer, including how the data are retrieved, manipulated, and communicated.
  - ○ The operating system of the various system computers and one or more applications specific to the task of making room reservations
- *Communication media:* This allows the various hardware components to communicate with each other.
  - ○ The network cabling and other devices that facilitate communication, such as routers
- *Procedures:* The procedures govern how the reservation agent and hotel managers should interact with the system.
  - ○ Instructions for how to get into the system, which data have to be entered, how to retrieve information, and how to generate reports
- *People:* In this system, people provide input for the system, control how the system is used, and interpret the information from the system.
  - ○ Customer, reservation agent, and hotel managers

Now that you know the basics of information systems, let us turn our attention to how information systems help businesses deal with the tremendous volume of information they must cope with every day.

How Information Systems Help Us Deal with Information

Businesses face an ever-increasing amount of information. Given the increasing complexity of today's business environment, this is unlikely to change any time soon. We are fortunate to have information systems to help us cope with this tsunami of information. Let's look at how information systems accomplish this.

First, information systems let us gather large amounts of data quickly, easily, and reliably. Think about your last trip to the grocery store. Today, most stores have electronic scanners that read a bar code (called the universal product code, or UPC) that is printed on most products. The checkout clerk runs each product across this scanner, which reads the UPC and electronically enters the fact that the product is being purchased into the system that facilitates the checkout process. (Eventually, these data also go into other systems, such as the inventory control system.) The system retrieves the item's price from a database, and the amount is added to the order's total. (This is an example of a point-of-sale information system.) All this happens in a fraction of a second, and many different clerks can be performing the same basic operation at one time. In addition, the data are entered very accurately. A large grocery store has tens of thousands of transactions per day, so being able to gather these data quickly and accurately is important.

Second, information systems allow businesses to store and organize very large amounts of data. Databases with multiple terabytes (approximately one trillion characters of data) are common. Information systems allow businesses to store volumes of data in an organized manner that allows for rapid retrieval. This simply would not be possible with manual systems.

STATS BOX 2.1:
GROWTH OF APPLICATIONS IN APPLE'S APP STORE

By any measure, Apple's iPhone has been very successful. One reason for its success is the large and growing number of applications, or "apps," available in Apple's App Store. These applications make the phone more useful to the owner, whether the app is work related or just a fun game. Figure 2.4 shows the steady growth of the number of available apps. Google and Amazon have similar app stores for Android and Amazon devices.

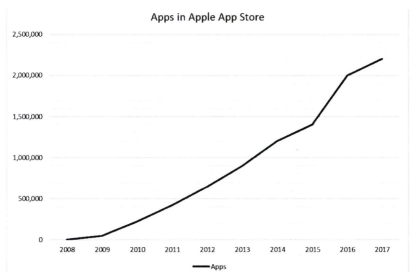

Figure 2.4 Available Apps in Apple's App Store
Source: http://en.wikipedia.org/wiki/App_Store_(iOS).

Third, information systems perform their data manipulations quickly, accurately, and consistently. As long as the hardware is operating correctly and the software is designed and implemented correctly, an information system is very consistent in its manipulations. Using our grocery store example, the checkout system will retrieve the same price for a given item every time that item is scanned (unless the price changes). It will also correctly calculate any necessary sales tax and will correctly total the customer's order. Again, this degree of speed, accuracy, and consistency simply cannot be matched with manual systems.

Finally, information systems let us retrieve and output information in a variety of forms, depending on what is useful to the user. The same information can be displayed on a screen, printed, or graphed. Different purposes may require different forms of displaying data; charts and graphs are good for showing large amounts of data at a glance, while printed reports are often better for showing details.

One important function of many business information systems is to enforce **business rules**. A business rule is a statement that defines or constrains an aspect of a business with the intent of controlling behaviors within the business. All businesses have rules that govern their operations. The following are some examples:

- A hotel reservation system that will not allow assigning a room that is already occupied

- A course registration system that does not allow registering for a course that is full

- An order entry system that automatically calculates the proper sales tax and adds it to the customer's invoice

BUSINESS EXAMPLE BOX 2.1

How Uber Provides On-Demand Service with Information Systems

Founded in 2009, Uber Technologies Inc. provides on-demand ride services in more than 600 cities worldwide. As the company name implies, technology is central to Uber's operations. In fact, technology is so important to Uber that the company describes itself as a "technology platform" (https://help.uber.com/h/738d1ff7-5fe0-4383-b34c-4a2480efd71e). Uber uses a smartphone app to connect drivers with those wanting a ride. When you want a ride from Uber, you request the ride using the app. The request goes out to nearby drivers. Once a driver accepts the request, the app gives you information about the driver (such as the driver's name, a description of his or her car, and the car's license plate number) and provides an approximate wait time. The app also provides a quote for the cost of your ride. As your driver heads toward your pickup location, the app shows you a map with the driver's progress. When your ride is completed, Uber's information system automatically charges your preselected payment method for the ride.

Although Uber's app is simple to use, the supporting information systems are complex. For example, Uber uses geolocation technologies to locate riders and drivers. Google Maps and other mapping technologies provide routing information that shows progress during the ride. SMS (short message service) technologies allow Uber to inform you when a driver accepts your ride request and when the driver is approaching the pickup location. Uber uses dynamic, demand-based pricing. Other systems process your payment for the ride and pay the drivers. This is only a partial list of the various systems that must work together seamlessly in order for Uber to provide its services. For a more detailed view of Uber's technology, see https://eng.uber.com/tech-stack-part-one/.

Source: Abrosimova (2014).

Information systems enforce business rules by not allowing violations to occur. Let's look at an example. Suppose your company had a business rule that said you could not accept an order from any customer who is more than 30 days past due on his or her bill. Only a supervisor can override this rule. The business's order entry system enforces this rule by not allowing sales representatives to enter orders from past-due customers. When such customers want to place orders, the system refuses to accept the order until a supervisor gives approval. Later, we will tell you about how information systems are analyzed and designed. One critical aspect of systems analysis and design is to properly understand business rules, which are then carefully built into the design of the system.

LEARNING ACTIVITY 2.4

Information Systems and Change

Research a process that has been substantially improved by information systems. (Registering for classes is one example.) Briefly describe the before and after processes. Describe how the process was improved. Was the process more efficient/effective for both the organization and its customers? How?

Here are some Web resources that might help you with your research:

- *CIO Magazine:* http://www.cio.com/tag/cio-digital-magazine/
- *New York Times* technology section: http://www.nytimes.com/pages/technology/index.html
- *Computer World:* http://www.computerworld.com
- *Information Week:* http://www.informationweek.com

  (*Note:* Your instructor may give you a specific example to research.)

How Information Systems Facilitate Organizational Change

There are many ways in which information systems help managers bring about organizational change. To help you understand how this occurs, we break down these ways into four categories: process improvements, automation, control, and information flow.

Process Improvements

The increasing use of information systems was partially responsible for the business process redesign movement that started in the 1990s and continues today. Information systems can help organizations improve both the efficiency and effectiveness of processes. For example, many companies use information to enable customer self-service, which means that individual customers interact with systems to perform their own customer-service activities. A classic example of this is the automated teller machine (ATM). In the past, when you needed cash, you would go into your bank and either cash a check or make a withdrawal. Now you simply find a convenient ATM, put in your card, push a few buttons, and get your cash. Some banks, such as Wells Fargo, even allow you to access the ATM using a smartphone app; you don't even need a card. The old process was less efficient from the bank's perspective because of the need for the teller's time. The ATM illustrates how information systems can bring about process improvements and control. Not only is the process more efficient, but it is also more effective due to the reduced number of errors and the increased convenience for the customer. Of course, there are many other such examples of information systems improving efficiency and effectiveness, including the course registration example at the beginning of the chapter.

Automation

Some processes have been totally automated. A good example of this is online ordering. Prior to the popularity of the Web, ordering something from a company typically involved either calling the company and placing the order with a sales representative or filling out and mailing in an order form, which was then entered into the company's order system by a clerk. Today, you simply go to the company's website, fill out an online form, and the order is directly entered into the order system. Even something as simple as buying gasoline is often fully automated. When you pull up to the pump, all you need to do is slide your credit or debit card through the slot, fill your tank, take your receipt, and go on your way. (Some gas stations even allow you to pay using a smartphone app.) In the past, an attendant would make an imprint of your card on a special form and would then fill out the relevant information. This form would go to the bank, which would do additional processing so that the gas station could be paid for your purchase.

Control

Information systems also enable organizational change by improving process controls. When properly designed and implemented, an information system can ensure that business rules are followed throughout a process. For example, an order entry system might refuse to accept an order for a customer whose account is past due. Returning to our gas station example, prior to automation, the station attendant was required to check a "hot list" of stolen or suspended credit cards before accepting a card as payment. As you might imagine, this business rule was often violated, especially when the station was busy. Today, the information system checks the status of the account before allowing the customer to pump any gas. The course registration system from the focusing story is another example of enforcing rules. Under the less-automated system, it was relatively easy to register for a class even if you did not have the necessary prerequisites. (Don't ask us how we know this!) Today's systems typically check prerequisites before allowing a student to register for a course. (This assumes that the prerequisites have been properly entered into the system.)

Information Flow

Finally, information systems improve communication and information flow in organizations. Workflow systems facilitate information flow throughout a work task. Consider a simple example of a grade change. The instructor enters the grade change into the information system. The system generates an email notifying the appropriate administrator that a grade change is pending her or his approval. The administrator reviews and approves or denies the request. If the request is approved, the system notifies the instructor and student, and the grade change is recorded and made permanent. Throughout the process, the system manages the flow of information and controls the process. Information systems also facilitate information sharing. Examples include document repositories and communication systems, such as email.

The ways in which information systems enable change combine to allow for changing organizational forms. To help you understand this, we discuss virtual teams and the role of middle managers. Members of virtual teams are not necessarily located in the same place; they may literally be spread across the globe. Information systems allow these teams to work together by providing communication functions such as email and videoconferencing, which allow the members to interact even though they are not colocated (in the same location). Other tools, such as shared calendars and document repositories, also help virtual teams function.

On a larger scale, information systems help companies flatten their organizational structure. In the past, many midlevel managers existed to monitor the activities of lower-level workers and to facilitate communication between lower and upper levels of the organization. Today, information systems can serve some of these same functions by enforcing business rules and facilitating communication throughout various processes. In addition, communication technologies such as email and websites improve communication flow across organizational levels and provide employees with

BUSINESS EXAMPLE BOX 2.2

AgTech—Making Farming More Efficient and Sustainable

As the world's population continues to grow, providing adequate food supplies is an ongoing problem. At the same time, societies across the globe are increasingly concerned about the environmental impact of food production. AgTech (the use of digital technology to improve agriculture) may be the key to increasing food production in an environmentally sustainable way. A wide array of information systems help gather and process information in order to increase yields and improve efficiency, especially with respect to resource use. For example, geographic information systems combined with other technologies allow farmers to precisely apply fertilizer to specific areas based on soil composition, weather, and other factors. Sensors and drones combine to provide information that lets farmers better determine how specific areas of their fields should be irrigated. Both of these examples improve the sustainability of agriculture by reducing resource use.

Some dairy farms are making extensive use of robots to mix and distribute feed to cows with minimal human intervention. Automated milking machines not only milk the cows but also monitor cows' nutritional needs. The milking machine communicates with the feed robots to adjust the mixture of the feed in order to deal with various health issues. These systems help the dairy farm maximize milk production without harming the health of the cows. In fact, one of the goals of these systems is to keep cows stress free since stress reduces milk production. From more precise irrigation to stress-free cows, AgTech holds considerable promise for supporting the food needs of a growing population while at the same time reducing the environmental impact of agriculture.

Sources: https://www.cbinsights.com/research/agriculture-tech-market-map-company -list/; https://www.youtube.com/watch?v=v761DILatzg; https://www.forbes.com/sites/ jenniferhicks/2016/12/31/take-a-look-at-how-technology-makes-smart-and-sustainble -farming/#6667d7bb3deb.

information that previously only existed at higher levels of the organization. As a result, many companies have flattened their organizational structures.

Our goal up to this point in the chapter has been to help you understand information systems and their role in organizations. In the next section, we provide brief overviews of some common information systems. Many of these are discussed in greater detail later in the book.

Common Information Systems

There are numerous different types of information systems in modern organizations; we will cover many of these in the rest of this book. For now, it is useful to get a glimpse of the range of information systems used by organizations. A useful way to do this is to classify information systems according to the impact or "reach" of the system, as shown in Figure 2.5. At the bottom of this triangle are personal applications, which are typically used by one person or a small group. At the top are global systems, the use of which spans multiple organizations across the world.

To further help you understand the range of information systems available today, we provide some brief examples of systems at each level of our triangle:

- *Personal applications:* These systems help make individuals' daily work more efficient and effective. Office automation systems (such as office suites like Microsoft Office) are included in this category. Other examples include note-taking systems such as Evernote or OneNote, to-do list systems, personal information managers, personal calendars, and drawing programs.

- ***Transaction processing systems (TPSs):*** These systems collect, monitor, process, report, and store large volumes of data that are created by business processes. The grocery store point-of-sale system we mentioned earlier is an example. Many organizations have a large number of TPSs. Other examples include payroll processing systems, invoicing systems, and inventory control systems. (Note that many of these stand-alone TPSs have been replaced by integrated enterprise systems, which we discuss later.) In the earlier days of information systems, most TPSs operated in batch mode, which means that they gathered all the data to be

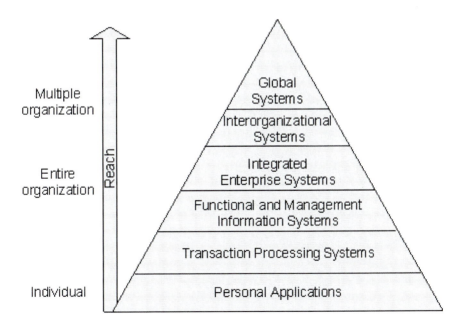

Figure 2.5 Levels of Information Systems
Source: Adapted from Turban and Volonino (2009), p. 43.

processed and then processed the data in one batch. The modern trend is toward online transaction processing (OLTP) systems, which process the data as soon as they are gathered.

- *Functional and management information systems:* These systems monitor, control, and analyze the operation of functional areas. Examples include financial management systems, sales force automation systems, materials requirements planning (MRP) systems, and benefits administration systems. As was the case with TPS, integrated enterprise systems have replaced many of these stand-alone systems.

- *Integrated enterprise systems:* Today, many organizations (particularly large organizations) have replaced many of their stand-alone TPS and functional systems with integrated, enterprise-wide systems that impact multiple functional areas. A stand-alone system is primarily used in isolation from other systems. An integrated system has multiple applications in a cohesive, interrelated system. For example, enterprise resource planning systems provide an integrated set of modules that carry out the information processing and reporting systems for the entire organization. Enterprise information systems are very important; we devote an entire chapter (Chapter 12) to them.

- *Interorganizational systems:* These span organizational boundaries to connect companies to suppliers and customers. **Electronic data interchange (EDI)** is at the heart of many of these systems. EDI allows the systems in one organization to directly interact with those in a partner organization. Many electronic business systems enable partner organizations to interact seamlessly and thus are considered interorganizational systems.

- *Global systems:* These are simply interorganizational systems that cross national boundaries. These systems are often more complex than other systems due to cross-national differences in language, currency, and culture.

Stand-alone systems are often integrated so that they can exchange data. For example, an accounting application may pull data from a transaction processing system. Such integration is very important to the smooth operation of an organization.

Chapter Summary

This chapter helped you learn how information systems help organizations operate effectively. This knowledge gives you a foundation that will be helpful in understanding the rest of the book. Here are the main points discussed in the chapter:

- Information systems combine technology, data, people, and processes to help collect, manipulate, store, organize, retrieve, and communicate information.

- In today's information-rich business environment, business professionals must be skilled at dealing with a variety of information systems.

- Systems are made up of components that work together to achieve a goal by taking inputs and processing them into outputs.
- The information processing cycle consists of input, processing, storage, output, and control.
- Information systems are made up of six critical elements: data, hardware, software, communication media, procedures, and people.
- Information systems help managers deal with information by improving how data are collected, organized, manipulated, and output.
- Information systems can help enforce business rules.
- Information systems facilitate organizational change through improving, automating, and controlling processes and improving information flow.
- Categories of common information systems include personal applications, transaction processing systems, functional and management information systems, integrated enterprise systems, and global systems.

Review Questions

1. Explain why business professionals need to understand information systems.
2. Define the term *system*.
3. Name the key system concepts discussed in this chapter.
4. Describe the information processing cycle.
5. Name and describe the six critical elements of an information system.
6. Why are people a critical element of an information system?
7. Contrast system and application software.
8. Name four ways in which information systems help managers deal with large volumes of information.
9. What is a business rule? How do information systems relate to business rules?
10. Name five ways in which information systems can facilitate organizational change.
11. Name and briefly describe six types of common information systems.

Reflection Questions

1. What is the most important thing you learned in this chapter? Why is it important?
2. What topics are unclear? What about them is unclear?
3. What relationships do you see between what you learned in this chapter and what you learned in Chapter 1?

4. How do information systems impact your life? Pick one information system and discuss how your life would change if it did not exist in a computerized form.

5. Think about your future career. How do you think you will use information systems? In what ways will better understanding information systems help advance your career?

6. In the text, we said that people are key components of information systems. How can people cause an information system to fail? Provide specific examples to back up your claims.

Additional Learning Activities

2.A1. Relate the information processing cycle to the class registration system described at the beginning of the chapter. Provide examples of the inputs required, the processing that occurs, outputs that are produced, data that are stored, and controls that should be in place.

2.A2. Use the information processing cycle to discuss a system that allows consumers to make purchases from an online store. (Your instructor may give you a different information system example to use.)

2.A3. Consider an information system that processes a company's payroll. Give specific examples of each of the critical elements involved in this information system. (The critical elements are data, hardware, software, communication media, procedures, and people.)

2.A4. Identify three business rules that you have encountered. For each rule, briefly discuss how information systems enforce the rule. (For example, a course registration system would block a student from registering for a course if he or she did not have the necessary prerequisites.)

2.A5. Find an example of how information systems facilitated organizational change. Using the categories presented in the chapter, discuss how the information system helped facilitate the change.

2.A6. Describe two examples of how an information system improved the efficiency or effectiveness of a business process. Be specific: What elements of the process were improved? How? Did the improvement benefit both the organization and its customers or suppliers?

2.A7. Find a specific example of an information system for each of the six levels of common information systems described in the chapter. For instance, Microsoft Excel would be an example of a personal applications. (*Note:* Do not use the examples provided in the chapter!)

References

Abrosimova, K. 2014. "Building an App like Uber: What Is the Uber App Made From?" *Medium*. https://medium.com/yalantis-mobile/uber-underlying -technologies-and-how-it-actually-works-526f55b37c6f.

Coopers. 2011. "Coopers 2011 Annual Report." http://www.coopers.com.au/static/ media/uploads/coopers_annual_report_2011.pdf.

Pauli, D. 2010. "IT and Beer: A Love Story." *CIO*, June 7. http://www.cio.com/ article/2417646/enterprise-resource-planning/it-and-beer--a-love-story.html.

Turban, E., and Volonino, L. 2009. *IT for Management: Improving Performance in the Digital Economy*. New York: John Wiley & Sons.

Glossary

Business rule: A statement that defines or constrains an aspect of a business with the intent of controlling behaviors within the business.

Control: A set of functions intended to ensure the proper operation of a system.

Electronic data interchange (EDI): A B2B e-business model focusing on the electronic exchange of information between two or more organizations using a standard format.

Equifinality: The idea that in an open system, there are many different potential paths to the final outcome.

Feedback: A process by which a system regulates itself by monitoring its own output.

Information system (IS): A combination of technology, data, people, and processes that is directed toward the collection, manipulation, storage, organization, retrieval, and communication of information.

Open system: A system that interacts with its environment.

Subsystem: A system that is part of a larger system.

System: A set of interacting components that work together to form a complex whole by taking inputs and processing them to produce outputs.

Transaction processing system (TPS): A system that collects, monitors, processes, reports, and stores data generated by an organization's transactions.

CHAPTER 3

Evaluating Information

Learning Objectives

By reading and completing the activities in this chapter, you will be able to

- Discuss why it is important both personally and professionally to be an informed information consumer
- Describe information overload, its consequences, and approaches for dealing with information overload
- Discuss the relationship between information overload and information evaluation
- List and describe the dimensions of information quality
- List and describe the elements of an information evaluation framework
- Given an information-related task, evaluate information for its usefulness and believability

Chapter Outline

Focusing Story: Biased Information in a Trusted Outlet
Learning Activity 3.1: How Good Is This Information?
Being a Smart Information Consumer
Learning Activity 3.2: My Online Life and Information Overload
Information Overload and the Need to Evaluate Information
Dealing with Information Overload
Learning Activity 3.3: Dimensions of Information Quality
Information Quality
Learning Activity 3.4: Evaluating Information Sources
Evaluating Information

Chapter Summary

Review Questions

Reflection Questions

Additional Learning Activities

References

Glossary

With the tremendous amount of information available today, information evaluation is an important skill. The goal of this chapter is to help you gain the knowledge and skills necessary for effective information evaluation.

FOCUSING STORY

Biased Information in a Trusted Outlet

Information is often biased—sometimes intentionally, sometimes unintentionally. This point was driven home to me personally many years ago. I was reading an article in a trade magazine that I read frequently. Generally, I found the magazine informative and useful. This particular article was about an output device called a plotter. A plotter is used to produce large-format drawings, such as architectural and engineering plans. I was quite knowledgeable about plotters, having sold and used them extensively. This particular article was about a special kind of plotter that used pencils rather than pens, inkjet, or laser technologies. To say the article was positive about pencil plotters would be a gross understatement. The author went on and on about how much better the pencil technology was than any of the others. This was puzzling to me, as I knew that other technologies had many advantages that were not mentioned in the article. For example, inkjet and laser-like plotters were much faster than pencil plotters. They were also more versatile with respect to the kinds of images they could produce. To be blunt, I questioned the sanity and knowledge of the author. After coming to the end of the article, I saw in small print a short "about the author" note. The author was the national marketing manager for the only company that manufactured pencil plotters (at that time). The reason for the article's glowing opinion of pencil plotters became quite clear. The author had a heavy bias for pencil plotters; the information in the article reflected this bias. I often wondered how many companies purchased pencil plotters because of that article; hopefully not many.

This story illustrates the importance of taking a critical view of information, especially when making important decisions. Being able to evaluate and understand information quality are important skills for business professionals. You will face many situations that will require you to gather information in order to make important decisions. Making these decisions based on biased or otherwise low-quality information can lead to serious consequences, such as spending thousands of dollars on an inferior plotter.

FOCUSING QUESTIONS

1. Give two examples of instances where you encountered biased information. What made you think the information was biased?
2. What would the consequences have been if you relied on the biased information?

LEARNING ACTIVITY 3.1

How Good Is This Information?

The focusing story related a situation in which bad information led to unfortunate outcomes. But what do we mean by "bad" information? In small groups, discuss the meaning of information quality. Develop a list of characteristics of "good" information.

After your discussion, your instructor will give you an information source, such as a blog or wiki. Evaluate the information contained in the source using the characteristics you developed as a guide.

Being a Smart Information Consumer

Being successful in today's knowledge society requires being a good information consumer. We are faced with an ever-increasing array of information. Being able to deal with that information is a key life skill. In Chapter 1, we discussed the concept of information literacy. You may recall that being able to effectively evaluate information is an element of information literacy. The goal of this chapter is to help you improve your information evaluation skills.

As is often the case, the amount of readily accessible information available online has both advantages and disadvantages. The obvious advantage is that we now have easy access to information that would have been quite time consuming and difficult to track down just a few years ago. Unfortunately, there are also a few downsides. One of the great things about the Internet is that there are almost no "gatekeepers" who determine what can be posted. However, this also means that there is no quality control. Almost anyone can post information about almost any topic. In more traditional media, evaluating the quality and correctness of information was the job of editors and publishers. Today, with respect to much of the information on the Internet, that responsibility shifts to the information consumer (in other words, you). So the ability to evaluate information is an important skill.

Often when we deal with something routinely, we tend to go into an autopilot mode; we act without really thinking. Being faced with so much information, we run the risk of using the information without thinking critically about it. When we are making small decisions, this is usually fine. However, when making higher-impact decisions, it is worthwhile to be a more discerning information consumer, especially by critically evaluating the quality of the information.

Information evaluation is the systematic determination of the merit and worth of information. Information evaluation skills will be important to you both personally and in your business career. Personally, you need to be able to sift through and evaluate many kinds of information. As you go through life, you will have to make many decisions, some big and some small. When facing a big decision, such as choosing a job or making a major purchase, the consequences of relying on bad information can be quite severe. As you saw in the focusing story, acting on bad information can lead to bad outcomes.

STATS BOX 3.1:
THE COST OF POOR INFORMATION QUALITY

Poor-quality information is costly. One study estimated that 75% of organizations believe that customer service quality suffers due to inaccurate information. According to that same study, human error is the most common cause of inaccurate data (Experian Data Quality 2016). Another study, conducted by the Data Warehousing Institute, estimates that poor-quality data cost organizations in the United States more than $600 billion per year (http://www.crmbuyer.com/story/44711.html?wlc=1278446605).

The need to intelligently deal with information is also important to your career. As is the case with your personal life, you will face many decisions throughout your career. Knowing how to evaluate the information you must deal with is particularly important. Much of your reputation and thus your career success depends on the outcomes of the decisions you make. Making decisions based on better information usually leads to better outcomes.

In business, we often use information to reduce uncertainty. The more uncertainty there is surrounding a decision, the more we seek information in order to reduce that uncertainty. This makes intuitive sense, but there is an underlying assumption that the information is of good quality. Poor-quality information is ineffective at reducing decision uncertainty.

Consider the example of hiring a new employee. When a manager is evaluating potential new employees, he or she gathers information about the person in order to increase the odds of making a good hiring decision. Information on the applicant's experience, education, and character all come into play. If this information is accurate, then the manager is better able to hire the right person. But what if the information on the applicant's resume is false? In this case, the likelihood of hiring the right person decreases.

The bottom line here is that it is important to be able to intelligently evaluate all sorts of information. In this chapter, we help you understand information quality and provide some approaches to evaluating information.

BUSINESS EXAMPLE BOX 3.1

Resume Fraud

Although resume fraud has been around for many years, instances of fraud often increase in times of high unemployment. Such fraud ranges from small embellishments to outright lies. Here are a few of the more common resume lies:

- Falsifying or exaggerating education, such as listing degrees that were not completed
- Omitting past employment
- Falsifying military records
- Enhancing job responsibilities or titles
- Falsifying credentials, such as certifications
- Exaggerating skills and accomplishments

What does this have to do with information evaluation? First, evaluating a job candidate's resume requires a critical eye in much the same way as evaluating any information source. Second, as is the case with all information evaluation, the amount of effort you should put into evaluation depends on the consequences of making a bad decision. For example, more effort should go into evaluating the resume of a potential executive than those of entry-level, part-time workers.

Here are a few tips for evaluating resumes:

- Ask the applicant for specific dates of employment and verify these dates.
- Seek out additional references through contacts within the organization or profession.
- Perform a Web search of the candidate, but allow the candidate to respond to any negative information. (Remember that it is easy to post false information about someone.)
- Look for inconsistencies, such as missing dates and employment gaps.
- Actually check with references to verify employment dates, job titles, and responsibilities.

As a job applicant, you should be sure to not fall into the trap of inflating your resume. Any short-term gains will be more than erased when the fraud is uncovered. More and more organizations are taking very hard lines on resume fraud, in part because it displays a commitment to ethical business practices. The bottom line is that resume fraud is not only unethical; it is also unprofitable in the long run.

Sources: Marquet, C. T., and L. J. B. Peterson. 2015. "Resume Fraud: The Top 10 Lies." *Marquet International LTD.* http://www.marquetinternational.com/pdf/Resume%20Fraud-Top%20Ten%20Lies.pdf; Tuna, C. 2008. "How to Spot Résumé Fraud." *Wall Street Journal,* November 13. http://www.wsj.com/articles/SB122653695797922735.

LEARNING ACTIVITY 3.2

My Online Life and Information Overload

We all face a daily torrent of information. The more "connected" you are, the more information you face. As you go throughout tomorrow, pay attention to how you deal with the information you face. Prepare a one- or two-page report that addresses the following questions:

1. What strategies do you use to determine what information is important and to reduce the amount of information you deal with?
2. How successful are these strategies?
3. How could you improve your approach to information filtering?

Information Overload and the Need to Evaluate Information

Herbert Simon (1971), the Nobel Prize–winning psychologist and economist, stated in 1971,

> In an information-rich world, the wealth of information means a dearth of something else: a scarcity of whatever it is that information consumes. What information consumes is rather obvious: it consumes the attention of its recipients. Hence a wealth of information creates a poverty of attention and a need to allocate that attention efficiently among the overabundance of information sources that might consume it.

Although he did not use the words "**information overload**," this is basically what he is talking about: being faced with more information than we can effectively process. The more information we have to sift through, the less attention we have to devote to other tasks. Information overload is a very real problem, in terms of both our business and personal lives. It reduces productivity, increases stress, and can actually lead to physical health problems.

Business managers bring some of this on themselves. Managers know the value of information and gather information for many different reasons (Butcher 1998):

- To improve decision making
- To justify decisions
- To verify previously acquired information
- To "play it safe" by making sure they do not miss any relevant information
- To use the information later

Add to this the amount of unsolicited information that managers face and you can see why information overload is a problem for many managers.

To better understand this, we will use the example of an information technology (IT) manager named Pat. Pat's company is getting ready to purchase a large number of laptop computers, and Pat has to decide which brand of computers to buy. (The company has already decided on the specifications needed.) Pat could easily become overloaded with information for this decision. She may begin reading reviews of the various brands, checking prices and specifications, and so on. She may reach out to her colleagues to see what their experiences have been with the brands being considered. While this is a big decision, Pat could easily become bogged down with more and more information. Being able to deal with these situations is important to being a successful manager.

Two major strategies for dealing with information overload are filtering and withdrawal (Savolainen 2007). *Withdrawal* essentially involves disconnecting from sources of information: not checking email, turning off the television, not surfing the Web, and so on. This may not always be a viable option for business professionals, so filtering may be a better choice for many of us.

Filtering information involves knowing what information we need and what information merits attention and use, which makes being able to evaluate information a critical skill in today's information-rich world. Most of us evaluate information almost constantly, but without really paying attention to how we do so. For example, we scan our email inboxes and choose which messages to open, which to save for later reading, and which to delete or ignore. We make these decisions, in part, based on an evaluation of the information we think is contained within the message. In most cases, we evaluate the information in email messages based on its relevance to whatever we are working on at the time. Relevance is one aspect of information quality, which we discuss later in the chapter.

If we dig a little deeper, we see that relevance is only one piece of the puzzle. Whether consciously or unconsciously, we evaluate other aspects of information when we decide what to do with it. If the information is too old, untrustworthy, or otherwise of questionable quality, we essentially ignore the information and do not use it (at least that is what we should do). As you can see, improving your information evaluation skills will help you better deal with information overload.

DEALING WITH INFORMATION OVERLOAD

How can you deal with the torrent of information you face every day? Fortunately, there are a number of techniques you can use to help avoid information overload. First, understand and identify your information priorities and needs. Once you have determined these, try to focus on the most relevant information. This can be difficult, especially when you see information that is not really relevant at the moment but may be later. To deal with these situations, it is a good idea to develop some organizational structure for this "may need later" information. There are some good technology solutions for this. If the information is mostly Web based, an application such as Pocket (https://getpocket.com) provides an easy means of saving items for later reading. You can also use a note-taking application such as Evernote (http://www.evernote.com) to save the Web page to read later and to make a quick note about the pages you have saved. Evernote lets you tag notes and organize them in notebooks, which can make recalling information easier. You can also use something like Google Docs to make a quick note or record a link for later use. Be sure to put something meaningful in the document so you can find it later. Finally, think about what information sources are the most useful and of the highest quality. Be sure to consider these sources first when faced with relevant information needs. This can save quite a bit of searching time.

LEARNING ACTIVITY 3.3

Dimensions of Information Quality

Information quality is an important, complicated topic. Because of this, there are many views on what constitutes "high-quality" information. Search the Web to discover different views on the dimensions of information quality. What, in your opinion, are the three most important dimensions of information quality? Why do you think these are the most important?

Information Quality

"Garbage in, garbage out." This old saying succinctly sums up the importance of information quality. As we mentioned in previous chapters, businesses rely on information to carry out business processes and to make decisions, both of which require good information. If you use bad information as the basis for a decision, you are probably going to make a bad decision. But just what does "good" information mean?

The issue of information quality is surprisingly complex. As you may have noticed when doing your research for Learning Activity 3.3, there are many different opinions regarding the meaning of information quality. We like the definition of **information quality** as information that is fit for its intended use. In other words, the information is useful toward the achievement of whatever task is at hand. While we like this definition, it is not particularly useful in helping us understand information quality. A more useful approach is to think about the dimensions of information quality: the characteristics of information that make it useful or not useful.

Dozens of studies have investigated the issue of the dimensions of information quality. As a result, there are many different lists of information quality dimensions. (Some of these studies are listed in the Further Readings section at the end of the chapter.) Richard Wang and Diane Strong (1996) developed a framework that is useful for understanding and evaluating information quality. (They used the term *data quality*, but the concepts apply to information quality.)

Wang and Strong put quality dimensions into four categories:

- *Intrinsic quality* includes dimensions of quality that are important regardless of the context or how the information is represented.

- *Contextual quality* includes the dimensions that may be viewed differently depending on the task at hand.

- *Representational quality* concerns how the information is provided to the user.

- *Accessibility quality* has to do with whether authorized users can easily access the information.

In this chapter, we focus on the first two categories. Figure 3.1 shows the dimensions in these categories, and Table 3.1 provides definitions for each dimension.

We need to make a few points regarding the information in Figure 3.1 and Table 3.1. First, there is considerable disagreement regarding the dimensions of information quality. It is possible (even likely) that your instructor will have a different perspective on which dimensions are most important. If you want to know more about this topic, we recommend that you read some of the articles in the References and Further Readings sections of this chapter. The articles by Lee, Strong, Kahn, and Wang (2002) and Knight and Burn (2005) both give nice overviews of prior research on information quality.

Second, we want to reemphasize the importance of considering context when thinking about information quality. Consider the example of stock price information. It is common for free information services (such as Yahoo! Finance) to delay stock price information by 15 minutes. If you are a casual investor, this usually is fine; the delayed information is acceptably current for keeping track of the value of your portfolio. However, if you are a professional stock day trader, a 15-minute delay is unacceptable (even a 15-second delay could be a problem) and would be considered poor-quality information.

Finally, information quality has a cost. On the surface, it may seem like we should want the highest-quality information possible. However, this typically is not true. Few individuals or organizations are willing to invest the resources necessary to ensure the highest possible information quality. More commonly, we want information that is of sufficient quality to carry out tasks effectively. In other words, we want "good enough" information quality. This is not to say that information quality is not important; quite the opposite is true. Information quality is critical to business success. However, it is also important to consider the costs of information quality and what level of cost is justified.

At a more micro level, a good way to think about the costs of information quality is to consider the possible consequences of poor-quality information. For more important, higher-impact decisions, it is worthwhile to pay much more attention to information quality than for lower-consequence decisions. If you are buying a house, you want very high-quality information. If you are buying a pack of notebook paper,

Figure 3.1 Information Quality Dimensions

lower-quality information is probably fine. We will talk more about this in Chapter 6, which covers decision making.

Table 3.1 Information Quality Dimension Definitions

Intrinsic Dimension	Definition: Extent to which the information is . . .
Accurate	Correct, free from error, and reliable
Believable	Regarded as true and credible
Objective	Free from bias
Consistent	Compatible with previous information
Understandable	Easily comprehended
Contextual Dimension	Definition: Extent to which the information is . . .
Relevant	Applicable and useful for the task at hand
Timely	Available in time to perform the task at hand
Comprehensive	Of sufficient depth and breadth for the task at hand
Current	Sufficiently up to date for the task at hand

Sources: Adapted from U.S. Department of Justice (2010) and Knight and Burn (2005).

It is easy to see how poor-quality information can negatively impact a business. Consider when you order a product from an online store. If the description of the product is inaccurate, you may end up with a product that does not meet your needs. If the inventory information is not current, you may not receive the product when expected. Biased reviews may lead you to order a poor-quality product. We could go on, but you probably have the idea. In almost any business situation, you can easily see the impact of poor-quality information.

Let's return to Pat, the IT manager who needs to pick a laptop brand. She needs to pay careful attention to the quality of the information she is using to make this decision. She clearly needs to have accurate information, but she also needs to get the information in a timely manner. Objective information is very important in this case. Pat probably would not want to rely on a vendor's sales representative for information on the durability of the laptops. One thorny issue in this situation is the completeness of the information. Pat needs to have enough information to make the decision while avoiding information overload. It is also important to have current information. Specifications and pricing information change often in the computer industry, so Pat needs to ensure that she has current information.

Now that you have some understanding of information quality, it is useful to gain a better understanding of how to evaluate information, which is the topic of the next section.

BUSINESS EXAMPLE BOX 3.2

Information Quality as an Ethical Issue

In 1986, the journal *MIS Quarterly* published Richard Mason's important article "Four Ethical Issues of the Information Age." One of these four issues was information accuracy. In the article, Mason relates the story of the March family, who were the victims of information inaccuracy. Despite the fact that for years the Marches had faithfully made their mortgage payments on time, the computerized system used by the bank for some reason failed to record one of the payments. This ultimately led to a foreclosure proceeding. Unfortunately, Mrs. March learned of the foreclosure while recovering from a heart attack. The news was such a shock that she suffered a stroke that almost took her life. The good news is that after considerable time and effort, the Marches were able to keep their home and actually won a substantial settlement from the bank.

Because of the degree to which our lives depend on information, Mason points out that the organizations responsible for the information have an ethical obligation to ensure and maintain the accuracy of the information.

We have personal experience with this; one of us was once denied a loan due to incorrect information in a credit report. One of the negative entries in the credit report was a default on a credit card that occurred at the age of 12, which was clearly inaccurate. It took quite a bit of time and effort to eventually clean up the credit report. The loan was to make a substantial retail purchase, so in this case the merchant also lost a sale. There are many other examples of inaccurate information causing everything from minor inconveniences to death. We agree with Mason that information accuracy is an ethical issue and an obligation for organizations that store and provide information.

LEARNING ACTIVITY 3.4

Evaluating Information Sources

You are thinking about investing in real estate. While doing some initial research, you obtain the following sources of information:

- A 2004 book on investing in residential real estate
- A local real estate broker
- A database of historical sales prices from your local tax collector

Rank these three sources based on how willing you would be to rely on the information from the source. Briefly justify your rankings.

Evaluating Information

Now that you understand a bit about information quality, the question of how to evaluate information comes into play. There are some elaborate methodologies for examining information that is internal to an organization's information systems. A full discussion of that topic is beyond our scope in this chapter but is discussed in more detail in Chapter 14. So we focus on how to evaluate information obtained from third parties, such as websites and published articles. Although we frame the discussion around external sources, the basic principles can also be applied to internal information.

A quick Web search for information evaluation strategies reveals many different approaches to evaluation. There are common themes that run through most of these strategies. Basically, there are two questions you need to answer: (1) Is the information useful? and (2) Is the information believable? In the next few paragraphs, we discuss the various "questions within questions" that you need to answer in order to evaluate information. Figure 3.2 illustrates our information evaluation framework.

As we noted earlier, filtering is one strategy for dealing with information overload. The ability to effectively evaluate information is important to being able to effectively filter information. Being able to quickly disregard poor-quality information is a big help in dealing with information overload.

Before getting into the details, it is important to understand that the evaluation of information is highly context dependent. You can only evaluate information within the context of your information needs. Consider Wikipedia as an information source. Anyone can add information to Wikipedia regardless of his or her credentials. If you are researching a topic for pleasure, Wikipedia is often a fine source of information. However, if you are researching a topic for a work task, we would caution against relying exclusively on Wikipedia. In the first situation, it really does not matter much if the information is slightly inaccurate, incomplete, or out of date. For a work-related task, however, inaccurate, incomplete, or old information may be completely unacceptable.

Figure 3.2 Information Evaluation Framework

Evaluating Usefulness

Before taking the time to assess the believability of information, you should determine whether the information is useful for the task at hand. If the information is not useful, then there is no need to assess its believability. To determine whether information is useful, evaluate whether the information is relevant, appropriate, and sufficiently current. Each of these is a "go, no-go" assessment. At any point, if you evaluate the information as not passing the test, there is no need to go further. For example, if the information is not relevant, you do not need to determine whether it is appropriate or sufficiently current.

Information relevance is the degree to which the information is pertinent to the task at hand. You can determine the relevance of information by asking yourself a simple question: Will this information help me accomplish my task? The answer to this question is often not a simple yes or no. There are varying degrees of relevance. Some information is highly relevant, while other information may only be tangentially relevant. With experience, you will be able to determine what degree of relevance merits further evaluation. To complicate matters further, relevance is context dependent. In some cases, information that does not seem relevant early in a task may become relevant as you move toward a solution. All this being said, relevance really does come down to figuring out whether the information helps you accomplish your task.

If the information seems relevant, then you should evaluate whether the information is appropriate: Is the information suitable for your purpose? For example, if you are researching a new technology when preparing a report for your manager, the information contained in a high school student's report may not be appropriate for your use. You will need to assess the level of detail and the depth of the information in light of your information needs. Again, this is a context-dependent question.

Currency is the final evaluation criteria related to usefulness. Assessing whether information is sufficiently current requires thinking about how current you need the information to be. If you are seeking information related to rapidly evolving topics, such as information technology, you may need information that is very up-to-date. For less volatile topics, older information may be fine. Unfortunately, determining the currency of Web-based information is often difficult. Many websites do not clearly indicate when the information was last updated. We caution you against relying too much on undated websites when you need up-to-date information.

Evaluating Believability

Once you establish that the information is sufficiently useful, you need to determine whether the information is believable. This requires assessing whether the information comes from a credible, objective source, is well supported, and is sufficiently comprehensive.

Evaluating the credibility of an information source can be tricky in many cases and relatively straightforward in others. For example, more formal publications, such as peer-reviewed journals, often include short author biographies, which can be helpful in assessing credibility. Often a quick search for information about the author can further help you evaluate credibility. If the author has written widely on the topic in reputable sources, he or she probably has sufficient expertise to merit using the information. In some cases, however, it is almost impossible to determine who wrote the information. We would be reluctant to trust information from such sources, unless it is provided by an organization with a solid reputation. If the information is provided by a respected organization, you can usually trust that the individual who created or compiled the information is knowledgeable on the topic.

The next step is to evaluate whether the information is objective. To determine whether information is objective, first consider the source of the information. An organization or individual who is credible may still have a bias or some agenda that makes the information less objective. Our opening story provides a good example of this. The author of that article undoubtedly had considerable expertise in plotters, but he also had a bias toward his own company's products, which tainted the information he provided. Another example is when an organization provides information on its own product or service. Using factual information from Dell's website is fine, but relying on Dell to provide an unbiased comparison of their computers to Hewlett-Packard's is a bad idea. You should also pay attention to the language used. If much of the information is presented using persuasive or emotional language, the information is probably not entirely objective. Language that is more fact based and neutral is more likely to be objective. Finally, if the topic is controversial, consider whether all sides of the issue are presented. If only one side is presented, the information is probably not entirely objective.

Evaluating the support for claims is also important. Begin by determining whether or not any support is offered. Claims without support should not be trusted. For example, we might say that this is the greatest information systems book ever written, but unless we present some evidence to back this claim, it is not believable. When support is offered, you should evaluate the quality of the support. Claims that are supported by credible sources, such as peer-reviewed journals, are usually believable. Also consider the reasonableness of the claim. There is a saying that extraordinary claims require extraordinary evidence. If a claim seems unreasonable or is widely different from other views of the topic, you should require more supporting evidence before believing the claim. Finally, think about whether the claim is testable. This does not mean that you have to actually test the claim, but if you can see no reasonable way to do so, be reluctant to rely on the information.

Our final evaluation criterion is whether the information is sufficiently comprehensive. Assessing comprehensiveness requires assessing the depth and breadth of the information. Breadth concerns whether all aspects of a topic are covered, while depth concerns the level of detail provided. When evaluating comprehensiveness, look for obvious gaps in the information. If it seems like something is missing, it probably is. Finally, consider whether there are unanswered questions. If there are, you will need to gather more information. Throughout your evaluation, keep in mind the context of your particular task; information that is sufficiently comprehensive for one task may be lacking for another.

All this probably seems like a lot of work. Keep in mind that the more information you evaluate, the more some of this will become second nature. Also, match the level of effort you put into evaluation against the importance of the task. The more important the task, the more worthwhile the effort put into evaluating the information.

Chapter Summary

In this chapter, you learned about information quality and information evaluation. The intent of the chapter was to give you an appreciation for the importance of information evaluation from both personal and professional perspectives and to help you gain the knowledge necessary to effectively evaluate information. Here are the main points discussed in the chapter:

- Being able to evaluate information is a key element of information literacy, which is an important skill for both our professional and personal lives.
- Career and personal success depends, in part, on the outcomes of the decisions we make. Our ability to evaluate the information we use to make these decisions affects the quality of our decisions.
- Information overload occurs when we are faced with more information than we can effectively process.
- Increasing our information evaluation skills helps us deal with information overload by reducing the amount of attention and time we devote to low-quality or nonuseful information.
- Intrinsic dimensions of information quality include accuracy, believability, objectivity, understandability, and consistency.
- Contextual dimensions of information quality include relevance, timeliness, completeness, and currency.
- Evaluating information concerns determining whether the information is useful and believable.
- Useful information is relevant, appropriate, and sufficiently current for the task at hand.
- Believable information is credible, objective, well supported, and comprehensive.

Review Questions

1. Briefly explain why information evaluation skills are important personally and professionally.

2. Explain the relationship between information and uncertainty in decision making. Use a decision-making example to illustrate your answer.

3. What is information overload? How is information evaluation related to information overload?

4. Briefly describe five reasons managers gather information.

5. Name and briefly describe two major strategies for dealing with information overload.

6. Explain the phrase "garbage in, garbage out" as it relates to information quality and decision making.

7. Name and briefly describe the four categories of information quality dimensions discussed in the chapter.

8. Contrast intrinsic and contextual information quality.

9. What are the two main questions that must be addressed when evaluating information?

10. Name and describe the elements of the information evaluation framework.

Reflection Questions

1. What is the most important thing you learned in this chapter? Why is it important?

2. What topics are unclear? What about them is unclear?

3. What relationships do you see between what you learned in this chapter and what you have learned in earlier chapters?

4. How does information evaluation relate to information systems?

5. How do you think information evaluation skills will be helpful in your future career?

6. Describe a situation where, looking back on it, you spent more time gathering information than you should have. How do you know when you've gathered enough information?

7. Why is information quality an ethical issue?

8. How do you decide how much effort to put into information quality/evaluation?

9. Why is context important to information quality and evaluation?

Additional Learning Activities

3.A1. Think about a situation in which you relied on poor-quality information. Briefly describe the situation and what poor-quality information you relied on. Identify the dimension(s) of information quality where the information was not of adequate quality. (For example, you might have taken a course that you thought was required, but you were looking at out-of-date requirements and the course was no longer required. This information was poor on the accuracy and timeliness dimensions of information quality.)

3.A2. A rubric is a set of rules for assessing something. For example, many instructors use rubrics for grading assignments. Develop a rubric for judging information quality. (For a rubric template, see http://www.edutopia .org/resource/editable-sample-rubric-download.)

3.A3. Many of you might have graduate school in your future. Choosing the right graduate school is a major decision-making task. Suppose you want to attend a full-time MBA program. Use the information evaluation framework to evaluate the information you would find in each of the following sources. For each information source, rate each dimension on a scale of 1 (lowest) to 5 (highest). Give a brief explanation of each of your ratings:

   a. Princeton Review's Graduate Business Schools website (http://www .princetonreview.com/business-schools-programs.aspx)

   b. A university's website about their MBA program

   c. A friend who recently got his MBA

   d. The admissions councilor for an MBA program

3.A4. For each of the following tasks, indicate on a scale of 1 (very little time) to 10 (a significant amount of time) how long you would spend evaluating the information you would use in completing the task. Briefly justify each of your ratings.

   a. Deciding where to go for a celebration dinner

   b. Deciding what pair of running shoes to buy

   c. Deciding what laptop to buy

   d. Deciding which of two postgraduation job offers to accept

3.A5. For each of the following tasks, indicate on a scale of 1 (very little time) to 10 (a significant amount of time) how long you would spend evaluating the information you would use in completing the task. Briefly justify each of your ratings.

   a. Deciding which item to make the "daily special" for a restaurant

   b. Deciding what employee to hire for a part-time, temporary job

   c. Deciding what employee to hire for a management-level job

   d. Deciding which outlets to use for a national marketing campaign

3.A6. In this chapter, you learned about information quality and information evaluation. Create a diagram that links the information quality dimensions to the information evaluation criteria.

References

Butcher, H. 1998. *Meeting Managers' Information Needs.* London: Aslib.

Experian Data Quality. 2016. *The 2016 Global Data Management Benchmark Report,* https://www.edq.com/globalassets/white-papers/2016-global-data-management-benchmark-report.pdf.

Knight, S., and J. Burn. 2005. "Developing a Framework for Assessing Information Quality on the World Wide Web." *Informing Science* 8: 159–72. http://inform.nu/Articles/Vol8/v8p159-172Knig.pdf.

Lee, Y., D. Strong, B. Kahn, and R. Wang. 2002. "AIMQ: A Methodology for Information Quality Assessment." *Information & Management* 40: 133–46.

Marquet, C. T., and L. J. B. Peterson. 2015. "Resume Fraud: The Top 10 Lies." *Marquet International LTD.* http://www.marquetinternational.com/pdf/Resume%20Fraud-Top%20Ten%20Lies.pdf.

Mason, R. O. 1986. "Four Ethical Issues of the Information Age." *MIS Quarterly* 10(1): 5–12.

Savolainen, R. 2007. "Filtering and Withdrawing: Strategies for Coping with Information Overload in Everyday Contexts." *Journal of Information Science,* 33(5): 611–21.

Simon, H. 1971. "Designing Organizations for an Information-Rich World." In *Computers, Communications and the Public Interest,* edited by Martin Greenberger, 40–41. Baltimore: Johns Hopkins University Press.

Tuna, C. 2008. "How to Spot Résumé Fraud." *Wall Street Journal,* November 13. http://www.wsj.com/articles/SB122653695797922735.

United States Department of Justice. 2010. *Information Quality: The Foundation for Justice Decision Making.* http://www.it.ojp.gov/documents/IQ_Fact_Sheet_Final.pdf.

Wang, R., and D. Strong. 1996. "Beyond Accuracy: What Data Quality Means to Consumers." *Journal of Management Information Systems* 12(4): 5–34.

Glossary

Accurate (information): The degree to which information is correct and free from error.

Believable (information): The degree to which information is regarded as true and credible.

Comprehensive (information): The degree to which information is of sufficient depth and breadth for the task at hand.

Consistent (information): The degree to which information is compatible with previous information.

Current (information): The degree to which information is sufficiently up-to-date for the task at hand.

Information evaluation: The systematic determination of the merit and worth of information.

Information overload: Being faced with more information than one can effectively process.

Information quality: The degree to which information is suitable for a particular purpose.

Objective (information): The degree to which information is free from bias.

Relevant (information): The degree to which information is applicable and useful for the task at hand.

Timely (information): The degree to which information is available in time to perform the task at hand.

Understandable (information): The degree to which information is easily comprehended.

CHAPTER 4

Gaining Strategic Value from Information

Learning Objectives

By reading and completing the activities in this chapter, you will be able to

- Present the main steps in the strategic planning process
- Identify competitive advantage frameworks and discuss their purposes
- Discuss methods for evaluating strategic initiatives
- Explain the concept of hypercompetition

Chapter Outline

Focusing Story: Health Care on My Cell Phone
Strategic Information Systems
Strategic Planning Process
Learning Activity 4.1: Trends in Top Management Concerns
Frameworks for Strategic Information Systems
Evaluating Strategic Initiatives
Critical Success Factors
Learning Activity 4.2: What Does This Company Need for Success?
Priority Matrix
Learning Activity 4.3: Competitive Advantage at TRIPBAM
Hypercompetition: Sustainability of Competitive Advantage
Learning Activity 4.4: Disrupting an Established Market!
Chapter Summary
Review Questions
Reflection Questions

FOCUSING STORY

Health Care on My Cell Phone

In the business world, a key goal for many companies is to achieve some form of competitive advantage over rivals. Of course, creating a new product that no one has ever thought of before, or a product that is so much better than previous ones, definitely gives an organization a competitive advantage (think of the Apple iPod, for example). However, it is often possible to also develop competitive advantages from creative uses of existing technologies. One of these exciting newer trends in the world of medicine is mobile health, also called mHealth.

mHealth offers health care services delivered via mobile technology, such as cellular or smartphones, tablets, or personal digital assistants (PDAs). Mobile health care services can include compliance (ensuring that patients follow their medication plans), information dissemination (providing caloric information for obese patients or sugar content for diabetic patients), or monitoring (measuring hypertension or cholesterol or tracking activity). Surveys conducted in 2015 suggest that 66% of Americans use apps to track their health and fitness daily, including diet/nutrition, medication reminders, symptoms, and physical activity. In 2017, it is estimated that mHealth apps generated US$26.56 billion.

The idea of mHealth is to provide health care services where they are needed, often to those who cannot access them. One application called text4baby from Voxiva helps prevent infant mortality by sending weekly text messages to young women about their babies' health. There are also mobile health screening programs at home for executives in Pakistan and at truck stops for truck drivers in Canada. mHealth smoking applications have been shown to help smokers quit smoking. Another company called Avacta developed a handheld device to detect dangerous flu diseases in the field without having to bring samples to laboratories for tests. In China and Malaysia, doctors' offices have started using less expensive text messaging instead of phone calls to remind patients of appointments; results include improved attendance by 7% in China and reduced nonattendance rates of 40% in Malaysia. An even more exciting potential for mHealth is in providing health services to remote regions of developing countries, which are facing constant growth of life-threatening chronic diseases (e.g., hypertension, obesity, heart disease, and diabetes) and communicable diseases. In developing countries, there are limited health care infrastructures, limited hospital resources, and not enough health care workers, particularly in remote regions. This is where mHealth can make a difference, because even in remote regions of developing countries, mobile phones are often available. In 2016, for example, the International Telecommunications Union (ITU) and the World Health Organization produced a report on how to use mobile phones to combat noncommunicable diseases like diabetes, labeled "Be He@lthy, Be Mobile: A Handbook on How to Implement, mDiabetes."

A new trend with mHealth is personal well-being, where individuals track their own health information with fitness trackers (like the Fitbit) or smart watches (like the Apple Watch). The devices are often worn 24 hours a day, seven days a week, collecting pulse rates, sleeping patterns, activities, and even food intake. Wrist wear is not the only type of personal health/fitness device, though it is the most common. Others include smart clothing and leg wear. Together, wearable fitness devices represent a market of close to US$14 billion in 2017. Who would have thought people would start wearing watches again?

FOCUSING QUESTIONS

1. What mHealth applications do you use?
2. What are the benefits of mHealth for existing health care organizations? For consumers?
3. How will fitness devices change the health of individuals in the future?
4. What new mHealth applications should companies develop in the future to help have better well-being in society?
5. What other day-to-day device could be transformed to change the competitive landscape?

Sources: http://mhealthshare.com/mfactsheet.htm; "Case Study: Organizations, Technology and PR Unite to Deliver Mobile Health Service Targeted at Moms and Moms-to-Be." 2010. *PR News* 66(45): 45; Contant, J. 2008. "Mobile Health Unit Rolls into Truck Stop." *OH & S Canada* 24(7): 21; "Dow University Launches Mobile Health Screening Program." 2010. *Financial Post,* October 15; Kahn, J. G., J. S. Yang, and J. S Kahn. 2010. "Mobile Health Needs and Opportunities in Developing Countries." *Health Affairs* 29(2): 252–58; "Wearable Fitness Trackers Market: Wrist Wear Product Type Segment Expected to Remain Dominant over the Forecast Period," Future Market Insights, 2017, retrieved December 20, 2017, from https://www.futuremarketinsights.com/reports/wearable-fitness-trackers-market; World Health Organization. 2016. "A Handbook on How to Implement mDiabetes." *World Health Organization and International Telecommunications Union,* https://www.itu.int/dms_pub/itu-d/opb/str/D-STR-E_HEALTH.09-2016-PDF-E.pdf.

Strategic Information Systems

Today, organizations need a wide variety of information systems for conducting their day-to-day business. For example, some information systems can be used for basic accounting services, such as payroll systems, or for communication support services, like electronic mail. In this chapter, we are interested in those information systems that are more specifically meant to provide organizations with competitive advantages. We call those business initiatives **strategic information systems.** Importantly, it is not necessary to have unique and proprietary information technology to make an initiative strategic; it is how the information systems are used that can provide the added value or strategic advantage organizations seek by implementing such initiatives.

Strategic Planning Process

The identification of strategic information systems should follow a structured set of steps, or a **strategic planning process.** Of course, there are situations when some techno-oriented individuals start using a new technology and believe everyone should have access to it to increase productivity of the workforce. When the BlackBerry and iPhone devices came out, many managers believed they needed them, even though they had no real idea why. Some companies gained real advantages from increased mobility, while others realized the devices did not really help their employees beyond being more accessible. Most large organizations, however, do have a strategic planning process in place. The goal of the strategic planning effort is to identify how the organization will use and manage its resources for strategic purposes (think competitive advantage). It provides a roadmap for decision making related to information systems. Figure 4.1 shows an example of the steps involved in a typical information systems strategic planning process. Notice how the process is iterative, with later steps in the process requiring managers to revisit earlier steps. In addition, there may be several phases involved within each of the stages (rectangles).

Step 1: Strategic Business Planning

Before an organization can decide what information technology (IT) initiatives can be used to gain a competitive advantage, it has to clearly identify what the mission of the organization is and how it is going to achieve this mission. The strategic business planning phase is often referred to as "Know Who You Are." Executives or leaders of the organization should perform strategic business planning on a regular basis. (How often this is varies substantially between companies.) The outcomes of strategic business planning sessions should include the mission and vision of the organization, its goals for the future, and the strategies that will be used to achieve those goals.

While strategic business planning is not specifically focused on information systems, it is essential to the IS strategic planning process because the organization needs to know what it is trying to achieve before it can identify how information systems

Figure 4.1 Sample Information Systems Strategic Planning Process

are going to help achieve those strategic objectives. The goal is to achieve a high level of alignment between the business side of the organization and its information systems. With high alignment, there will be a high level of fit between the priorities and activities of the IS function and the strategic goals of the organization.

LEARNING ACTIVITY 4.1

Trends in Top Management Concerns

The alignment of business and information systems objectives is a key concern for top managers. Every year, a survey is conducted among members of the Society for Information Management (SIM) about senior managers' top concerns about information technology. The most recent survey (Kappelman et al. 2017) highlights IT and business alignment as one of the top priorities, with all priorities being ranked in following order:

1. Alignment of IT with the business
2. Security/Cybersecurity/Privacy
3. Innovation
4. Agility/Flexibility (IT)
5. Agility/Flexibility (Business)
6. Cost Reduction/Controls (Business)
7. Cost Reduction/Controls (IT)
8. Speed of IT Delivery/IT Time-to-Market
9. Strategic Planning (Business)
10. Productivity/Efficiency (Business)

For this learning activity, find previous IT Key Issues and Trends Studies by visiting *MISQ Executive* through your library's website, or use those provided to you by your instructor. Identify the trends in top management concerns, as these studies go back in time to the early 2000s. Identify reasons you think might have led to which issues were of greater concern at different times. Be prepared to defend your reasons to the class.

Step 2: Information Systems Assessment

Once managers know the main strategic goals of the organization, they need to identify the current state of information systems resources in the organization. This phase is sometimes referred to as "Know Where You Start." It is important to conduct a proper assessment of resources because these resources could enable information systems managers to meet or surpass some strategic objectives or, conversely, constrain the organization regarding what it can do. For example, if the organization has been collecting data about its customers for a very long time but never used those data, there might be some great potential for new systems that will make use of these data. (We will discuss customer relationship management [CRM] systems in Chapter 12.) On the other hand, the lack of certain resources may also constrain what an organization can achieve. For example, if all individuals in the IT group are trained on a particular system, replacing the system with technology that is completely different may create a very disruptive situation for the organization, which may even impact profits for some time. The outcome of the **information systems assessment** is a picture of the current state of information systems resources in the organization. Depending on the assessment, it may be necessary for the organization to revise its strategic goals.

As you can see, information systems resources are not limited to just technology. There are three categories of resources: technical resources, which include hardware, software, and networks; data and information resources, such as databases; and human resources, which would include the skills and personal characteristics of the information systems employees, the user community, and the management, as well as the structure of the organization and its incentive systems.

Step 3: Information Systems Vision

In the first step, the executives of the organization developed mission and vision statements for the organization as a whole. Given those statements and the information systems resources identified in the second phase, information systems managers must now develop a vision specifically for information systems. For this and the following steps, the senior information systems person in the organization must gather not only employees of the information systems group, including individuals with technical skills, but also functional managers. Functional managers work in other areas of the organization, such as accounting or marketing, and are likely to be the end users of the information systems initiatives that will be identified later. They therefore need to be part of the information systems strategic planning process from the start.

The **information systems vision** should be a broad statement of how the organization should use and manage its information systems for strategic purposes. It basically suggests that organizations need to "Know Where They Want to Go." Clearly, the information systems vision has to be aligned with the organization's mission, vision, and strategies, which may require revisiting the organization's strategies. An example of an IS vision statement could be "We will strive to offer leading-edge but tested technologies to our functional areas, provide leadership in managing external and internal data, and promote technologies that will enhance the competitive advantage of our firm." Of course, each organization is unique, and the statements will be more specific to each company. Nevertheless, the statement should define what role the information systems should play in the organization.

Step 4: Information Systems Architecture

In most organizations, an information systems vision is likely to already exist. Therefore, the previous phase involves modifying it if needed. Similarly, most large organizations will already have selected an information systems architecture. **Information systems architecture** specifies how information systems resources should be used and how they should work together. It is the "Know How You Are Going to Get There" phase. We will discuss information systems architectures in more depth in Chapter 7 (Transmitting Information). The development of an architecture may require managers to revisit the information systems vision if, for example, the architecture cannot support the vision that was established.

The selected information systems architecture will provide some guidelines for future uses, acquisitions, and the management of information resources. It is therefore general enough to provide guidelines for several years but specific enough to offer actionable guidelines. Consider the following architectural statement: "We will strive to provide a technology environment that will allow a variety of vendors to interact with our systems independently of their technology platforms." The statement clearly points to the need for interoperability of technology, which is the ability of heterogeneous systems to communicate with one another. Therefore, acquisition of software or hardware that limits interoperability is not consistent with the selected architecture. Architectural guidelines could include statements about all information resources, including hardware, software, and networks; the way data are stored, protected, and managed; and how information systems human resources are managed, such as whether information systems work can be outsourced.

Step 5: Strategic Initiatives Identification

The ultimate goal of the information systems strategic planning process is to identify strategic information systems initiatives that will provide competitive advantages to the organization. These initiatives tend to be longer term (two to five years), although some strategic initiatives can be launched rapidly. It should be noted that strategic initiatives can be about systems, but most of the time they involve much more than technology, which means they may result in a new strategic direction for the organization. For example, when an organization decides to implement customer relationship management systems, installing software and hardware is not enough; employees must be trained to be highly customer oriented if the implementation is to succeed.

There are many frameworks that can be used to identify **strategic information systems initiatives**, and we will discuss several of them in the next section of this chapter. As you learn how to use the frameworks to identify initiatives, however, keep in mind that the initiatives that are identified need to be aligned with the IS vision and the strategic goals of the organization.

Advantages of IS Strategic Planning Process

The identification of strategic initiatives is in itself an important goal of the information systems strategic planning process. There are, however, several other benefits from using a structured approach to identify strategic initiatives:

- *Improved communication:* Having stakeholders involved in the planning process allows everyone to provide input into initiatives that will potentially affect individuals in different areas of the organization. By providing documented discussions of the advantages and disadvantages of each initiative, overall communication inside the organization is improved.

- *Improved coordination:* Since various stakeholders are involved in the planning process, they develop a shared mental image of the initiatives, their purposes, and their advantages and disadvantages. Furthermore, each member of the planning team gets a clear picture of everyone's responsibility. This improves overall coordination of the efforts related to the initiative, both before and during the implementation.

- *Improved decision making:* When a structured approach is used for identifying strategic initiatives, a clear set of guidelines and criteria for selection of initiatives are established. For example, initiatives have to be aligned with the goals of the organization. The result is that decision making is more consistent over time with respect to which strategic initiatives are supported and, more importantly, why.

Frameworks for Strategic Information Systems

The last phase of the strategic planning process is the identification of strategic initiatives. As previously discussed, each phase is actually composed of several steps. In this section, we look more specifically at a number of frameworks or tools that can be used to identify strategic information systems initiatives.

Information Systems SWOT Analysis

Most students will have discussed **SWOT (strengths, weaknesses, opportunities, and threats) analyses** in one of their management or marketing classes. SWOT analyses can be used for strategic information systems planning, just like for other areas of the organization. While the technique of a SWOT analysis has existed for some time now, the basic concepts remain the same. Table 4.1 summarizes the components of a SWOT analysis, with some example statements that could be applied to Amazon.com.

When considering the use of a SWOT analysis for the purpose of identifying potential strategic information systems initiatives, it is important to consider factors beyond technology in the strengths, weaknesses, opportunities, and threats. Say, for example, a firm has a great idea for implementing an information system to improve the sales cycle by providing mobile devices to sales representatives. If one of their weaknesses is that their customer base is limited to military agencies where mobile devices may not be allowed on the facilities for security reasons, then this may not be a good initiative for the organization. On the other hand, if one of their opportunities is to have a more physical presence with customers (which may seem contradictory to the use of electronic media), it may be that changes in technologies available at home can free up more time for sales representatives to visit their clients. The important point is that you should not limit yourself to thinking only about technology when you perform a SWOT analysis.

Table 4.1 SWOT Analysis Components

Component	Description	Example for Amazon.com
Strengths	What gives the organization advantages over others in its industry?	Leadership position in online retailing
Weaknesses	What creates disadvantages for the organization relative to others in its industry?	Increased size of the company requires more investments
Opportunities	What activities or factors could help the organization get new advantages over others in its industry?	Expanding to services instead of just retailing
Threats	What activities or factors could create disadvantages or troubles for the organization relative to others in its industry?	Increasing global competition from online retailers

How do you identify information systems strategic initiatives from a SWOT analysis? Of course, you can look at the opportunities and see which ones can be achieved with the implementation of information systems. However, you can also look at weaknesses and see if you can remove or reduce those weaknesses via better use of information systems. Similarly, ask yourself, How can the organization reduce external threats by making better use of information systems? How can it make better use of its strengths through new information systems? All these ways to look at the SWOT elements can allow managers to identify a number of initiatives. Not all of them will be viable, but at this point, we are only focused on identifying them.

SWOT ANALYSES IN PRACTICE

Does a SWOT analysis seem too basic to you? While it is true that SWOT analyses are more often discussed in academia, they do find their way into the real world. If you use a search engine and type "SWOT analysis examples," you will find many real-world companies that have been analyzed using this framework. For example, *Entrepreneur* proposes key questions to ask to develop a SWOT analysis for a sales organization. For strengths, they suggest asking, "What does your team do better than anyone else? . . . What benefits do your customers get from working with you? . . . What does your product or solution offer that your competitors can't? . . . Do you have unique processes, products, or services that set you apart?" For weaknesses, they suggest asking, "What does the competition see as your biggest weakness? . . . What do your customers regard as a weakness in your sales methods, product or service? . . . When you lose a sale, why did it happen?" Questions for opportunities include "What do you see as a good opportunity that will strengthen your business? . . . In what segment of your market are clients consistently making purchases? . . . What high margin products or services can you expose to a broader market? . . . Have you noticed a change you can exploit in your market? . . . Is there a market you can enter with greater profits potential?" Finally, questions to evaluate threats include "Does more than 25% of your sales revenue come from less than 10% of your customer base? . . . What recurring challenges do your sales people face? . . . Is there a competitor that consistently beats you in the marketplace? . . . How much bad debt are you carrying? . . . Are sales meeting expectations?"

Source: SWOT Analysis Examples, 2016, *Entrepreneur,* https://www .entrepreneurmag.co.za/advice/business-plans/business-plan-research-and -preparation/swot-analysis-examples/.

Porter's Five Competitive Forces Model
Porter's Five Competitive Forces Model is one of the most popular frameworks for analyzing a firm's competitive position by looking at the major forces that shape an organization's competitive environment. An adaptation of the framework is presented in Figure 4.2. The original purpose of the model is to analyze how competitive an industry is and therefore determine if a particular market (product, service, geography, etc.) could be attractive for an organization to consider. It could also be used to reevaluate a company's competitive position if one of the competitive forces changes—for example, if a major merger changes the level of rivalry in a particular industry.

The original model was developed back in 1979 but was later updated by Michael Porter in 2008. Some have argued that the model focuses too much on a perfect yet simple market situation where there is a relative static structure (where competition does not fluctuate very much; Recklies 2015). Yet while there have been some

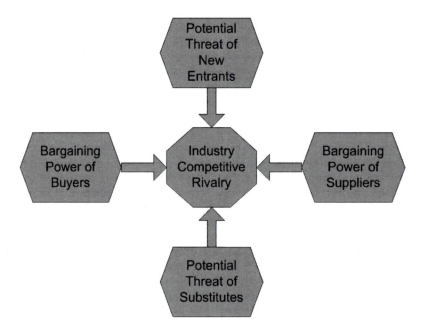

Figure 4.2 Porter's Five Competitive Forces Model
Source: Adapted from Porter (1979, 2008).

criticisms, the Five Forces model is still used as a way to analyze a firm's competitive position in today's business world. For example, Martin (2017) looks at the Five Forces model for Under Armour (http://www.underarmour.com) and concludes the company's position was weak on competitive rivalry and threats of new entrants but strong on bargaining power of suppliers, bargaining power of customers, and threat of substitutes.

In the context of information systems, we can use Porter's Five Competitive Forces model to identify strategic information systems initiatives. Table 4.2 shows how each of the forces could be examined from a strategic information systems point of view.

Porter's Value Chain Analysis

Porter proposed another framework that could be useful in identifying strategic information systems initiatives. In a **value chain analysis**, managers identify all the activities that the organization must perform to conduct its business (Porter 1996). As each activity is performed, the organization adds value to the product or service it delivers. Clearly, all industries and organizations are likely to have their own value chain. Porter identified two broad categories of activities in the value chain: primary and support. *Primary* activities are directly related to the creation, processing, or delivery of the product or service. *Support* activities are those overall tasks that

Table 4.2 Porter's Five Competitive Forces Model and Strategic Information Systems

Competitive Force	Description	Desired Level	Strategic Information Systems	Examples
Potential threat of new entrants	How easy is it for new companies to enter the market in which the organization operates?	Low—no new companies can enter the market.	How could you use information systems to increase barriers to entry in the organization's market?	Create barriers to entry—leverage data about customers that others cannot access, creating information asymmetry.
Bargaining power of buyers	What is the ability (or market power) of the organization's buyers (customers) to reduce its competitive position (e.g., by bringing prices down)?	Low—customers cannot dictate lower prices or better conditions.	How could you use information systems to reduce the buyers' power of negotiation?	Create switching costs—give customers value-added services such as personalization or lower costs (through economies of scale) that will make them loyal to the organization.
Bargaining power of suppliers	What is the ability (or market power) of the organization's suppliers to reduce its competitive position (e.g., by bringing prices up)?	Low—suppliers cannot dictate higher prices or better conditions.	How could you use information systems to reduce the suppliers' power of negotiation?	When there are few suppliers, this tends to be a high barrier. Use information systems to aggregate buying power with others (e.g., online exchanges) or reduce the cost of buying (electronic procurement).
Potential threat of substitutes	What is the likelihood that other products of equal of superior value will be available?	Low—no products can substitute for the organization's products (or services).	How could you use information systems to make your products unique or make customers unwilling to use substitutes?	Create switching costs so customers will not be willing to use substitutes (personalization, lower costs, etc.) or use information systems to create unique or patented products such as proprietary systems (like Google applications or Apple products).
Industry competitive rivalry	What is the current level of competition in the industry?	Low—there is limited competition.	How could you use information systems to ensure that competition is limited in the industry?	Use information systems to differentiate the organization's products so that there are few or no competitors.

make it possible for the organization to function but that are not directly involved in the product or service. Figure 4.3 shows a typical value chain in a manufacturing firm. Note that many organizations today are in the service industry, and their value chain would be completely different. We will discuss service industry firms in the next section.

How could you use a value chain analysis to identify strategic information systems initiatives? Porter identified two major ways to create competitive advantages in the value chain: lower the costs of performing an activity or add more value to the final products and services in an activity. Therefore, for every activity in their value chain, managers can ask themselves, How can I use information systems to perform this activity at a lower cost? How can I use information systems to improve the value added from this activity to the final product or service? If we take the example of marketing a product, in what ways can information systems reduce marketing costs? The organization could use electronic marketing through social networks or electronic mailings. What about adding value to the product? Well, the organization could make its products more personalized. For example, instead of selling cute teddy bears, the organization could create online profiles for the teddy bears that would make them have their own online "lives," making the product more attractive than the other teddy bears that do not have online lives.

There are a lot of opportunities for managers to examine the activities of their organization in order to identify potential strategic uses of information systems. But now think of extending this outside of the organization's value chain to its suppliers and customers. With more and more organizations linked electronically, are there possibilities for the activities of members of an organization's value system (upstream and downstream value chains) to be improved via technology? That is what the giant retailer Wal-Mart is doing when it manages its inventory not only within its organization but within its suppliers as well. (See Chapter 12, Enterprise Information Systems, for a story about this.)

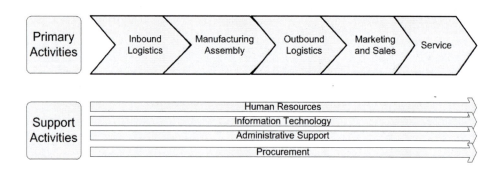

Figure 4.3 Sample Value Chain in Manufacturing Firm
Source: Adapted from Porter (1996).

Virtual Value Chain

As discussed in the previous section, many firms today are mainly information-based organizations. Think about what Google offers as a product. The company creates and offers software tools to individuals and companies. In addition, the company offers information to individuals through its search engine as well as information to organizations via its analytical software that provides an analysis of traffic on organizations' websites.

Instead of looking at activities that turn raw materials into a final product, as in manufacturing organizations, the **virtual value chain** looks at activities that turn raw data into useful information (Piccoli 2008). An example of an information-based business is consulting. Consulting firms' main outputs are information and knowledge-based reports and documents they provide to their clients about specific questions of interest, specific analyses regarding their own business or certain markets they are considering, or even reports about general industry trends. In the business of consulting, professionals regularly gather substantial amounts of data and information and then organize and store them in some useful way (retrievable, indexed, etc.). When the organization is asked to provide consulting on a specific topic, the professionals in the firm identify and retrieve the relevant information from a repository (where it is stored), synthesize the information (rendering it useful), and then distribute it to the client. Figure 4.4 shows an example of a virtual value chain.

Similar to the other frameworks discussed so far, an analysis of the virtual value chain can help identify strategic information systems initiatives. Managers can ask themselves in what ways information systems can make gathering, organizing, selecting, synthesizing, and distributing less expensive and add more value to the firm's information. For example, within the human resources (personnel) department, information could be distributed more rapidly to employees using an intranet (discussed in Chapter 7). Are there better ways to gather information and data for

Figure 4.4 Virtual Value Chain: Handling Information
Source: Adapted from Piccoli (2008).

the human resources department? One could imagine, for example, collecting work hours (time sheets) for remote employees via website applications as opposed to paper forms. Similarly, are there better ways to organize and select information within the human resources department? It may be that a new system could be implemented for identifying information requirements for employees who travel internationally. As you can see, different questions can lead managers to the identification of potential strategic information systems. And we only discussed the human resources department! This can be extended to all departments that require gathering, organizing, selecting, synthesizing, and distributing of information.

Evaluating Strategic Initiatives

In the previous section of this chapter, we used a variety of frameworks to identify potential strategic information system initiatives that the organization should consider. In theory, we should at this point have a significant number of initiatives identified. Not all of them will be implemented, as some simply cannot be done (for example, they might require technology that does not exist yet), and others are not worth doing (for example, they might be too costly with only limited benefits). We therefore need to rank the initiatives, or at least eliminate those that cannot or should not be considered. There are several tools that can be used for doing this analysis, and we will discuss two: the critical success factors method and the priority matrix. Both methods can be used for evaluating the viability of strategic information systems initiatives, although the priority matrix provides a more in-depth analysis.

Critical Success Factors

Critical success factors (CSFs) are those few important considerations that must be achieved for the organization to survive and be successful (i.e., achieve its mission). These are not about technology (in general), but more about business objectives. In other words, CSFs must be in line with the organization's vision and mission. Organizations usually have just a few critical success factors, and top management typically identifies these.

Identification of CSFs is a process in itself that resembles brainstorming sessions where top managers sit together with a moderator who helps them develop a short list of the main factors necessary for the company's success. The key questions asked to start the discussion are similar to these: What needs to happen for our organization to increase its revenues? What are the most important actions we need to take to be more competitive? What is needed for us to be more successful? These questions just help start the discussion, which subsequently involves deliberations among the executives, identification of potential obstacles, and mostly the development of priorities among the most important factors for the organization's success.

Imagine that you are an executive at your school involved in developing strategies for the future of the school. Your group of school executives would have to ask themselves, What is needed for the school to be a leader in education? The group would probably identify factors such as the following:

1. Having the highest quality students possible (Having no students is not a good idea; having poor-quality students does not help the university be successful.)
2. Having the best possible faculty
3. Providing a close link to the community

Once the critical success factors are identified for the organization, managers can map their proposed strategic information systems initiatives to the CSFs. Initiatives that do not support the CSFs of the organization should not be considered as top priorities. This ensures that the organization achieves the business and IT alignment discussed earlier in the chapter and that the planning team is able to prioritize initiatives in a consistent way. In fact, consulting firms often suggest that businesses use CSF to ensure they meet their strategic objectives and highlight the importance of tracking the CSFs on a regular basis (Paulo 2017; Reilly 2016).

LEARNING ACTIVITY 4.2

What Does This Company Need for Success?

The purpose of this activity is to get some practice identifying critical success factors. Your instructor will assign you to groups, and each group of students will act as a top management team from one of two companies: Lyft (http://www.lyft.com) or Spotify (http://www.spotify.com). Your job is to brainstorm critical success factors for the company.

Priority Matrix

The **priority matrix** allows managers to evaluate potential initiatives and prioritize them along two key dimensions: the ease of implementation and the potential returns. The ease of implementation includes several factors such as costs, time required, efforts required, or the actual complexity of the system. The potential returns can be in terms of revenues, market shares, savings, reputation, and so on. Figure 4.5 shows a sample priority matrix.

Looking at Figure 4.5, you can easily identify which strategic information systems initiatives should be given higher priority by managers. **Imperatives** are initiatives that should be relatively easy to implement—for example, because they cost little or the technology is already implemented—and have the potential to bring high returns to the organization. **Quick wins** represent initiatives that do not have much

STATS BOX 4.1:
CSFS FOR IMPLEMENTING WEB PORTALS IN SAUDI ARABIA

Critical success factors (CSFs) can be used for the organization as a whole, as we described in this chapter, but also sometimes for specific projects. In this example, researchers explored the CSFs for the implementation of Web portals in two Saudi organizations: the Saudi Food and Drug Authority (SFDA) and the Saudi Stock Exchange. A Web portal usually provides a point of access to integrated information and services. Both organizations had launched portals that provided several services to their constituents. In the table below, the researchers identified 21 CSFs based on rankings where 1 = critical, 2 = very high importance, 3 = high importance, 4 = moderate importance, and 5 = low importance. The researchers who developed this list interviewed a large number of managers and looked for factors that emerged as the most commonly mentioned for success.

Ranking	Critical Success Factor	Mean Value
1	Strong communication inward and outward	1.00
2	User acceptance	1.00
3	Top management support	1.33
4	Clear goals and objectives	1.33
5	Project monitoring and controlling	1.33
6	Requirements analysis	1.33
7	Defining the portal architecture	1.67
8	Dedicated resources	1.67
9	Selection of the appropriate portal package	2.00
10	Process and application integration	2.00
11	Prototyping	2.00
12	Flexible project structure	2.00
13	Project management	2.00
14	Portal design	2.33
15	Change management	2.33
16	Team competencies and skills	2.67
17	Portal strategy	2.67
18	User training and education	2.67
19	Business process reengineering	2.67
20	Organizational culture	3.00
21	Portal engineering roadmap	3.00

Recall that in the chapter we suggest there should be only a few CSFs in an organization (three to five). Having 21 items to worry about is unlikely to be very productive. Since CSFs should focus on the "critical" ones, managers might consider only items 1 to 8. Alternatively, they can merge some items together, as recommended by the researchers who developed this list. For example, they suggest merging five factors into one called project management (project monitoring and controlling, change management, project management, team competencies and skills, and user training and education).

Source: Al-Mudimigh, Zahid, and Talal (2011).

upside potential but are easy to implement (low or no cost, low or no difficulties involved, limited effort, etc.). They are called quick wins because the organization can get some visible impacts without much effort. The initiatives may not be the top priorities, but since they can be implemented rapidly and easily, it is worth considering them. The initiatives in the **evaluate** quadrant need to be discussed and evaluated thoroughly by managers. Some of them will be implemented and others will not. In the end, it may depend on how many initiatives are on the table and what resources are available to the organization to implement these initiatives. Finally, the "**stay away**" quadrant includes what many say are lost causes—initiatives that would be difficult to implement and would have limited potential returns.

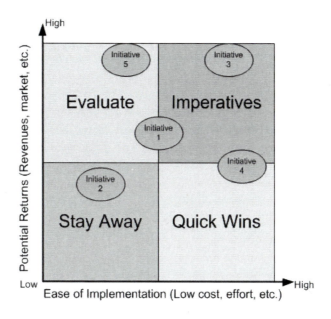

Figure 4.5 Sample Priority Matrix

LEARNING ACTIVITY 4.3

Competitive Advantage at TRIPBAM

This activity requires you to complete a competitive analysis of TRIPBAM (Piccoli and Pigni 2016). The case may be provided to you by your instructor. Use one of the frameworks discussed to (1) identify the competitive position of TRIPBAM, and (2) identify three strategic information systems initiatives you believe the company should consider.

Source: Piccoli, G., and F. Pigni. 2016. "TRIPBAM: Leveraging Digital Data Streams to Unleash Savings." *Communications of the Association for Information Systems* 39(25). Retrieved from https://aisel.aisnet.org/cais/vol39/iss1/25.

Hypercompetition: Sustainability of Competitive Advantage

Most of the frameworks discussed previously to help identify potential strategic information systems initiatives were developed with the idea that firms can create competitive advantages that differentiate them from other organizations over time. Today, however, the pace of change in information technologies and other innovations is faster than ever. This has led some individuals to question the sustainability of any competitive advantage a firm obtains through its initiatives. This is the concept of **hypercompetition**.

In his 1994 book *Hyper-Competition,* Richard D'Aveni suggests that any competitive advantage an organization has will be rapidly eroded by competitors and that focusing on trying to sustain competitive advantages could be a deadly distraction for organizations. Instead, he suggests that organizations should seek to create disruptions in the market through a series of initiatives. He identifies seven strategic moves that organizations should consider to compete in hypercompetitive markets; these are called D'Aveni's 7 Ss, which are summarized in Table 4.3.

While many companies have not adopted the 7 S framework of hypercompetition, it can still be used to identify strategic information systems initiatives. Think about new ways that an organization can try to maximum customer satisfaction (superior stakeholder satisfaction) using information systems. For example, a new customer relationship management system (Chapter 12, Enterprise Information Systems) can be used to determine what customers prefer in their interactions with the organization. Similarly, new Web 2.0 technologies (Chapter 7, Transmitting Information) can be used to seek new knowledge directly from potential customers (strategic soothsaying). As you learn about the various technologies and information systems available today and in the near future in the next chapters, remember how they can be used for strategic purposes.

Table 4.3 D'Aveni's 7 *S*s

Strategic Move	Description
Superior stakeholder satisfaction	Maximizing customer satisfaction by adding value strategically
Strategic soothsaying	Using new knowledge to predict or create new windows of opportunity
Positioning for speed	Preparing the organization to react as fast as possible
Positioning for surprise	Preparing the organization to respond to the marketplace in a manner that will surprise competitors
Shifting the rules of competition	Finding new ways to serve customers, thereby transforming the industry
Signaling strategic intent	Communicating intentions in order to stall responses by competitors
Simultaneous and sequential strategic thrusts	Taking steps to stun and confuse competitors in order to disrupt or block their efforts

Source: D'Aveni (1994).

LEARNING ACTIVITY 4.4

Disrupting an Established Market!

The purpose of this activity is to practice some of the concepts discussed in this chapter. Your instructor will assign you to groups, ideally the same groups used for Learning Activity 4.2. Each group represents a senior management team at Lyft (http://www.lyft.com) or Spotify (http://www.spotify.com). Your team is tasked with selecting one of the 7 *S*s from D'Aveni's framework and specifically targeting it to find a way for Lyft to better compete with Uber (http://www.uber.com) or Spotify to better compete with Pandora (http://www.pandora.com). The team must then identify a specific strategic initiative that will be used to implement the selected strategy.

Once this activity is completed, all initiatives proposed by the groups in the class should be prioritized using the critical success factors identified in Learning Activity 4.2.

Chapter Summary

In this chapter, we discussed how organizations can obtain competitive advantages by implementing strategic information systems. We started by discussing the strategic planning process, which involves more than just planning about information technology, and then explored various frameworks that can help managers identify strategic information systems initiatives. We then discussed how managers can evaluate which strategic initiatives to implement and concluded with a discussion of hypercompetition, or the idea that competitive advantage cannot be sustained but that organizations should try to achieve market disruptions instead.

Here are the main points discussed in the chapter:

- There are five main steps in the strategic planning process:
  1. Strategic business planning
  2. Information systems assessment
  3. Information systems vision
  4. Information systems architecture
  5. Strategic initiatives identification

- We discussed four frameworks that can be used to identify strategic information systems initiatives. The SWOT analysis is used for managers to identify strengths, weaknesses, opportunities, and threats for the organization. Porter's Five Competitive Forces Model helps managers analyze the organization's competitive position by looking at five major forces in the firm's competitive environment: threats of new entrants, threats of substitutes, bargaining power of buyers, bargaining power of suppliers, and industry rivalry. Porter's value chain helps managers identify all the activities that the organization must perform to conduct its business. Finally, the virtual value chain looks at activities that turn raw data into useful information instead of looking at activities that turn raw materials into a final product like in manufacturing organizations.

- We discussed two methods for evaluating strategic initiatives: the critical success factors method, and the priority matrix. Critical success factors (CSFs) are those few important considerations that must be achieved for the organization to survive and be successful (i.e., achieve its mission). The priority matrix allows managers to evaluate potential initiatives and prioritize them along two key dimensions: the ease of implementation and the potential returns.

- Hypercompetition is when competitors rapidly erode competitive advantages; in this case, organizations should focus on market disruptions instead of trying to sustain competitive advantages.

Review Questions

1. What is a strategic information system? How is it different from a strategic information system initiative?
2. What is the purpose of the strategic planning process, and what are its main steps?
3. What are the main advantages of using an information systems strategic planning process?
4. What do the SWOT analysis, Porter's Five Competitive Forces Model, and Porter's value chain model have in common?
5. What are the key differences between the traditional value chain model and the virtual value chain?
6. How can a SWOT analysis be used for identifying strategic information systems initiatives?
7. What is the purpose of the Porter's Five Competitive Forces Model, and how can it be used for information systems strategic planning?
8. What are critical success factors (CSFs), and how should they be used to evaluate strategic initiatives?
9. What is the priority matrix, and how should it be used to evaluate strategic initiatives?
10. What is hypercompetition, and how can D'Aveni's 7 Ss framework be used in that context?

Reflection Questions

1. What is the most important thing you learned in this chapter? Why is it important?
2. What topics are unclear? What about them is unclear?
3. What relationships do you see between what you learned in this chapter and what you have learned in earlier chapters?
4. Why do you think the information systems strategic planning process is an iterative process?
5. If the strategic planning process has the benefits of improved communication, coordination, and decision making, could it be used or applied by students for group projects? How?
6. In what situations in your personal life could you apply a SWOT analysis (not for a specific course)?
7. How are the virtual value chain and the traditional value chain similar and different?

8. How does the priority matrix relate to critical success factors?

9. Do you believe that hypercompetition exists today? If so, do you think it will continue to happen in the future?

10. Looking back over the content of the chapter, why do you think it is important to discuss strategic initiatives in the context of introducing information systems?

Additional Learning Activities

4.A1. Use the priority matrix to rank initiatives identified in Learning Activity 4.4. Compare the results of your analysis with the results of the analyses conducted in Learning Activity 4.4. Be prepared to discuss the differences.

4.A2. This activity requires you to complete a competitive analysis of Uninor. The case may be provided to you by your instructor or found online.

Bose, Indranil. 2017. "Persevere or Exit: What Is the Right Strategy?" *Communications of the Association for Information Systems* 41(12). Retrieved from https://aisel.aisnet.org/cais/vol41/iss1/12.

4.A3. Find the mission statements for Amazon.com and your school. Compare the two statements and identify similarities and differences. Why are there differences?

4.A4. Complete Table 4.1 with at least five new statements for each of the SWOT components for Amazon.com.

4.A5. Conduct a virtual value chain analysis to identify potential strategic information systems in the hotel industry.

References

Al-Mudimigh, A. S., U. Zahid, and A. A. Talal. 2011. "A Framework for Portal Implementation: A Case for Saudi Organizations." *International Journal of Information Management* 31(1): 38–43.

D'Aveni, R. 1994. *Hyper-competition.* New York: Free Press.

Kappelman, L., E. McLean, V. Johnson, R. Torres, Q. Bguyen, C. Maurer, and M. Snyder. 2017, December. "The 2016 SIM IT Key Issues and Trends Study." *MIS Quarterly Executive* 16(1): 47–80.

Martin, M. 2017. "Porter's Five Forces: Analyzing the Competition." *Business News Daily,* June 26. Retrieved December 20, 2017, from https://www.businessnewsdaily.com/5446-porters-five-forces.html.

Paulo, S. 2017. "Examples of Critical Success Factors." *Bizfluent,* September 26. Retrieved December 20, 2017, from https://bizfluent.com/list-5968674-examples-critical-success-factors.html.

Piccoli, G. 2008. *Information Systems for Managers.* Hoboken, NJ: Wiley.

Porter, M. E. 1979. "How Competitive Forces Shape Strategy." *Harvard Business Review* 57(2): 137–45.

Porter, M. E. 1996. "What Is Strategy?" *Harvard Business Review* 74(6): 61–78.

Porter, M. E. 2008. "The Five Forces That Shape Strategy." *Harvard Business Review* 86(1): 78–93.

Recklies, D. 2015. "Porters Five Forces—Content, Application, and Critique." *TheManager.org*, November 20. Retrieved December 20, 2017, from http://www.themanager.org/2015/11/porters-five-forces/.

Reilly, M. 2016. "How to Determine Critical Success Factors for Your Business." *ClearPoint Strategy*, June 20. Retrieved December 20, 2017, from https://www.clearpointstrategy.com/how-to-determine-critical-success-factors-for-your-business/.

Glossary

Bargaining power of buyers: In Porter's Five Competitive Forces Model, determines the ability of the organization's buyers (customers) to reduce the organization's competitive position.

Bargaining power of suppliers: In Porter's Five Competitive Forces Model, determines what is the ability of the organization's suppliers to reduce its competitive position.

Critical success factors (CSFs): The few important considerations that must be achieved for the organization to survive and be successful (i.e., achieve its mission).

Evaluate: In a priority matrix, the initiatives that need to be discussed and evaluated thoroughly by managers.

Hypercompetition: When competitive advantages are rapidly eroded by competitors and organizations should focus on market disruptions instead of trying to sustain competitive advantages.

Imperatives: In a priority matrix, the initiatives that should be relatively easy to implement and have the potential to bring high returns to the organization.

Industry competitive rivalry: In Porter's Five Competitive Forces Model, determines the current level of competition in the industry.

Information systems architecture: Specifies how information systems resources should be used and how they should work together.

Information systems assessment: The step of planning process where the organization identifies the current state of information systems resources in the organization.

Information systems vision: A broad statement of how the organization should use and manage its information systems for strategic purposes.

Opportunities: In a SWOT analysis, determines the activities or factors that could help the organization get new advantages over others in its industry.

Porter's Five Competitive Forces Model: Framework to help managers analyze the organization's competitive position by looking at five major forces in the firms' competitive environment: threats of new entrants, threats of substitutes, bargaining power of buyers, bargaining power of suppliers, and industry rivalry.

Positioning for speed: In D'Aveni's 7 Ss framework, a strategy about preparing the organization to react as fast as possible.

Positioning for surprise: In D'Aveni's 7 Ss framework, a strategy about preparing the organization to respond to the marketplace in a manner that will surprise competitors.

Potential threat of new entrants: In Porter's Five Competitive Forces Model, determines how easy is it for new companies to enter the market in which the organization operates.

Potential threat of substitutes: In Porter's Five Competitive Forces Model, determines the likelihood that other products of equal or superior value are available.

Priority matrix: Framework that allows managers to evaluate potential initiatives and prioritize them along two key dimensions: the ease of implementation and the potential returns.

Quick wins: In a priority matrix, the initiatives that do not have much upside potential but are easy to implement.

Shifting the rules of competition: In D'Aveni's 7 Ss framework, a strategy about finding new ways to serve customers, thereby transforming the industry.

Signaling strategic intent: In D'Aveni's 7 Ss framework, a strategy about communicating intentions in order to stall responses by competitors.

Simultaneous and sequential strategic thrusts: In D'Aveni's 7 Ss framework, a strategy about taking steps to stun and confuse competitors in order to disrupt or block their efforts.

Strategic information systems: Information systems specifically meant to provide organizations with competitive advantages.

Strategic information systems initiatives: Detailed (usually two- to five-year) plans for implementation of systems that may result in a new strategic direction for the organization.

Strategic planning process: Structured set of steps to identify strategic information systems.

Strategic soothsaying: In D'Aveni's 7 Ss framework, a strategy about using new knowledge to predict or create new windows of opportunity.

Stay away: In a priority matrix, the initiatives that would be difficult to implement and would have limited potential returns.

Strengths: In SWOT analysis, asks what gives the organization advantages over others in its industry.

Superior stakeholder satisfaction: In D'Aveni's 7 *S*s framework, a strategy about maximizing customer satisfaction by adding value strategically.

SWOT analysis: Framework used by managers to identify strengths, weaknesses, opportunities, and threats for the organization.

Threats: In SWOT analysis, determines what activities or factors could create disadvantages or troubles for the organization relative to others in its industry.

Value chain analysis: Framework to help managers identify all the activities that the organization must perform to conduct its business.

Virtual value chain: Framework that looks at activities that turn raw data into useful information instead of looking at activities that turn raw materials into a final product like in manufacturing organizations.

Weaknesses: In SWOT analysis, determines what activities create disadvantages for the organization relative to others in its industry.

SECTION II

Managing Information

CHAPTER 5

Storing and Organizing Information

Learning Objectives

By reading and completing the activities in this chapter, you will be able to

- Discuss the purpose of a database management system
- Decide whether it is better to store data using a database management system or another alternative, such as a spreadsheet
- Explain the basic structure and components of relational databases
- Describe the purpose of foreign keys in a relational database
- Discuss the purpose of a relational database schema and explain its notation
- List and describe a number of online databases
- Understand what Big Data is and how businesses can use it to make more informed decisions

Chapter Outline

Focusing Story: The Database behind Facebook
Learning Activity 5.1: Data for an Amazon Order
Overview of Relational Databases
Learning Activity 5.2: Connecting Data Elements
Databases versus Spreadsheets: When to Use a DBMS
Database Diagrams
Learning Activity 5.3: Finding Business Databases Online
Online Databases
Big Data
Chapter Summary

Review Questions

Reflection Questions

Additional Learning Activities

Glossary

Throughout this book, the focus has been on information. Much of the information used by businesses is stored in databases. While there are different schemes for storing data, much of the data you will deal with is stored in relational databases. Databases may seem pretty mysterious, but they are actually not hard to understand at a basic level. In this chapter, we will help you learn about how relational databases store data. We will help you learn how to construct, populate, and retrieve data from databases using Microsoft Access in Appendices C and D.

<hr>

FOCUSING STORY

The Database behind Facebook

Odds are you are one of the more than 2 billion active users of Facebook. If so, you probably know how to "friend" people and post photos, videos, and status updates. What you may not know is that there is a giant database that keeps track of all this information. Here is a partial list of what Facebook's database must track:

- Almost 1 billion objects, such as pages, groups, events, and communities
- More than 30 billion pieces of content, including links, posts, photos, notes, videos, and new stories
- Friend connections among the more than 2 billion active users (The average user has well over 100 friends.)

Source: https://newsroom.fb.com/company-info/.

Keeping track of all this information requires a very complex database design, in addition to a robust infrastructure. Facebook uses a variety of tools to create and manage its data, including Apache Cassandra, which manages data across hundreds of servers; Apache Hive, which facilitates summarizing and retrieving data in very large databases; and Scribe, which reliably delivers billions of Facebook messages each day.

While you may never have to deal with databases this large, you will probably have to use databases throughout your work life. Much of the information you will need to access in order to do your job will be stored in relational databases. Relational databases underlie many of the applications discussed throughout this book, including enterprise resource planning, customer relationship management, and supply chain management systems, which you will learn about in Chapter 12. (Note that Facebook uses other types of database technologies in addition to relational databases.)

FOCUSING QUESTIONS

1. Identify the information elements that are part of a Facebook profile.
2. What information do you think Facebook uses to determine what friend suggestions to make?

LEARNING ACTIVITY 5.1

Data for an Amazon Order

Suppose you are ordering something from Amazon.com. What pieces of data (for example, your name) does Amazon need to fulfill your order?

STATS BOX 5.1:
DIGITAL DATA

How much digital data exists? This is a big, complicated question, given that according to IBM, 2.5 quintillion bytes of data are created every day. In fact, 90% of the data stored in the world was created in the last two years. (This includes business and personal data, such as digital photos, music, and video.) A quintillion is a 1 followed by 18 zeroes. According to IDC's annual Digital Universe study, there are currently 4,400 quintillion bytes of data stored worldwide. That number is expected to become 44,000 quintillion bytes by 2020. The amount of data collected is only expected to grow as more sensors, websites, and other means of collecting data increase by the day. With the ever-expanding glut of digital data, you can understand why efficient ways to store, organize, and retrieve the data are increasingly important.

Source: https://www-01.ibm.com/common/ssi/cgi-bin/ssialias?htmlfid= WRL12345USEN.

Overview of Relational Databases

Databases and Database Management Systems

A **database** is an organized collection of data. In this chapter, we focus on a particular type of database called a relational database, because this is the dominant type of database for business applications. These databases can store different types of "information," including text, numbers, documents, images, and videos. Given the amount and variety of information that businesses deal with, well-structured databases are a must for any business.

Typically, a database is managed by a **database management system (DBMS)**. A database management system provides the means for creating, maintaining, and using databases. For most of you, the "using" part is the most important aspect of a DBMS, although you may create small databases. Professional database designers and administrators handle the creation and maintenance tasks in most organizations.

There are many database management systems used by businesses. Smaller database-oriented tasks can be handled by a personal DBMS, such as Microsoft Access or OpenOffice Base. Larger, more complex databases require an enterprise-level DBMS, such as Oracle, MySQL, Microsoft SQL Server, or IBM's DB2. Each of these has its advantages and disadvantages, but all are quite capable. Oracle has been the market leader for many years, but the others are widely used in business.

Databases are integral elements of information systems. Most information systems today use multitiered architectures that divide processing into different elements. Multitiered architecture refers to the database server, the Web server, and applications, all existing on different computers. You will learn more about this in Chapter 7. Without going into too much detail, applications handle the processing of data, while the DBMS is responsible for managing the data. As shown in Figure 5.1,

Figure 5.1 Interaction between Applications and Databases

the application requests data from the DBMS, which provides the requested data. The application can then manipulate the data (such as reducing inventory when a product is ordered) and send updated data to the DBMS. The DBMS updates the actual databases according to the update sent by the application. It is possible to do all this within the application, but most large systems use the multitier approach.

LEARNING ACTIVITY 5.2

Connecting Data Elements

In Learning Activity 5.1, you came up with a list of data that Amazon would need to process an order. Take those elements and group similar items together and name each group of elements. For example, the customer's name and address might be in a group called Customer.

Databases versus Spreadsheets: When to Use a DBMS

Many people get a little confused about whether to use a spreadsheet (such as Microsoft Excel) or a DBMS (such as Microsoft Access) for storing and organizing information. One reason for this confusion is that both store information in tables of rows and columns. This similarity is a bit misleading, however. The two applications have very different purposes, strengths, and weaknesses.

Spreadsheets are fine for very simple data storage tasks such as keeping simple lists, like a personal contact list or a home inventory. Unfortunately, spreadsheets have a number of limitations that make them unsuitable for more complex data storage. Some of the problems you might run into if you use a spreadsheet for data storage include the following:

- Unnecessary data duplication
- Inconsistent data
- Difficulty in data retrieval and search
- Poor data integrity
- Difficulty in relating different data elements (such as customers and orders)

The problems of unnecessary data duplication and poor data integrity are particularly troubling. (Data integrity problems include inaccurate, inconsistent, and out-of-date data.) Some studies indicate that most complex spreadsheets have errors. (See http://panko.shidler.hawaii.edu/SSR/index.htm for a good overview of these studies.) While not all of these errors are due to data issues (for example, formulas could be incorrect), many are. Most database management systems have methods for keeping data up to date and consistent. While data stored in databases are not perfect, they typically are of higher quality than data stored in spreadsheets (or in other formats, such as documents, pictures, or videos).

Using an out-of-date version can also be a problem with spreadsheets. Businesses sometimes make bad decisions because someone has relied on an old version of a spreadsheet. Often this is due to data not being updated, but there can be other changes that make a spreadsheet out of date. Reports from database management systems draw data directly from databases, which typically contain current information. It is worth noting that spreadsheets can be built to connect to a database to avoid the problem of outdated data.

Because spreadsheets are relatively easy to use and require less planning than database management systems, it is tempting to use a spreadsheet for managing information. For all but the simplest tasks, this is a mistake. In the long run, you are usually much better off taking the time to plan and design a proper database, especially as the amount of information being stored increases.

Databases are good at storing and organizing information. Spreadsheets are good for analyzing and displaying information visually. A complete information solution requires both. Fortunately, it is relatively easy to extract data from a database and import them into a spreadsheet for analysis, so you do not have to make an "either/or" choice. Use a database to store the information; use a spreadsheet to make sense of the information.

Now that you have a general idea of the purposes of databases and their relationship to information systems, we can get into more detail about how relational databases function.

Relational Databases

A **relational database** stores data in the form of connected tables. Tables are made up of records (rows) and fields (columns). A **record** is a set of fields that all pertain to the same thing, while the **fields** represent some characteristic of the thing. An example may make this easier to understand. Consider Table 5.1.

Table 5.1 Instructors Table

InstructorID	Last Name	First Name	Email
1	Smith	Sadie	ssmith@school.edu
2	Jones	Maggie	mjones@school.edu
3	Thurman	Annie	rthurman@school.edu
4	Wilson	Fred	fwilson@school.edu

Each row represents a single instructor. Each column represents a characteristic. The first row of data (not counting the headings) contains data about the instructor named Sadie Smith. The table stores four characteristics (fields) about the instructors:

- Identification Number (InstructorID)
- Last Name
- First Name
- Email Address

Fortunately, this structure makes intuitive sense for most of us. Things get a little more complicated when we need to store data about multiple things. Take a look at Figure 5.2, which shows a small database about course offerings. This database stores data about three "things" that are related to each other: sections, courses, and instructors. Since we want to store data about three things, we have three tables. This is a key feature of relational databases. Each table stores data about a separate thing. This structure allows for flexibility when retrieving data while minimizing redundancy. When storing data, unnecessary redundancy can be a bad thing because redundancy can lead to inconsistencies. By storing each piece of information only once, we ensure that the data are consistent. We explain more about redundancy and consistency later in this chapter.

In order for a database to work, we need some way to uniquely identify each record. You might think that we could use the instructor's name for this purpose, but this will not work because two instructors might have the same name. Sometimes there is a natural choice for this unique identifier called the **primary key**. For example, student ID numbers might be a good choice for a database that tracks members of a student organization. Sometimes, however, you might simply make up an identifier. Since the identifier typically does not store any meaningful data (other than to

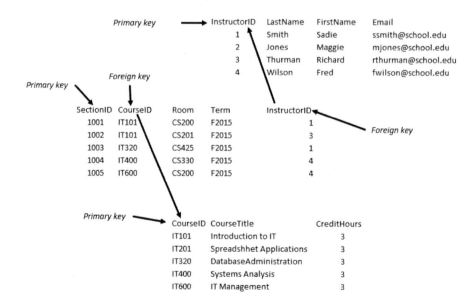

Figure 5.2 A Small Database

identify a row), making up a number is not a problem. Each table in a database has a primary key. Sometimes a primary key is made up of more than one field. We call this a *composite primary key*.

You might have noticed that earlier we said that the tables in our database are related to one another. For example, the Sections table is related to the Instructors table and the Courses table. In a relational database, these connections are implemented by **foreign keys**, which are fields that reference a primary key in a related table. For example, the CourseID field in the Sections table references the CourseID field in the Courses table. This cross-referencing is called a *relationship*. The arrows in Figure 5.2 show how the foreign keys reference the primary keys.

These cross-referencing foreign keys make it easy to combine data contained in multiple tables. See if you can answer this question: What is the title of the course being taught in section 1001? This is a pretty easy question to answer. Section 1001 is Introduction to IT. All you have to do is look at the CourseID in the Sections table and then find the matching CourseID in the Courses table. There is another foreign key in the Sections table. InstructorID references the primary key of the Instructors table. While there are a number of very formal, precise rules that govern relational database design, if you understand this cross-referencing scheme, you understand the basics of relational databases. Even very large, complex databases follow this same basic structure. They just have more tables and fields.

There is an additional characteristic of relational databases that we need to discuss. For reasons that are beyond our scope, in a relational database, each row/column intersection can store at most one item of data. For example, if there is more than one section of a course, you must have a separate record for each section.

There are some other rules that govern relational database design. These rules, which are called *normal forms*, are in place to ensure data consistency by eliminating unnecessary redundancy. While the particulars of these rules are beyond our scope, we want to use a simple example to show the relationship between redundancy and data consistency. Consider the data shown in Table 5.2.

Answer the following question about Table 5.2: What is Instructor #1's last name? You really cannot be sure of the answer to this question. This instructor's last name is Smith in the first row and Jackson in the third row. We do not really know which one is correct. This inconsistency, which we call an *anomaly*, results from storing the instructor's name in multiple rows. Compare this structure to the one in Figure 5.2. The earlier structure prevents these inconsistencies by storing each item of data only once. (The exception is the foreign key.) This is why each table stores data about one "thing." To summarize simply, if you only store a data element in one place, you cannot have inconsistent values. One of the values could be incorrect (for example, an instructor's name could be misspelled), but that is a different problem than inconsistency.

Sometimes a particular row in a table can be related to at most one row in a related table. For example, in most businesses, a specific order can only be related to

Table 5.2 Redundancy Example

SectionID	CourseID	CourseTitle	InstructorID	LastName	FirstName
1001	IT101	Introduction to IT	1	Smith	Sadie
1002	IT101	Introduction to Computers	3	Thurman	Maggie
1003	IT320	Database Administration	1	Jackson	Sadie
1004	IT400	Systems Analysis	4	Wilson	Fred
1005	IT600	IT Management	4	Wilson	Fred

one customer. If we look at this from the other direction, a specific customer can be related to more than one order. This is an example of a *one-to-many* relationship.

Many-to-many relationships also exist. In these relationships, a specific row can be related to multiple rows in a related table. But in contrast to the one-to-many relationship, this is true in both directions. Consider the example of students registering for course sections. A specific student can be registered for more than one section (each for a different course), and a specific section can have more than one student registered for it. This is known as a many-to-many relationship.

Because of the structural rules of relational databases, many-to-many relationships require creating a new table that links the two related tables. Not surprisingly, these are called *linking* or *intersection* tables. Figure 5.3 shows a linking table for student registrations. The purpose of the Registrations table is to link a student to a section. You can see that Student #1 (Pat Johnson) is registered for four sections (1001, 1002, 1004, and 1005). Section 1001 has three students registered (1, 2, and 4).

Although they are more unusual, one-to-one relationships also exist. In these relationships, a specific row in a table can be related to at most one row in a related table. This is true in both directions of the relationship. For some businesses, the relationship between customers and accounts could be a one-to-one relationship. (It could be a one-to-many relationship for other businesses.)

As you might imagine, using the actual data to show the structure of a database only works for very small databases. For larger databases, we illustrate structure using database schema diagrams, which we discuss next.

Database Diagrams

Database designers use several different diagrams when coming up with the design of a database. Here we are interested in a view that shows tables, fields, and relationships. (Note that we often call fields *attributes* when discussing database models. We are

Students

StudentID	LastName	FirstName	Email
1	Johnson	Pat	pjohnson@school.edu
2	Gonzales	Joreg	jgonzales@school.edu
3	Andrews	Annie	aandrews@school.edu
4	Goldman	Beau	bgoldman@school.edu
5	Simpson	Lois	lsimpson@school.edu

Sections

SectionID	CourseID	Room	Term
1001	IT101	CS200	F2015
1002	IT101	CS201	F2015
1003	IT320	CS425	F2015
1004	IT400	CS330	F2015
1005	IT600	CS200	F2015

Registrations

SectionID	StudentID
1001	1
1001	2
1001	4
1002	5
1002	1
1003	3
1003	2
1004	1
1004	3
1004	5
1004	2
1005	1
1005	5

Figure 5.3 Many-to-Many Linking Table Example

going to stick to *fields* to make things less confusing.) Some people call these diagrams *entity-relationship diagrams (ERDs),* while others call them *database schemas.* There are technical differences between the two, but both essentially show the data elements and the relationships among them, which is what we care about here.

Figure 5.4 shows a diagram for a database that stores wish lists for customers. Each rectangle shows the name of the table at the top. Each field is included inside the rectangle. The primary key is indicated by the PK in the left-hand column. Foreign keys have FK beside them to the left. Since tables can have more than one foreign key, the FK notations are numbered. Recall that the foreign keys relate a row in one table to a row in a related table. For example, the field "CategoryID" in the Products table refers to a CategoryID value in the Categories table.

You might find the notation for the WishList table a little confusing. This is an example of a linking table. It links two other tables together. These types of tables are needed to control unnecessary redundancy. Many linking tables have composite primary keys (primary keys composed of more than one field). In our notation, each field in the primary key is boldfaced, underlined, and has PK next to it, as is the case

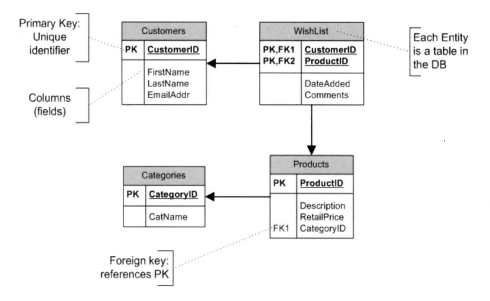

Figure 5.4 Database Diagram

with CustomerID and ProductID in the WishList table. Together, CustomerID and ProductID serve as the primary key of the WishList table. Separately, however, each of these fields acts as a foreign key. You can tell this because of the FK1 and FK2 next to CustomerID and ProductID, respectively. The CustomerID value in the WishList table refers to the CustomerID of the specific customer to whom the WishList item is assigned. ProductID in the WishList table serves a similar purpose. An arrow between the tables shows relationships between tables graphically. The direction of the arrow indicates the direction of referencing (from the foreign key to the corresponding primary key).

Note that this is only one way to show a database diagram. Your instructor may prefer another, such as crow's foot notation, IDEF1X, or Chen's notation. We use this particular notation simply because it is well implemented in Microsoft Visio and other programs. Once you have the logical design, you have most of the information necessary to create a database, especially for simple applications. More complex applications require additional information, but that is beyond our scope here.

Being able to read a database diagram is important, even if you never design or build a database. The diagram is a key to understanding the structure of the database, which is useful when retrieving data from a database or if you have the job of a programmer or systems analyst and you need to work with a database administrator to create or modify the database as part of a project. Learning how to create a database design is beyond the scope of this chapter but is covered in Appendix E.

LEARNING ACTIVITY 5.3

Finding Business Databases Online

Your campus library likely has a variety of business-related online databases. (See http://guides.lib.vt.edu/subject-guides/bus for an example.) Visit your library's website and find its list of business databases. Identify and briefly describe one database for each of the related purposes:

- Economic statistics
- Industry information
- Demographic statistics
- Business-related news articles

ITUNES MATCH

As people purchase more and more electronic devices to play their digital music, it has become necessary to have a central repository in which to store these songs. One such repository, provided by Apple, is iTunes Match. This service catalogues all the digital songs that you have purchased and stores them in the cloud. "Stored in the cloud" means that rather than being stored on one of your devices, such as a laptop, the songs are stored online, which makes them available to all of your devices. When logged onto a device that utilizes iTunes Match, it then allows for the music to be streamed directly from the cloud or downloaded onto the device.

With a number of people utilizing iTunes Match, how does Apple go about storing all this information? Apple's iTunes database has 4.3 million songs stored. If the song that a person owns is part of this database, an indicator that the person owns that song is stored rather than the song itself. The only copies of songs that have to be stored separately are those that Apple does not already have in its database. This centralized database approach allows Apple to keep its database storage needs low while providing a centralized service for the many people who want to use it.

It should be noted that Amazon, Google, Spotify, and others utilize a similar process to catalogue their music libraries as well.

Source: https://www.apple.com/itunes/itunes-match/.

Online Databases

So far in this chapter, we have primarily discussed relational databases that store text and numeric data related to business operations. There are other types of databases that are quite useful for performing research; many of these are accessible through the Internet. You may have used some of these when working on a research paper for class. These databases can also be quite useful in your professional life. For example, if you are a marketing professional, you can use these databases to gather information about prospective clients or competitors. Demographic databases are important for understanding markets. For example, retail organizations use demographic databases to gather data to help decide where to locate new stores. These databases serve a different purpose than the databases we discussed earlier. Rather than being containers for raw data, these online databases contain pointers to sources of information.

Knowing what databases exist and how to use them can be very beneficial to you, both personally and professionally. Here are just a few examples of situations you might face and databases that might be helpful. Most of these resources are available through libraries.

- Researching a career
  - The United States Bureau of Labor Statistics (http://www.bls.gov/data/) has a searchable database of employment, pay, and benefit statistics and occupation growth projections.
  - Job search sites such as AllianceQ, Monster.com, CareerLink, and CareerBuilder .com maintain databases of job openings. You can usually search these databases by a variety of criteria, including occupation and location.
- Preparing for a job interview
  - Article databases such as ABI/Inform and LexisNexis Academic (often available through your university library's website) are useful for finding news articles about a company and its executives.
  - The Business and Company Resource Center (often available through your university library's website) maintains databases of company- and industry-related information.
- Gathering information on customers or competitors
  - The Business and Company Resource Center is also useful for learning more about customers and competitors.
  - Hoovers.com provides extensive information about companies and industries.
- Conducting market research
  - In addition to many of the above, the United States Census Bureau (http://www.census.gov) provides access to a variety of demographic and economic data.

- Economic forecasting, investment planning, and portfolio management
  - Wharton Research Data Services (WRDS) is essentially a portal that provides a Web-based interface to databases of financial information, including the following:
    - *Compustat:* Company financial items such as income statements and balance sheets
    - *CRSP:* Historical stock and mutual fund prices and U.S. Treasury interest rates
    - *Global Insight:* United States and international macroeconomic data
  - Federal Reserve Economic Data (FRED) (http://research.stlouisfed.org/fred2/) provides more than 21,000 time-series data sets, including interest rates, inflation, and economic growth.

Big Data

A chapter covering databases would not be complete without a discussion of Big Data. **Big Data** is something of a buzzword that refers to the vast amount of data (often measured in terabytes or petabytes) that are created and stored that have grown beyond the capabilities of traditional data processing tools and applications. The meaning of Big Data is not rigorously set and will be subject to change over the years as technology evolves. In essence, due to the increasing number of ways that data are created through sites like Facebook.com and Google.com, and due to sensors being installed in cars, homes, and businesses, there is so much data being stored that new technologies and practices are required to analyze them. This increased amount of data has provided businesses with new opportunities to analyze the data to identify trends that will help them make better business decisions. However, there are some challenges that must be overcome in order to capitalize on the increased availability of data. Such challenges include the following:

- How should the data be stored?
- How do data from various sources integrate with one another?
- How are data retrieved and disseminated?

The answers to all these questions were pretty straightforward with a relational database. But in the case of Big Data, new solutions may be required. It should be noted that storing the data necessary to conduct Big Data can be done using traditional relational databases. However, in this section, we discuss an alternative method to relational databases along with some of the strengths they provide.

BIG DATA AT FACEBOOK

Many of you probably enjoy using Facebook (or at least know people who do). A single user alone has hundreds of friends, and when they log on to Facebook, they want to see an update specific to them. Imagine now that there are more than one billion Facebook users, and each of these users has a unique set of friends. Facebook is successful at selecting the correct posts and making recommendations based on each individual's interactions with the website. This success is due to utilizing Big Data in such a way to very quickly select the updates that a given user will want to see as well other recommendations customized for him or her based on previous visits to Facebook. Thanks to advances in Big Data, you are able to enjoy this and many other services that bring together the interaction of millions, if not billions, of users in one service.

Storing Data

In a relational database, data are stored in a way that ensures data integrity as records are inserted, updated, and deleted. However, one of the trade-offs with storing data in this fashion is performance. As the amount of data being stored, and then ultimately retrieved, grows as large as it has in this era of Big Data, it may be necessary to sacrifice some levels of data integrity in order to keep performance at an acceptable level. While a normalized database is stored in a highly structured way, in a Big Data implementation, data can be stored unstructured. This is done using either a network-attached storage (NAS) model or a direct-attached storage (DAS) model. The NAS model utilizes a series of file servers that can easily expand to grow capacity and high-speed connections between them. The DAS model keeps the data more centralized. This approach allows for faster access time when it comes to processing but limits the scalability of data size. Hybrid approaches can also be used. Data stored permanently could utilize the NAS model, while temporary data that needs to be access more quickly could be stored using the DAS model.

Data lakes are an emerging approach to storing the massive amounts of data generated and collected by organizations. Data lakes store huge volumes of data in their original formats by giving each data element a unique identifier and tagging it with descriptors that tell users what it is about. In most data repositories, data structure and requirements are defined up front. In a data lake, data structures and requirements are not defined until the data are needed. The bottom line is that the best ways to store, organize, and use large volumes of data are still emerging. Time will tell if data lakes are important long term or just an interesting method that will lead to further advancements.

Integrating Data

With data coming from a variety of different sources, it is necessary to ensure that records from various different data sources can be combined to make sense of the data.

This process is referred to as the E/T/L process, which stands for extract, transform, and load. We will go into more detail about the E/T/L process in Chapter 14, but we will briefly discuss it here for the purpose of Big Data. The first step in this process is to extract, or retrieve, the data from the various locations in which it was stored or gathered. This involves identifying the sources of the various data that are needed to make the decisions required. Due to the vast amount of data that could be stored, it is important to strategically identify what data are needed for making business decisions. The recommendations discussed in Chapter 4 would be followed.

Once the necessary data have been identified and extracted, it is then necessary to transform the data. This is the process where the data are modified and combined in such a way that records from various different sources can be combined. For example, one data source may provide data that are stored at the second-by-second transaction level. However, this may need to be combined with other data that are stored in a daily summarized manner. In order to combine them, the data will need to be transformed in such a way that the two different levels will make sense when combined. It may make sense to summarize the transaction-level data to daily summarized data and analyze at that level. Or it may make sense to take the summarized data and create a way for it to be combined at the transaction level. Whatever decisions are made should be done in such a way to be in alignment with a business's strategy. However, once data are transformed to be summarized at a level higher than the transaction level, it is impossible to desummarize. Much caution at this decision-making stage is recommended. Once the transformation of the data has occurred, the data must then be stored. This is the load process. Loading is a matter of writing the data to a disk in a fashion that can be readily retrieved as necessary. An illustration of this process is provided in Figure 5.5.

Retrieving and Disseminating Data

One of the advantages of Big Data is the ability to analyze the data that are being stored to make informed business decisions. If the data are stored in a relational database, then SQL will be utilized to query the data. However, if it is stored in an unstructured format, it is necessary to retrieve the data in a manner other than SQL. One way this is done is by utilizing what is called NoSQL, which some interpret as "Not only SQL." NoSQL allows for greater scalability and efficiency in storing and retrieving data. With NoSQL, one approach to querying data is to assign all attributes keys. This allows for the dynamic creation of a table for a given query. Then, when that query is over, a new dynamic creation can be utilized depending on the question being answered. This method of retrieving data then results in the ability to analyze data in an ad hoc fashion without necessarily needing to know what questions will be asked prior to the creation of the database structure.

Regardless of how the data are stored or queried, as discussed above, it is still necessary to interpret and share these results. One manner for doing so in an easy-to-utilize fashion is through data analytics. Data analytics utilizes the data that the

Extract, Transform, Load (ETL)

Figure 5.5 The Extract, Transform, Load Process
Source: https://commons.wikimedia.org/wiki/File:Extract,_Transform,_Load_Data_Flow
_Diagram.svg.

company has available and uses statistical analysis through various tools to make business-related decisions. This could include forecasting future sales, graphically displaying information about the organization through charts and graphs, and tracking metrics that the organization has deemed important for its success. The important aspects necessary for a company to use data analytics are to possess the necessary data, understand how it relates to the business problems, and then statistically interpret the data.

Chapter Summary

In this chapter, you learned about databases, which are critical to the operation of information systems. The intent of the chapter was to help you gain an appreciation of the importance of databases, with a special emphasis on relational databases. Here are the main points discussed in the chapter:

• Database management systems provide the means for creating, maintaining, and using databases.

- Spreadsheets are good for storing simple lists of information. However, they have a number of limitations that render them less effective for more complex data management.
- A relational database stores data in the form of connected tables. Tables are made up of records and fields.
- In a relational database, a record is a set of fields that all pertain to the same thing, while the fields represent some characteristic of the thing.
- In a relational database, foreign keys are fields that reference the primary keys in related tables.
- A database diagram shows the logical structure of a relational database, including its tables, fields, and relationships among tables. Primary and foreign keys are also indicated.
- There are many online databases that store a vast array of information. These databases include article databases, market and economic databases, and databases of demographic and governmental information, among other topics. Examples include LexisNexis Academic (article database), Federal Reserve Economic Data service (economic data), and Monster.com (employment database).
- Big Data provides a new opportunity to analyze information and identify trends that can help businesses make better-informed decisions.

Review Questions

1. What are the main functions of a database management system?
2. Name five potential problems that might arise from using a spreadsheet for data storage.
3. Briefly describe how a software application interacts with a database management system in a multitiered architecture.
4. Briefly describe how relational databases store information.
5. What are the main elements of a relational database?
6. In a relational database, what is the function of a primary key?
7. In a relational database, what is the function of a foreign key?
8. What is the purpose of a database diagram?
9. What are the main elements of a database diagram?
10. Name and briefly describe four online databases.

Reflection Questions

1. What is the most important thing you learned in this chapter? Why is it important?

2. What topics are unclear? What about them is unclear?

3. What relationships do you see between what you learned in this chapter and what you learned in previous chapters?

4. Compare and contrast data storage using electronic spreadsheet software and database management systems.

5. Suppose you need to keep track of some data. How would you decide whether to use a spreadsheet or database management system to store the data?

6. As a user of databases, why is it useful to understand how relational databases are structured?

7. What challenges do you think arise as organizations collect the amount of data necessary to conduct the analyses provided by Big Data?

Additional Learning Activities

5.A1. You have just been elected chair of one of your clubs. Your first task is to design a form to keep track of information about your members. For now, you just need to track basic information: member's name, email address, mobile phone number, and join date. You want to be able to see the information about multiple members at one time. To keep things simple, you are going to keep the information on paper (at least for the moment). Sketch out a format for how you would store this information.

5.A2. Suppose that you want to store the club member information from the previous question on a computer. Would you use a database (such as Microsoft Access) or a spreadsheet? Explain your choice.

5.A3. Identify the data elements necessary for you to register for a course. Group these elements into tables. Draw a sketch showing how these tables might relate to one another.

5.A4. Identify the tables and fields that would be a database that stores information for the purchase order form shown in Figure 5.6. (*Note:* "Extended" is the extended cost, or quantity multiplied by cost.) Draw a sketch showing how these tables might relate to one another.

5.A5. Use the database shown in Figure 5.7 to perform the following tasks:

    a. Name the tables in this database.

    b. For each table, list its fields and primary key.

    c. List the foreign keys.

    d. For each foreign key, list the table to which it refers.

5.A6. Use the database shown in Figure 5.8 to perform the following tasks:

    a. Name the tables in this database.

    b. For each table, list its fields and primary key.

    c. List the foreign keys.

    d. For each foreign key, list the table to which it refers.

5.A7. You are probably thinking about your future career. One element of your career choice is finding out what industry (or industries) interests you. Visit your library's website and identify three online databases that provide information that can help you evaluate an industry. Briefly describe each database and explain why you think it would be useful in this task.

PURCHASE ORDER FORM

PO No.:	12548	**Date:** 11/3/2014
Vendor ID:	87459	
Name:	Bithlo Books	
Address:	27 E. SR 50	
	Bithlo, FL 32158	

ISBN	Title	Qty	Cost	Extended
1-55860-294-1	Database Modeling & Design	5	10.00	50.00
3-12368-998-2	Guide to the Outback	7	12.00	84.00
2-78912-437-5	Sports Heroes of the 1700's	2	16.25	32.50
	TOTAL COST			**166.50**

Figure 5.6 Purchase Order Form

Figure 5.7 Customer Activity Database Design

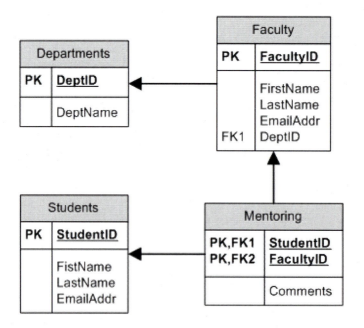

Figure 5.8 Mentoring Database Design

Glossary

Big Data: The vast amount of data that are created and stored that have grown beyond the capabilities of traditional data processing tools and application.

Database: An organized collection of data.

Database management system (DBMS): A set of programs that control the creation, maintenance, and use of databases.

Field: In a relational database, stores data about a single characteristic of a record.

Foreign key: In a relational database, a field (or fields) that references the primary key of a related table.

Primary key: In a relational database, the unique identifier of a record.

Record: In a relational database, a set of related fields.

Relational database: A data store that organizes data in connected two-dimensional tables.

CHAPTER 6

Analyzing Information for Business Decision Making

Learning Objectives

By reading and completing the activities in this chapter, you will be able to

- Discuss the importance of having good decision-making skills
- Explain how decision-making changes depending on organizational level
- Discuss the role of information in decision making
- Contrast structured, semistructured, and unstructured decisions
- Apply a decision-making methodology
- Choose the appropriate technology tool for a given decision-making task

Chapter Outline

Focusing Story: How a Spreadsheet Saved Me (a Lot of) Money
Learning Activity 6.1: Information and Decision Making
The Importance of Good Decision-Making Skills
Learning Activity 6.2: What Kind of Information Do I Need?
Using Information for Decision Making
Types of Decisions
A Decision-Making Process
Learning Activity 6.3: What Kind of Information Do I Need?
Information Retrieval and Analysis Tools
Learning Activity 6.4: "What If" I Get a 75% on the Final?
Chapter Summary
Review Questions
Reflection Questions

Making good decisions requires information, but that is not enough. You must also be able to analyze information. In this chapter, we want to help you understand the basics of business-oriented decisions and the process by which they are made. In Chapter 14, you will learn about systems specifically designed to support decision making. Here the focus is on understanding more about the decision-making process and the tools that can help you retrieve and analyze information as part of that process.

A **decision** is simply a choice among alternatives. We make many decisions each day. Sometimes these decisions are trivial, such as deciding what to eat for lunch, while others have enormous consequences, such as deciding whether to accept a job offer. Regardless of the importance of the decision, making the decision requires retrieving and analyzing information.

FOCUSING STORY

How a Spreadsheet Saved Me (a Lot of) Money

A number of years ago, I was fortunate to have some excess money I wanted to invest. This was during the boom years of real estate, so that was a natural possibility to explore. "Flipping" houses (buying a house, making improvements, and then selling at a profit) was quite popular, and I was a big fan of some of the house-flipping shows on television. While on a run, I noticed a small house that looked like a good candidate for flipping. The house seemed to be ideal: It was well within my budget; it was in a good, stable, family-oriented neighborhood; and it was close to my home. So I called the real estate agent and arranged for a showing. Despite a number of cosmetic issues, the house was well built, and I could easily envision how to improve it. After viewing the house and researching the potential value, I created a simple spreadsheet that analyzed the investment potential of the house. I did a "what-if" analysis that examined a range of possible scenarios: worst case, best case, and expected. For example, in the best-case scenario, I estimated that I would have to own the house for 6 months before I could sell it. In the worst case, I estimated it would take 18 months. After "running the numbers," it became pretty clear that the investment was not worth the risk (at least to me). The best-case outcome was that I would make around $10,000, but if the worst-case scenario came true, I would lose well over $10,000. The expected scenario would only result in a profit of about $5,000. Some people would have made this investment, but I decided that under this range of possibilities I did not want to invest the time, effort, and money required to improve the house. This turned out to be a good decision; the housing bubble burst at about the time I would have been trying to sell the house. In fact, the house remained for sale for a very long time after I looked at it.

FOCUSING QUESTIONS

1. What role did information play in this decision?
2. An electronic spreadsheet was very helpful in making this decision. What would have been different if spreadsheet software was not available?

LEARNING ACTIVITY 6.1

Information and Decision Making

Suppose that you are in the market for a new apartment. (Your instructor may give you a different decision-making problem.) How would you go about making the decision of which new apartment to choose? What information would you gather? What would be the consequences of making a bad decision? Be prepared to share your answers in class.

The Importance of Good Decision-Making Skills

Good decision making requires good information along with good decision-making skills, processes, and tools, which is the primary focus of this chapter. The ability to make good decisions is one of the skills that sets apart successful business professionals. There is no escaping decision making. Being able to make sound decisions that result in positive outcomes is a critical skill for a successful business career. Analytical reasoning skills and the ability to solve complex problems are among the most highly sought-after qualities for potential employees. These skills are directly related to being able to make good decisions.

Interestingly, while decision-making skills are important at all levels of business, they are increasingly important as one moves up the "organizational ladder." Why is this? First, decisions made by higher-level managers tend to be more complicated. The more complex a decision, the more skilled one must be in order to make effective decisions. Second, higher-level decisions typically have greater impacts. Consider this example. The store manager for a fast-food restaurant makes decisions such as hiring and scheduling hourly workers and ordering products. A district manager may decide about local marketing campaigns and choose suppliers. A corporate executive might make decisions about national marketing campaigns and whether to introduce new products. Deciding whom to schedule for the morning shift is much easier than deciding whether to roll out a new product. In addition, a bad decision on scheduling has relatively minor consequences, while bad product decision can cost millions of dollars.

Let us be quite clear about the importance of decision making. Virtually everything in this book is related, to some degree, to making better decisions. All the systems we discuss, all the tools you will learn about, and all the information skills you will gain are directed toward helping you better understand and use information so that you can make better decisions. To paraphrase Herbert Simon, Nobel Prize–winning economist and technologist, nothing is more important for the well-being of society than that decision making and problem solving be well done.

LEARNING ACTIVITY 6.2

What Kind of Information Do I Need?

You will face many different types of decisions throughout your business career. Some decisions are well defined and have clear alternatives and information requirements. Others are much less clear. For each decision, answer the following questions:

- What information would you need in order to make the decision?
- How confident are you that you have accurately identified the needs? Why do you feel this way?

Decisions

1. You are the manager of a fast-food restaurant. How many hamburger buns should you order for tomorrow?
2. You are the manager of a retail store and you need a new shift manager. Which employee should you promote?
3. You are an executive for a technology company. Should your company develop a new wearable technology to compete with devices such as Apple Watch?

Using Information for Decision Making

Information and decision making are inextricably linked; many of our information needs are related to decision making, and making good decisions requires information. Insufficient, inaccurate, or untimely information has detrimental impacts on decision making. You need good information to understand the objectives of a decision, the constraints that limit the number of alternatives, and the alternatives themselves. You also need information to forecast the potential outcomes of each alternative. Finally, information provides the means for comparing and selecting among the alternatives. If you have inadequate information related to any of these, your ability to make the proper decision is limited.

BUSINESS EXAMPLE BOX 6.1

Why Do Managers Make Bad Decisions?

If decision-making skills are so important to business professionals, why are so many bad decisions made? There is a variety of reasons, including the following:

- Poor decision-making skills
- Time pressures (perception that there is not enough time for systematic decision making)
- Relying too much on intuition rather than engaging in systematic decision making
- Being overconfident in decision-making skills, intelligence, or knowledge of the decision context
- Going with the group (groupthink)
- Addressing the wrong objective

Decision-making biases also play a role in making poor decisions. A *decision-making bias* is a cognitive tendency that causes the decision maker to make an incorrect decision. Here are a few of the more common decision-making biases:

- *Negativity bias:* Giving more weight to negative than to positive experiences or information.
- *Confirmation:* Searching for information that supports preconceptions.
- *Loss aversion:* Making losses more important than equal gains.
- *Bandwagon:* Tending to do or believe something because many others do or believe the same thing.
- *Gambler's fallacy:* Believing that random events are influenced by previous random events.

Being aware of these biases is the first step in overcoming them.

Types of Decisions

As a business professional, you will face many different types of decisions. Information systems can help you with these decisions. Before getting into how information systems can help you, it may be helpful to understand how information needs vary for different types of decisions. Herbert Simon (1960) developed a widely used view of decisions as falling along a continuum from highly structured to unstructured. (Simon called these *programmed* and *nonprogrammed*, but others have used *structured/unstructured*, which we prefer.) **Structured decisions** are routine and repetitive and often have well-defined procedures for dealing with them. **Unstructured decisions**, in contrast, are novel and do not have agreed-upon procedures for making the decisions. **Semistructured decisions** are somewhere in between the two extremes; they have elements that are structured and elements that are unstructured. For structured decisions, we know what information we need and how to use that information. For unstructured decisions, we are not sure exactly what information we need, nor do we know exactly how to use the information. This is important to grasp, as it helps us understand how different types of information systems can help with decision making.

A complementary view comes from Anthony (1965), who developed a framework of managerial activity that is made up of three categories: strategic planning, managerial control, and operational control. *Strategic planning* entails choosing the organization's objectives and deciding how to achieve them; predicting the future of the organization and its environment; and using creative, nonroutine thinking. *Managerial control* involves ensuring the efficient, effective use of resources in achieving the objectives laid out in strategic planning. *Operational control* makes sure that the tasks of the organization are being conducted efficiently and effectively. These tasks typically are routine and well defined.

Gorry and Scott-Morton (1971) combined Simon's framework with Anthony's framework. This resulted in the framework shown in Table 6.1. Examples of relevant information systems are shown in each row/column intersection. As you can see, information systems are useful at all levels of managerial activity and for all types of organizational decisions.

Let's look at this from the perspective of information needs. Operational control has narrow, well-defined information needs that can be anticipated. Furthermore, the information often comes from internal sources or from external sources that are

Table 6.1 Gorry and Scott-Morton's Information Systems Framework

	Operational Control	Managerial Control	Strategic Planning
Structured	Accounting systems (accounts payable/receivable), order processing, inventory control, order processing	Human resources reporting, short-term forecasting	Investment analysis, distribution system analysis
Semistructured	Production planning	Budget variance analysis	Compensation planning
Unstructured	Cash management, project management	Budget preparation, sales planning	New product planning, social responsibility planning

Source: Adapted from Gorry and Scott-Morton (1971) and Rainer and Turban (2008).

easily accessed. In contrast, strategic planning's information needs often are broad and poorly defined and come from both internal and external sources.

Operational, structured decisions often do not require any human intervention. Transaction processing systems (TPSs) can deal with these decisions using predetermined rules and processes. There is little or no judgment involved. For example, an order-processing program can "decide" to allow a customer to place an order if the customer's credit card company accepts the charges but will block the transaction if the charge is denied.

While some managerial decisions are structured, many are semistructured. Semistructured decisions can be supported through systems that allow flexible information retrieval. We can anticipate some information needs but cannot create a program capable of making the decision without relying on human judgment. Since we can anticipate some information needs, information systems often have predefined reports that managers can run to retrieve necessary information. However, it is also important to allow for more flexibility through ad hoc querying, which lets managers retrieve information on the fly. These decisions also require tools that allow for flexibility in analyzing the information once it is retrieved.

Strategic planning often involves unstructured decisions. It is very difficult to anticipate the information needs of managers involved in strategic planning. They may need information ranging from simple, prebuilt reports from internal sources to economists' projections on the future of the economy. In addition, it is hard to determine what the managers will do with the information once they have it.

It is important to understand that as the amount of structure in a decision decreases, the need for flexibility increases. Very structured decisions require little flexibility in terms of information systems. In contrast, the highly unstructured decisions typical of strategic planning require information systems that offer great flexibility.

A Decision-Making Process

Many different decision-making processes exist, each with its own set of proponents. There are many similarities across the various processes. Most seem to fit well with Simon's classic intelligence/design/choice model, so we start this section with a brief discussion of that model and then provide a more detailed process that you can use to make better decisions.

The intelligence phase of Simon's model includes those activities that alert decision makers that there is a need to change the current state. Intelligence, in this context, involves sensing conditions and predicting what conditions will require action. The design phase involves developing alternative approaches to bringing about the required change or achieving the required goals. The most effective and efficient alternative is selected in the choice phase. Some believe that it is worthwhile to add a fourth phase, implementation, in which the activities in the chosen alternative are carried out. Table 6.2 provides some examples of information systems that can be used at each stage of Simon's model.

While we like Simon's model very much, it may be worthwhile to expand his model to provide more actionable details.

Identify and Clearly Define the Problem

In many ways, this is the most critical phase in the decision-making process. If you do not clearly define the problem to be solved, you may spend considerable time and energy in solving the wrong problem. A good problem definition should produce a clear, concise problem statement that describes both the initial state (where you are now) and desired state (where you want to be).

One common issue with problem definition is confusing the core problem with symptoms of the problem. For example, a sales manager might notice that sales from new representatives are decreasing. This could be a symptom of poor training, poor selection of new representatives, or a number of other underlying problems. There are techniques you can use to get at the core problem. The "5 Whys" is a popular example that is easy to understand and apply. To use the technique, simply start with the apparent problem or issue, such as "our sales are declining." Then ask yourself (or your group) "why?" and keep asking "why?" until you uncover the root cause of the problem. By the way, there is nothing magical about the "5" in 5 Whys. It is fine to ask more than five questions to get at the root cause. One criticism of the 5 Whys is that it is sometimes too simple to uncover causes in some situations. Also, the technique does not allow for identifying multiple root causes. Despite its limitations, the 5 Whys remains an effective and popular technique for uncovering root causes.

Having a well-defined, concise problem statement has other benefits as well. One important benefit is that it allows all parties to agree on the core problem. This

Table 6.2 Information Systems and Decisions Stages

Phase	Information System
Intelligence	Data analysis (spreadsheets, statistical software, visualization) Communication systems Data retrieval and document management systems
Design	Group support systems Communication systems Document management systems Data analysis systems (spreadsheets, statistical software, visualization)
Choice	Data analysis systems
Implementation	Project management systems Data analysis systems Communication systems

is very helpful in later phases. In addition, such a statement enables more effective communication of the problem to various stakeholders.

Determine Requirements and Goals

Once you have your problem well defined, you should define the decision's requirements. **Requirements** are the conditions that any acceptable solution must provide. The key word here is *must*. Most decisions have conditions that must be met and conditions that are desirable but not required. One major benefit of having well-defined requirements is that they often help you eliminate infeasible alternatives early in the decision-making process. For example, if you have an absolute budget for a new automobile, you can quickly eliminate many possibilities on the basis of cost.

In contrast to requirements, **decision goals** go beyond the minimum, essential requirements. One way to distinguish between requirements and goals is to think of requirements as "must haves" and goals as "like to haves." Interestingly, goals often conflict with one another. Consider the example of deciding on a new car. Goals might include low cost, excellent fuel efficiency, and high performance. While these are all reasonable goals, fuel efficiency and performance may be in conflict. Another interesting aspect of goals is that they sometimes suggest new requirements. Also keep in mind that as you analyze your decision, you may realize that an original requirement is actually not required and is therefore a goal. For example, when searching for an apartment, you may originally consider having two bathrooms a requirement. However, if you would choose a one-bath apartment that was fantastic in every other aspect, the "two baths" requirement is really a goal.

Identify Alternatives

Once you understand your problem's requirements and goals, it is time to identify **alternatives**. An alternative is a method for transforming the current condition into the desired state. An alternative often goes through two stages: generation and refinement. Brainstorming is often used to generate alternatives, but there are other methods that can be effective. For example, the *nominal group technique* is a structured method for reaching consensus within a group while encouraging input from all group members. While the technique was developed to help groups reach consensus, it can also be used to generate alternative solutions to a problem. Regardless of the method used to identify alternatives, it is important to provide clear descriptions of each alternative. These descriptions should plainly show how the alternative solves the problem and how it is different from other alternatives.

Define the Criteria

Decision criteria are objective measures of the requirements and goals that help you discriminate among the alternatives. Criteria are used to determine how well each alternative meets a particular goal or requirement. It is important that each criterion be independent of other criteria. (It should stand alone.) Also, each goal and requirement should be represented by at least one criterion. You should also avoid redundant criteria. Finally, you should try to use relatively few criteria (keeping in mind that each requirement and goal must be represented by at least one criterion) to keep things manageable.

LEARNING ACTIVITY 6.3

What Kind of Information Do I Need?

Suppose that you are in the market for a new vehicle. Establish at least five requirements and goals (five combined). For each requirement and goal, determine one or more criteria. Be prepared to share your answers.

Select a Decision-Making Technique/Tool

There are many decision-making tools that can be applied to various decision-making situations. While it is beyond our scope here to give a comprehensive list, we offer several that are easy to understand and apply while also being quite useful. The book's website gives some resources for learning more about decision-making tools.

The techniques vary in their complexity and level of subjectivity. Generally, you want to use the simplest appropriate decision-making technique. Be sure to also consider the importance of the decision. More important decisions usually benefit from more complex, sophisticated techniques.

Pros/Cons Analysis

Pros/cons analysis is conceptually simple and requires no mathematical skills. You simply list the advantages and disadvantages of each alternative and then choose the alternative with the strongest advantages and weakest disadvantages. This technique is good for simple decisions that have a small number of alternatives and few discriminating criteria. Where this method gets tricky is in figuring out what "strongest" and "weakest" mean operationally. Also, this method is highly subjective. Despite its weaknesses, a pros/cons analysis is often quite helpful in choosing among alternative courses of action.

Paired Comparisons

The paired comparisons technique, as the name implies, requires you to evaluate each alternative against all other alternatives. There are various ways you can carry out this analysis. In its simplest form, it is kind of like a single-elimination sports tournament. Start by picking one pair of alternatives. Compare the two using the criteria you established earlier. The losing alternative is out of the "tournament." Pair the winner against the next alternative. Keep doing this until only one winning alternative remains.

This method, while simple, is inferior to the more sophisticated variation of paired comparisons. In the more complex variant, you build a matrix, such as the one shown in Figure 6.1. The top row of the matrix is partially grayed out because it represents

	A	B	C	D
A				
B	A			
C	A	C		
D	D	D	D	

Figure 6.1 Paired Comparisons Matrix

duplicate comparisons. The diagonal is grayed out because there is no need to compare an alternative to itself. Each remaining cell indicates which of the two alternatives is better. (This is easier if you assign a letter to each alternative.) Once all the comparisons are done, choose the alternative with the most "wins." In our example, you would choose alternative D.

You can also indicate the strength of the "win" by entering a number following the better alternative. Use a scale such as 0 (no difference) to 5 (major difference). Add up all the numbers for each alternative and convert them to a percentage. Choose the alternative with the highest percentage.

Decision Matrix

The decision matrix technique is widely used in business, especially for choosing among projects or products. The decision matrix uses a grid that lists all the alternatives in the first column and all the criteria in the first row, as shown in Table 6.3. Fill in the grid by rating each alternative on the criteria using a scale to indicate how well the alternative scores on the criterion. In our example, we use a 10-point scale, with 10 indicating that the alternative satisfies the criterion very well. Add up the scores for each alternative; choose the one with the highest total score.

The above example considers all criteria to be of equal importance. If this is not the case, you can use a weighted version of the decision matrix. To do this, assign each criterion a weight relative to its importance. One way to do this is to distribute 100% across the criteria, as shown in Table 6.4. Once you have the weights and the ratings for each alternative, multiply each score by that criterion's weight. The sum of these is

Table 6.3 Unweighted Decision Matrix

	Cost	Quality	Experience	Flexibility	Complete	Score
Proposal 1	6	8	4	7	8	33
Proposal 2	8	6	5	8	8	35
Proposal 3	4	4	6	6	9	29
Proposal 4	1	8	7	6	9	31

Table 6.4 Weighted Decision Matrix

	Cost	Quality	Experience	Flexibility	Complete	Score
Proposal 1	6	8	4	7	8	7.00
Proposal 2	8	6	5	8	8	7.10
Proposal 3	4	4	6	6	9	5.65
Proposal 4	1	8	7	6	9	6.20
Weight	*0.25*	*0.30*	*0.10*	*0.10*	*0.25*	

the overall score for the alternative. Complete this operation for each alternative and choose the one with the highest sum.

Evaluate the Alternatives Using the Criteria

Once you have chosen a decision-making tool, apply it to evaluate each of the alternatives. It is very important that you use your criteria when assessing the alternatives. This may seem obvious, but sometimes the criteria get lost along the way and are not used effectively.

Check That the Solution Solves the Problem

It is worthwhile to validate the chosen alternative to make sure that it actually solves the original problem. Be sure that the alternative will bring about the desired state, meets all requirements, and best achieves the goals.

It is important to understand that the entire process is dependent on the problem definition. If the problem is poorly defined, you are likely to develop inappropriate requirements and goals, which leads to incorrect criteria. If you have the wrong criteria, your alternative evaluation will be faulty, and you are likely to make the wrong choice. So each step in the process is dependent on the steps that precede it. Because of this, it is important to ensure that each step is carried out correctly.

Information Retrieval and Analysis Tools

Now that you understand more about the relationship between decision structure and information needs, we can discuss how information systems help with decision making. In this section, we discuss two categories of tools: information retrieval and information analysis tools. (There are other information and communication tools that are helpful for decision making, such as email and knowledge management systems, but we discuss these in Section III). It is worth noting that the tools we discuss here can be considered components of a decision support system, which we cover in Chapter 14.

When you analyze information, the information has to come from somewhere. Often this information comes from an organization's databases, so you need tools to help you retrieve the information you need. Information may also be stored in organizational documents. Information retrieval tools include database management systems, reporting tools, and document management tools. As we discussed in Chapter 5, one element of database management systems is data retrieval, which is called *querying*. Creating complex database queries requires specialized knowledge, so many managers use reporting tools such as Business Objects or Crystal Reports to generate reports to support their decision making. These **reporting tools** typically allow users to create reports visually rather than requiring special commands. This allows managers to quickly generate reports as they refine their information needs. Figure 6.2 shows a Business Objects screen. The user simply drags data objects from the left-hand pane to the Results Objects area to create a query, which serves as the basis of the desired report.

Managers sometimes need information that is stored in documents such as memos and policy documents. **Document management systems** include functions that help users locate and retrieve such documents. There are multiple aspects to a document management system. Some help with the creation of the document, either directly or through integration with other systems. There also must be some means to capture the document. (Place the document into the document management system.) Not all documents originate from a computerized system. Nondigital documents must be scanned so that they can be managed by the document management system. Once the document is in the system, it needs to be indexed to facilitate faster and easier retrieval.

In addition, document management systems help with versioning (keeping track of various versions of a document). Some document management systems help workers share documents. The system may also help with distributing documents properly.

LEARNING ACTIVITY 6.4

"What If" I Get a 75% on the Final?

"What grade will I get if I score a 75% on the final?" You have probably asked yourself a similar question. While you can certainly figure this out without a computer, a properly designed spreadsheet can make this much easier. Create a spreadsheet that calculates your overall score in the course using the weightings for various factors as indicated by your instructor. Bring the spreadsheet to class, either electronically on your device or with knowledge of the formulas you used. Be prepared to discuss.

Spreadsheets are a type of decision support system. (We will discuss decision support systems more in Chapter 14.) The electronic spreadsheet played an important role in introducing the use of personal computers to businesses. For an interesting

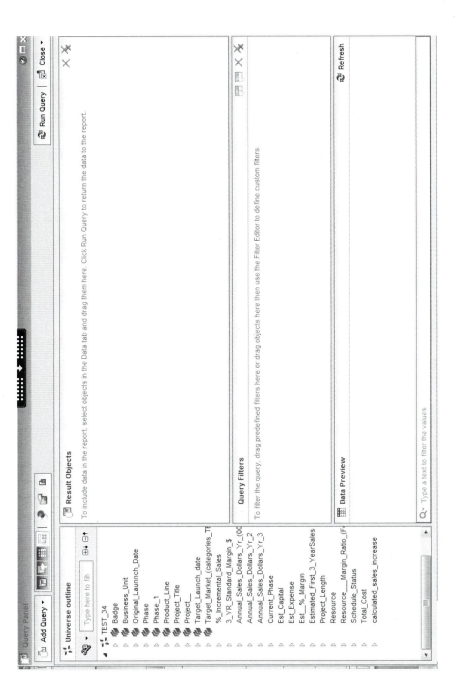

Figure 6.2 SAP Business Objects Screen

history of the electronic spreadsheet, see http://dssresources.com/history/sshistory.html.

In terms of decision support, spreadsheets provide two very important functions: "what-if" analysis and goal-seek analysis. **"What-if" analysis**, which is a form of sensitivity analysis, involves seeing how changes in one or more input variables impact the value of one or more outcome variables. For example, if you are purchasing a car, you can see the impact of changing the interest rate of your loan on the monthly payment, as shown in Figure 6.3. You can change any of the input variables to see a range of possible outcomes.

Some electronic spreadsheet software (such as Microsoft Excel) offers ways to quickly generate a number of scenarios so that you can see the impact of various changes on outcome variables. Excel's Scenario Manager is an example. Figure 6.4 shows a Scenario Manager summary for our car payment calculator. There are three scenarios showing the monthly payment, total payments, and total paid for three payment periods: 36 months, 48 months, and 60 months.

Goal seeking is the opposite of what-if analysis. In a what-if analysis, you specify changes to the input values to see the impact on the outcome variables. When performing a **goal-seek analysis**, you specify the value of the outcome variable you seek (the goal) and the spreadsheet software determines the value of a particular input that will produce the desired output. Suppose that you have set a budget of $400 per month for your new car, you have received a price quote of $25,000 for the model you

	A	B	C	D	E	F	G
1							
2	Purchase price	20,000.00		Interest rate	0.06		
3	Down payment	2,000.00		Period (months)	48		
4	Trade in	2,000.00					
5	Amount financed	16,000.00					
6							
7	Monthly payment	375.76					
8	Total payments	18,036.50					
9	Total paid	22,036.50					
10							

Figure 6.3 Spreadsheet Example

	A	B	C	D	E	F	G	H	I
1									
2		Scenario Summary							
3				Current Values:	36 Months	48 months	60 months		
5		Changing Cells:							
6		Months		48	36	48	60		
7		Result Cells:							
8		Payment		375.76	486.75	375.76	309.32		
9		TotalPayments		18,036.50	17,523.04	18,036.50	18,559.49		
10		TotalPaid		22,036.50	21,523.04	22,036.50	22,559.49		
11		Notes: Current Values column represents values of changing cells at							
12		time Scenario Summary Report was created. Changing cells for each							
13		scenario are highlighted in gray.							
14									

Figure 6.4 Scenario Manager Summary

want to buy, and your current car is worth $2,000 as a trade-in. You could use goal-seek analysis to determine the down payment you would have to provide in order to meet your monthly payment goal. The "before" (original) and "after" for this example is shown in Figure 6.5. (Note that we are only showing part of the spreadsheet.) As you can see, you would need almost $6,000 for a down payment to achieve your payment goal.

The reason that spreadsheets can provide such useful tools is that in building the spreadsheet, instead of putting in numbers for some of the cells, you put in relationships in the form of formulas and functions. Figure 6.6 shows the formulas and functions for our car-buying spreadsheet. Because the spreadsheet is built around the formulas and functions, changing one of the input variables quickly shows us the impacts on all related values. If you want to learn more about using spreadsheets, please see Appendix F.

Original

	A	B	C
1			
2	Purchase price	25,000.00	
3	Down payment	2,000.00	
4	Trade in	2,000.00	
5	Amount financed	21,000.00	
6			
7	Monthly payment	493.19	
8	Total payments	23,672.91	
9	Total paid	27,672.91	
10			

After Goal-Seek Analysis

	A	B	C
1			
2	Purchase price	25,000.00	
3	Down payment	5,967.87	
4	Trade in	2,000.00	
5	Amount financed	17,032.13	
6			
7	Monthly payment	400.00	
8	Total payments	19,200.00	
9	Total paid	27,167.87	
10			

Figure 6.5 Results of Goal-Seek

	A	B	C	D	E
1					
2	Purchase price	25000		Interest rate	0.06
3	Down payment	2000		Period (months)	48
4	Trade in	2000			
5	Amount financed	=B2-SUM(B3:B4)			
6					
7	Monthly payment	=PMT(E2/12,E3,B5)*-1			
8	Total payments	=B7*E3			
9	Total paid	=B8+SUM(B3:B4)			
10					

Figure 6.6 Spreadsheet Showing Formulas

While spreadsheets can perform many types of statistical analysis, they typically are unable to apply more sophisticated statistical methods. When more advanced techniques are needed, you must turn to dedicated statistical software, such as SPSS, Stata, R, and SAS (among others). These applications have the capability to analyze a large number of data points quickly and accurately. Some applications specialize in particular families of statistical techniques. For example, SmartPLS

STATS BOX 6.1:
THE COST OF SPREADSHEET ERRORS

Spreadsheets are widely used analytical tools. Unfortunately, electronic spreadsheets often contain errors that can prove costly. F1F9, a large financial modeling and training firm, estimates that almost 90% of corporate spreadsheets contain meaningful errors. These errors could cost as much as $10 billion annually. Here are a few examples of the costs of spreadsheet errors:

- Eastman Kodak Co. had to restate its income statement in 2005 due to several errors. One of the most severe was an $11 million error in an employee's severance pay package. The error was caused when too many zeroes were added to the employee's severance accrual.

- A spreadsheet error caused the London 2012 Olympic organizing committee to oversell tickets to synchronized swimming events by 10,000 tickets. The error was caused when a staff member entered 20,000 rather than 10,000 into a spreadsheet.

- A cell formatting misunderstanding led to the United Kingdom's intelligence agency, MI5, bugging more than 100 wrong phones.

- In 2013, the "London Whale" disaster led to JPMorgan Chase suffering $6 billion in trading losses and was due in part to an Excel spreadsheet showing underestimating risks from various investments.

You can learn more about these and other costly spreadsheet errors at http://www.eusprig.org/stories.htm.

(http://www.smartpls.de) specializes in a technique called *partial least squares.* Others have broad capabilities ranging from simple descriptive statistics to very complex, sophisticated statistical methods such as time-series analysis for economic forecasting. Many include programming languages that can be used to develop custom algorithms. These applications vary widely in their complexity. Some are intended only for expert users with in-depth knowledge of statistics and the program itself. Others are specifically intended for more casual users.

There are also software tools that help you visualize data. While most statistical software applications have some **data visualization** capabilities, there are also programs that are intended specifically for data visualization. Visualizing data can help you uncover trends and relationships in data that might be less apparent when viewing the data in tables. Figure 6.7 shows a variety of graphs on sales based on customer and location. These charts were produced using Tableau, a popular visualization application. It is worth noting that spreadsheet software can produce charts but typically are not as powerful or flexible as dedicated visualization software.

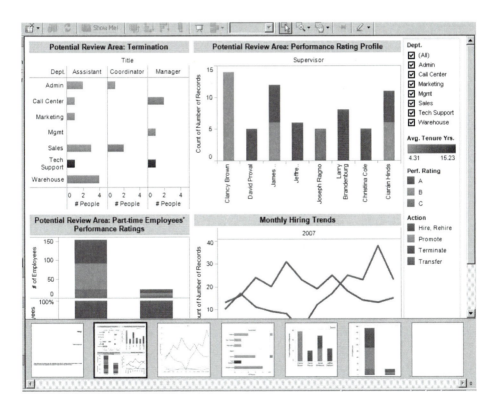

Figure 6.7 Visualization Example

Source: http://public.tableausoftware.com/download/workbooks/Hiring-Terminating-Trends_022?format=html.

Chapter Summary

The focus of this chapter is using information for decision making. We discussed a variety of tools that can be used to help retrieve, analyze, and understand information when making decisions. We also presented a systematic process for making decisions. Finally, we provided you with several techniques that are helpful in decision making.

Here are the main points discussed in the chapter:

- Good decision making requires good information and good decision-making skills, processes, and tools.

- Decision-making skills are critical to a successful business career. These skills are highly sought after by business employers.

- Decision-making skills become increasingly important as one moves to higher levels of responsibility in a business. This is because decisions made at higher levels are more complex and have greater impacts.

- Making good decisions requires good information. Insufficient, inaccurate, or untimely information hurts decision making.

- Information impacts the following with respect to decision making: the constraints that limit the number of alternatives, the alternatives themselves, the forecast of the potential outcomes from each alternative, and the means for comparing and selecting among the alternatives.

- Structured decisions are routine and repetitive and often have well-defined procedures for making them. Unstructured decisions are novel; we do not know exactly how to go about making them, what information is needed, or how to use that information. Semistructured decisions have elements of both structured and unstructured decisions.

- Decision making can be done by completing the following steps:

  1. Identify and clearly define the problem.
  2. Define the requirements and goals of the decision.
  3. Identify alternatives.
  4. Define the decision criteria.
  5. Select the appropriate decision-making tools.
  6. Evaluate the alternatives using the criteria.
  7. Check that the solution solves the problem.

- Many information analysis tools exist, including tools for information retrieval, information analysis, knowledge management, and communication.

- Information retrieval tools include database management systems, reporting tools, and document management tools.

- Information analysis tools include electronic spreadsheets, statistical software, and data visualization tools.

Review Questions

1. Explain why decision-making skills are more important at higher levels of an organization.
2. Compare and contrast structured, semistructured, and unstructured decisions.
3. Explain the relationship between decision type (structured, semistructured, unstructured) and managerial activity (strategic planning, managerial control, operational control).
4. Name and briefly describe the phases of Simon's model of decision making.
5. For each phase of Simon's model of decision making, give an example of an information system that supports the phase.
6. Name the phases in the detailed decision-making process described in the chapter.
7. Contrast requirements and goals in the context of decision making.
8. Name and briefly describe the decision-making tools discussed in the chapter.
9. Name and briefly describe the information retrieval tools discussed in the chapter.
10. Compare and contrast the "what-if" and "goal-seek" analyses.

Reflection Questions

1. What is the most important thing you learned in this chapter? Why is it important?
2. What topics are unclear? What about them is unclear?
3. What relationships do you see between what you learned in this chapter and what you have learned in earlier chapters?
4. Think about a difficult or important decision you have had to make. What made the decision difficult? How could the material in this chapter have helped you make that decision?
5. Think about a time when you made a poor decision. What could you have done that would have led to a better decision?
6. Briefly discuss how a reporting tool can be used to help you make semi-structured and unstructured decisions.
7. Why are document management systems useful when making unstructured decisions?
8. How can following a disciplined decision-making process (such as the one described in this chapter) help you justify a decision?
9. How do you decide how much time and effort to put into making a decision?

10. Suppose that you have several job offers from which to choose. Describe how you would go about deciding which one to accept.

Additional Learning Activities

6.A1. Suppose you have three decisions to make:

   a. What elective class to take in your final semester

   b. Which of several postgraduation job offers to accept

   c. Where to go for your graduation trip

   Rank each decision according to how much time and effort you would put into making the decision. Explain your rating. Be prepared to share your answers in class.

6.A2. Suppose that have three job offers from which to choose.

   a. Determine the requirements and goals for deciding which offer to accept. (Have at least five total requirements and goals.)

   b. Determine the criterion you would use to measure each requirement/goal.

   c. Which decision-making tool would you use to make this decision? Why?

6.A3. Suppose that you are a marketing manager who needs to decide among several different advertising outlets.

   a. Determine the requirements and goals for deciding which outlet to use. (Have at least five total requirements and goals.)

   b. Determine the criterion you would use to measure each requirement/goal.

   c. Which decision-making tool would you use to make this decision? Why?

6.A4. Go to the course website and locate the Car Buying spreadsheet. Use the spreadsheet to determine the monthly payment for two different interest rates for two different periods (for example, 6% and 8% for 36 and 60 months). For each combination, report the monthly payment, total payments, and interest paid. Briefly describe how you could use this spreadsheet when car shopping.

6.A5. Go to the course website and locate the Monthly Commission spreadsheet. Determine how many units you would have to sell to earn $3,000 in commission payments. How did you go about solving this problem? How long did it take you? Be prepared to share your experience in class.

6.A6. Go to the course website and locate the What-If spreadsheet. Follow the instructions in the spreadsheet.

6.A7.   Go to http://simile-widgets.org/ and select one of the links on the right (Exhibit, Timeline, Timeplot, or Runway). Look at the visualization it created. Then click on one of the More Live Examples underneath the visualization that is on that page. Prepare a paragraph that discusses the following: 1. Which dataset did you chose? 2. What story did you want the visualization to tell? 3. How effective was the visualization in telling that story? 4. How effective was the visualization in helping you better understand the data? Be prepared to discuss your experience.

6.A8.   Pick four competing elective classes that you might take next semester. (You can only take one of the four.) List the classes, then do the following:

a.   Prepare a paired comparison matrix to show which class you would take.

b.   Prepare an unweighted decision matrix with at least three criteria (such as time of day, or your interest in the class).

c.   Prepare a weighted decision matrix using the criteria from (b).

Which of the three methods was the most effective? Why?

References

Anthony, R. N. 1965. *Planning and Control Systems: Framework for Analysis.* Cambridge, MA: Graduate School of Business Administration Harvard University.

Gorry, A., and M. Scott-Morton. 1971. "A Framework for Information Systems." *Sloan Management Review* 13(1): 56–79.

Rainer, R. K., and E. Turban. 2008. *Introduction to Information Systems: Supporting and Transforming Business.* 2nd ed. New York: John Wiley & Sons.

Simon, H. A. 1960. *The New Science of Management Decision.* New York: Harper & Row.

Glossary

Data visualization: A visual representation of data with the goal of clearly communicating or better understanding the meaning of the data.

Decision: A choice among alternatives.

Decision alternative: A method for transforming the current condition into the desired state.

Decision criteria: Objective measures of decision requirements and goals that discriminate among the alternatives.

Decision goal: Desired decision solution requirements that go beyond the minimum, essential requirements.

Document management system: A system that assists with managing, locating, retrieving, and tracking documents.

Goal-seek analysis: An analysis that determines the value of a particular input variable that will produce the desired output (the goal).

Reporting tools: Information systems tools that allow users to create reports without knowing special commands.

Requirement (decision): A condition that any acceptable solution must provide.

Semistructured decision: A decision for which some elements are structured and others are unstructured.

Structured decision: A decision that is routine and repetitive and often has well-defined procedures for making the decision.

Unstructured decision: A decision that is novel and therefore has no agreed-upon, well-understood procedure for making the decision.

"What-if" analysis: An analysis that involves seeing how changes in one or more input variables impact the value of one or more outcome variables. Also known as *sensitivity analysis*.

CHAPTER 7

Transmitting Information

Learning Objectives

By reading and completing the activities in this chapter, you will be able to

- Discuss key components and characteristics of networks
- Explain the different types of networks
- Explain what the Internet is and what it is used for
- Identify the main networking architectures and infrastructures
- Describe various Web 2.0 and Web 3.0 concepts

Chapter Outline

Focusing Story: I Want My Own Wi-Fi!: The Emergence of the Mi-Fi
Learning Activity 7.1: How Does That Car Drive Itself?
Introduction and Definitions
Types of Networks
Learning Activity 7.2: Broadband in Developed Countries
The Internet
Learning Activity 7.3: Who Is Using the Internet?
Learning Activity 7.4: A Future Internet? Internet2 and Business
Networking Architectures
Learning Activity 7.5: Architectures and Principles
Communicating Information in Modern Organizations
Learning Activity 7.6: Web 3.0 versus the Internet of Things
Chapter Summary
Review Questions

FOCUSING STORY

I Want My Own Wi-Fi! The Emergence of Mi-Fi

The interconnected world as most students know it—with easy and often free access to the Internet from home, school, the coffee shop, the airport, and even on the train—is actually fairly recent. We used to need cables (wires) to connect to other systems and the Internet. Really.

But now that we have tasted the freedom of the wireless world, people want more and more. However, there are places in this country that lack the access many in a university environment may take for granted. That's where Mi-Fi comes in. Some people utilize a device the size of a credit card (but thicker) to provide an Internet connection anywhere. Other people utilize their smartphones as a mobile hot spot to take advantage of the data that they are already paying for on their wireless phone plan. A Mi-Fi network can support typically up to five users or devices (like an iPhone, a laptop, an iPad, a gaming device, or a Web camera) within 30 feet of the router. The routers are fairly inexpensive (free to $100 per router, plus the data plan) and run on batteries that can be recharged. (Some examples of these products can be found at http://www.verizonwireless .com/internet-devices/ and https://www.freedompop.com.)

Two experiences of the authors of this text exemplify how Mi-Fi has been utilized to enable business and education to occur in previously impractical locations. The first involves a friend of one of the authors who runs a side business from his farm property creating webpages. Prior to Mi-Fi, his best option was to utilize dial-up or satellite Internet technology. At his office job, he connected via a high-speed Internet connection, and his clients expected that he could do the same as part of his business services. As it became obvious that dial-up and satellite Internet were not going to cut it for him to continue his side business, he decided to try a Mi-Fi connection. This proved to be the perfect solution. Although it was much more expensive than a cable or DSL connection, it ultimately allowed him to keep his business running.

A second example concerns education. Distance learning is a growing trend in higher education that capitalizes on the broadband connections to the Internet that most people have access to. However, one author's experience is that students in rural areas such as Indian reservations and farm country were having a hard time participating in the requirements of distance education. To address these concerns, the author recommended that the students try utilizing Mi-Fi connections. Sure enough, students who adopted these solutions were able to participate in classes and get the level of education they expected from a public university.

These two examples show how utilizing Mi-Fi opens doors in ways that were before impractical, if not impossible. Think about all the other avenues this opens up.

FOCUSING QUESTIONS

1. What potential challenges exist for using Mi-Fi for business?
2. What other creative business uses can you think of for Mi-Fi?
3. What do you think could be the next evolution in wireless networks?

LEARNING ACTIVITY 7.1

How Does That Car Drive Itself?

For this learning activity, watch the following two YouTube videos. While you do, make a list of all the different pieces of information and technology that are required in order for a car to drive itself. After you have done this, find out where that information comes from and how it interacts with other information in order for a car to successfully drive itself. Be prepared to discuss your list in class.

- https://www.youtube.com/watch?v=CqSDWoAhvLU
- https://www.youtube.com/watch?v=TsaES--OTzM

Introduction and Definitions

To begin our discussion of **networks**, we should first define what a computer network is. Basically, it is a collection of interconnected devices that allow users and systems to communicate and share resources. The devices can be computers, servers, routers, or a wide variety of other telecommunication devices.

Network Components and Characteristics

Setting up a network requires a variety of devices, and depending on which devices are used, a different type of network is established. For example, the wireless networks discussed in the focusing story require a Mi-Fi router to set up the network and devices that have wireless network adapter cards, like the Apple iPad or most laptops, to connect to it.

A **router** is an intelligent device that controls the flow or transmissions in and out of a network. It takes its name from its main purpose, which is routing traffic to appropriate devices on the network (by using a routing table that contains address information for the devices on the network) or to other networks. Routers oftentimes include connections for Ethernet cables while also allowing wireless signals that many devices in businesses and homes use. See Table 7.1 for a list of common router manufacturers and links to their current product lines.

We have been talking about devices having specific addresses. How is that done? It is the result of each device having a **network interface card (NIC, or network adapter)** that provides physical access to a device because it has a unique ID written on a chip that is mounted on the card. Wireless NICs, just like wired NICs, also have their own unique addresses. The network adapter for wired networks is where you plug in an Ethernet cable on your computer.

Finally, basic networks can also make use of **repeaters** to retransmit a data signal that it receives after eliminating noise in the signal and regenerating it for strength. These are often used when the signal from a wireless router weakens and is not usable in certain parts of a building or property that are some distance away from where the router is located.

Types of Networks

Wired versus Wireless Networks

There are many ways to categorize networks. First, networks can be wired or wireless. Wired networks make use of physical cables, which can be copper wires (like the lines to your phones at home or the Ethernet cable we talked about in the previous section), coaxial cables (like the ones used for cable television), or fiber-optic cables (which are made of glass fiber and transmit using light signals) (see Figure 7.1). The possible speed of transmission increases from wires to coaxial cables to fiber-optic cables, with fiber-optic cables allowing speeds hundreds of times faster than coaxial cables and thousands of times faster than basic wires.

There are also quite a few **wireless networks** besides the Wi-Fi you are used to. All of them make use of frequencies to transmit data (and voice). For example, some transmissions are done using microwaves that must be placed no more than

Table 7.1 Router Manufacturers

Manufacturer	Product Line
ASUS	http://www.asus.com/us/Networking/Wireless-Routers-Products/
Belkin	http://www.belkin.com/us/Products/Network-Accessories/c/WSNTWLS/
D-Link	http://us.dlink.com/product-category/home-solutions/connect/routers/
Linksys	http://www.linksys.com/us/c/wireless-routers/
NETGEAR	https://www.netgear.com/home/products/networking/wifi-routers/

30 miles apart, since they must "see" each other to transmit. The satellites used for data transmissions are typically 22,000 miles in space above the equator. (They are called *geosynchronous satellites* because they keep a relative position to the earth.) Those are the same systems that send you satellite radio signals, GPS coordinates, and TV signals from remote locations. Infrared communication can also be used to create a wireless network for devices in close proximity. For example, wireless mice, keyboards, and other such devices often use infrared to connect to one another. Radio signals are also used for connecting devices. Think of your cordless phone or garage door opener. **Cellular networks** also use radio communication technologies to offer another wireless alternative. As you know, cell phones connect to a local antenna that relays calls from one area to the next. Finally, **Bluetooth** is another standard that uses short-wavelength radio transmissions to connect devices (like we discussed for infrared technology) such as wireless mice, keyboards, or headphones.

With all the wireless technology options, what is a wireless, or Wi-Fi, network? First of all, **Wi-Fi** is a name owned by the Wi-Fi Alliance. Today it has become standard terminology to refer to a wireless network that you can access with one of your wireless devices, such as a laptop or smartphone. Wi-Fi networks also make use of radio technology, but in a different way than some of the technologies discussed above. A Wi-Fi network consists of a wireless access point (WAP, or hotspot) that is itself connected to a wired network (see Figure 7.2). The WAP sends the transmissions it receives from wireless devices to a wired device connected to the Internet.

Broadband Networks

Another way to classify networks is by whether they are baseband or broadband; these classifications refer to the speed and frequency of the bandwidth of the network. Today, the networks you use to connect to the Internet are likely to be broadband networks. They are faster, with download speeds (transfers from the servers to your computer) in megabytes per second, although most broadband networks today transfer at rates in gigabytes per second. The types of networks that are classified as broadband include the familiar DSL (digital subscriber lines) types of networks and cable connections, as well as some you may not have heard of, like integrated services digital network (ISDN) and T-lines. We discuss these networks in greater depth in Appendix H.

Figure 7.1 Types of Cables. From left to right: coaxial, Ethernet, fiber optic
© istock.com/piotr_malczyk, © istock.com/hatchapong, © istock.com/zentilia

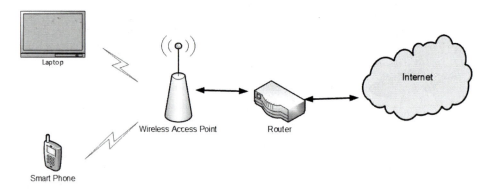

Figure 7.2 Wireless Network

Network Coverage

Networks can also be classified as a function of the area of coverage or geography of the network. The two most significant ones are the local area network (LAN) and the wide area network (WAN), but other variations exist. See Table 7.2 for a list of different terms you might hear when people discuss types of networks.

Table 7.2 Network Types (Geographical Classification)

Type of Network	Description	Notes
Local area network (LAN)	A network that connects devices in a limited geographical area (a local area of usually fewer than five kilometers).	Most organizations use many LANs interconnected via backbone networks (see below).
Wide area network (WAN)	A network that connects devices over a large geographic area, which can span any distances you can imagine, from city-wide to continent-wide to worldwide.	These networks can be implemented via private networks or public transmission systems, such as the Internet.
Personal area network (PAN)	A network connecting personal devices to a personal computer (i.e., mouse, microphone, printer, etc.) over a very short distance.	Often uses USB connections (wired) or Bluetooth or infrared technologies (wireless).
Home area network (HAN)	A network used within a home office, allowing PCs to share devices such as printers, routers, or scanners.	Sometimes referred to as an office area network (OAN).
Backbone network (BBN)	A network that serves to interconnect other networks (like LANs) or network segments (subnetworks).	Often used in large buildings or areas that have multiple LANs that need to communicate together.

LEARNING ACTIVITY 7.2

Broadband in Developed Countries

The percentage of the population in a country that has access to broadband networks can have a significant impact on the use of applications such as electronic business, electronic government, and other network-dependent applications. According to the Organisation for Economic Co-operation and Development (OECD) data shown below, the United States has more than 100 broadband subscriptions per 100 people. In other words, in a group of 100 U.S. citizens, there would be more than 100 broadband connections to the Internet. As you can see, this is not the same for all countries in the developed world.

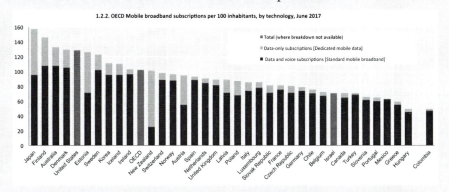

1.2.2. OECD Mobile broadband subscriptions per 100 inhabitants, by technology, June 2017

For this learning activity, identify and be prepared to discuss the following:

- Why do you think some industrialized countries have more broadband subscriptions than others?
- What new opportunities emerge when essentially an entire country is connected to the Internet with broadband connections?
- What different opportunities exist in countries where the majority of people do not have access to the Internet via broadband connections?

Source: Based on data from the OECD: OECD Broadband Portal, http://www.oecd.org/sti/broadband/broadband-statistics/.

Local area networks (LANs) connect devices in a limited geographical area (a local area of usually fewer than five kilometers). Examples include homes, departments, a school, or a floor of a large office building. Because of the limited geography, LANs can offer very good transmission speeds, especially for wired LANs. To be part of the LAN, a cable must connect the NIC of the computer or device with the router/bridge/switch of the LAN's **hub** (for wired LANs). The most popular LAN technology today is Ethernet, which is represented in Figure 7.3, although some alternatives do exist.

Wide area networks (WANs) connect devices over a large geographic area, which can span any distance you can imagine, from city-wide to continent-wide to world-wide. Unlike LANs, WANs often make use of various communication media (like phone lines, coaxial cables, and satellite) as well as several different providers (phone company and cable company), even for one given network.

The Internet

One network we have yet to discuss is the Internet. The **Internet** is a publicly accessible worldwide network of networks. One way to explain how the Internet works is to think of a road system (Van Slyke and Bélanger 2003). In many countries, there are interstate highway systems that link major cities together. These interstate highways intersect one another to form a complex road system. However, not every place in the country is accessible directly from an interstate highway. Smaller roads branch off from the highways to allow travelers to reach virtually any area of a country. The Internet works in a similar way. Main connections, called the *Internet backbones,* carry the bulk of the data traffic on the Internet. Networks from major Internet service providers (ISPs) make up the backbone. These networks extend across the globe in a similar way that interstate highway systems extend across many countries.

Figure 7.3 An Ethernet Local Area Network

For the Internet to allow global traffic, routers are used to interconnect the various networks together. Every host or computer that is a full participant (permanently connected) on the Internet has a unique address called an *IP (Internet Protocol)* address. Appendix H includes more details on the Internet's protocols and addressing, but it is important to note that the IP addressing scheme most students have seen (such as 128.192.68.1) is outdated because it has run out of addresses to allocate to businesses, organizations, and countries. It is called **IPv4** (for version 4). The new IP addressing scheme is called IPv6. In simple terms, **IPv6** expands the IP address size from the current 4 bytes (the four sections of the address above) to 16 bytes (such as 2002:1AC4:DB32:EF10). In fact, on Thursday, February 3, 2011, the **Internet Assigned Numbers Authority (IANA),** the organization responsible for assigning IP addresses, assigned the last blocks of IPv4 addresses.

The Internet started as a project by the United States Defense Advanced Research Projects Agency (DARPA) in collaboration with universities. The Internet then grew by absorbing various networks worldwide. Today, the Internet has grown so much that there are more than one billion host computers connected, based on data collected by the Internet Systems Consortium, which is the developer of the open source infrastructure software BIND DNS (see Figure 7.4). One of the core characteristics of the Internet that has contributed to this growth is interoperability, which is the

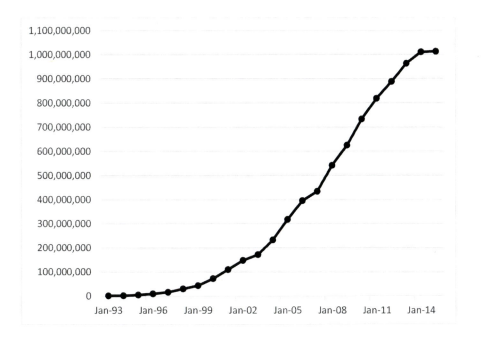

Figure 7.4 Number of Hosts Connected to the Internet as of January 2017
Source: Based on data from the Internet Systems Consortium, ISC Domain Survey, https://www.isc.org/network/survey/.

ability of heterogeneous (different) systems to communicate with one another. For example, systems based on different hardware platforms and running different software can communicate together on the Internet if they use the Internet's protocols (described in Appendix H).

LEARNING ACTIVITY 7.3

Who Is Using the Internet?

The Internet is truly a global phenomenon, with connectivity in almost every country in the world. In 2017, the International Telecommunications Union (ITU) reported that more than 84% of European households, 65% of American households, and even 18% of African households have access to the Internet at home. This represents a wide variety of individuals with different languages, cultures, and applications. For this activity, find statistics about Internet users in terms of gender, age, culture, language, or other characteristics that your instructor will provide you. Be prepared to discuss the following in class:

1. How is usage of the Internet likely different around the world? Why would there be such differences (or why are there no differences)?

2. What is the likely future of the Internet in terms of diversity? How will that affect businesses? Governments? Societies?

Source: ICT Facts and Figure 2017. Retrieved December 16, 2017, from https://www.itu .int/en/ITU-D/Statistics/Pages/stat/default.aspx.

Internet Applications

The Internet is a network, not an application. When asked what the Internet is, students often describe it as a place where there is all this information you can access. But this definition actually refers to the **World Wide Web (the Web)**. They are *not the same!* The Web is one application using the Internet as its carrying network. Examples of other applications that make use of the Internet include email, file transfer, instant messaging, Internet telephony, and desktop videoconferencing. Table 7.3 briefly describes some of these other traditional Internet-based applications. Later in the chapter, we will discuss more recent applications, labeled as Web 2.0 applications.

The Web allows users to access an amazing variety of resources using the infrastructure of the Internet. The Web is the result of work performed by Tim Berners-Lee at CERN (the European Organization for Nuclear Research), who proposed the hypertext transfer protocol (HTTP) to interconnect files on the Internet. That is why many Web addresses start with "http," indicating that the page is located on a server that supports the hypertext transfer protocol. You are also certainly familiar

Table 7.3 Traditional Internet-Based Applications

Application	Description
World Wide Web (the Web)	Graphical interface to worldwide resources.
Electronic mail (email)	Allows users to send and receive messages through computer networks.
Instant messaging	Allows multiple users to communicate synchronously by sending and receiving short text messages online.
Voice over IP (Internet telephony)	Allows voice data to be sent over an IP-based network, such as the Internet.
Desktop videoconferencing	Allows individuals in different locations to communicate via voice and video on personal computers.
Peer-to-peer file sharing	Allows file sharing between specific individuals or systems across the Internet.
Online application sharing	Allows users to share documents, calendars, or other applications using websites.
File Transfer Protocol (FTP)	Allows users to move files back and forth between nodes on the network. FTP is *anonymous* when files are loaded on such public sites.

with hyperlinks, the (often) underlined blue links that allow you to navigate back and forth between pages or to a specific section of a Web page. When you click on a link, your browser sends a request to the Web server that houses the requested page. The server then sends the document over the Internet to your browser. Figure 7.5 illustrates how the Web application makes use of the Internet.

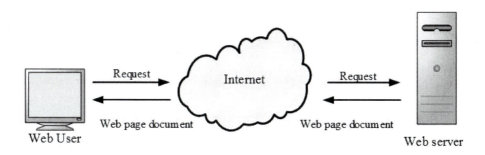

Figure 7.5 The Internet and Web

BUSINESS EXAMPLE BOX 7.1

Internet Application of the Day: Get a Degree Online!

Ever heard of the University of Phoenix or DeVry University? You might have seen ads about the completely online degree programs available at these and many online universities where one can get an associate, bachelor's, master's, or even PhD degree. Online leaning is not new, but it has grown substantially because it offers a cost-efficient way to deliver education and allows institutions to have a broader reach to individuals who would otherwise not be able to attend school. One organization has identified more than 28,000 programs from online schools covering more than 130 possible areas of studies in the United States. As previously stated, online degrees are no longer limited to "online universities" but have become standard offerings from many traditional universities. Some highly ranked online programs belong to Penn State, Boston University, and Indiana University, for example. A 2015 survey reveals that online education is no longer an exception, with more than one-quarter of students taking online courses (28%). The survey finds that in public institutions, the portion of undergraduate students is even higher, at 72.7% taking online courses (Online Learning Consortium, 2015). Therefore, it is likely that you will be taking at least one online course during your program of study (you likely already have). You therefore know that the biggest challenges are to maintain interaction with the instructor and other students and to remain up-to-date and motivated.

Every year the *U.S. News & World Report* has been providing rankings of different undergraduate and graduate programs worldwide. Consistent with their increasing popularity, therefore, online programs are now included in the *U.S. News & World Report*'s rankings. Their rankings for online degrees include "Best Online Bachelor's Programs" and best online rankings for a variety of graduate programs, including MBA, engineering, nursing, and many more. One important factor to consider when choosing an online degree is to select one that has been accredited by a recognized organization. Online degrees, facilitated by the rise of the Internet, have clearly changed the availability of education, providing a broader reach to degrees for individuals with limited availability (e.g., working full time) or unable to physically attend class due to geographical constraints (e.g., living in remote areas) or physical disabilities. Costs can be lower, but some online degrees can be very expensive as well. For example, for an online master's degree in information technology, the *U.S. News & World Report* suggests that the per-credit costs vary from $440 to $1,500.

Importantly, many hiring managers now consider online degrees on equal footing with on campus degrees if the online degree is accredited by a reputable accreditation agency, comes from a university that also has a traditional on-campus presence, and has an established brand or reputation. Knowing this information is important to prospective students who may be deciding to invest their time and money in pursuing an online degree.

Sources: Kumar, Sunil. 2015. "5 Common Problems Faced by Students in eLearning and How to Overcome Them." *eLearning Industry.* Retrieved December 20, 2017, from https://elearningindustry.com/5-common-problems-faced-by-students-in-elearning -overcome; "100 Best Online Colleges for 2018–2019." *The Best Schools.* Retrieved December 20, 2017, from https://thebestschools.org/rankings/best-online-colleges/; "Best Online Programs." *US World and News Report.* Retrieved December 20, 2017, from https://www.usnews.com/education/online-education; "Do Employers Value Online Learning?" 2013. *Ed Tech Magazine,* September. Retrieved March 28, 2015, from http:// www.edtechmagazine.com/higher/article/2013/09/do-employers-value-online-learning -infographic; "Online Information Technology Master's Degree." *US World and News Report.* Retrieved December 20, 2017, from https://www.usnews.com/education/online -education/information-technology-masters-degree; "Online Report Card—Tracking Online Education in the United States 2015." *Online Learning Consortium.* Retrieved December 20, 2017, from https://onlinelearningconsortium.org/read/online-report-card -tracking-online-education-united-states-2015/.

Internet versus Intranet

Most organizations today, including businesses, schools, and governments, use an **intranet**. It sounds similar to "Internet" because it is the use of Internet technologies and related applications inside an organization. This means that security controls are in place to ensure that only individuals inside the organization have access to the applications on the intranet.

LEARNING ACTIVITY 7.4

A Future Internet? Internet2 and Business

The Internet has been in existence since the early 1970s. It has grown into a worldwide network that is used extensively for commercial purposes (among other things). Some researchers, however, believe that it is important to have an Internet-like network that is not overwhelmed by commercial users so that they can rapidly exchange research information between researchers, the military, and academics. That is the role of **Internet2**, which was created by a consortium of research and education institutions, industry leaders, and government agencies. Internet2 is a trademark of the University Corporation for Advanced Internet Development (UCAID). The organization has more than 200 members and operates the **Internet2 network**, a fiber optics–based network used for high-speed transfers between research institutions and for testing and researching networking technology. For this activity, research the most up-to-date status of the Internet2 project. Discuss its potential implications for businesses.

The Internet of Things

An emerging trend with respect to the Internet is referred to as the **Internet of Things (IoT)**. The Internet of Things capitalizes on the ever-increasing number of household and everyday objects that connect to the Internet. As each device is connected to the Internet, it is able to be uniquely identified through its IP address. It can then communicate with other computers and Internet-connected devices. This has the potential to make significant changes in such areas as health care, automobiles, and the home. Imagine if someone with heart issues had an internal monitor connected to the Internet that kept doctors informed of his or her heart status in real time. In the automobile industry, cars are parking and even driving themselves. This is all done due to the interconnectivity of various devices in the car (as you likely learned in Learning Activity 7.1). Another example of the Internet of Things includes wiring household devices to the Internet, such as thermostats that regulate the temperature of the house and door locks. Nest is a thermostat that learns when you are home or away and the desired temperature for your house and then automatically sets itself based on your patterns. It also allows users to control the temperature of the house from anywhere they are if they have an Internet connection. As more devices connect to the Internet, more possibilities emerge for changing the way we live our lives. Think of your fitness trackers that can encourage you to exercise or apps on your smartphone to lock/unlock or even start your car remotely. How does the app communicate with the car? Via the Internet. That's just the tip of the iceberg for IoT.

Networking Architectures

Architecture

An architecture is a layout or blueprint for how devices are supposed to work together. **Networking architectures** can then be implemented as specific **networking infrastructures**. The infrastructure includes the actual hardware, software, and networking components that support the processing and transfer of information. In this section, we focus on the higher-level picture, the networking architectures, which each have specific advantages and disadvantages. Some architectures have been in existence for a long time (e.g., historical architectures). These include the mainframe, client/server computing, and peer-to-peer networks. Others are more recent (e.g., modern architectures), such as cloud computing and virtualization. We describe these in this section but first explain key principles that should be considered in selecting an architecture.

Architectural Principles

When deciding on an architecture, managers must ensure first and foremost that the architecture will support the business objectives of the organization (ensuring information technology [IT] and business alignment, as discussed in Chapter 4). Then managers must also consider certain architectural principles, such as the following:

- *Ease of implementation:* Some architectures are easier to implement than others. For example, the SaaS (software as a service) architecture we describe below requires limited effort by the organization wishing to use it.

- *Flexibility/interoperability:* In some situations, it is important to be able to make changes to how devices are interconnected or which devices are connected to which ones. Some architectures allow for more flexibility concerning devices that are connectable.

- *Control:* Organizations often want to maintain a certain degree of control over which devices can connect and how they are connected to the network. In the days of the mainframe, where everything was connected to one large central computer, organizations had complete control. Today, they must evaluate how much control they need as they make decisions on which architecture to use.

- *Scalability:* When the number of users or devices increases or decreases substantially, it is important for organizations to be able to grow or reduce the size of the network accordingly. This is the concept of **scalability,** and it is a core consideration in selecting an architecture. In fact, the client/server architecture described below overtook the old mainframe architecture we just described partly because it offered substantial scalability.

- *Maintainability:* Once an architecture has been implemented, it must be maintained by installing software patches, upgrading equipment, and replacing equipment when it fails. Maintenance is a task that requires responses 24 hours per day, 7 days per week. One principle that may affect organizations' choices of architecture is how to minimize having to perform this maintenance themselves.

- *Security and reliability:* All technology decisions should take into consideration security, including reliability of the systems, and architectures are no exception. For example, most experts consider a peer-to-peer architecture, where files are shared, as one of the least-secure options for networking. We will discuss security in depth in Chapter 8.

Client/Server Architecture

In the **client/server architecture**, processing and storage tasks are shared and distributed between two types of network systems: clients and servers. **Clients** are processes that request services from servers. **Servers** provide services to clients by responding to their requests. Most computers can perform client or server services, even if we mostly think of clients as the personal computers we use to access larger machines called servers.

An example can help clarify the concept of sharing the workload among clients and servers (see Figure 7.6). When you search the Web for information, you are using a browser on your personal computer. The browser is acting as a client that makes requests to a Web server when you click on a hyperlink, asking for that page to be sent to you. The Web server receives the request and sends the documents back to your

Figure 7.6 Client/Server Computing Architecture

browser. Now assume that you need information about prices in that document. The Web server may send a request to a database server for the information, and then it sends it along with the other documents to your browser. The browser then displays the requested document. In this case, the client (browser) requests services but also performs the task of displaying the results (presentation task). The Web server receives the requests, makes its own request to the database server (data task), and then packages it to send it back to you (processing or logic task). For servers and clients to communicate, even when they are on different technology platforms, they require some software that can understand each technology's specific formats and communication protocols and translate them into the other platform's formats and protocols, enabling interoperability. This is the role of middleware.

Peer-to-Peer Architecture
The **peer-to-peer architecture** is used substantially on the Internet, but not as much in organizations. In a peer-to-peer network, all systems are equal (acting as both clients and servers), sharing their resources with one another. The sharing of resources can include processing power, disk storage, and network bandwidth. Most students are familiar with Napster, the music-file-sharing system, a prime example of peer-to-peer networking.

Wireless Architecture

In the wired versus wireless networks section, we discussed how wireless networks are set up. Organizations must evaluate several decisions regarding what to support and whom to allow on the network when they choose to implement a wireless architecture. Think of your university's wireless network. Who should have access to it? If everyone, is it your tuition fees that pay for the network? Which devices should be allowed on it? What level of security should be provided? All these issues have to be discussed and decided upon by the network architects of your university before they make the wireless network available.

One important decision organizations have to make when considering wireless architectures they want to support is what policies to implement with respect to employees bringing their own wireless devices and using them for work and/or personal purposes. This is referred to as **BYOD (bring your own device)** policies. These devices include smartphones, tablets, and even personal laptops, which some employees prefer to use over office computers. Because these devices are not controlled by the organization, some companies are concerned about the possible security issues. They are also concerned about employees using the devices for purposes other than work during work time. Yet at the same time, most organizations recognized the increased productivity that has resulted from employees using their devices anytime, anywhere. Additional Learning Activity 7.A1 at the end of the chapter proposes a case study that explores BYOD use in classrooms.

Service-Oriented Architecture

A more recent architecture that has gained substantial interest in the business world is **service-oriented architecture (SOA)**. It is a model or a set of design principles of how to take data from heterogeneous systems and create reusable services. The services can be used in different systems with different technology platforms. Think of an invoice as a service. The accounts payable department probably has a system generating invoices. The shipping department, however, also has a system that handles invoices for products that are ready to ship. The two departments can make use of the same service, an invoice, with each of their own applications, independent of where and on which platform their applications are. Figure 7.7 shows how SOA works.

As with all architectures, it is important to realize that SOA is not a product itself but an architecture or, in this case, a way to design how devices are interconnected. Note also that the layer that allows SOA to work is similar to middleware, which we discussed previously. Because SOA is a vague architecture and requires some coding (using the middleware), it is often too broadly defined by organizations. This can lead to poor implementation, where reusability is not really achieved and the potential gains are not realized. While it seems easy when looking at Figure 7.7 to connect the various heterogeneous systems together, it takes time to make sure that all the different data fields and formats can be "understood" and translated by the middleware.

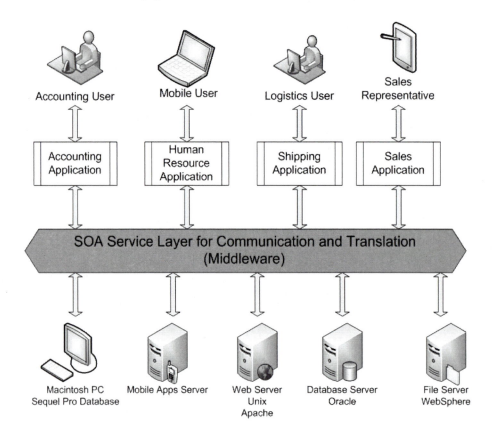

Figure 7.7 Sample Service-Oriented Architecture (SOA) Layout

Furthermore, in some organizations, those who "own" the data may not agree to let various systems access their data and services.

Cloud Computing

One of the most popular architectures that has appeared in the last few years is cloud computing, also known as "on-demand computing" or "utility computing." In **cloud computing**, an organization acquires or rents computing resources from providers instead of having its own locally managed hardware and software (see Figure 7.8). Using the Internet, the organization is able to increase or decrease its computing resources when the needs arise or decrease. What can be acquired via the cloud? Virtually any computing resource, from hardware for storage and processing, to backup services, to specific applications. Clearly, the cloud includes the SaaS we discuss later in this chapter and much more. The main providers of cloud services are large organizations with resources to spare, such as Google, IBM, AT&T, Microsoft Azure, and Amazon Web Services (AWS), although specialized providers also exist. You are likely

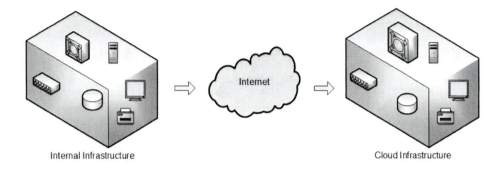

Internal Infrastructure   Cloud Infrastructure

Figure 7.8 Cloud Computing

familiar with use of the cloud to store documents if you have used Dropbox, Google Drive, iCloud, or one of the many other similar services available to you today. You can further explore these in Additional Learning Activity 7.A6 at the end of the chapter.

The four main forms of cloud computing are IaaS, PaaS, SaaS, and recently BPaaS (business process as a service). The interaction among these first three forms is displayed in Figure 7.9.

Infrastructure as a Service (IaaS)

The availability of cloud computing has provided the ability to offer infrastructure as a service (IaaS), which is an Internet-based computer operating system that is maintained and updated by a third party at a remote location. Utilizing a system such as this allows businesses to pass the running of their computer systems to another company so they can focus on their business competencies. Companies that offer these services usually utilize virtualization, which is discussed below, to provide many different operating systems on one server. It also allows for the dynamic scaling of infrastructure when demand increases in areas such as online storage and backup. Some examples of companies providing IaaS are Amazon.com and Symantec.

Platform as a Service (PaaS)

Another service provided by the ubiquity of Internet connections is known as platform as a service (PaaS), which provides a cloud-based platform for running websites and databases and executing programming languages. In the current Internet era, it is important for systems to be operational 24 hours per day and 365 days per year. If a company wants to keep its system up at this level, it needs to invest not only in staff whose job it will be to provide this level of uptime but also in backup systems that provide redundancy when electronic systems inevitably need maintenance or even fail. Third parties that provide these services are able to gain efficiencies of scale by spreading the cost of supporting a system like this over many customers, thus reducing the total number of systems needed (though virtualization) as well as the

Figure 7.9 Cloud Infrastructure Services

personnel necessary to run it. Examples of companies that provide this service are Google's App Engine and Microsoft's Azure.

Software as a Service (SaaS)

Another architecture or model of computing is **software as a service (SaaS)**, which is basically the acquisition (or rental) of software via a subscription model (see Figure 7.10). SaaS, often called "software on demand," allows organizations to rent software from a provider, frequently using the Internet to access this software application. SaaS software tends to be mostly straightforward applications that businesses need but that do not provide specific competitive advantages. For example, the most popular SaaS applications include customer relationship management software, sales force automation, human resources management software, and desktop applications (like word processing). One form of SaaS that you are likely familiar with is Google Docs. Others include Web meeting technologies such as Cisco's WebEx, customer relationship management technologies such as Salesforce.com, and enterprise resource planning software such as SAP Business ByDesign.

Business Process as a Service (BPaaS)

A newly emerging delivered service is **business process as a service (BPaaS)**, which utilizes the SaaS, IaaS, and PaaS already used by the company. BPaaS provides companies with a way to provide services in a streamlined fashion that adapts and grows as the businesses' needs to provide services change and expand. BPaaS infrastructures are implemented in such a way to allow multiple languages to be displayed to the

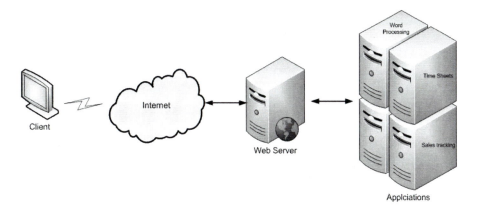

Figure 7.10 Software as a Service

end user and to scale very rapidly as business grows. These business processes include any processes that a company may provide, including email, package shipping, and customer credit management. One of the largest providers of BPaaS is ADP, a payroll processing company. By utilizing ADP's payroll processing BPaaS, companies can focus on the products and services they are in business to offer and let ADP handle their payroll processing needs.

Virtualization

Another recent trend in computing architectures is virtualization. As can be seen in Figure 7.11, **virtualization** allows one physical device such as a server or computer to operate as if it is several machines. Virtualization software creates virtual environments called *virtual machines* on the hardware platform. Each virtual machine can then run its own operating system and applications. If you own a recent Apple Mac computer, its operating system allows you to perform virtualization so you can run a Windows operating system on your Mac.

LEARNING ACTIVITY 7.5

Architecture and Principles

The purpose of this activity is to further explore one of the networking architectures discussed in this chapter. More specifically, the goal is to map each architectural principle to one of the networking architectures that your instructor will assign to you. Perform necessary research as a group and clearly highlight how the given architecture ranks on each architectural principle (high, medium, low), and make sure to describe why. For example, you could state that the client/server architecture ranks high on scalability because clients and servers can be added to the network easily and as needed. Prepare a presentation for the class.

Figure 7.11 Virtualization

Communicating Information in Modern Organizations

The previous section briefly reviewed some of the most used or most recent networking architectures. How do we make use of these architectures? Well, they serve as the communication backbone for all the applications that organizations employ to perform tasks. These tasks are called *business processes,* and we will dedicate Chapter 11 to discussing them more in detail. In this section, however, we want to continue our discussion about the communication applications running on networks with a review of the more recent Web 2.0 applications.

Web 2.0

Web 2.0 refers to the second generation of applications on the Internet. The main difference between the initial set of applications, like email or Web surfing, and Web 2.0 applications is the addition of interactivity, where the user becomes a participant in the interaction. For example, through **wikis** like Wikipedia (http://www.wikipedia .org), users can participate in the design of the site by adding their own definitions and corrections to the information. The set of technologies referred to as Web 2.0 includes wikis, social networking, blogs, mashups, Twitter, and much more. Table 7.4 presents a list of some popular Web 2.0 technologies and their descriptions.

Table 7.4 Popular Web 2.0 Technologies

Web 2.0 Technology	Description	Examples
Wikis	Website that allows individuals to jointly create and edit Web pages about a chosen topic.	• Wikipedia: http://www.wikipedia.org • Set up your own wiki: http://www.wikispaces.com/
Instant messaging and presence awareness	Allows several individuals to communicate via real-time text-based messages. **Presence awareness** indicates when colleagues are currently online and connected.	• AOL Instant Messaging: http://www.aim.com • Yahoo Messenger: http://messenger.yahoo.com
Collaborative content	Allows several individuals to contribute to and share stored data and documents such as text documents, movies, pictures, calendars, and more. The collaborative content systems control for user access and versioning, avoiding two users from changing a document simultaneously.	• Doodle (calendar): http://www.doodle.com • Google Docs (documents): http://docs.google.com
Web conferencing (voice, video, and data)	Allows individuals to conduct live meetings via the Internet, including training sessions or sales presentations. All participants use their own computers to connect to the meeting and can use voice (voice over IP) and/or video, as well as send files, use instant messaging, or even share their personal desktop with others.	• Skype: http://www.skype.com • Google+ Hangouts: https://hangouts.google.com/
Social networking	Allows individuals to participate in a community of users (individuals or organizations) where they are connected with one another via links (e.g., friendship or business relationships).	• Facebook: http://www.facebook.com • LinkedIn (business social network): http://www.linkedin.com
Blogs	Allows individuals to write commentaries or opinions on anything they want on websites that others can read. Usually, blogs are updated regularly and allow others to leave comments. The name comes from "Web log."	• Create your own blog: http://www.blogger.com; http://www.wordpress.com
Twitter (microblogging)	Allows individuals to write tweets, which are short text messages on their user page for others to "follow." Initially up to 140 characters, this was increased to 280 in late 2017. Twitter is very popular among celebrities to share their day-to-day activities with fans.	• Twitter: http://www.twitter.com

continued

Table 7.4 Popular Web 2.0 Technologies (*continued*)

Web 2.0 Technology	Description	Examples
RSS (Really Simple Syndication)	Allows individuals to receive frequently updated information like blogs or news headlines directly on their personal computers.	• Search your university's news pages for where you can sign up to receive news as a RSS feed. • Yahoo! Sports (RSS feed): http://sports.yahoo.com/top/rss

As you can see from Table 7.4, there are many interesting Web 2.0 technologies that are changing the way we interact with organizations and with one another. Individuals are increasingly connected via technologies, with many advantages and disadvantages.

THE POWER OF WIKINOMICS (CROWDSOURCING)

You have heard of wikis and Wikipedia, but what if you could take advantage of everyone's voluntary contributions to knowledge for business purposes? This is referred to by some as **crowdsourcing** or **mass collaboration,** where individuals voluntarily come together to solve a problem. Others have given it the name **wikinomics.** More specifically, in a book called *Wikinomics: How Mass Collaboration Changes Everything* (2007), Don Tapscott and Anthony Williams give the example of Goldcorp.

Goldcorp, a Canadian mining company with a 50-year-old mine considered to be tapped out, needed to clearly identify new deposits, but in-house geological experts did not seem to be able to find them. The company's CEO, Rob McEwen, then took a very unusual step by publishing all proprietary geological data on the Web (mining is usually a very secretive industry). He challenged "Web prospectors" in a contest to find new mining deposits and offered $575,000 in prize money. Approximately 1,000 individuals from 50 countries examined the available information, and 110 target locations were submitted to Goldcorp; 50% of them were previously unknown to the company. The amazing result is that 80% of the newly identified deposits yielded substantial quantities of gold.

Netflix, the online movie rental company, offers another example of the creative use of wikinomics. One of the company's core strengths is providing users recommendations of movies they may like based on what they have watched or placed in their rental "queue" (list of movies they want shipped to them in order of preference). Up to 60% of their rentals were driven by these recommendations. Netflix had their own developers working on this recommendation system, which they called CineMatch. The company, however, wondered if others could develop an even better algorithm, so they turned to the Web and launched a contest where teams could register on the company's website, download the data from a large number of customers' rental preferences, and propose their own recommendation algorithm. If the teams could improve CineMatch's prediction accuracy by *10%* or more, they would receive $1,000,000. Netflix would also offer a yearly progress prize of $50,000 for teams with the greatest improvements that year. The competition was announced in October 2006 and was set to end on October 2, 2011. On September 2009, one team received the $1,000,000 grand prize for improving the CineMatch algorithm by approximately 10.10%.

Another example comes from the Boston Marathon bombing. On April 15, 2013, during the Boston Marathon, a bomb was detonated near the finish line, killing 3 people and injuring an estimated 264 others. Luckily for the investigators, there are commercial cameras all around the area where the bombing took place. However, there were holes, or blind spots, in what these cameras recorded. This is where the crowdsourcing came in. Police were able to tap into the approximately 500,000 people watching the marathon and the videos they were recording. These people all provided digital recordings, which helped with the investigation. Unfortunately, crowdsourcing didn't work as well for the investigation. A second group of people thought they would help the investigators review the vast number of videos they had. This resulted in an innocent person being suspected of committing the crime based on an overzealous ambition to help find the person who set off the bomb (Wadhwa 2013).

Web 3.0

Web 2.0 technologies are all around us today, but a new technology is emerging into the marketplace: **Web 3.0**. If Web 2.0 introduced interactivity and user participation, what is Web 3.0 bringing to us? The semantic Web. This is when computer systems start to understand the meaning (semantics) of information and data. In other words, the systems will consider the context of the information to give meaning to other information or data connected to it. For example, when you search the Web today, you have to identify which keywords are likely to give you the information you need. In the semantic Web, the systems will understand what you need and give you exactly that information. Searches will become much more intelligent and results much more personalized. For example, Google implements this when you search for restaurants on your smartphone and it suggests local restaurants you might enjoy based on such information as your location, prior searches, and restaurants you have previously clicked on.

LEARNING ACTIVITY 7.6

Web 3.0 versus the Internet of Things

You may have noticed that the Web 3.0 and the Internet of Things are similar in nature. For this learning activity, identify two ways that Web 3.0 is being used and two ways that the Internet of Things is being used. Identify how these

STATS BOX 7.2:
DIFFUSION OF INNOVATIONS TIMELINE

Social networking is everywhere, and there is no doubt about its popularity. What is quite interesting is that it achieved this status very rapidly compared to other major innovations. The table below compares how long it took various technologies to achieve 150 million users. Of course, in the days of the telephone, there were fewer people, so this is not a scientific analysis. Yet it does tell something about today's interconnected world.

Innovation	Year Introduced	Year Reached 150 Million Units	Years It Took
Telephone	1876	1965	89
Television	1928	1966	38
Cellular phone	1983	1997	14
iPod	2001	2008	7
Facebook	2004	2009	5
Snapchat	2014	2016	2

As of January 2015, Facebook has more than 1.39 billion active users, and more than half of them log on to their accounts every day! The average user has more than 300 "friends," and overall, American users spend 40 minutes per day on Facebook.

Sources: Constine, J. 2014. "American Users Spend an Average of 40 Minutes per Day on Facebook." *TechCrunch,* July 23. http://techcrunch.com/2014/07/23/facebook-usage-time/; Kokalitcheva, K. 2015. "Facebook Passes 1.39B Monthly Active Users, 890M Daily Active Users, and Half a Billion Mobile-Only Users." *Venture Beat News,* January 28. http://venturebeat.com/2015/01/28/facebook-passes-1-39b-monthly-active-users-and-890m-daily-active-users; Novet, J. 2016. "Snapchat by the Numbers: 161 Million Daily Users in Q4 2016, Users Visit 18 Times a Day." *NovetVentureBeat,* February 2, 2017. https://venturebeat.com/2017/02/02/snapchat-by-the-numbers-161-million-daily-users-in-q4-2016-users-visit-18-times-a-day/.

implementations are similar and how they are different. Be sure to pay attention to how the understanding of information and data (semantics) are used with each of these technologies. Be prepared to discuss your lists of similarities and differences with the class.

Chapter Summary

In this chapter, we discussed networking concepts and how information is transmitted. We first defined networks and discussed various types, including the Internet and the Web. We then discussed networking architectures and concluded with Web 2.0 technologies and Web 3.0.

Here are the main points discussed in the chapter:

- A network is a collection of interconnected devices that allow users and systems to communicate and share resources. The network requires connecting devices such as routers, bridges, or switches. Each device on the network requires a network interface card (NIC, or network adapter). Repeaters and hubs can be used to regenerate signals on networks.

- Networks can be classified as wired (using physical connections) or wireless (using airwaves for connections). Wireless networks include Wi-Fi, microwave signals, satellite signals, infrared signals, and radio signals, including cellular networks and Bluetooth. Networks can also be classified as local area networks (LANs), which connect devices in a limited geographical area, or wide area networks (WANs), which connect devices over a large geographic area like a city, a country, or the world. Other networks include personal area networks (PANs), home area networks (HANs), virtual private networks (VPNs), and backbone networks (BBNs).

- The Internet is a publicly accessible worldwide network of networks. It uses routers to interconnect the various networks together, and every host or computer that is a full participant (permanently connected) on the Internet has a unique address called an IP (Internet Protocol) address. The Internet is a network, not an application. The many applications that can make use of the Internet include the Web, which is a graphical interface to worldwide resources, as well as electronic mail, instant messaging, voice over IP (Internet telephony), desktop videoconferencing, peer-to-peer file sharing, online application sharing, file transfers (FTP), newsgroups, and many more.

- Network architectures describe how devices are supposed to work together. Every architecture has its advantages and disadvantages in terms of ease of implementation, flexibility and interoperability, control, scalability, and security and reliability. The main networking architectures we discussed include client/server architecture, where processing and storage tasks are shared and distributed between clients and servers; peer-to-peer architecture, where systems are equal in sharing their resources with one another; wireless architecture, which defines how devices are to be connected to the wireless network; service-oriented architecture (SOA), which allows data from heterogeneous systems to be used to create reusable services; cloud computing architecture, which allows an organization to acquire computing resources from providers instead of having its own locally managed hardware and software; and the virtualization model, where one physical device can operate as if it is several machines.

- Web 2.0 refers to the second generation of applications on the Internet where the user becomes a participant in the interaction. Web 2.0 technologies include wikis, which allow individuals to jointly create and edit Web pages about a chosen topic; instant messaging and presence awareness, which allow several individuals to communicate via real-time text-based messages with presence awareness indicating when colleagues are currently online and connected; collaborative content, which allows several individuals to contribute to and share stored data and documents; Web conferencing, which allows individuals to conduct live meetings via the Internet; social networking, which allows individuals to participate in a community of users connected with each other; blogs, which allow individuals to write commentaries or opinions on anything they want on websites others can read; mashups, which allow users or developers to combine data or applications from several sources to create new ways to view data or new aggregated results; Twitter, which allows individuals to write short text messages of up to 280 characters on their user page for others to "follow"; and RSS, which allows individuals to receive frequently updated information like blogs or news headlines directly on their personal computers.

Review Questions

1. What is a network?
2. What are the key components and characteristics of a network?
3. What is a wireless network, and what are some examples of it?
4. What are the differences between local area networks (LANs) and wide area networks (WANs)?
5. What is the Internet, and what is the difference between the Internet and the World Wide Web?
6. What is the role of network architectures, and what principles should managers take into consideration when evaluating network architectures?
7. Briefly explain each of the networking architectures presented in the chapter.
8. Explain what Web 2.0 means and provide three examples of Web 2.0 technologies.
9. What is Web 3.0? What other terminology is often related to Web 3.0?
10. What is the Internet of Things?

Reflection Questions

1. What is the most important thing you learned in this chapter? Why is it important?
2. What topics are unclear? What about them is unclear?
3. How can the architectures discussed in this chapter be used to create competitive advantages for the organizations we discussed in Chapter 4?
4. Why do many individuals confuse the Internet with the World Wide Web?
5. Why does it make sense for companies to use architectures like cloud computing?
6. What issues could exist when companies use architectures like cloud computing?
7. Do you think we will eventually live in a completely wireless world, or will there always be wired networks? Why?
8. In your opinion, which architectural principle is most important in deciding on a network architecture?
9. Is the Internet likely to continue growing in terms of users, hosts, and connected networks?
10. How can a business use Web 2.0 technologies for competitive advantages?

Additional Learning Activities

7.A1. This activity requires you to complete a case analysis regarding BYOD (bring your own device) as implemented in classrooms. The case can be accessed online or may be provided by your instructor.

Sipior, Janice C., James Bierstaker, Q. Chung, and Johnny Lee. 2017. "A Bring-Your-Own-Device Case for Use in the Classroom." *Communications of the Association for Information Systems* 41(10). Retrieved from http://aisel.aisnet.org/cais/vol41/iss1/10.

7.A2. This activity requires you to complete a case analysis regarding social networking. The case may be accessed through your university website, the Ivey Business School business case website (https://www.iveycases.com), or the Harvard Business School cases website (https://cb.hbsp.harvard .edu/cbmp/pages/home), or it may be provided to you by your instructor.

Aggarwal, Ridhima, Stephen E. Chick, and Francoise Simon. 2017. "PatientsLikeMe: Using Social Network Health Data to Improve Patient Care." *INSEAD*, January. Product number: IN1312-PDF-ENG.

7.A3. As a group, research Web 3.0 and develop a presentation for fellow students that can clearly explain what it is and how it is being utilized.

7.A4. Locate two undergraduate or master's degree programs that use the Internet and Web to completely replace face-to-face meetings. Describe each of the programs, including the network-enabled applications they use, and identify how they could make even better use of Web 2.0 technologies to increase the interactivity of their programs.

7.A5. Research voice over IP (VoIP) products. Select and download two of them that either are freeware (available for free) or offer a test version. Use the two products several times and identify their main advantages and weaknesses. Prepare a recommendation report for which one would be most useful for (a) students and (b) a small business. Make sure to discuss why.

7.A6. Use one of the cloud storing applications discussed in the chapter (Dropbox, Google Drive, iCloud) to share documents with your classmates. Prepare a document discussing the advantages and disadvantages of using the cloud for your schoolwork and for business.

7.A7. This activity requires you to complete a case analysis regarding cloud computing. The case can be accessed online or may be provided by your instructor.

Cain, James, Matt Levorchick, Alan Matuszak, Allan Pohlman, and Douglas Havelka. 2015. "eLoanDocs: Riding the Tide of Technology without Wiping Out." *Communications of the Association for Information Systems* 36(38). Retrieved from http://aisel.aisnet.org/cais/vol36/iss1/38.

7.A8. This activity requires you to complete a case analysis regarding Web 2.0. The case may be accessed through your university website, the Ivey Business School business case website (https://www.iveycases.com), or the Harvard Business School cases website (https://cb.hbsp.harvard.edu/cbmp/pages/home), or it may be provided to you by your instructor.

Steenburgh, T., and J. Avery. 2008. "CASE: UnME Jeans: Branding in Web 2.0." *Harvard Business Case,* November 12. Product number: 9-509-035.

References

Tapscott, Don, and Anthony D. Williams. *Wikinomics: How Mass Collaboration Changes Everything.* Penguin, 2008.

Van Slyke, C., and F. Bélanger. 2003. *Electronic Business Technologies.* New York: John Wiley & Sons.

Wadhwa, T. 2013. "Lessons from Crowdsourcing the Boston Bombing Investigation." *Forbes,* April 22. http://www.forbes.com/sites/tarunwadhwa/2013/04/22/lessons-from-crowdsourcing-the-boston-marathon-bombings-investigation/.

Glossary

Backbone network (BBN): A network that serves to interconnect other networks (like LANs) or network segments (subnetworks).

Blog (Web log): A website that allows an individual to write commentaries or opinions on anything for anyone to read.

Bring Your Own Device (BYOD): A policy regarding the use of personally owned wireless devices (laptops, tablets, and smartphones) by employees in the workplace.

Bluetooth: A wireless network that uses short-wavelength radio transmissions to connect devices such as wireless mice, keyboards, or headphones.

Business process as a service (BPaaS): Provides companies with a way to provide services in a streamlined fashion that adapts and grows as the businesses' needs to provide services change and expand.

Cellular networks: Networks that use radio communication over local antennas to relays calls from one area to the next.

Client/server architecture: A computing model where the processing and storage tasks are shared and distributed between clients and servers.

Clients: Processes that request services from servers.

Cloud computing: A computing model where an organization acquires or rents computing resources from providers instead of having its own locally managed hardware and software. Also known as *on-demand* or *utility computing*.

Collaborative content: A situation in which several individuals contribute to and share stored data and documents.

Crowdsourcing: Mass collaboration of information to solve a problem. Also known as *wikinomics*.

Desktop videoconferencing: A system allowing individuals in different locations communicate via voice and video on personal computers.

Electronic mail (email): Applications used to send and receive messages through computer networks.

File Transfer Protocol (FTP): A system allowing users to move files back and forth between nodes on the network.

Home area network (HAN): A LAN used within a home office, allowing PCs to share devices such as printers, routers, or scanners.

Hub: A form of repeater that has multiple ports to connect many devices together.

Instant messaging: A system allowing multiple users to communicate synchronously by sending and receiving short text messages online.

Instant messaging and presence awareness: A system allowing several individuals to communicate via real-time text-based messages with presence awareness indicating when colleagues are currently online and connected.

Internet: The publicly accessible worldwide network of networks.

Internet Assigned Numbers Authority (IANA): The organization responsible for assigning IP addresses.

Internet of Things (IoT): The connection of physical everyday objects to the Internet that allows them to communicate with one another and other computers.

Internet2: A consortium of research and education institutions, industry leaders, and government agencies that operates the Internet2 network.

Internet2 network: A fiber optics–based network used for high-speed transfers between research institutions and for testing and researching networking technology.

Intranet: The use of Internet technologies and related applications inside an organization.

Internet Protocol Version 4 (IPv4): An older IP addressing scheme that uses 4 bytes for addresses (such as 128.192.68.1) that ran out of addresses to allocate.

Internet Protocol Version 6 (IPv6): A new IP addressing scheme that uses 16 bytes.

Local area network (LAN): A network to connect devices in a limited geographical area (usually fewer than five kilometers).

Mashup: A situation in which users or developers combine data or applications from several sources to create new ways to view data or create new aggregated results.

Mass collaboration: More than one individual gathering information. Also known as *wikinomics* or *crowdsourcing*.

Network: A collection of interconnected devices that allow users and systems to communicate and share resources.

Network architecture: The layout or blueprint for how devices are supposed to work together.

Network infrastructure: The actual hardware, software, and networking components that support the processing and transfer of information.

Network interface card (NIC, or network adapter): Provides physical access to a device because it has a unique ID written on a chip that is mounted on the card.

Online application sharing: A system allowing users to share documents, calendars, or other applications using websites.

Peer-to-peer architecture: A computing model where all systems are equal (acting as both clients and servers), sharing their resources with one another.

Peer-to-peer file sharing: File sharing between specific individuals or systems across the Internet.

Personal area network (PAN): A network connecting personal devices to a personal computer (e.g., mouse, microphone, printer) over a very short distance.

Really Simple Syndication (RSS): A format allowing individuals to receive frequently updated information like blogs or news headlines directly on their personal computers.

Repeater: A device that retransmits a data signal that it receives after eliminating noise in the signal and regenerating it for strength.

Router: An intelligent device that controls the flow or transmissions in and out of a network.

Scalability: The ability to grow or reduce the size of the network as required.

Servers: Processes that provide services to clients by responding to their requests.

Service-oriented architecture (SOA): A computing model or set of design principles of how to take data from heterogeneous systems and create reusable services.

Social networking: Individuals participating in a community of users connected with one another.

Software as a service (SaaS): An architecture or model of computing where the acquisition (or rental) of software is done via a subscription model.

Twitter: A technology allowing individuals to write short text messages of up to 280 characters on their user pages for others to "follow."

Virtualization: A computing model that allows one physical device, such as a server or computer, to operate as if it is several machines.

Voice over IP (Internet telephony): Voice data sent over an IP-based network, such as the Internet.

Web 2.0: The second generation of applications on the Internet where the user becomes a participant in the interaction.

Web 3.0: Computer systems that understand the meaning (semantics) of information and data, resulting in more intelligent searches and more personalized results. Also known as the *semantic Web*.

Web conferencing: A technology allowing individuals to conduct live meetings via the Internet.

Wide area networks (WANs): A network connecting devices over a large geographic area, such as a city, a country, or the world.

Wi-Fi: The network name owned by the Wi-Fi Alliance; a wireless network that uses radio technology.

Wikinomics: A term to describe when individuals voluntarily come together to solve a problem online. Also known as *crowdsourcing*.

Wikis: Web pages individuals jointly create and edit about a chosen topic.

Wired network: A network that makes use of physical cables (copper wires, coaxial, or fiber-optic cables) for connections.

Wireless network: A network that makes use of frequencies to transmit signals.

World Wide Web (the Web): The graphical interface to worldwide resources available on the Internet.

CHAPTER 8

Securing Information

Learning Objectives

By reading and completing the activities in this chapter, you will be able to

- Discuss the relationship between risk management and information security
- Explain the various types of threats to the security of information
- Identify the main goals of information security
- Discuss the different categorizations of security technologies and solutions
- Explain the basic functioning of security technologies and solutions, such as passwords and password managers, two-factor authentication, firewalls, biometrics, encryption, virus protection, and wireless security
- Discuss the main purposes and content of security policies

Chapter Outline

Focusing Story: My Mac Is More Secured than Your Windows-Based PC!
Introduction and Definitions
Learning Activity 8.1: How Protected Is Your Computer?
Information Security Threats
Learning Activity 8.2: What Do Hackers Break into the Most?
Learning Activity 8.3: Detecting Phishing
Security Technologies and Solutions
Learning Activity 8.4: How Strong Is Your Password?
Learning Activity 8.5: Biometrics on the PC
Learning Activity 8.6: Breaking the Encryption
Learning Activity 8.7: Where's the Security?
Chapter Summary
Review Questions

FOCUSING STORY

My Mac Is More Secured than Your Windows-Based PC!

I am sure some of you have heard it and probably even shared the rumors with others. If you get a Mac (an Apple computer with a Macintosh operating system), you are much less likely to have security breaches than if you get a regular PC—plus they're really cool. We might agree with the cool part, but what is the status of Apple computer security?

For quite a while, there were few viruses and other such programs (called *malware*) that targeted Mac systems. That resulted in a reputation that Mac systems were substantially safer than Windows-based PCs. Experts do recognize that this is still true; Apple computers are less likely to be victims of viruses, but they also warn that this does not mean there are no security issues! One Mac lover and security researcher named Charlie Miller revealed in the spring of 2010 that he had identified 20 security vulnerabilities in Apple's software, each of which could result in the computer being compromised (taken over). Miller first hacked an iPhone in 2007 and then a MacBook Air in two minutes at a competition in Vancouver a few months later.

When Apple released the iPhone in 2007, it generated new interest in Apple's platforms and might have attracted the attention of many more hackers who had targeted Microsoft's platforms before. As a result, many hackers started to identify security flaws in the iPhone, such as the ability to bypass the phone's PIN by placing it in recovery mode or the ability to extract encrypted data using basic forensic software (i.e., software used by investigators to perform such tasks as logging into a computer or recovering lost or deleted files). This software is available for free online, and a YouTube video even explains how to do this. Of course, Apple released fixes for these security issues as soon as they could. Nevertheless, as a result of these issues, many firms that deal with sensitive data, such as law firms, decided iPhones were too risky to use. In the summer of 2010, new security issues surfaced with the release of the iPad. One group of computer experts discovered a flaw that allowed them to uncover 114,000 email addresses, including those of prominent officials in companies, politics, and the military. What they did is guess numbers that identified iPads connected to AT&T's mobile network. In 2017, Mac users started being victims of **ransomware** when hackers used the "Find My iPhone" feature with a bunch of iCloud usernames and passwords they stole to remote-lock users' devices.

In the end, however, it is still true that Macs face fewer attacks. One reason is that Macs still only accounted for less than 7% of the worldwide market for personal computers in late 2017, making this a much smaller pool of potential victims.

FOCUSING QUESTIONS

1. Why is forensic software available online to everyone?
2. Why are security issues in iPhones and iPads of concern to Mac users?
3. Will a larger market for Apple platforms change this security landscape?
4. Can the Apple Watch create new security issues for Mac users?

Sources: Ante, S. E. 2010. "AT&T Says iPad Owners' Email Data Was Breached." *Wall Street Journal,* June 10: B.1; Ante, S. E., and B. Worthen. 2010. "FBI to Probe iPad Breach—Group That Exposed AT&T Flaw to See Addresses Says It Did a 'Public Service.'" *Wall Street Journal,* June 11: B.1; Chin, M. 2017. "Some Mac Users Are Getting Hit with Ransomware—Here's What to Do." *Mashable,* September 22. Retrieved from http://mashable.com/2017/09/22/icloud-hack -find-my-mac/#JzWi0I19TmqY; Greenberg, A. 2010. "The Mac Hacker Strikes Again." *Forbes* 85(6): 40; Monroe, I. 2010. "Worms in the Apple?" *ABA Journal* 96(3): 33; Hooper, L. 2007. "iPhone: Apple's Worm?" *CRN* 1256 (December 10): 16; Clover, J. 2017. "Apple's Shipments Down in Q3 2017 amid Continuing PC Market Decline." *MacRumors,* October 10. Retrieved from https://www .macrumors.com/2017/10/10/apple-mac-shipments-down-q3-2017/.

Introduction and Definitions

Information security is an important topic for everyone in today's interconnected world. What is **information security**? It is defined as the set of protections put in place to safeguard information systems and/or data from security threats such as unauthorized access, use, disclosure, disruption, modification, or destruction.

Risk Management

Before discussing information security, it is important to understand that information security is one aspect of risk management that organizations pursue. No matter what efforts an organization may make to provide the best security possible, or which technologies and tools it might invest in, there will always security risks involved. **Risk management** is the process of identifying, assessing, and prioritizing the security risks an organization may face. As a result of this process, organizations may decide to accept the risks, try to mitigate or prevent those risks by investing in security protections, or share the security risks with another organization—for example, by buying insurance. Organizations can refer to different standards for risk management that are available from organizations like the Project Management Institute, the National Institute of Science and Technology, and the International Standards Organization (ISO).

While security and risk management do go hand in hand, they have a few differences as well. **Security** is focused on protecting the assets a company has from both external and internal threats. External threats such as hackers and viruses threaten the valuable information a company collects while in business. Security must be able to secure these data from attacks to ensure the company can run smoothly without interruption. Internal threats are important to guard against as well. For example, security must monitor the network to make sure that policies are not being breached in a harmful way (either deliberately or accidentally) and that employees are only able to access systems they are authorized to. Risk management has a broader focus, analyzing and balancing risks with the resources available to mitigate them. Risk management determines where the company is most vulnerable and how likely it is to be affected by a risk. While weighing these risks, the company looks at the cost of addressing these issues and makes decisions based on both the financial aspect and the acceptable level of security needed to protect different areas in the company. A graphical representation of how a multitude of threats work together to increase risk is presented in Figure 8.1.

In this chapter, the focus is on the steps that can be taken to mitigate or prevent risks. That is the essence of why information security steps are taken. First various high-level information security concepts are discussed. This is followed by a

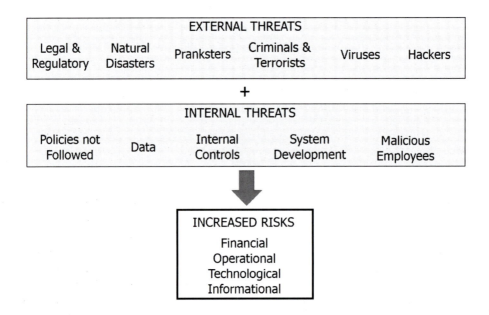

Figure 8.1 Threat Types and Causes That Lead to Increased Risk Exposure

discussion of various information security threats and, finally, by solutions to these threats. It is important to note that some of the solutions are employed to counteract multiple threats. There is not a direct one-to-one relationship between threats and solutions.

Information Security Concepts

Whether you need to secure your own computer to prevent a virus from destroying your files or an organization needs to secure access to its data and servers to ensure that hackers cannot get information about its clients, the core concepts of security remain the same.

First, security is not only about technology but also about management and people. It is possible to acquire the best-ever security tools, but if employees do not use them or, even worse, decide to bypass the security protections mandated by the organization, the systems and data are vulnerable to attacks or security failures. Top-to-bottom commitment to security in the organization is needed to ensure that security tools are properly used and security policies are followed adequately.

Second, the world of information security is somewhat unfair. How many security weaknesses does the hacker need to break into a system? One. How many security weaknesses does the organization or individual need to fix or protect against? All of them. This is referred to as **asymmetrical security warfare**. One party must do everything to protect oneself, while the other party (the attacker) only needs to find the one weakness.

Third, as a result of having to protect the computer systems and data from all possible weaknesses, security for individuals, and even more so for organizations, requires what is called *defense in depth*. **Defense in depth** means that there must be multiple layers of security protections in place. For example, if you have very important data on your computer, such as personal financial information, defense in depth would mean having a lock on the computer, a password to access it, a firewall to protect it against breaches from the Internet, and even encryption of the data so it is unreadable without the passcode or password. We will discuss all these technologies in this chapter. Below we explore various levels of security protection in depth.

Security Levels

The concept of defense in depth refers to multiple layers of protection, which can include multiple devices performing similar functions. Similarly, there must exist protection technologies and policies to secure stored information as well as information in transit. Some like to refer to three main levels: (1) protection of the information itself, (2) protection of the computer on which the information is stored, and (3) protection of the network to which the computer is connected. A more fine-grained set of **security levels** is shown in Figure 8.2. In this case, data can only be accessed with proper authorization for the data, the application that uses the data, the host computer on which the data are stored, and the network to which the host is connected.

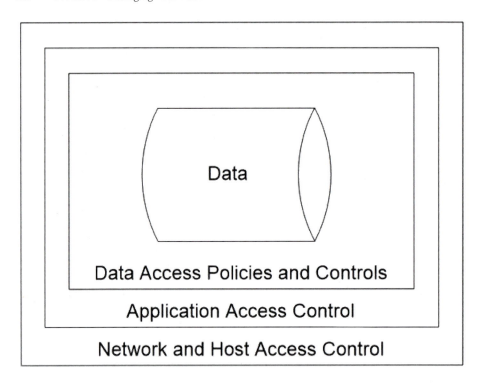

Figure 8.2 Access Levels for Information Security

An example of securing access to data could be the university grade-entry application that your instructors use. In order to give you a grade for the semester, the professor needs to have access to the university's network with a user ID and password. To change grades, the instructors are required to connect to a specific application on a specific system, which also requires the use of a user ID and password. In addition, only authorized users (instructors) are able to access the grade-entry application. The student data are protected through an additional level of security, since only certain instructors are allowed to change certain grades for certain students. At many universities, an employee ID is required in addition to the user ID and password when accessing specific information about students. Finally, data can be encrypted at the data level, providing yet another level of security. In this case, the instructor (or her computer) will need to have software to handle the encrypted information and make it legible.

How Protected Is Your Computer?

For many individuals, students and nonstudents, security is the job of information technology (IT) specialists and something they do not feel comfortable handling themselves. However, many studies show that the weakest link in security is these same individuals who fail to perform basic steps in securing their computers, data, and networks. Does this describe you? Let's see how secure your computer is with this learning activity.

1. Visit the following website and click the "Download Now" button and select your operating system to download Saner, a tool to check how protected your computer is: http://www.secpod.com/saner-endpoint-security-personal.html.

2. After installing the tool, it will automatically scan the computer for vulnerabilities and noncompliant configurations.

3. Note any vulnerabilities or noncompliant configurations it indicates and bring to class for discussion. After this, you can click "Remediate All," and it will attempt to fix the identified issues.

Information Security Threats

Most people think of information security as unauthorized access to individual or organizational data or systems. But it is much broader; it also includes dealing with natural disasters, such as earthquakes and fires, as well as dealing with any threats to computerized systems, such as viruses, hackers, and accidental loss of data or systems.

There are a large number of **security threats** to individuals and organizations alike, particularly today, as most people are connected to the Internet on a regular if not permanent basis. Threats are often broadly categorized as denial of service, unauthorized access, and theft and fraud. **Denial-of-service threats** are those that render a system inoperative, limit its capability to operate, or make data unavailable. **Unauthorized access threats** refer to someone accessing systems and/or data illegally. **Theft and fraud threats** are related to the loss of systems or data due to theft or fraudulent activities.

Denial of Service

Security threats that can cause denial of service can result from intentional acts, careless behavior, or even natural disasters. While natural disasters such as earthquakes, tornadoes, hurricanes, or fires cannot be prevented and can completely destroy systems or data, a careful security **disaster recovery** plan will include steps to recover from such disasters (backups, duplicate systems, etc.). Careless behavior can include forgetting to perform proper backups of one's computer, not installing security updates to an operating system, or failing to update one's antivirus software. Often, individuals even turn off security features because they find them annoying. Was this the case in Learning Activity 8.1? Did you remove password protection from your PC? Did you forget to update your operating system software? No one should underestimate the potential security issues that careless behaviors can generate. What solutions exist to protect against these? Education is the first one, and the second is the automation of security tools and updates so that the user does not have to perform security tasks or is prevented from reducing the effectiveness of the current security of the systems and data.

The last category of denial-of-service security threats includes those that are intentional. Some threats could be fairly simple, like vandalism from a disgruntled employee who reformats a server's main drive or starts a fire in the computer room. Others can involve sophisticated tools meant to disrupt use of or destroy systems or data. These threats include viruses and other malware, ransomware, and break-ins (also unauthorized access, as discussed in that section).

Viruses and Other Malware

Viruses have been around for several decades and have become a major issue for all organizations, as well as individuals. It is likely that at least one person in your class has been a victim of a virus. Two of the authors have at some point in time had computer virus issues. Viruses are often referred to as **targets of opportunity**, which means they are sent out to find any victim they can.

What are viruses? What do they look like? **Viruses** are computer programs designed to perform unwanted events. Some cause minor harm, such as sending undesirable messages. Others are very destructive, deleting all files on a computer or creating so much traffic on a network that it crashes and cannot be used by its customary users. The lines of code that make up a virus can be embedded into other files, or they can be attached to the initial boot sectors of disks or USB drives (so they automatically infect anyone using that device).

What the virus looks like is called the **virus signature**; it is the particular bit patterns that can be recognized, which is how virus detection software knows your computer has contracted a virus. If viruses are embedded into a legitimate file, they are often called **Trojan horses**. If they can propagate themselves throughout the Internet with no user intervention, they are referred to as **worms**. A **stealth virus** is a more advanced virus that changes its own bit pattern to become undetectable by virus scanners. Some viruses are downloaded when users access certain websites. Browsers today often protect you from downloading what is called **active content** (for example, ActiveX programs). However, when asked, many users simply say yes to downloading any content from a website. Once viruses are installed on a computer, it may be difficult to remove them. (We discuss later how to do this.) Viruses can also modify themselves as they move to other computers, changing their signatures to become less easy to detect. These are called **polymorphic viruses**. Finally, **spyware** (which we discuss in Chapter 9) is a form of virus, since the software logs everything users do on their computers, unbeknownst to them.

There are also **virus hoaxes** on the Internet. These are not viruses but false virus alerts being sent and resent by individuals. Their consequences include either substantial unnecessary network traffic or unwanted actions by users (for example, telling users that certain files must be deleted to avoid the virus). Usually, unsophisticated users who panic at the idea that they might have caught a virus propagate these hoaxes. In case of doubt, the best action is to go to the website of the company that built the targeted application and search for virus hoaxes.

Ransomware

One kind of attack that has gained popularity in recent years is ransomware. Ransomware is software that is installed on the victim's computer via viruses, unauthorized access, or phishing (clicking on a link; see Learning Activity 8.3). Once installed, ransomware attacks the computer by encrypting the data on the computer until an appropriate password is provided. Without the password, the owner of the computer cannot access the data. The hacker who sent the ransomware demands a ransom, generally in the form of **bitcoins**, in order to provide that password. If the computer owner does not pay the ransom, then he or she cannot access the data on his or her own computer, as it is being held ransom. In 2017, there was a rise of 250% in ransomware attacks, with the United States being the hardest hit by those attacks (Cuthbertson 2017).

It is interesting that hackers demand to be paid in bitcoins. In order to understand why, it is first necessary to understand what bitcoins are. Bitcoins are cryptocurrency (a currency that utilizes encryption) that relies on the **blockchain** to track the transactions they are involved in. The blockchain provides a secure network where users can conduct transactions anonymously, eliminating the need to have trust between parties. In fact, because the blockchain does not require trust between individuals who use it, it doesn't require individuals to know who each other are. It creates a way to remain anonymous in the execution of transactions. Because bitcoins use this blockchain technology that provides anonymity, criminals feel safe demanding payment this way. Prior to bitcoins, electronically sending payments required banks or financial institutions where the identity of customers was known. Thus the anonymity provided by bitcoins opened the door for a new way for hackers to make money through computer vulnerabilities.

Unauthorized Access (Break-Ins)

Unauthorized access involves illegal access to systems, applications, or data. One of the biggest worries for organizations is theft of data, including customer information, trade secrets, or other important information regarding the organization, its business partners, or its employees. Unauthorized access through break-ins can also be used to damage information or applications on a system, leading to a type of denial of service.

When thinking of unauthorized access, we often imagine a hacker who lives on the margins of society and tries to access an organization's data files to do something good for the world or to prove he can. However, the reality is that organizational insiders often perpetrate unauthorized access; they have the knowledge needed to hack into the systems to obtain information, such as credit card numbers. Some incidences of unauthorized access are difficult to identify because they are passive, such as recording transmissions. By doing so, a hacker can obtain passwords, which can then be used to access information on an organization's systems through a valid account. Breaks-ins can also be used to actively modify the system or data being hacked—for example, creating false account information for fraud purposes, downloading customer data, or changing the content of messages to falsely implicate the company in certain events or to delay negotiations on an important contract. Figure 8.3 shows the differences between passive and active unauthorized access. Active break-ins can also be used to install software that waits for instructions from the hackers to attack other machines. This is like having a dormant agent on one's computer. If many computers are then used for conducting attacks, we call them **distributed denial-of-service (DDOS) attacks.**

Active Unauthorized Access

Passive Unauthorized Access

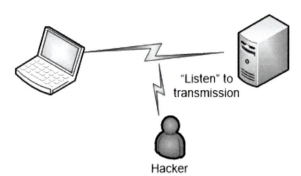

Figure 8.3 Passive versus Active Unauthorized Access

Why would anyone perform such malicious acts? Some may be disgruntled employees. Others may attack a given target for political reasons—for example, protesting a company's stand on some issue. The groups who perform such actions often use the term **hacktivism**, which involves finding information that, if revealed, will advance human causes. However, these and other denial-of-service attacks by hackers continue to be very damaging to organizations. Any downtime in computer systems or networks can mean lost sales and lost revenue for companies or major losses in productivity if employees cannot perform their normal duties.

How is hacking actually performed? It requires a combination of skills and patience. Most of the tools available for hacking are unfortunately easy to find on the Internet, but not everyone has the skills, patience, or intent to perform break-ins. Software, such as **sniffers**, can be used to map information on someone's network and identify weaknesses in computers and networks. When you performed Learning Activity 8.1, the scanning software identified **open ports** on your computer. This means that some specific applications are installed and running on your computer. Once this is known, a hacker can test the targeted system for vulnerabilities (like unpatched software), and if a vulnerability is found, he or she can exploit it. Hackers often do this using **spoofing**, which means they pretend to be someone else (or another computer). In an email message, you can easily spoof an address by simply changing the information in the "From" line to reflect the name of the person you want to impersonate. This is not very sophisticated, and many individuals are able to detect such simple spoofing. More advanced spoofing can be done at the IP address level by changing the source (sender's) IP address to look like it comes from a different address. This is done by changing the information in the address field of the IP packet. A **packet** is a small unit of data that flows through networks, allowing for the transmission of messages. Hackers usually spoof IP addresses when they launch spamming denial-of-service attacks so that the attacks cannot be traced back to them.

LEARNING ACTIVITY 8.2

What Do Hackers Break into the Most?

Hackers have been increasingly making the news for stealing information from a number of large companies. For this learning activity, visit http://www.verizonenterprise.com/verizon-insights-lab/dbir/ and download Verizon's latest Data Break Investigations Report. As you are reading the report, do the following and be prepared to discuss in class:

1. List the targets of hackers and how many report incidents there were.
2. Determine which of these incidents were of the greatest concern to consumers.
3. Create various ideas for how you can protect yourself from hackers seeking to gain access to information you have shared with organizations.

Spamming involves sending emails to many individuals at once, sending unsolicited commercial email to individuals, or targeting one individual computer or network and sending thousands of messages to it.

What are vulnerabilities? They are often called *software security holes.* All operating systems and applications have them. The Internet is again a source of information, since vulnerabilities are documented. Software patches (updates) are meant to address these vulnerabilities once they are found. When new software is made publicly available, it usually takes very little time for hackers to identify the security holes. The software developers then have to quickly react by developing fixes, which are made available to users via download on the software developers' website. Unfortunately, many users do not update their operating systems fast enough or even turn off automatic updates.

Finally, it is important to reiterate that many unauthorized access situations arise because users have access to someone else's legitimate passwords and accounts. In many cases, individuals are negligent about protecting their passwords. In other cases, individuals can be tricked into giving out this (and other) information. This is

BUSINESS EXAMPLE BOX 8.1

Even Big Technology Companies Can Be Hacked

One would think that large technology companies should have the resources and expertise not to be victims of hackers, right? Well, in September 2017, Equifax, one of the three largest credit bureaus, reported having been the victim of hackers. Equifax stated that the cybersecurity breach affected close to 143 million persons in the United States, which represents approximately half of the country's population.

The information that was accessed included names, birth dates, addresses, social security numbers, and even driver's license information. All of these are considered personally identifiable information. The files that were accessed also affected citizens of Canada and the United Kingdom. Because of its size and the type information accessed, many consider this breach to be one of the worst to date in history. However, it is unfortunately not the only one. In 2017, some key companies that also suffered breaches include Saks Fifth Avenue, UNC Health Care, InterContinental Hotels Group, Kmart, and Verizon, to name a few. In the case of Equifax, the breach happened between May and July, and the company informed the public in September. This is actually considered fairly rapid in terms of disclosing a major breach. Equifax now offers credit file monitoring, credit reports, ID theft insurance, and various scanning services for free to those affected.

Source: Yurieff, K. 2017. "We Still Don't Have Assurance from Apple That iCloud Is Safe." *CNN Tech,* September 10. http://money.cnn.com/2017/09/08/technology/equifax-hack-qa/index.html.

referred to as **social engineering** (and sometimes called *phishing*). Examples of social engineering actions include tricking someone into telling you his or her password by claiming to be someone with rights to know it or tricking someone into sending you an important file or opening a link to a dangerous website. Sophisticated social engineering can even involve listening to lunch conversations among unsuspecting professionals with privileged information. Today, most Internet users are familiar with phishing through email messages sent from hackers pretending to be banks or large companies such as eBay.com, PayPal, or Amazon.com. The problem is that for most individuals, it is hard to identify whether such emails are phishing emails when they actually have an account with those companies.

Even when a system has been hacked, organizations do not necessarily know that this has happened unless a problem occurs immediately. Some organizations have tools to detect hacking attacks, which we will discuss in the next section of this chapter. The hacker, however, will often start the attack by erasing audit logs that would show what has happened and installing **rootkits**, or software that will allow him to have unfettered access to everything on the system, including adding, deleting, and copying files. Hackers often install **backdoors**, allowing them to reaccess the system at their will. Finally, they can install victimization software, such as **keystroke capture programs** that will log all information entered into the computer, spyware, attack software for denial-of-service attacks, or other remote tools to control the systems that have been hacked.

Theft and Fraud

Theft and fraud concerning information have become important concerns for companies. We discussed some fraud and theft of data in the unauthorized access discussion. Two additional issues need to be explored regarding theft and fraud: theft of software or hardware devices that increasingly contain huge amounts of information and theft of data using small hardware devices.

Theft of software usually occurs when employees copy legitimate software installed on their company's servers to bring home or to give to someone else. These copies do not carry licenses and are therefore illegal copies. This is a major concern for organizations, and many have started to perform audits of installed software. The best security control for this problem, though, is user education. Many employees do not see a problem with copying software this way, although it is illegal. Other organizations provide only personal computers that do not allow saving to any external mediator devices, preventing software from being copied.

As hardware has become more portable and powerful, theft of hardware has become an increasing concern for organizations. Think of how much data can be stored on a laptop, tablet, or even a personal digital device like an iPhone. Besides the cost of the hardware itself, organizations have to worry about the information contained on these devices as well as the access that the devices often have to the organization's internal systems.

LEARNING ACTIVITY 8.3

Detecting Phishing

There are many ways to detect phishing emails. Look for the following common problems to identify phishing emails:

1. The email is not addressed to you directly.
2. The email is addressed to you using your email account info (without the @ provider).
3. The email does not have a personalized salutation (i.e., Dear Bélanger).
4. When you hover the mouse over the hyperlink, the site does not seem to be from the proper company. (Look at the domain name.)
5. When you hover the mouse over the hyperlink, the site seems to be located in another country.
6. The email contains poor grammar and spelling mistakes real companies would not make (we hope).
7. The email makes you feel your response is urgent or something bad is going to happen.

Read more about phishing at the following sites:

* http://www.antiphishing.org/
* http://www.spamlaws.com/phishing.html

Then test your skills detecting phishing emails here: https://www.sonicwall .com/en-us/phishing-iq-test. You can also identify the problems mentioned above in the sample phishing email in Figure 8.4.

Finally, theft of data is also possible thanks to storage devices with ever-increasing capacities. Today, a small USB thumb drive can contain gigabytes of data. Think of a complete list of all of an organization's customers, with addresses and historical purchases; this can fit easily on a thumb drive. An individual can install software that automatically copies everything on a device when the USB thumb drive is inserted. There have been reports of such tools being inserted into computers in hotel business centers, in kiosk devices in shopping malls, and others. A nonemployee roaming an office could easily copy tons of files if allowed in with the device and not supervised while in the organization's offices.

Summary of Security Threats

Before a manager can evaluate security measures and come up with a proper security plan, she must identify all the threats to security that her organization faces. We presented some of the most common security threats in this section. There are, however, other threats to security that can occur.

From: customer.center@BankOfAmerica.com
To: belanger@vt.edu
Date: Oct-22–10 2:36 PM
Subject: Online Banking Alert
Your Online Banking Is Blocked! Please Take Immediate Action.

Dear Belanger,

　　We recently reviewed your account and we suspect that your Bank of America account may have been compromised by an unauthorized person. Protecting the security of your account is our primary concerns. Therefore, as a preventive measure, we have temporarily limited access to important account features.
　　To restore your online account access, we need you to confirm your information at the following website within 48 hours of receiving this email. It is very important that you update your information within this time frame if you do not wish your online access to be placed on hold.
　　https://www.bankofamerica.com/update/
　　We thank you for your rapid attention to this matter.

Figure 8.4 Example of a Phishing Email

Every year a number of organizations and institutes conduct surveys to identify the state of cybersecurity. In a recent one, the Ponemon Institute, in collaboration with Accenture, published its "2017 Cost of Cybercrime Study." They highlighted the growth of cyberattacks in general year to year, with ransomware attacks having more than doubled over the previous year. They suggest that the costs of cyberattacks represented more than US$21 million in the United States, US$11.15 million in Germany, and US$10.45 million in Japan, to name a few countries. And of course, not all intrusions are reported because companies do not want to spend the energy on reporting incidents, are afraid of negative publicity or competitors taking advantage of the incidents, or do not believe law enforcement can help or would be interested.

The following is a list of the security breaches that occurred most often in 2017 in order of prevalence (i.e., those reported most often listed first):

1. Malware (e.g., viruses, worms, botnets)
2. Web-based attacks
3. Denial of services
4. Malicious insiders
5. Malicious code

6. Phishing and social engineering

7. Stolen devices

8. Ransomware

9. Botnets

Source: Ponemon Institute. 2017. "2017 Cost of Cybercrime Study: Insights on the Security Investments That Make a Difference." Retrieved December 20, 2017, from https://www .accenture.com/t20170926T072837Z__w__/us-en/_acnmedia/PDF-61/Accenture-2017 -CostCyberCrimeStudy.pdf.

Security Technologies and Solutions

Security Goals

Before we discuss each of the security tools, we need to briefly mention that all tools and policies are meant to address one or more core security goals, which are known as CIA: confidentiality, integrity, and availability.

Confidentiality involves making sure that only authorized individuals can access information or data. **Integrity** involves making sure that data are consistent and complete. For example, as a message is transmitted, its content must not be modified unwillingly during the transmission. Finally, **availability** involves ensuring that systems and/or data are available when they are needed. For systems to be considered highly available, the organization must protect them from disruptions not only due to security threats such as denial-of-service attacks but also due to power outages, hardware failures, and system upgrades.

There are two additional goals of security to consider: authentication (or authenticity) and nonrepudiation. **Authentication** is basically making sure that the parties involved are who they say they are and that transactions, data, or communications are genuine. **Nonrepudiation**, which is particularly important in e-commerce, refers to making sure one cannot renege on his or her obligations—for example, by denying that he or she entered into a transaction with a Web merchant. In e-commerce, digital signatures and encryption are used to ensure that the goal of nonrepudiation is met.

Preventive, Corrective, and Detective Controls

A large number of security technologies and solutions exist to address the threats we have discussed so far. One way to classify the security solutions and tools (often called *security controls*) is to consider whether they are preventive, detective, or corrective controls. The goal of **preventive controls** is to stop or limit the security threat from happening in the first place. For example, **antivirus software** scans computers and programs and alerts users if potential viruses exist before they can infect files or computers. The goal of **detective controls** is to find or discover where and when security threats occur. For example, **audit logs** can be used to track access to a system to see if multiple false attempts are made from a particular user ID. Finally, the goal of **corrective controls** is to repair damages after a security problem has occurred. An example is the antivirus software previously discussed, which can remove a virus, quarantine the file with the virus, or simply delete the problematic file.

Physical Security versus Logical Security

Security solutions can also be classified as physical or logical. **Physical access controls** are those security solutions that involve protecting physical access to systems, applications, or data, whereas **logical access controls** include security solutions that protect access to systems, applications, or data by ensuring users or systems are authenticated and allowed to have such access.

Physical access controls can include locks for laptops, locked computer rooms, and secured rooms for backup storage. Once devices are no longer needed, software programs called *drive shredders* should be used to make sure that all discarded disk drives cannot be read again. Physical security also involves ensuring that wiring closets, where all the routers and connections are located, are properly locked and secured. Another important aspect of physical security is selection of personnel. Remember that insider abuse is one of the most significant security threats. Organizations must ensure that only proper personnel have access to key information systems and data. Organizations should run background checks on such personnel and provide appropriate training. Several surveys have identified onsite contractors as a major threat to security for organizations.

Logical access controls use many technologies to require authentication of users and systems trying to access specific applications, networks, data, or computers. These include user profiles, biometrics, firewalls, and encryption.

User Profiles

User profiles are one of the main solutions used to prevent unauthorized access to systems, data, and applications. Users are assigned profiles that consist of a user identification (self-selected or assigned by the organization) and a set of privileges. Once the user confirms his identification, he can access the system, application, or data with the level of privileges given to him. For example, faculty can view student data but cannot modify some of those data (such as personal addresses). This is considered the **principle of least privilege**. Give users only access to what they need and no more!

User profiles require that individuals be differentiated from one another using one or several levels of identification: possession, knowledge, or trait.

- *Possession* is when an individual owns a form of identification. For example, your driver's license, your student ID, and your passport are possession forms of identification.

- *Knowledge* is when an individual needs to know something to gain access. Passwords are a good example of knowledge required to access systems. Combining possession and knowledge, such as requiring a personal identification number (PIN) with a banking card, provides more security.

- *Traits* require recognition of physical or behavioral human characteristics, such as a fingerprint or a signature style, to gain access to systems, data, or applications. This is part of biometrics, which will be described in the next section.

LEARNING ACTIVITY 8.4

How Strong Is Your Password?

Passwords are one of the most used security solutions to control access to systems, applications, and data. We have no doubt that you have several passwords you use on a regular basis. But how strong are these passwords? Let's see what a strong password is.

1. Select two passwords you use frequently and test their level of security using one of the following password checkers:
   - https://howsecureismypassword.net/
   - http://www.passwordmeter.com
2. Read the information on how to create a strong password:
   - https://support.google.com/accounts/answer/32040?hl=en
3. Create a strong password. Test it. Do not use it for your accounts!
4. Bring the following to class:
   - The level of security of your two passwords (Be honest, but do not tell the passwords!)
   - The strong password you created and what it stands for

User profiles remain one of the most used security solutions for access to systems and data. Yet there are many issues with using user profiles for authentication. First, users often use words or numbers that are easy to remember for their passwords. Many systems today will not accept such passwords, which can be easily "broken" with a **dictionary attack**, where all words of several dictionaries in multiple languages are tested as passwords with numbers before and after the words. With this method, it often takes only a few seconds for a password to be discovered. The second problem is that users also write their passwords down on a sticky note taped to their computer or taped to the inside of their desk drawers because they have too many passwords to remember. Alternatively, they use the same password for everything. If someone finds out about it, all systems the user accesses are compromised. Password recovery can be a problem too, since it is often easy to know the name of a person's pet, family members, school attended, or city of birth, as well as birthday or important numbers. Just think how much of that information can be found on social networking sites like Facebook!

To increase the effectiveness of user profiles, security systems now often require users to change their passwords regularly, such as every one, three, or six months. Many systems will not allow more than a few attempts at entering a password before they block access to the user account. Most systems also require the use of strong passwords. As you discovered in Learning Activity 8.4, strong passwords require a mix of uppercase letters, lowercase letters, alphanumeric characters, and numbers. Tools exist to help manage passwords. For example, **password crackers** are available online for various systems to recover passwords that are forgotten. Of course, they can also be used to crack someone else's password—for example, on a stolen laptop. There are also password generators that can help you generate strong passwords. Even with all these tools, however, most individuals still create poor passwords. SplashData has been analyzing millions of leaked passwords over the years and reporting the most popular each year. Every year we continue to see that most users still have really weak passwords; the top 20 passwords for 2017 are shown in Table 8.1.

Many security professionals now recommend password managers (previously called wallets) to ensure that users have stronger passwords. Password managers are applications that users can install on their devices (computer or mobile device) to store and organize passwords. The passwords are encrypted, and the user needs to only remember one strong password to have access to the database of his or her other passwords. There is a debate in the field of security whether this is the best approach. Some argue that it finally allows users to make use of strong passwords for all their accounts. Others claim that it renders users vulnerable to having their passwords hacked if the database is hacked (even if encrypted). For example, Windows 10

Table 8.1 Top 20 Worst Passwords in 2017

Rank	Password	Rank	Password
1	123456	11	admin
2	password	12	welcome
3	12345678	13	monkey
4	qwerty	14	login
5	12345	15	abc123
6	123456789	16	starwars
7	letmein	17	123123
8	1234567	18	dragon
9	football	19	passw0rd
10	iloveyou	20	master

Source: Kooser, A. 2017. "'Starwars' Appears on List of Worst Passwords of 2017." *C/net,* December 19. Retrieved December 20, 2017, from https://www.cnet.com/news/worst-passwords-2017-star-wars-splashdata-list/.

was bundled with a password manager called Keeper, but in December 2017, Tavis Ormandy reported a bug that would allow someone to break into the password manager (Chirgwin 2017). The security issues were quickly fixed—in fact, within eight days—but this reinforces the debate on whether or not password managers are the ultimate password security solution. Nevertheless, as password managers grow in popularity, many different solutions are being offered. Table 8.2 shows the "Best Password Managers of 2018" as evaluated by *PC Magazine*. There are also free password managers, with some of the highest-ranked ones also shown in Table 8.2. Most free password managers are "toned-down" versions of commercially available ones.

Two-Factor Authentication

As you can see from the discussion of passwords and password managers, cybersecurity experts are still trying to find the best way to provide security for everyone. One approach that has gained popularity in the last few years is **two-factor authentication** (2FA). With 2FA, you add an extra step to logging into an application or device that goes beyond using your username and password (the first factor of authentication), which is meant to add another layer of security. This extra step (the second factor of authentication) can be an app on a trusted device (such as Google Authenticator or Duo), a token on a security device users carry with them, a phone number that you trust to receive calls or text messages, or verification codes that are generated for one-time use only.

Many applications you currently use allow for 2FA. For example, Apple uses it for various log-ins with your Apple ID. Google, LinkedIn, Amazon.com, some banks, and many other large organizations from which you access services online have

Table 8.2 Best Password Managers Examples for 2018

Password Manager	Website
Dashlane	https://www.dashlane.com
Sticky Password Premium	https://www.stickypassword.com
LogMeOnce Password Management Suite Ultimate 5.2	https://www.logmeonce.com
Keeper Password Manager & Digital Vault	https://keepersecurity.com/
Free Password Managers	
LastPass	https://www.lastpass.com
LogMeOnce Password Management Suite Premium 5.2	https://www.logmeonce.com

Source: Rubenking, N. J. 2017. "The Best Password Managers of 2018." *PC Magazine,* December 7. Retrieved December 20, 2017, from https://www.pcmag.com/article2/0 ,2817,2407168,00.asp.

started to make use of 2FA. For example, the university of one of this book's authors requires two-factor authentication for access to the university's systems. It's not even an option; it's mandatory.

Virus Protection

Viruses are one of the most prevalent security threats in organizations. You should not underestimate the amount of money involved in terms of support personnel time involved in fixing virus problems. Fortunately, today antivirus software has become very easy to use and to keep up to date. Recall that a virus has a signature: the bit pattern that represents the virus. Antivirus software looks for these signatures or variations of them in files and systems. If they are found, the software can remove the virus, quarantine the file, or delete the file. The software can even detect viruses in emails and files as they are loaded but before they are opened. Once a new virus is identified, it usually takes fewer than 24 hours for specialists to decode it and write a protection for it. But viruses are easy to write, with several tools for writing viruses available online. Symantec, one of the leading providers of antivirus software, states that there are now more than one million computer viruses in existence.

Unfortunately, most antivirus programs are primarily reactive. They only detect existing viruses or ones that look similar to an old virus archived in the software's database. Newer virus protection tools, called **behavioral-based antivirus protection tools**, look for suspicious behaviors in programs instead of just a virus's signature. One of the most important protections, however, remains user education about updating software and not downloading unknown executable files to computers.

Biometrics

Another security method used to authenticate users and control access to systems, data, and applications is **biometrics**, which use human traits and characteristics to recognize individuals. While they go beyond possession and knowledge, biometrics can be used in conjunction with these to provide strong security—for example, requiring a card with a password and a fingerprint to have access to certain data. Fingerprinting is a low-cost example of biometric technology. There are several other biometric technologies, which can be classified as **physiological biometrics** (those that use physical traits) or **behavioral biometrics** (those that use behavior). Table 8.3 briefly describes these security solutions.

LEARNING ACTIVITY 8.5

Biometrics on the PC

For this learning activity, start with the list of biometric solutions provided in Table 8.3 and utilize the Internet to list how well each of these could be implemented on your personal computer to provide authentication. Be prepared to discuss this list with the class.

Table 8.3 Sample Biometric Solutions

Physiological Biometrics		Behavioral Biometrics	
Fingerprint recognition	Analyzes ridges and valleys (minutiae) on the surface tips of human fingers.	**Signature recognition**	Analyzes the signature. **Static signature recognition** compares scanned or ink signatures with stored signatures; **dynamic signature recognition** analyzes not only the signature but how it is written using pressure points—how much an individual pushes on the pen when she writes her name.
Facial recognition	Analyzes facial features or patterns (faceprints).	**Gait recognition**	Analyzes the walking style or gait of individuals.
Finger geometry recognition	Analyzes 3D geometry of the finger.	**Keystroke recognition**	Analyzes rhythm and patterns of keystroke of individuals on keyboards.
Hand geometry recognition	Analyzes geometric features of the hand, such as length of fingers and width of the hand.		
Iris/retina recognition	Analyzes features (eyeprints) in the iris or the patterns of veins in the back of the eye (retina).		
DNA recognition	Analyzes segments from an individual's DNA.		
Odor recognition	Analyzes an individual's odor to determine identity.		
Voice recognition (speaker recognition)	Analyzes voice to determine the identity of a speaker (who is speaking); different from speech recognition (what is being said).		
Ear recognition	Analyzes the shape of the ear.		

Source: Based on information provided by Griaule Biometrics, available at http://www
.griaulebiometrics.com/en-us/book/understanding-biometrics/introduction/types/
behavioral.

Law enforcement agencies have used fingerprinting for a long time to identify criminals. Today, many laptops have fingerprinting scanners to restrict access or replace passwords. Iris scanning offers some of the best security because the iris is unique among all individuals. (The iris is the colored portion of the eye.) Immigration services in the United States use fingerprinting for noncitizens and iris scanning for frequent travelers who have special cards identifying them as trusted travelers. The English government in the United Kingdom has a large database of earprints because it is said that no two ears are the same. In recent years, we have seen a significant growth in the use of biometrics with mobile devices. Most recent smartphones allow you to use a fingerprint in lieu of a passcode to turn on your phone. Several devices now even support use of an iris reader as well as facial recognition. For example, BioID (mobile.bioid.com) offers authentication on your smartphone via facial recognition; you can log in to applications with "face log-in."

Biometrics are used in one of two ways: authentication or identification. In **authentication**, also called *one-to-one matching*, the goal is to match the individual with his or her stored biometric data. Fingerprint biometrics on laptops are good example of that. The recent mobile biometrics just discussed also fit in that category. In **identification**, also called *one-to-many matching*, the goal is identify an individual from an entire population of individuals with stored biometric data. An example is facial recognition at airports used to identify potential terrorists entering a country from a database of facial prints stored by law enforcement agencies. The processes of authentication and identification are shown in Figures 8.5 and 8.6.

Firewalls

At the beginning of the chapter, you tested your computer security using an online tool. The software was looking for whether your computer was letting information out about itself and whether there were open ports or software applications running. The best protection against these potential problems is a firewall, and if your computer's firewall was running and up-to-date, your computer should have indicated that your computer was "stealth" (not visible to outsiders).

A **firewall** is a computer or a router that controls access in and out of the organization's networks, applications, and computers. The term *firewall* comes from the construction industry, where it represents a wall built with fire-resistant materials. If a fire starts in one room of a building, it won't spread to other rooms if firewalls are used. In computer security, firewalls control the transmissions that are attempting to enter and/or leave the organization's networks or computers, as shown in Figure 8.7.

There are several types of firewalls, which vary in how they control access into and out of the organization. Table 8.4 lists various terms used to describe firewalls.

Firewalls are great security tools, but they cannot handle all security threats. For example, they cannot protect an organization from a virus that is attached to a message with an appropriate destination and source addresses or that is introduced

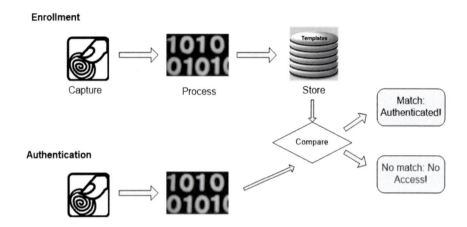

Figure 8.5 Authentication in Biometrics

Figure 8.6 Identification in Biometrics

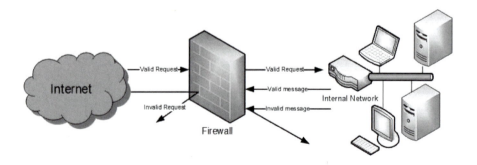

Figure 8.7 Firewall

by an individual on a portable storage device. Firewalls also cannot prevent hackers from exploiting an unsecured computer; keep disgruntled employees from copying sensitive information; or stop employees from losing sensitive data loaded on an unsecured laptop, thumb drive, or smartphone, for example. Nevertheless, firewalls are part of the main line of defense for organizations. Consistent with the principle of defense in depth, different firewalls should be implemented at different locations in the organization, as shown in Figure 8.8.

Figure 8.8 A Firewall Architecture for Defense in Depth

Table 8.4 Firewall Types and Terminology

Firewall type	**Packet-level firewall** (also called screening router firewall)	A firewall that works at the network level, looking at information within the data packets (see Appendix 1). If the source address of the packet is from an "acceptable" computer, the firewall will let the message through, assuming that the destination address is also a valid internal address.	Easy to implement and prevents most basic attacks such as email bombing and other denials of service. Sophisticated attacks can often bypass these.
	Application-level firewall (One form is called a *proxy server.*)	A firewall that verifies access to applications. Users must log into the firewall before they can access applications inside the organization (from outside).	More complex to install and manage. Slows down communication but provides better security than a packet-level firewall.
	Firewall appliance	A firewall that is self-contained. In other words, the hardware and software are built to perform only one function, that of a firewall.	Very useful for small businesses with limited technical knowledge that require more protection than a simple host firewall on their personal computers.
Firewall location	**Internal firewall**	A firewall used between departments or divisions inside the organization.	Organizations can use these to isolate departmental data and provide greater defense and in-depth protection.
	External firewall	A firewall used to protect access to the internal network and computers of the organization.	This is the type of firewall usually referred to in most definitions.
	Host (personal) firewall	A firewall installed on a computer.	Good option for all computers. In addition to protecting the computer from outsider attacks and warning of arrival of malicious files, the personal firewall often offers privacy features.

Firewall technology	Static firewall	A firewall with predetermined ways of dealing with transmission requests based on application types and ranges of IP addresses.	Easy to implement.
	Dynamic firewall	A firewall that manages requests as they occur, deciding on both denials and permissions as they arrive.	More difficult to manage but much more flexible.

STATS BOX 8.1:
SECURITY POLICY VIOLATIONS

Even when security is a top priority for organizations, employees can often find ways to not follow or to violate security policies, such as by encrypting email or bypassing security controls such as firewalls, restricted access, or automatic logoff systems. In a survey of more than 700 senior IT and business decision makers in the United States and Canada, DataMotion found that three quarters of employees violate security policies at least occasionally (Hutton 2015).

Rendering Data Unreadable: Encryption

Encryption, also known as *cryptography,* is the use of mathematical algorithms to convert a message or data into scrambled information that makes it unreadable. The original message is called **plaintext**. The converted or unreadable text is called **ciphertext**. When the ciphertext is converted back to plaintext, this is referred to as **decryption**. The algorithm used to convert the message is called the **cipher**. The **encryption or decryption key** is information known only by the proper users of the encryption tool.

The ciphers used in Learning Activity 8.6 are very simplistic. Ciphers used in encryption are much more complicated and use complex algorithms (not simply adding numbers and letters). The strength of an encryption technique is related to the length of the key. This is usually expressed in the number of bits the key has. The larger the size of the key, the more secure the encryption. This is because larger keys are harder to break since there are more combinations of bits possible. Today, keys in commercial use are 256 bits or longer. It is estimated that with advances in technology, a 64-bit key can be broken in a day or less. Understandably, a 256-bit, or even 1024-bit, key is much more secure.

Types of Cryptography

There are two main types of cryptographic systems used today: asymmetric or symmetric, as shown in Figure 8.9. The systems are based on whether the same key is issued to encrypt and decrypt the data. In **asymmetric encryption**, two keys are used. The public key is used to encrypt messages. It is sent to any person or system with whom one wishes to exchange encrypted messages. Using the public key, anyone can encrypt messages for the intended recipient, who will then use his or her private key to decrypt those messages. The public key and the private key are linked (forming a **key pair**), but only the recipient has the private key. This is also called *public key cryptography*, since one of the keys can be shared with anyone (public).

In **symmetric encryption**, the same key is used to encrypt and decrypt data. In this case, individuals have to be very careful with whom they share their encryption keys because these individuals or companies will also be able to decrypt their

---

LEARNING ACTIVITY 8.6

Breaking the Encryption

Security technologies are unlikely to be able to prevent all unauthorized access to data, applications, and systems. One way to provide additional protection for important data is through encryption. Before we discuss encryption in depth, let us explore what makes data unreadable.

Part 1

Given the plaintext a b c d e f g h I j k l m n o p q r s t u v w x y z and the resulting ciphertext b c d e f g h I j k l m n o p q r s t u v w x y z a, what is the cipher?

Part 2

Using the cipher, convert the words "computer lab closed."

Part 3

Using the following cipher and your personally selected keys below, convert the text "Fun for Spring Break."

Key selection:

1. Pick a number from 1 to 5.
2. Pick a sign (+ or −).
3. Pick a symbol (!,@,#,$,%,^,&,*).
4. Use this cipher to encode: new letter = original letter (sign selected) number, spaces replaced with symbol selected.
5. Compare your results with classmates.

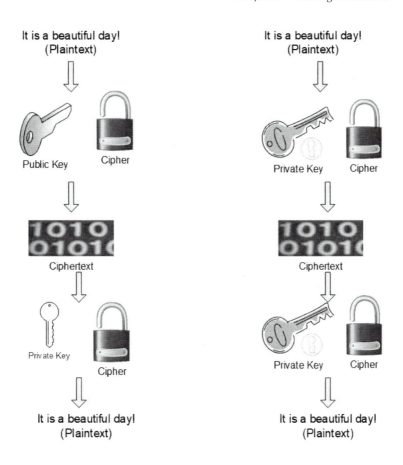

It is a beautiful day!
(Plaintext)

Public Key   Cipher

Ciphertext

Private Key
Cipher

It is a beautiful day!
(Plaintext)

It is a beautiful day!
(Plaintext)

Private Key   Cipher

Ciphertext

Private Key   Cipher

It is a beautiful day!
(Plaintext)

Figure 8.9 Symmetric versus Asymmetric Encryption

messages. It is very efficient, but it requires that both parties know the key and no one else. The problem is therefore how to distribute the key without having it intercepted by others. This is why both types of encryption are often used together, with public key encryption used to distribute a secret key to a party you wish to interact with. Once the secret key is received, it can be used for symmetric encryption, since both parties know it. Finally, it is important to realize that encryption can be used for more than transmission of data. It can be used to protect data on servers and computers. For example, you could encrypt your data on your personal computer so that no one could access it without the proper key.

Encryption has many applications for securing data and transmissions. One of them is the **virtual private network (VPN)**. A VPN is a connection that makes use of an open wired network such as the Internet but that provides a secured channel through encryption and other security features. It is often used for employees to securely connect to their organizations from remote locations. VPNs function through the use of encryption. When the employee wishes to connect to the company's internal network, she requests a VPN connection. After inputting secret information, the employee's computer establishes an encrypted session with the company's server. (This is called a *handshake.*) Once both computers share the secret key (which is only for that session), all transmissions are encrypted until the VPN connection is dropped.

Web and Credit Card Security

Encryption is also used for protecting information in business transactions online. When you shop online and have to enter your credit card information, you typically look for the lock icon or the https:// in the URL to indicate that the site is secure. If you double-click on the icon, you will see the security certificate that was issued to the website by a certificate-issuing organization such as VeriSign. Figure 8.10 shows a sample certificate located in the Internet options of a browser application. This certificate includes a public key, which is sent to your browser when you connect to this secure Web page. The browser can then generate a secret key and send it to the server using the public key encryption, since only the server can decrypt this information (via the private key). Once the server receives the secret key, your browser and the server can communicate securely using this secret key (called a *session key*). The transmissions will be encrypted until the current session is dropped.

One major change in electronic payments has been the rise of credit cards with chip technology. Europay, MasterCard, and Visa (EMV) have worked together to develop chip card standards and technology, which involves using chips instead of the old magnetic stripes. The cards can be used via either contact chips (inserted into a chip reader) or contactless technology (the card only needs to be in proximity to the reader). The technology allows data to be stored on the chip embedded in the credit card. The data is then secured with both hardware and software security measures. For example, there a verification method can be programmed into the card itself, allowing accept or decline decisions to be more dynamic. However, as with every security technology, the use of chips is not a guarantee that your information is completely secured (Bukhari 2017).

Wireless Security

Because more and more individuals are connecting their devices to the Internet and connecting to their organizations via wireless networks, we need to briefly discuss the additional issues related to wireless security. In reality, all the security solutions discussed so far can be used in the wireless environment. However, because the wireless networks typically broadcast their communications over the "airwaves," they are more susceptible to security breaches since they can be intercepted without physical connections to the devices.

The best protection for wireless networks remains encryption. The standards for wireless encryptions are numerous, and the most popular ones in America are called

Figure 8.10 Sample Security Certificate

WEP and WPA. **WEP, Wired Equivalent Privacy**, is an older encryption algorithm, which today can be easily cracked within minutes (with proper knowledge and software tools). **WPA, Wi-Fi Protected Access**, replaced WEP with a more powerful encryption algorithm. However, this has been replaced by WPA2, which provides an even more powerful encryption algorithm and is widely available in most routers. So when setting up a home wireless network, users should select WPA2 encryption if their devices support it. A further protection for home wireless networks is to disable the broadcasting of the network's ID (SSID). Only with knowledge of the network's name can someone find it and connect to it (along with the WPA2, WPA, or WEP encryption key information). The next improvement in wireless security is an extension to WPA2 called Robust Security Network (RSN), which uses even more sophisticated encryption.

BUSINESS EXAMPLE BOX 8.2

How to Respond to a Security Crisis

While certain individuals in an organization are more concerned about being hacked (usually a chief-level officer or a security person), many believe that it is unlikely to happen to them. But what if it does? How should a company react? Organizations can learn from what happened to Heartland Payment Systems in 2008–9 and from how they reacted.

Heartland Payment Systems, a financial transaction company, discovered in late 2008 that their system, which contained the information of more than 600 million credit card holders, had been hacked. Unfortunately, the company did not have a security crisis plan in place. Fortunately, they were quick to act and hired a crisis response corporation. The first order of business? To develop a plan to deal with employees, Wall Street, the media, and the customers and to do it quickly as opposed to waiting weeks or months after the breach happened. The company decided that it was better to provide full disclosure about what happened and be transparent about what was being done to address the situation. The company and their consultant agreed on two key objectives: (1) to show that they were going above and beyond expectations in terms of responsibility and accountability to deal with the huge data loss and (2) to develop a leadership position on dealing with identity theft after the crisis was over.

To achieve their objectives, the officers of the company quickly announced what type of data was hacked and what was not, conducted a great number of media interviews, and contacted a large number of their customers directly. They also discussed the situation with influential financial bloggers and industry analysts, created a dedicated website, and communicated all this to their employees fully and clearly.

In the end, the company was mainly successful in handling the crisis. They then explored new security programs and formed a security group. They also shared some of their key lessons learned: "Be prepared," "Have a war room," and "Figure out how you can make a difference in a bad situation."

Source: "Case Study: Credit Card Payments Company 'Runs to the Light' as Security Breach Puts Reputation and Profits in Jeopardy." 2010. *PR News* 66(35).

Security Policies

Most medium to large organizations today have security policies that describe *what* the general security guidelines are for the organization. **Security policies** tend to be for internal use and include a number of **security procedures**, which are specific statements describing *how* to implement the security policies. For example, a security policy could be "All users must change their passwords every two months." One of its related security procedures could then describe steps to be taken to change one's password. Another procedure could involve an automated system to force users to change their passwords every two months, while an additional one could include actions that should happen if a user attempts to enter an unacceptable (not strong) password. A security policy should have clear goals and objectives, a detailed list of security policies and procedures, and a list of actions for the enforcement of procedures.

Even with the best policies and procedures in place and with the best security technologies available, an organization may not be well protected if its users and employees fail to follow the policies and procedures or fail to use the technologies properly. This is where security education and training become very important. Users must be made aware of the risks involved, the tools available, and the consequences of not performing the proper security behaviors that are asked of them. Refer to the book's website for several tips on how to secure your computer, network, and data properly.

LEARNING ACTIVITY 8.7

Where's the Security?

Now that we have explored all the security threats and solutions, we need to see how they fit together. For this learning activity, you need to map the threats to security and the goals of information security to the security solutions available. Prepare a table that contains the following information:

1. *Column 1:* List all the main security threats discussed.
2. *Column 2:* List all the security solutions that can address each of the security threats you have identified. (There might be many solutions for each threat.)
3. *Column 3:* For each security solution in column 2, indicate which security goal is met by the security solution.

Chapter Summary

In this chapter, we discussed the security of information. We first defined information security and described the threats to information security. We then discussed the technologies and solutions related to information security and concluded the chapter with a discussion of information security policies.

Here are the main points discussed in the chapter:

- There are three main categories of information security threats: denial of service, unauthorized access, and theft and fraud. Denial-of-service threats are those that render a system inoperative, limit its capability to operate, or make data unavailable. They include intentional acts, such as viruses, malware, and computer attacks; careless behavior, such as a lack of backups; and natural disasters. Unauthorized access threats refer to someone accessing systems and/or data illegally. Theft and fraud threats are related to the loss of systems or data due to theft or fraudulent activities, including illegal downloading or copying of software and theft of data using small hardware devices.

- There are three main goals that security tools and policies are meant to address: confidentiality, integrity, and availability (CIA). Confidentiality involves making sure that only authorized individuals can access information or data. Integrity involves making sure that the data are consistent and complete. Availability involves ensuring that systems and/or data are available when they are needed. Two additional goals are authentication (or authenticity) and nonrepudiation. Authentication means making sure that the parties involved are who they say they are and that transactions, data, or communications are genuine. Nonrepudiation refers to making sure one cannot renege on his or her obligations— for example, by denying that he or she entered into a transaction with a Web merchant.

- Security solutions and tools (also called security controls) can be classified as preventive, detective, or corrective controls. The goal of preventive controls is to stop or limit the security threat from happening in the first place. The goal of detective controls is to find or discover where and when security threats occurred. The goal of corrective controls is to repair damages after a security problem has occurred. Security controls can also be classified as physical or logical. Physical access controls are those security solutions that involve protecting physical access to systems, applications, or data, whereas logical access controls include security solutions that protect access to systems, applications, or data by ensuring users or systems are authenticated and allowed to have such access. Physical access controls can include locks for laptops, locked computer rooms, and secured rooms for backup storage. Logical access controls include user profiles, biometrics, firewalls, encryption, virus protection, and wireless security.

- There are many security solutions. The security solution of user profiles requires users to be assigned profiles that consist of a user identification (self-selected or assigned by the organization) and a set of privileges. Two-factor authentication requires an additional step before individuals have access to their devices and applications. Biometrics use human traits and characteristics to recognize individuals to grant them access or to identify them among other individuals. Firewalls are computers or routers that control access in and out of the organization's networks, applications, and computers. Encryption, also known as cryptography, is the use of mathematical algorithms to convert a message or information into a scrambled message or information that makes it unreadable. Antivirus software looks for virus signatures (patterns) in files and systems to prevent them from being executed. Wireless security is mostly done through encryption, such as WEP, WPA, WPA2, and RSN.

- Security policies describe what the general security guidelines are for an organization, including procedures, enforcement mechanisms, objectives, and also list actions for the enforcement of procedures.

- Risk management is the process of identifying, assessing, and prioritizing the security risks an organization may face and deciding whether to accept the risks, mitigate the risks, or share the security risks by buying insurance.

Review Questions

1. Briefly explain the three main goals of security and the additional two discussed in the text.

2. What is a denial-of-service attack, and what kind of events can lead to such an attack?

3. Explain how unauthorized access threats can occur.

4. Define preventive security controls, detective security controls, and corrective security controls. Provide two examples of each.

5. What are the various purposes of biometrics and how do they work?

6. What is a firewall and how does it work?

7. What are the two types of encryption discussed in the chapter and how do they differ?

8. How does antivirus software work?

9. What are the key steps required for wireless security?

10. What are security policies and procedures, and how are they related?

Reflection Questions

1. What is the most important thing you learned in this chapter? Why is it important?

2. What topics are unclear? What about them is unclear?

3. For each of the following security threats, suggest one preventive, one detective, and one corrective security control.

   - A virus is affecting the organization's intranet.
   - A hacker accesses consumer data on the company's database server to commit fraud.
   - A disgruntled employee steals trade secrets from the company's computers.
   - A construction worker breaks the data communication and electrical cables coming into the company's building.

4. Which biometric technologies are better used for identification and which are better used for verification? Explain why.

5. Explain what happens when you request your antivirus software to scan your hard drive.

6. A friend wants to send you encrypted messages. She asks you to send her both your public and private keys. What should your response be? Why? What should you send her? How will you send it? Does it matter?

7. List at least three security threats that a firewall will not protect a company against. Explain why.

8. Is a virtual private network a network or a security tool? Explain.

9. What do you believe are the most serious security concerns for the different types of networking architectures discussed in Chapter 7?

10. If an organization decides to accept a security risk instead of trying to mitigate it, would this still be considered risk management? Why or why not?

Additional Learning Activities

8.A1. Identify all the security threats individuals can face when using social networking sites such as Facebook, LinkedIn, Instagram, and others. Create a table that lists the threats, your estimate of how serious each threat is (low, medium, high), and a suggestion for how such sites should go about addressing these security threats.

8.A2. Perform research on encryption software that individuals can use for emails, their hard drives, or even mobile devices. Create a table that lists the various features of each major vendor and the costs for individual users like you. Then select one of the products and try it. Be prepared to discuss the advantages and disadvantages of the product you selected both for you as a student and for businesses that might want to use it.

8.A3. Read Appendix I, which discusses how to implement a security plan for an organization. Select a local small business that has at least 10 employees and develop a security plan for this business.

8.A4. Find your university's security policy and identify the main components of this policy. Be prepared to discuss the following:

a. What threats are referred to?

b. What security technologies are included in the policy?

c. Select one example each of a specific policy and a specific procedure.

d. Who is responsible for ensuring that you, as a student, follow the policy?

e. What happens if you do not follow the policy?

8.A5. Compare and contrast the security policy you found in Learning Activity 8.A4 with the templates for security policies provided by the SANS organization: http://www.sans.org/security-resources/policies/.

8.A6. Read the article by A. S. Horowitz, "Top 10 Security Mistakes," *Computerworld*, July 9, 2001, http://www.computerworld.com/article/2582953/security0/top-10--security--mistakes.html. Briefly explain each of the 10 mistakes. Then answer the following questions:

a. Where do we stand today on these security mistakes?

b. Why have we not improved more?

c. What is the possible role of technology in handling these "mistakes"?

8.A7. Research the ransomware Wannacry. Prepare a report of its history, its main victims, and what experts suggest companies do to avoid becoming a target of such ransomware.

8.A8. This activity requires you to complete a case analysis regarding security breaches. The case may be accessed through your university website, the Ivey Business School business case website (https://www.iveycases.com), or the Harvard Business School cases website (https://cb.hbsp.harvard.edu/cbmp/pages/home), or it may be provided to you by your instructor.

Dubé, L. 2016. "Autopsy of a Data Breach: The Target Case." *International Journal of Case Studies in Management* 14(1). Product number: HEC130.

8.A9. As computing technology changes, so do the threats to the security of information. Research the current state of threats, including spear-phishing and advanced persistent threats. Create a table with four columns. The first column should contain the name of the new threat. The second column should contain a definition of this new threat. The third column should identify how this threat builds on existing threats discussed in this chapter. Finally, column four should list what makes this threat different than existing threats discussed in this chapter. Be prepared to discuss these findings in class.

8.A10. In Chapter 7 Additional Learning Activity 7.A6, you used a cloud application (Dropbox, Google Drive, iCloud) to share documents with your classmates. Explore more in depth the security issues that have arisen to date with the particular cloud application you used.

References

Bukhari, J. 2017. "That Chip on Your Credit Card Isn't Stopping Fraud after All." *Fortune*, February 1. Retrieved December 20, 2017, from http://fortune.com/ 2017/02/01/credit-card-chips-fraud/.

Chirgwin, R. 2017. "Windows 10 Bundles a Briefly Vulnerable Password Manager." *The Register*, December 18. Retrieved December 20, 2017, from https://www .theregister.co.uk/2017/12/18/windows_10_bundles_vuln/.

Cuthbertson, A. 2017. "Ransomware Attacks Rise 250 Percent in 2017, Hitting U.S. Hardest." *Newsweek*, May 23. Retrieved from http://www.newsweek.com/ ransomware-attacks-rise-250-2017-us-wannacry-614034.

Hutton, M. 2015. "Annual DataMotion Survey Reveals Employees Violating Security and Compliance Policies and Major Mobile Vulnerabilities." *DataMotion*, March 4. http://www.datamotion.com/2015/03/annual-datamotion-survey -reveals-employees-violating-security-compliance-policies-major-mobile -vulnerabilities/.

Glossary

Active content: Executable files on websites.

Antivirus software: Programs that look for virus signatures or variations of them in files and systems.

Application-level firewall: A firewall that verifies access to applications by requiring users to log into the firewall before they can access applications inside the organization (from outside).

Asymmetrical security warfare: One party must do everything to protect itself, while the other party (the attacker) only needs to find the one security weakness.

Asymmetric encryption: A type of encryption that uses two keys: a public key for encrypting and a private key for decrypting.

Audit logs: Software programs that can scan for unexpected actions to detect potential hackers.

Authentication: A process by which the identity of a transacting party is verified.

Authentication (biometrics): A type of security that matches the individual with his or her stored biometric data.

Availability: System and/or data are available when needed.

Backdoors: Ways for hackers to reaccess the compromised system at will.

Behavioral-based antivirus protection tools: Programs that look for suspicious behaviors in programs instead of just a virus's signature.

Behavioral biometrics: Biometrics that use human behaviors.

Biometrics: Technologies that use human features to recognize individuals and grant them access.

Bitcoins: A cryptocurrency or currency that utilizes encryption based on the blockchain technology.

Blockchain: A network where transactions can be tracked but do not require trust between the transacting parties, thus allowing anonymity.

Cipher: An algorithm used to encrypt and decrypt plaintext.

Ciphertext: An encrypted (unreadable) message.

Confidentiality: Making sure that only authorized individuals can access information or data.

Corrective controls: Controls meant to repair damages after a security problem has occurred.

Decryption: Converting ciphertext back to plaintext.

Decryption key: A key used to convert the unreadable text into its original form.

Defense in depth: Multiple layers of security protections in place.

Denial-of-service threats: Threats that render a system inoperative or limit its capability to operate or make data unavailable.

Detective controls: Controls meant to find or discover where and when security threats occur.

Dictionary attack: When all words of several dictionaries in multiple languages are tested as passwords with numbers before and after the words.

Disaster recovery: Procedures and tools to recover systems affected by disasters and destruction.

Distributed denial-of-service attacks (DDOS): When many computers are being used for DOS attacks.

DNA recognition: A type of security that analyzes segments from an individual DNA.

Dynamic firewall: Manages the requests as they occur, deciding on both denials and permissions as they arrive.

Dynamic signature recognition: A type of security that analyzes not only the signature but how it is written using pressure points.

Ear recognition: A type of security that analyzes the shape of the ear.

Encryption: The application of a mathematical algorithm to a message or information that scrambles that message or information to make it unreadable.

Encryption key: A key used to convert the text into an unreadable form.

External firewall: A firewall used to protect access to the internal network and computers of the organization.

Facial recognition: A type of security that analyzes facial features or patterns (faceprints).

Finger geometry recognition: A type of security that analyzes 3D geometry of the finger.

Fingerprint recognition: A type of security that analyzes ridges and valleys (minutiae) on the surface tips of human fingers.

Firewall: A computer or a router that controls access in and out of the organization's networks, applications, and computers.

Firewall appliance: The hardware and software to perform firewall function.

Gait recognition: A type of security that analyzes the walking style or gait of individuals.

Hactivism: A type of hacking in which hackers try to find information that, if revealed, will advance human causes.

Hand geometry recognition: A type of security that analyzes geometric features of the hand, such as length of fingers and width of the hand.

Host firewall: A firewall installed on a computer.

Identification (biometrics): Identifying an individual from an entire population of individuals with stored biometric data.

Information security: A set of protections put in place to safeguard information systems and/or data from security threats such as unauthorized access, use, disclosure, disruption, modification, or destruction.

Integrity: When data are consistent and complete.

Internal firewall: A firewall used inside an organization, between departments or divisions.

Iris/retina recognition: A type of security that analyzes features (eyeprints) in the iris or the patterns of veins in the back of the eye (retina).

Key pair: A linked public key and private key.

Keystroke capture programs: Software that logs all information entered into a computer.

Keystroke recognition: A type of security that analyzes the rhythm and patterns of individuals' keystrokes on keyboards.

Knowledge (in security access): When an individual needs to know something to gain access.

Logical access controls: Security solutions that protect access to systems, applications, or data by ensuring users or systems are authenticated and allowed to have such access.

Nonrepudiation: Making sure a party cannot renege on obligations—for example, by denying that he or she entered into a transaction with a Web merchant.

Odor recognition: A type of security that analyzes an individual's odor to determine identity.

Open ports: In the context of telecommunications, it means a port (specific application) configured to accept traffic.

Packet-level firewall: A firewall that controls access by looking at the source and destination addresses in data packets. Also called *a screening level firewall.*

Packets: Small units of data that flow through networks, allowing for the transmission of messages.

Password crackers: Software used to recover forgotten passwords.

Personal firewall: A firewall installed on a given personal computer.

Physical access controls: Controls that involve protecting physical access to systems, applications, or data.

Physiological biometrics: Using physical traits to identify individuals.

Plaintext: Original message before it is encrypted.

Polymorphic viruses: A virus that modifies itself each time it infects a computer to void detection.

Possession: When an individual owns a form of identification.

Preventive controls: Controls meant to stop or limit the security threat from happening in the first place.

Principle of least privilege: A form of access control in which users are only given permission to access the minimum amount of information required to complete their jobs.

Ransomware: Software that is installed on the victim's computer via viruses, unauthorized access, or phishing that attacks the computer by encrypting the data on the computer until an appropriate password is provided.

Risk management: The process of identifying, assessing, and prioritizing the security risks an organization may face and deciding whether to accept, mitigate, or share the security risks.

Rootkits: Software that allows hackers to have unfettered access to everything on the system, including adding, deleting, and copying files.

Security: Protection against security threats.

Security levels: The layers of protection technologies and policies used to secure stored information.

Security policies: Statements describing what the general security guidelines are for an organization.

Security procedures: Specific statements describing how to implement the security policies.

Security threats: Broadly categorized as denial of service, unauthorized access, and theft and fraud.

Sniffer: Software that monitors transmissions, capturing unauthorized data of interest.

Social engineering: Tricking individuals into giving out security information. Also called *phishing.*

Spamming: Sending emails to many individuals at once, sending unsolicited commercial email to individuals, or targeting one individual computer or network and sending thousands of messages to it.

Spoofing: Pretending to be someone else (or another computer) to enter a system or gain attention.

Spyware: A form of virus that logs everything users do on their computers, unbeknownst to them.

Static firewall: A firewall that has predetermined ways of dealing with transmission requests.

Static signature recognition: A security measure that compares scanned or ink signatures with stored signatures.

Stealth virus: A more advanced virus that changes its own bit pattern to become undetectable by virus scanners.

Symmetric encryption: A form of encryption where the same key is used to encrypting and decrypting data.

Theft and fraud threats: Threats related to the loss of systems or data due to theft or fraudulent activities.

Traits: Physical or behavioral human characteristics needed to gain access to systems or data.

Trojan horses: Viruses embedded into a legitimate file.

Two-factor authentication: Also known as 2FA, this requires two layers of authentication, with the first typically being a username and password followed by a second factor such as an app on a trusted device, a security token, calls or text messages on a trusted phone, or one-time verification codes.

Unauthorized access threats: Individuals who access systems and/or data illegally.

User profile: Assigned profiles that consist of a user identification, a password, and a set of privileges.

Virtual private network (VPN): A connection that makes use of an open wired network such as the Internet but that provides a secured channel through encryption and other security features.

Virus: A computer program designed to perform unwanted events.

Virus hoaxes: False virus alerts sent and resent by individuals.

Virus signature: Bit patterns of the virus that can be recognized.

Voice recognition (speaker recognition): A security measure that analyzes voice to determine the identity of a speaker; different from speech recognition (determining *what* is being said).

Wi-Fi Protected Access (WPA): A recent and powerful encryption algorithm for wireless security. It has a newer version called WPA2.

Wired Equivalent Privacy (WEP): A protocol that uses encryption established via a pre-shared key known to the router and the wireless device or computer on a wireless network.

Worms: Viruses that propagate themselves throughout the Internet with no user intervention.

CHAPTER 9

Protecting the Confidentiality and Privacy of Information

Learning Objectives

By reading and completing the activities in this chapter, you will be able to

- Understand the various threats to information privacy
- Identify technologies and solutions used to protect the confidentiality and privacy of information
- Explain how information privacy is a component of the PAPA ethical framework
- Discuss the relationship between information privacy and information security

Chapter Outline

Focusing Story: Perceptions of Anonymity

Introduction and Definitions

Information Privacy Threats

Learning Activity 9.1: Privacy and Smartphones

Data Collection

Learning Activity 9.2: Concern for Information Privacy

Learning Activity 9.3: Privacy Pizza

Consequences of Privacy Violations

Technologies and Solutions for Information Privacy

Anonymous Browsing

Learning Activity 9.4: Surveillance Societies around the World

Learning Activity 9.5: Privacy Policy Creation

FOCUSING STORY

Perceptions of Anonymity

Internet service providers and email services can and do track a lot of what you say and do online. The big question is whether they use that information or not. Remember those times you are asked to click "I Agree" to access some services online? What are you exactly agreeing to? Even when your personal information is removed before searching or browsing, it is sold to a third party; it may not be as "anonymous" as you think. Moreover, what about the information that is collected about your purchasing habits from your credit card company? What are they allowed to "sell" to others? All of these situations can be problematic when multiple different pieces of information are joined together. Large data sets of information about you and others, which are called metadata, can be easily "mined" today to find patterns, even if they have been stripped of personal data— which is supposed to make them "anonymous data." Let's see some examples.

In a study of credit card transactions conducted over three months in 10,000 stores by 1.1 million individuals, researchers only had access to the date of the transactions, the amount charged, and the name of the stores (Singer 2015). This means that the data were "anonymized," since there were no names or account numbers. Yet by using four random pieces of information, including publicly available information on sites like Twitter and Instagram, the researchers were able to reidentify 90% of the users of those credit cards.

Location information is now commonly collected, in particular by your smartphones and tablets. One study was conducted to see how much anonymous data from using Google Maps (with settings allowing location information to be sent) would reveal about two users (Pangburn 2017). Within a few days of starting to collect the location information and using publically available information like mortgage information, LinkedIn, and Google Street View, the expert was able to identify one person exactly (with all kinds of personal information available) and one close enough (where he or she worked and lived).

Older studies were also able to identify users from "anonymous data," including identifying Netflix users in 2008, hospital patients in Washington State in 2013, and celebrities using taxis in New York in 2014 (Singer 2015). In another study, researchers identified 50 individuals who participated in a study of genomes by matching the anonymous genome data with publicly available information (Miller 2013). Another study of mobile users in 2013 by two universities found that they could uniquely identify 95% of 1.5 million individuals from 15 months of mobility data (Pangburn 2017).

FOCUSING QUESTIONS

1. What is the role of publicly available data in this story?
2. What are the possible consequences of being identified from one's browsing or searching habits?
3. What can you do when you are on the Internet that will protect your privacy?

Sources: Miller, G. 2013. "Scientists Discover How to Identify People from 'Anonymous' Genomes." *Wired,* January 29. Retrieved December 27, 2017, from https://www.wired.com/2013/01/your-genome-could-reveal-your-identity/; Pangburn, D. J. 2017. "Even This Data Guru Is Creeped Out by What Anonymous Location Data Reveals about Us." *Fast Company,* September 26. Retrieved December 27, 2017, from https://www.fastcompany.com/3068846/how-your -location-data-identifies-you-gilad-lotan-privacy; Singer, N. 2015. "With a Few Bits of Data, Researchers Identify 'Anonymous' People." *New York Times,* January 29. Retrieved December 27, 2017, from https://bits.blogs.nytimes.com/ 2015/01/29/with-a-few-bits-of-data-researchers-identify-anonymous-people/.

Introduction and Definitions

Privacy of information is the confidentiality of the information collected by organizations about the individuals using their services (Van Slyke and Bélanger 2003). It can also be defined as one's ability to control information about oneself (Bélanger, Hiller, and Smith 2002). From an individual's perspective, it refers to a desire to control or influence data about oneself (Bélanger and Crossler 2011). Privacy of information is a very important concept for individuals and organizations alike. Many students may have faced issues with the privacy of their information when friends posted something about them on Facebook or Twitter without their prior approval. This may have been just for fun or may have caused some tensions between friends. However, as students move to the workplace, they will realize that organizations need to be even more keenly aware of information privacy concepts, since workers, professionals, and managers have access to and deal with great amounts of information on a daily basis. Therefore, everyone has to be concerned not only about their own information privacy but also about the privacy of information of others, including customers, employees, business partners, students, parents, children, and more.

Information Privacy Threats

There are many possible threats to information privacy—for example, dealing with collection and unauthorized secondary use of data, improper access to data, and errors in data (Smith, Milberg, and Burke 1996). Inaccuracies or **errors in data** can have serious impacts on individuals—for example, those applying for jobs or loans. **Improper access to data** deals more with the security of information, as discussed in the previous chapter with the security threat of unauthorized access. The information privacy threats of data collection and unauthorized secondary use, however, are worth discussing in more depth.

LEARNING ACTIVITY 9.1

Privacy and Smartphones

Most students today have smartphones. Depending on the settings on these devices, it is likely that location information is associated with every picture taken. The following video demonstrates how this happens and the possible implications. Please watch the video and answer the questions below: https://www.youtube.com/watch?v=N2vARzvWxwY.

Discussion Questions

1. What could people do with the information that is available on the pictures?
2. Who should educate people about this?
3. What else could be geotagged on your phone?
4. Why would all consumers not disable this feature?
   - Is there a reason not to?
   - What is the trade-off?

Data Collection

The collection of data from individuals is not a new concern, and the concept of privacy has been explored and discussed for centuries. One of the major differences today, however, is that as communications and information have been digitized, it has become easier and faster to collect ever-increasing amounts of information. Specifically, with the advent of advanced information and communication technologies, the **data collection threat** means that data can be collected, aggregated, and analyzed at a faster pace and in larger volumes than ever. Of a greater concern sometimes is the fact that data can be collected without anyone's awareness—for example, through the use of cookies. **Cookies** are small text files that store information on your computer about you or your computer when you browse or enter information into certain websites.

Another hidden data collection approach is **clickstream data**, which tracks online browsing behaviors. The tracking is done by software that looks at the IP address of the computer connecting to a site, identifying what page the computer connected from, what page it goes to after the current one, how often it connects to this site, and whether actual purchases are made from this site. Thorough analysis of this data can then give marketers an indication of successful and unsuccessful online ads, referring sites, and other information on the preferences of each user. Customized ads can also be delivered to the consumer's screen. Interestingly, it's likely no one would agree to be followed in his or her buying decision process in a physical retail store. Imagine someone walking with you and observing you as you stroll through a Wal-Mart and look at various products! Yet online tracking of consumers is a regular occurrence.

The proliferation of data sources, tools to manipulate these data, and online sites collecting data in today's interconnected society leads to more data being available and to individuals being increasingly concerned about the privacy of their information. Current technology allows easy loading of information from online forms directly into databases. For companies, this is a major advantage, since the data are loaded immediately (faster) and accurately (no transcribing errors and no problems dealing with unreadable writing; Van Slyke and Bélanger 2003). However, as more information is being stored online, consumers are becoming increasingly concerned with losing control of how their information is being collected and used.

Information privacy is also an important concern for corporations. The increased ability to store consumer information makes corporations targets for hackers trying to gain access to the vast amount of consumer information that they store, causing an increase in the number of breaches that companies are experiencing. For example, customers who

---

LEARNING ACTIVITY 9.2

Concern for Information Privacy

A number of reports and studies relate the various concerns that individuals and organizations have about information privacy. For this learning activity, search the Internet for statistics on the level of concern either individuals or organizations have about sharing information electronically. Note any benefits reported as trade-offs that might overcome these concerns for sharing information. Be prepared to discuss your findings in class.

shopped at Target during December of 2013 provided their credit card information to Target. Hackers then attacked Target's point-of-sale terminals to gain access to this information (McGrath 2014). Over the years, as discussed in Chapter 8, many other large organizations have been hacked, compromising individuals' personal information.

Secondary Use of Information

Unauthorized secondary use of information refers to the use of data for purposes other than those for which they were originally collected. For example, you enter your information on a website to register for the warranty of your new digital camera, but then the company uses your information to send you marketing ads about its other products. Information privacy refers to having some level of control over these potential secondary uses of one's personal information. *Function creep* is another term used to refer to data being used for other functions beyond those purposes for which they were collected. Often, individuals are given the option to opt in or opt out of secondary use on websites. When you **opt in**, you have to specifically state that you agree that your data can be used for other purposes, often to receive special deals or information from partner companies. When you **opt out**, you have to make sure you tell the company you do not want your data shared with others or used for other purposes. The trick is that sometimes you have to click a box to opt out and sometimes you have to unclick one. If you forget, by default you are agreeing to let the companies share or use your information.

In summary, when information collection and use are not regulated, individuals have the responsibility of protecting their own (or others') information, particularly in the United States. However, it is often the case that individuals are not aware of the risks or do not know how to protect their own information. Often people make a choice to give this information because it provides convenience or personalization of one's online experience. These preferences do vary around the world.

LEARNING ACTIVITY 9.3

Privacy Pizza

Your instructor will present a video titled *Privacy Pizza* in class or may direct you to the course website for you to watch the video individually before class. As you watch the video, make notes on the types of information and technologies that are discussed and/or used in the video. The *Privacy Pizza* video can also be found at https://www .aclu.org/ordering-pizza. Be prepared to answer the following questions:

1. Do you think access to the various types of information identified is regulated or not?
2. For the technologies identified, are the technologies widely available today?
3. How likely is it that a pizza shop/company can use such technologies?
4. What can someone do to avoid this situation from happening to him or her?

STATS BOX 9.1:
PERCEPTIONS OF MONITORING

The focusing story showed that we are not as anonymous online as we wish we were. At the same time, it seems many people realize they are being monitored by their government. For example, the Pew Internet and American Life Research Center found that 70% of Americans believe it is "very likely" or "somewhat likely" that their emails and phone calls are being monitored by the government (Olmstead 2017). The survey shows some differences based on age, with more 18- to 50-year-olds (78%) believing they are being monitored compared to older adults (65% for 50- to 64-year-olds and 56% for 65-year-olds and older). Men were also more likely than females to think they were being monitored, but there were no differences across political affiliations.

Source: Olmstead, K. 2017. "Most Americans Think the Government Could Be Monitoring Their Phone Calls and Emails." *Pew Research Center,* September 27. Retrieved December 23, 2017, from http://www.pewresearch.org/fact-tank/2017/09/27/most-americans-think-the-government-could-be-monitoring-their-phone-calls-and-emails/.

Consequences of Privacy Violations

Individual Consequences: Identify Theft

Everyone can face serious consequences when people take their personal information for fraudulent activities. This is the concept of **identity theft**. Identity theft cases have been increasing substantially in recent years. The Javelin Strategy and Research Center (https://www.javelinstrategy.com) reported in 2015 that there were more than 12.7 million identity theft victims in 2014 in the United States. Their studies also show that as the ability to pay for products electronically using smartphones has emerged, the likelihood of having money stolen where the transaction occurs has also increased. In addition to these high-tech methods of identity theft, it is important to protect yourself from low-tech methods of identity theft as well, including the stealing of wallets, mail, and other physical documents that contain people's personal information. As seen in the previous chapter, transmitting information online is relatively secure, but as new mobile technologies are emerging, this is changing. Furthermore, what happens after the information is received by local organizations can sometimes not be as secure. Identity theft can have several negative consequences for individuals, including financial, social, and emotional impacts.

Students are often concerned that their data are being stolen from the Web when they acquire some goods or services online. In reality, as stated in the previous paragraph, the risks are greater that fraudsters or identity thieves access large amounts of information from unsecured databases. Often individuals who illegally access these data then resell it on the black market. It is difficult to have precise numbers on the size of this market, but various researchers and centers have identified the value of your information on the black market. How much would you be willing to pay for the following?

- A valid credit card number with a security code
- Valid bank account details, including the PIN (personal identification number)
- A valid Social Security number
- A completely new (valid) identity

The best way for individuals to protect themselves from identity theft is to follow basic security guidelines and common sense. The Identity Theft Resource Center (http://www.idtheftcenter.org), a not-for-profit organization, has been created to help identity theft victims and offers very useful information about protection against identity theft and what to do if it happens to you.

The following are some examples of the recommended actions:

- Do not use your Social Security number unless it is absolutely needed.
- Shred everything that has any data about you.
- Place outgoing mail at the post office or locked collection box.
- Password protect financial accounts with strong passwords and two-factor authentication, if available.
- Really check the statements you receive.
- Request photo identification when someone asks for your information, and do not give it out over the phone, Internet, or mail unless you initiated the contact.
- Destroy digital data by going beyond a simple delete.
- Limit the information provided on your checks.
- Request your free annual credit report and check it.

Organizational Consequences: Company Reputation

For organizations, information privacy violations also have serious consequences. There are, however, two sides to the issue here. Organizations have the responsibility of protecting their customers' data, but they are sometimes the ones infringing on the privacy of their clients.

If organizations fail to protect the privacy of their customers' information, then their reputations can suffer. There are many examples of companies' reputations being at stake. In 2017, for example, the Transportation Security Administration (TSA), which handles security at airports in the United States, had thousands of documents relating to their activities leaked from a password-less backup drive. The same year, close to 14 million records of Verizon customers were exposed by being stored on

STATS BOX 9.2:
FRAUD TYPE FROM IDENTITY THEFT

Every year, the Federal Trade Commission (FTC) collects information on identity theft complaints and on fraud committed with someone else's identity in the United States. The figure below shows the types of fraud that are committed this way, computed from FTC complaint data. As can be seen, wire-transfer fraud is by far the most common type of fraud being committed. This involves stealing money by intercepting the electronic communications between two financial institutions, such as banks. Other large categories of fraud include credit cards, bank account debits, and most recently, prepaid cards.

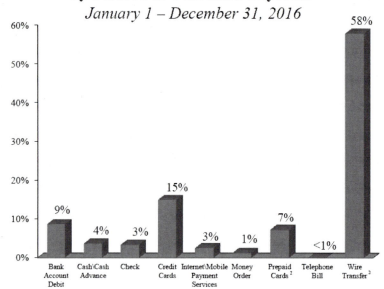

Consumer Sentinel Network Fraud Complaints by Method of Consumer Payment[1]

January 1 – December 31, 2016

Types of Fraud Committed through Identity Theft

[1]Percentages are based on the total number of CSN fraud complaints for each calendar year where consumers reported the method of payment: CY-2014 = 366,770; CY-2015 = 243,915; and CY-2016 = 241,886. Of the total, 19% reported this information during CY-2016, 19% in CY-2015 and 23% in CY-2014.
[2]Prepaid Cards includes a significant number of complaints from data contributor Green Dot, and Wire Transfer includes a significant number of complaints from data contributors MoneyGram International and Western Union. This may affect the distribution of the reported methods of payment.
[3]The amount paid is based on complaints reporting values from $0 to $999,999.

Source: Based on data published by the Federal Trade Commission. 2017. "Consumer Sentinel Network Data Book." Retrieved December 22, 2017, from https://www.ftc.gov/system/files/documents/reports/consumer-sentinel-network-data-book-january-december-2016/csn _cy-2016_data_book.pdf.

an unprotected cloud storage server, the National Security Agency was breached for gigabytes of data, and as discussed in chapter 8, Equifax was hacked and more than 143 million consumer records were breached (Whittaker 2017). In addition, there are many more instances, just in that year.

The costs of privacy breaches can be enormous for the companies involved. First, they may lose current and future customers. Second, they have to repair the breaches. And third, they have to compensate customers for their potential identity theft issues. In order to deal with the breach they faced in 2017, Equifax incurred more than US$87.5 million, with more costs forthcoming. They had to provide breach victims with monitoring services, but even more costly may be the more than 240 lawsuits they face and the losses from companies withholding their business from them. Following the announcement of the breach, their third-quarter profits in 2017 fell 27%. There are also investigations into Equifax executives selling stocks before the breach was announced to the public (Cowley 2017).

Finally, but not least, privacy breaches in organizations can directly impact the organization if the information that is leaked concerns the organizations' patents, trade secrets, or other intellectual property.

Technologies and Solutions for Information Privacy

Now that we understand the broad concepts of information privacy threats, it is important to further discuss the particular roles that technology can play in both infringing on information privacy and protecting one's information privacy. One technology that we will discuss is cookies. Some of the tools that we describe in this section, however, are more like approaches to information privacy rather than tools. For example, a privacy policy on a website is more about the content and whether it is applied properly than about technology to create a policy. Similarly, privacy seals and government regulations toward privacy are ways to protect you online, but they are more like tools and techniques than they are technologies.

Cookies and Cookie Managers

Websites often use cookies, small text files located on your computer, to temporarily (or sometimes for as long as you have your computer) store information about you, your accounts, and your computer. Information is stored in a cookie every time you enter information and are asked, "Do you want this to be remembered?" Cookies provide convenience to individuals. Because the information is stored on the computer, you do not have to retype all the account information or addresses or even remember your password to access a website that has stored information in the cookie file. Information not typed in can also be stored in cookies. For example, the website can record information such as your IP (Internet Protocol) address, the domain name of your computer, the length of time you stay on a specific Web page, and so on. When the user accesses one of the addresses in the address range of the website that

STATS BOX 9.3:
THE BLACK MARKET FOR STOLEN IDENTITIES

Identity theft is an increasingly prevalent issue because of the value of people's information. However, this information cannot be sold through traditional business channels. Therefore, a black market has emerged for people's information, with different values for different pieces of information. It is often called the "dark web." For example, when Yahoo was hacked in 2013, three entities are believed to have paid $300,000 each for a copy of the database that was stolen. Two of these are believed to be spammers (Goel and Perlroth 2016). While getting these kinds of data from the dark web is not easy, Symantec (2014) conducted a study to see how much different stolen information is worth, which is presented in the table below. More recently, *CNN Tech* (Larson 2017) suggested that trades focus on what they call "fullz," or full identity packets, which include names, dates of birth, social security numbers, and credit card information, for $20 or less. Some bigger fullz's that include financial data, prior addresses, medical history, or criminal history can cost more than $100. How much of these data do you think Equifax had on you?

Stolen Information	Value
Credit card	$0.50 to $20.00
Email account	$0.50 to $10.00 per 1,000 accounts
Scan of passport	$1.00 to $2.00
Cloud account (command and control centers)	$7.00 to $8.00
Gaming account	$10.00 to $15.00
Social network	$2.00 to $12.00 per 1,000 followers
Hotel reservation/train ticket/airline ticket	10% of asking price
Online gift card	50% to 60% of nominal value

Sources: Goel, V., and N. Perlroth. 2016. "Hacked Yahoo Data Is for Sale on Dark Web." *New York Times,* December 15. Retrieved December 23, 2017, from https://www.nytimes.com/2016/12/15/technology/hacked-yahoo-data-for-sale -dark-web.html; Larson, S. 2017. "What Cybercriminals Do with Stolen Social Security Numbers." *CNN Tech,* September 19. Retrieved December 23, 2017, from http://money.cnn.com/2017/09/19/technology/business/equifax-breach -social-security/index.html; Symantec. 2014. *Underground Black Market: Thriving Trade in Stolen Data, Malware, and Attack Services.* http://www.symantec.com/ connect/blogs/underground-black-market-thriving-trade-stolen-data-malware -and-attack-services.

stored the cookie, the browser transmits all the information retained in the cookie to the server of the website the user is currently browsing. Any item used to personalize your experience on the Web uses a set of cookies.

In terms of technologies to deal with cookies, there are many options. The simplest option is the settings you use on your Internet browser. The privacy settings allow you to state whether or not you allow cookies and what types of cookies should be automatically accepted. If you set your computer to be superprivate, most cookies will not work, and then many websites will not allow you to use their pages. If you set it your privacy settings too low, then most information about you and your computer will be stored and can be used by websites. The right balance depends on your privacy preferences. Different operating systems and browsers have different ways to deal with cookies. One organization, AboutCookies.org (http://www.aboutcookies.org) shows you different ways to control or delete cookies from your computer.

There are also **cookie managers** that can be downloaded for free or for a fee. These give you more details about which cookies are stored and what is stored in them and allow you to delete them. Table 9.1 shows you sample cookie managers, but many more exist on the Web. Finally, many new antivirus, antispyware, and other security programs automatically scan for and delete unnecessary cookies.

Anonymous Browsing

Given individuals' mounting concerns over information privacy, one approach that has been suggested is to use anonymous browsing. This can be done on computers, laptops, tablets, and even smartphones. The idea is to not allow websites to track what you are doing online, which is often used by advertisers to create targeted ads for you.

Table 9.1 Sample Cookie Management Tools

Name	Description	Creator and Link
One Smart Cookie	Cookie manager	http://download.cnet.com/One-Smart-Cookie/3000-2144_4-10260690.html
Cookie Monster	Cookie manager	AMPsoft: http://www.ampsoft.net/utilities/CookieMonster.php
Cookie Pal	Cookie manager	http://download.cnet.com/Cookie-Pal/3000-2144_4-10008248.html
IECookiesView	Cookie manager	NirSofer: http://www.nirsoft.net/utils/iecookies.html
Maxa Cookie Manager	Freeware cookie manager	Maxa Research: http://www.maxa-tools.com/cookie.php

There are a few things you can do to leave less of a trail when you are browsing the Web. First, as previously discussed, you can make sure that cookies are either blocked or deleted. You can also adjust the settings so your browser does not send location information to websites you are surfing. Chrome, Safari, and Firefox have specific settings for this. For Microsoft browsers, you can use your computer's privacy settings. Third, you can use an anonymous search engine (like DuckDuckGo) or turn off the settings that "personalizes" your searches. By getting more "personal" search information, you are also giving your search engine your preferences. Just think of how much Google knows about you already! You can also make sure your social networks, like Facebook, are not allowed to provide you with personalized ads, but that does not mean they won't track you. One of the authors of this book always uses anonymous browsing, which is available for most browsers (for example, there is InPrivate browsing on Internet Explorer and Incognito browsing in Chrome). There are also private browsers like the Tor browser (https://www.torproject.org/), which uses a complex open network so that websites cannot track and analyze your Web traffic. For smartphones and tablets, there are also different ways to use private browsing. For example, the Safari app on the Apple platforms can be set to use private browsing, but you do this within Safari instead of in the privacy settings. When looking at your opened Safari windows, you can see a "Private" option on the bottom left; clicking this allows you to set Safari in private browsing mode.

Unfortunately, even when trying to cover your tracks with anonymous browsing, you may still be tracked. A journalist and some experts in Europe acquired "anonymous" browsing history from three million German individuals and started analyzing them (Hern 2017; Price 2017). Close to three billion URLs revealed the identity of most of those individuals and specific information on their browsing habits, including some that most people would really not like to reveal.

LEARNING ACTIVITY 9.4

Surveillance Societies around the World

We discussed privacy as having consequences for individuals and organizations. Privacy can also have global aspects as well. However, the concern for privacy and how it influences people's decisions is different in various countries. Visit the EMC Privacy Index (http://www.emc.com/campaign/privacy-index/index.htm) and explore the different infographics available. As you do so, be prepared to answer the following questions:

1. In what contexts are people most willing to trade their privacy? Least willing?
2. In which countries are people most willing to trade their privacy for services? Least willing?
3. What is a paradox, and how does it affect people in different information-sharing contexts?

LEARNING ACTIVITY 9.5

Privacy Policy Creation

This activity will allow you to explore the contents of privacy policies. Based on the following scenario, create an appropriate policy.

Scenario: Two of your best friends from class have asked you to join them in a new venture. They are starting to sell customized, high-quality, university-branded apparel to fellow students and mostly to wealthy alumni. They want you to be the chief technology officer, and you have enthusiastically joined with them. As you oversee the development of the website for the company, which you are outsourcing, you have been asked to provide a privacy policy regarding your handling of customer data. This policy will be on the website at the bottom of the pages in small print.

Activity

1. Go to one of these sites (or another tool that you find online) to help generate a privacy policy:
   a. PrivacyPolicies.com: http://privacypolicies.com/
   b. Free Privacy Policy: http://www.freeprivacypolicy.com
   c. Shopify Policy Generator: https://www.shopify.com/tools/policy-generator
2. Bring your resulting policy to class (if the activity is performed before class).
3. Be prepared to discuss how you created your policy and which decisions you had to make.

Privacy Statement or Policy

Most serious companies who do business online have privacy policies. A **privacy policy** is a statement that describes what the organization's practices are with respect to the privacy of its customers. In general, most privacy policies include some or all of the following information:

- What data are collected
- How the data are collected
- What the organization is doing with the data
- Why it is collecting the data
- What other companies it may or may not share the data with
- What actions the company is taking to protect the data
- How you can access the data the company has about you and how you can fix errors
- Whether you can opt out

The information contained in the privacy policies of companies usually follows the **fair information practices (FIP) principles** set forth by the Federal Trade Commission (FTC) and a number of other organizations. These principles are derived from a number of studies, guidelines, and reports coming from a variety of countries. The FIP principles provide guidance for how to deal with personal information and include (1) notice/awareness, (2) choice/consent, (3) access/participation, (4) integrity/security, and (5) enforcement/redress. Table 9.2 shows how the FIP principles can be mapped to what privacy policies include.

It is important to note that privacy policies, like the privacy seals we will discuss below, are considered self-regulation mechanisms for information privacy. This means that most companies are not legally required to have a policy. **Self-regulation** is often an attempt by industry leaders to avoid government regulations. In this case, businesses do not want the government to impose privacy rules they would have to follow. Instead, they suggest that privacy policies provide sufficient protection for individuals. Do you think this is true? Well, the first question you should ask is, who reads privacy policies? Research clearly shows that most individuals never read privacy policies on websites. Now that you know what policies contain, do you feel protected? What would you do if a company failed to follow its own policies? The **Federal Trade Commission (FTC)** is in charge of ensuring that privacy policies are respected. However, there is no "privacy policy police." It is up to consumers to make complaints to the FTC in the United States. With enough complaints about a particular site, the FTC will investigate. So if you find that a company fails to follow its own policy, you must turn to the FTC with your complaint in the United States or the privacy and data protection regulators of European countries, the European Commission or the EU Commission Data Protection Working Group. Companies dealing with customers in Europe have to be aware that the privacy laws are more stringent there

Table 9.2 Mapping Fair Information Practices to Privacy Policies

Fair Information Practices	Privacy Policies
Notice/awareness	What data we are collecting How the data are collected What we are doing with the data Why we are collecting the data Which other companies we may or may not share the data with
Choice/consent	How you can (or cannot) opt out of us collecting these data about you
Access/participation	How you can access the data we have about you
Integrity/security	What actions we are taking to protect the data
Enforcement/redress	How you can fix errors in our data about you

than in the United States. To allow international business to prosper, however, a Safe Harbor program was developed so that companies in the United States can certify their practices with the U.S. Department of Commerce if they host or use European customers' data in the United States. More details on this program can be found at the Safe Harbor page at Export.gov: http://www.export.gov/safeharbor/.

BUSINESS EXAMPLE BOX 9.1

Privacy and Facebook

Which students are not on Facebook? Not many, right? Everyone seems to be on Facebook. Why? It's easy to communicate with so many people, so fast, from anywhere, and at any time. It's a great place to share pictures and keep in touch. It's addictive. Facebook is currently the most commonly used social networking site by adults.

Facebook likes to collect information on their users because it is the company's business model. Using profiles, Facebook is able to offer targeted marketing for companies. Facebook clearly says that it does not provide the information directly to its clients but rather uses its access to your information to provide targeted advertising for its clients. Think about the information available: what you like; where you shop; when you date; when you break up; when someone in your family gets a job, gets fired, or gets married; and so on. So is information privacy an issue on Facebook? Some say, "Yes, but I don't care." Others say, "No, not at all." And few, very few say, "Yes, and I quit." Where do you stand?

Let us look at some of the complaints against Facebook. In 2006, Facebook released a newsfeed application that displayed changes to a friend's page directly to your computer without you having to access his or her page. In 2007, Facebook released an application called Beacon that showed information on your page (available to all your friends) when you performed actions on partner sites, such as what movie you rented on Netflix or what you bought on eBay. Following class actions and a settlement, Facebook discontinued this application but launched a similar program called Connect, which is intended to have better privacy settings.

In spring 2010, Facebook changed settings to allow private information from users to be displayed to all users irrespective of the initial choice of keeping this private, including job title, music preferences, school attended, and home city. The information is also shared with selected business partners of Facebook through the "instant personalization" application. After complaints, Facebook offered ways to control this setting (opt out), but many users never changed them. It is apparently not an easy task to change the settings. As a result, European Union regulators filed complaints against Facebook, alleging that users did not have effective control over their information. The Federal Trade Commission also started to investigate and later asked the company to simplify privacy controls for users (which the company did) and to provide more opt-in rather than opt-out options (which the company did not do).

Lawsuits abound against Facebook regarding privacy and its tracking and use of data it collects. For example, in 2014, Facebook began battling a class-action lawsuit in Vienna due to its privacy practices. The primary goal of the class-action lawsuit is for Facebook to provide fundamental privacy rights such as simplifying privacy policies, providing users with more information about how their information is used, and limiting how long ad-click data are retained. In 2015, a class action lawsuit was filed against the company in Austria for illegal tracking of users' data. In 2016, a lawsuit was filed based in the state of Illinois suggesting that Facebook's photo-tagging system violates a law about biometric information. In 2017, Facebook was linked to Russian propaganda during the 2016 United States presidential elections. In the wake of these events, some individuals have argued that with the amounts of detailed personal data Facebook has about each user, there are huge challenges for the privacy of these users (Parakilas 2017).

Interestingly, while Facebook continues to face complaints regarding its own privacy practices, it does offer Facebook users a way to report privacy rights violations users feel they are a victim of (photo, video, or other): https://www .facebook.com/help/contact/144059062408922.

Sources: Best, J. 2014. "Facebook Forced to Respond to Privacy Complaints of 25,000 Europeans." *ZDNet,* August 21. http://www.zdnet.com/article/facebook-forced-to -respond-to-privacy-complaints-of-25000-europeans/; Cowan, J. 2010. "Why We'll Never Escape Facebook." *Canadian Business* 83(10): 28–33; Gelles, D., and M. Palmer. 2010. "Facebook in Privacy Action." *Financial Times,* July 8:16; "Getting Personal. But Too Personal? Facebook's Mark Zuckerberg on What Information People Should Share—and Who Gets to Decide." 2010. *Wall Street Journal,* July 7; Gibbs, S. 2015. "Class Action Privacy Lawsuit Filed against Facebook in Austria." *The Guardian,* April 9. Retrieved from https://www.theguardian.com/technology/2015/apr/09/class-action -privacy-lawsuit-filed-against-facebook-in-austria; Guynn, J. 2016. "Facebook to Face Privacy Lawsuit over Photo Tagging." *USA Today,* May 5. Retrieved from https://www .usatoday.com/story/tech/news/2016/05/05/facebook-photo-tagging-lawsuit-faceprints -privacy-illinois/83999984/; Hamaker, C. 2010. "Facebook Fans Pay Price in Privacy." *Rural Telecommunications* 29(4): 8; Lenhart, A., K. Purcell, S. Smith, and K. Zickhur, 2010. "Social Media & Mobile Internet Use Among Teens and Young Adults." *P. I. a. A. L. Project;* Lyons, D. 2010. "Facebook's False Contrition: A Business Built on Your Data." *Newsweek* 155(23); Lyons, D. 2010. "The High Price of Facebook: You Pay for It with Your Privacy." *Newsweek* 155(22); Menn, J. 2010. "Technology and Society: Virtually Insecure." *Financial Times,* July 28: 7; Parakilas, S. 2017. "We Can't Trust Facebook to Regulate Itself." *New York Times,* November 19. Retrieved from https://www.nytimes.com/2017/ 11/19/opinion/facebook-regulation-incentive.html.

Privacy Seals

Privacy seals offer companies another attempt at self-regulation regarding privacy of consumers and a way to reassure consumers about transacting with them online. The way it works is that some company or organization, such as the Better Business Bureau, develops a seal program with a **security seal**—a logo that companies can post on their website if they follow certain rules, such as BBBOnline. There are several **seal programs** that businesses can participate in to show their commitment to trust-worthiness (i.e., this website can be trusted). These seals are also called **reputation seals** and are issued by such sites as TrustArc (previously called TRUSTe) (http://www.trustarc.com) and WebTrust. Security seal programs assure consumers that the website follows a set of security procedures protecting their data; examples include those offered by VeriSign (http://www.verisign.com) and McAfee Secure (https://www.mcafeesecure.com/). Privacy seals ensure that the website follows certain privacy guidelines, such as ESRB Privacy Online (http://www.esrb.org/privacy/). Even

---

LEARNING ACTIVITY 9.6

Why Your Advisor Can't Talk to Your Parents

Legislation exists to protect information privacy of individuals in a number of specific cases, such as individuals' health and financial information, as well as information about children and students. The purpose of this activity is to allow you to explore how your information privacy is protected and to better understand the difference between legitimate and inappropriate uses of information.

1. Go to the Family Educational Rights and Privacy Act (FERPA) website for students: http://www.ed.gov/policy/gen/guid/fpco/ferpa/students.html. FERPA protects the privacy of student education records. This link is available on the book's website.

2. Read the information on the main page. Pay particular attention to the types of information covered by FERPA and individuals to whom protected information can be released.

3. Answer the following questions and be prepared to discuss them in class:

   a. What types of information are protected under FERPA?

   b. Under what conditions may school officials provide protected information to parents? In your opinion, how do these conditions relate to the concept of "owning" your personal data?

   c. Why do you think FERPA was created? What problem did it solve?

   d. Compare the protections afforded by FERPA to the privacy policies you examined in Learning Activity 9.5. What elements do they have in common? How are they different? Which has stronger protections?

general trust seals often deal directly with privacy. For example, TrustArc states to consumers, "Certified companies that display our privacy seal demonstrate compliance with our Certification Standards and their commitment to privacy protection, instilling confidence and trust in users of their products and services" (http://www .trustarc.com). Seals are supposed to instill consumer confidence in the website, but studies have shown that even experienced Web users are less familiar with privacy and security seals than with security technologies (Cheskin 1999). In general, only 25% of consumers seem to recognize seal features on websites (Harris Interactive 2001), and many users will acquire goods or services independent of whether trust seals are present or not (Bélanger et al. 2002). There are many other seal programs, some specific to other areas of the world, such as TrustUK for the United Kingdom and eTICK for Australia.

Government Information Privacy Regulations

Even though information privacy is largely our responsibility as individuals, there are specific situations where governments have created regulations to protect information privacy. In fact, there are actually many such regulations throughout the world. For example, the **Data Protection Directive** regulates how personal data are processed and protected in the European Union. In the United States, there are many privacy laws as well. Some that students might be more familiar with include the **Gramm-Leach-Bliley Financial Services Modernization Act of 1999 (GLBA)**, which regulates use of private information by financial institutions; the **Family Educational Rights and Privacy Act (FERPA)** discussed in Learning Activity 9.6; the **Children's Online Privacy Protection Act of 1998 (COPPA)**, which prevents websites from collecting personally identifiable information from children without parental consent; and **HIPAA**, the **Health Insurance Portability and Accountability Act**, which protects your medical information (and requires you to sign a form at the doctor saying you are aware of their privacy practices). Table 9.3 describes a few of these privacy protection regulations. Note that there are many more privacy regulations around the world that are not included in the table.

Mobile Information Privacy

The threats to information privacy and the related solutions discussed in this chapter apply to most digital environments. However, many researchers have claimed that information privacy is even more of an issue in mobile settings, such as in the use of your smartphone or tablet. Why? Because in the mobile environment, additional information is often being collected without users being aware of this. In addition, the mobile environment has fewer regulations, most users have enormous amounts of personal information on their devices, and users often download apps without considering what the apps can do (Bélanger and Crossler 2013). If you think about

Table 9.3 Sample Privacy Regulations

Law	Source
Children's Internet Protection Act of 2001 (CIPA)	http://www.fcc.gov/guides/childrens -internet-protection-act
Children's Online Privacy Protection Act of 1998 (COPPA)	https://www.ftc.gov/enforcement/ rules/rulemaking-regulatory-reform -proceedings/childrens-online-privacy -protection-rule
Electronic Communications Privacy Act of 1986 (ECPA)	https://epic.org/privacy/ecpa/
Family Educational Rights and Privacy Act (FERPA)	http://www2.ed.gov/policy/gen/guid/fpco/ ferpa/index.html
Gramm-Leach-Bliley Financial Services Modernization Act of 1999 (GLBA)	https://www.ftc.gov/tips-advice/business -center/privacy-and-security/gramm-leach -bliley-act
Health Insurance Portability and Accountability Act (HIPAA)	http://www.hhs.gov/hipaa/index.html

BUSINESS EXAMPLE BOX 9.2

COPPA in Practice

As discussed earlier, COPPA was enacted to protect children's personal information. The law requires that online services or websites in the United States have parental consent before they can collect any **personally identifiable information (PII)** from children below the age of 13. The law was later updated to clarify the scope of what is covered by COPPA (you can find out more by going to the website listed in Table 9.3), which now includes mobile apps.

In August 2017, a lawsuit was filed against the Walt Disney Company, claiming that it was violating COPPA with many of its smartphone apps. The lawsuit alleged that apps like Where's My Water? 2 or Moana Island Life collect information from children (such as location, browsing history, and personal information) without the consent of their parents. The lawsuit includes more than 40 apps. The Federal Trade Commission (FTC) is the regulating agency that can fine companies for such violations. In fact, the FTC had previously fined a Disney subsidiary $3 million for violations to COPPA with online games in 2011.

Source: Ciaccia, C. 2017. "Disney Apps Spying on Children, Lawsuit Claims." *Fox News,* August 9. Retrieved December 23, 2017, from http://www.foxnews.com/tech/2017/08/ 09/disney-apps-spying-on-children-lawsuit-claims.html.

it, most smartphones and smartphone apps collect location information on a constant basis, knowing exactly where the phone is at all times of the day, unless you change the settings to limit this sharing of information. For example, camera apps on your smartphone will tag where and when each picture was taken, creating a trail of where you have been.

Experts suggest that protecting your privacy on your smartphone involves several steps. Here is a list of steps recommended by PrivacyPolicies.org (http://www.privacypolicies.org). First, use only a recognized app download provider (Apple App Store, Google Play, etc.) by using a setting that does not allow downloads from unknown sources. Second, use settings that limit what apps have access to. Third, install security apps on your smartphone, particularly for Android phones (e.g., Bit-defender, F-Secure, etc.). Fourth, secure your lock screen with a PIN or password. Most experts believe a swipe is too easy to break. Fifth, use features like Find My Phone and Remote Wipe to do exactly that: find your phone if you lose it and remote wipe all information if your phone is not returned to you. Finally, don't use public networks, at least for anything important.

Privacy and Ethics

As discussed at the beginning of the chapter, information privacy and confidentiality are not new issues, but the increased use of technology has created new concerns about the use of data, and not only information privacy concerns. In the mid-1980s, Mason (1986) suggested that the increased use of information technologies, which was labeled the Information Age, would lead to four major concerns about the use of information: privacy, accuracy, property, and accessibility (PAPA). Table 9.4 shows the **PAPA framework**. The framework can be used by managers to consider areas of concern about information they handle in their organizations.

LEARNING ACTIVITY 9.7

PAPA, Privacy Policies, and FERPA

This activity is meant to bring together various concepts you have learned throughout the chapter. First, you must review the privacy policies you created earlier in this chapter and the information on FERPA regulations you read earlier. Answer the following questions and be prepared to discuss them in class:

1. How is each element of the PAPA model addressed in the privacy policy? Are any aspects of PAPA not addressed? Which ones (if any)?
2. How is each element of the PAPA model addressed by FERPA? Are any aspects of PAPA not addressed? Which ones (if any)?
3. Explain how the conditions under which a university can disclose information to parents relate to the property element of PAPA.

Table 9.4 PAPA Ethical Framework: For Students

PAPA Component	Description	Questions to Ask Yourself
Privacy	How the confidentiality of the data collected about you is maintained	• What information about you must you reveal to others? • What information should others be able to know about you—with or without your permission? • How is your information protected?
Accuracy	Whether the data about you is what it is supposed to be and does not include errors	• Who is responsible for the accuracy of your information? • Who is accountable for errors about your information? • How do you remedy errors about your information?
Property	Who owns the data about you	• Who owns your information? • Who has the legal rights to your information? • How is the distribution of your information regulated?
Accessibility	Who has access to the information systems and the data that they hold about you	• Who can have access to your information? • Which companies can have access to your information? • What safeguards are in place when someone accesses your information?

Source: Mason (1986).

Ethical Decisions

"A man without ethics is a wild beast unleashed on the world." This quote from the French writer Albert Camus nicely sums up the importance of ethics. While philosophers may argue about the definition of ethics, at its core is the idea of doing the right thing—standards of behavior that tell us how we should act. Since decision making is choosing among alternatives, ethical decision making is considering standards of conduct when making choices. Ethical decision making requires work, as doing the right thing often does. The work is worth the effort. If you always strive to make ethical choices, you will be a success. Many authors have proposed various procedures for making ethical decisions. One of them, the PLUS framework, was originally proposed by the Ethics Resource Center, which is now the Ethics & Compliance Initiative (https://www.ethics.org).

The PLUS framework is a set of questions to help in making ethical decisions. The questions ask whether an alternative

- [P] is consistent with organizational policies, procedures, and guidelines
- [L] is acceptable under applicable laws and regulations

- [U] conforms to universal values such as empathy, integrity, and justice
- [S] satisfies your personal definition of what is good, right, and fair

Keeping the PLUS questions in mind, follow these steps (adapted from the original framework):

1. Define the problem.
    a. Why do you need to make a decision? What outcome do you want from the decision?
    b. Does the current situation violate any PLUS criteria?
2. Identify alternatives.
    a. Try to identify three or more alternatives.
3. Evaluate the alternatives.
    a. What are the positive and negative consequences that flow from each alternative? Consider "positive" and "negative" from the perspective of those impacted by the decision.
    b. How probable is it that those outcomes will occur?
    c. Consider whether each alternative will create or resolve any violations of the PLUS criteria.

LEARNING ACTIVITY 9.8

Making Ethical Decisions

The following scenarios describe some decisions that have ethical issues. For each question, state what decision you would make and why you would make that decision. Be prepared to discuss your answers in class.

1. You need some special software for a school project. The software is available in the school's computer labs, but going to the lab is inconvenient. You can purchase the software at the bookstore, but your friend has the software and is willing to loan you the installation DVDs. Would you borrow the DVDs?
2. One of your coworkers is using his work computer for his part-time business. You become aware of this. Should you report your coworker?
3. You are the chief information officer for your company. As part of your duties, you are in charge of safeguarding data about your customers. The vice president for marketing is interested in trading information about your customers with another company. (In exchange, your company will receive information about the other company's customers.) The marketing VP thinks this trade will increase your company's revenue. Should you provide the customer information?

4. Make the decision.

5. Implement the decision.

   a. Minimize negative consequences to the greatest extent possible.

   b. Communicate the reasoning behind the decision to those affected by the decision.

6. Evaluate the decision.

   a. Did the decision improve the situation that led to the need for the decision?

   b. Were any new problems created by the solution?

   c. Are any PLUS considerations resolved or introduced by the new situation?

If you keep the following in mind throughout the decision-making process, you will be much more likely to make ethical decisions:

- Who are the stakeholders for this decision or its outcomes? Try to think broadly about this. Often, stakeholders may not be readily apparent.

- Could someone be damaged by this decision? If so, consider whether there are alternatives that can reduce this harm. Sometimes your decisions will harm people; tough decisions often do. However, by considering the impact on others and trying to develop ways to minimize the harm, you will often be able to soften the blow.

- What alternatives are available? How do the outcomes from those alternatives impact each stakeholder group? For each alternative, consider which option
  - Produces the greatest good and the least harm
  - Best respects stakeholders' rights
  - Leads you to act as the type of person you want to be

- How can you implement the decision with the greatest attention to stakeholders' concerns? Decisions often have uncomfortable outcomes. This applies to ethical decisions as well. The way in which you carry out the decision can have a significant impact on the level of harm to any individual stakeholder.

While information systems cannot make you an ethical decision maker, they can help reduce some of the extra work that sometimes comes from ethical decision making. For example, suppose you are tasked with cutting expenses for your company. A spreadsheet can help you analyze various alternatives for doing so. Information systems also contain the data and information you may need for developing and analyzing alternative courses of action.

Ethical decision making is worth the effort. Leadership requires followers, and if you always strive to make ethical decisions, the people you lead will trust you to have their interests in mind, even when making difficult decisions. When those you lead trust you, you can be a great leader.

Relationship between Security and Privacy

In the previous chapter, we discussed information security. After reading this chapter on information privacy, you should realize that these concepts are very much related in practice. Security is the protection of information against threats such as unauthorized access to data, falsification of data, or denial of service. A company can provide every security protection possible against these threats to your information without necessarily having the intent of protecting the confidentiality of your information. Thus information privacy is different from information security, even if these concepts are often used interchangeably.

Chapter Summary

In this chapter, we discussed information confidentiality and privacy. We first described the threats to information privacy and the consequences of privacy violations for individuals and organizations. We then discussed the technologies and solutions related to information privacy. We concluded the chapter with a discussion of the PAPA framework and of the relationship between security and privacy.

Here are the main points discussed in the chapter:

- There are four main categories of threats to information privacy: data collection, unauthorized secondary use of data, improper access to data, and errors in data.

- We identified several technologies used to infringe on and/or protect information privacy, such as cookies, cookie managers, privacy statements and policies, trust seals, and government regulations.

- Information privacy is one of the four components of the PAPA ethical framework, which includes privacy, accuracy, property, and accessibility. The framework can be used to identify concerns about the use of information.

- Information privacy and information security are related concepts, since it is mandatory for the information to be secured before it can be private. The reverse is not necessarily true, since information that is protected from a security standpoint can still be shared with others, infringing on the privacy of the information.

- Ethical decision making considers standards of behavior when making decisions.

Review Questions

1. Explain briefly the four main threats to information privacy.
2. What is the difference between opt-in and opt-out options in privacy policies?
3. What are some of the possible consequences of privacy violations?
4. What are cookies, and what should individuals do about them?
5. What is the purpose of privacy policies or statements? Who regulates them?

6. What are the fair information practice principles? What is their purpose?
7. What are privacy seals, and what is their purpose?
8. Briefly describe some of the key regulations protecting information privacy in the United States.
9. What is the PAPA framework? Explain its components. What is its purpose?
10. Describe the PLUS approach to ethical decision making.

Reflection Questions

1. What is the most important thing you learned in this chapter? Why is it important?
2. What topics are unclear? What about them is unclear?
3. Are there any overlaps between the information privacy threats discussed in the chapter and the components of the PAPA framework?
4. How are privacy policies, cookies, and privacy seals related?
5. Imagine a well-known online retailer reveals that a hacker successfully accessed the personal information of 500 of its consumers. Is this a threat to privacy or security for the consumers? Explain.
6. Give examples of five types of data that could be stored in a cookie set up by your university when you browse the main student pages.
7. What is the difference between information privacy and information security? Can one exist without the other?
8. Why are data collection and secondary use of information threats to information privacy?
9. Can businesses be victims of identity theft? Why or why not?
10. How can information and communication technologies help make ethical decisions?

Additional Learning Activities

9.A1. This activity requires you to complete a case analysis regarding information privacy. The case may be accessed through your university website, the Ivey Business School business case website (https://www.iveycases.com), or the Harvard Business School case website (https://cb.hbsp.harvard.edu/cbmp/pages/home), or it may be provided to you by your instructor.

McGee, H., N.-M. Hsieh, and S. McAra. 2016. "Apples: Privacy vs. Safety (A)." *Harvard Business School Case,* February 10. Product number: 9-316-069.

9.A2. This activity allows you to explore two privacy seal programs in greater depth. First, visit five websites and note which privacy seals are common to the websites. Identify trends. Do better sites use particular seals? Then select the two most popular privacy seals and find their websites. Identify the requirements and costs for organizations to participate in each of the two seal programs and create a comparison table that includes whether a fee is charged (high/low), policies for affixing the seal, disclosures required, consumer redress options, and any other important information.

9.A3. This activity requires you to listen to an interesting series of broadcasts on information privacy presented on the National Public Radio's *All Things Considered* program called "The End of Privacy." Listen to each segment and then write a short essay on one of these questions:

a. Is privacy still possible? Why?

b. Is real-time tracking a concern for privacy or a security advantage? Why or why not?

c. Is social networking worth the privacy risks? Why or why not?

d. Can online information about you come back to haunt you? How?

- October 26, 2009—Online Data Present a Privacy Minefield (7 minutes, 49 seconds)
  - http://www.npr.org/templates/story/story.php?storyId=114163862
- October 27, 2009—Is Your Facebook Profile as Private as You Think? (5 minutes, 47 seconds)
  - http://www.npr.org/templates/story/story.php?storyId=114187478&ps=rs
- October 28, 2009—Digital Bread Crumbs: Following Your Cell Phone Trail (7 minutes, 50 seconds)
  - http://www.npr.org/templates/story/story.php?storyId=114241860
- October 29, 2009—Digital Data Make for a Really Permanent Record (7 minutes, 46 seconds)
  - http://www.npr.org/templates/story/story.php?storyId=114276194

9.A4. Select two websites you regularly transact with or send information to. Obtain their privacy policies and map them to the fair information practices and privacy policy contents as done in Table 9.2. Do all privacy policies include the proper content? Explain.

9.A5. Investigate two of the laws discussed in this chapter in greater depth (COPPA, HIPAA, FERPA, etc.). Draw a table that shows how each law addresses the fair information practices principles.

9.A6. Much of the discussion in this text focused on laws and individual behaviors related to privacy that were very United States–centric. Research laws and privacy behaviors for individuals in another part of the world (e.g., Europe, Asia, Africa, and South America). Compare the privacy laws and behaviors of individuals to those discussed in this chapter. How are they the same? How are they different?

9.A7. With the permission of one of your good friends, search the Web to find everything you can about him or her. Then share your findings with your friend. How much information were you able to collect? When adding all the pieces of information together, what have you learned about your friend that you did not know before? How did your friend react to the information you found? Was your friend aware that so much was available about him or her on the Web?

9.A8. Compare and contrast the information privacy threats discussed in the chapter with the components of the PAPA framework. Identify any overlaps and differences.

9.A9. Think of a time when you had to make a decision that was unclear from an ethical perspective. Apply the PLUS model to the decision. Prepare a two-page reflection paper that comments on the following:

- Why the decision was unclear ethically
- The effectiveness of the PLUS model

References

Bélanger, F., and R. E. Crossler. 2011. "Privacy in the Digital Age: A Review of Information Privacy Research in Information Systems." *MIS Quarterly* 35(4): 1017–42.

Bélanger, F., and R. E. Crossler. 2013. "Research in Progress: The Privacy Helper ©2013: A Tool for Mobile Privacy." *Workshop for Information Technology and Systems* (WITS), Milan, Italy.

Bélanger, F., J. S. Hiller, and W. J. Smith. 2002. "Trustworthiness in E-Commerce: The Role of Privacy, Security, and Site Attributes." *Journal of Strategic Information Systems* 11(3/4): 245–70.

Cheskin. 1999. "eCommerce Trust Study." Cheskin Research and Studio Archetype/Sapient, January. http://experiencecurve.com/articles/ecommerceTrustCheskin.pdf.

Cowley, S. 2017. "Equifax Faces Mounting Costs and Investigations from Breach." *New York Times,* November 9. https://www.nytimes.com/2017/11/09/business/equifax-data-breach.html.

Harris Interactive. 2001. "Why Some Companies Are Trusted and Others Are Not: Personal Experience and Knowledge of Company More Important than Glitz."

PR Newswire. http://www.prnewswire.com/news-releases/why-some-companies
-are-trusted-and-others-are-not-personal-experience-and-knowledge-of
-company-more-important-than-glitz-72260317.html.

Hern, A. 2017. "'Anonymous' Browsing Data Can Be Easily Exposed, Researchers
Reveal." *The Guardian,* August 1. Retrieved December 27, 2017, from https://
www.theguardian.com/technology/2017/aug/01/data-browsing-habits-brokers.

Mason, R. O. 1986. "Four Ethical Issues of the Information Age." *MIS Quarterly*
10(1): 5–12.

McGrath, M. 2014. "Target Data Breach Spilled Info on as Many as 70 Million Customers." *Forbes,* January 10. http://www.forbes.com/sites/maggiemcgrath/2014/
01/10/target-data-breach-spilled-info-on-as-many-as-70-million-customers.

Price, E. 2017. "Your 'Anonymous' Browsing Data Is Not Very Anonymous." *Life-
hacker.com,* August 3. Retrieved December 27, 2017, from https://lifehacker.com/
your-anonymous-browsing-data-is-not-very-anonymous-1797490806.

Smith, H. J., S. J. Milberg, and S. J. Burke. 1996. "Information Privacy: Measuring
Individuals' Concerns about Organizational Practices." *MIS Quarterly* 20(2): 167.

Van Slyke, C., and F. Bélanger. 2003. *Electronic Business Technologies.* New York: John
Wiley & Sons.

Whittaker, Z. 2017. "These Were 2017's Biggest Hacks, Leaks, and Data Breaches."
ZDNet, December 18. Retrieved December 22, 2017, from http://www.zdnet
.com/pictures/biggest-hacks-leaks-and-data-breaches-2017/.

Glossary

Accessibility: Refers to who has access to the information systems and the data that they hold.

Accuracy: When data are what they are supposed to be and do not include errors.

Children's Internet Protection Act of 2001 (CIPA): A law that regulates access to offensive content over the Internet on school and library computers.

Children's Online Privacy Protection Act of 1998 (COPPA): A law that prevents websites from collecting personally identifiable information from children without parental consent.

Clickstream data: Tracking of online browsing behaviors.

Cookie manager: A software application that allows you to view which cookies are stored on your computer and what's in them and gives you the ability to delete them.

Cookies: Small text files located on your computer to store information about you, your accounts, and your computer.

Data collection threat: A privacy threat resulting from the fact that data can be collected, aggregated, and analyzed at a faster pace and in larger volumes than ever, without individuals' awareness.

Data Protection Directive: A law that regulates how personal data are processed and protected in the European Union.

Electronic Communications Privacy Act of 1986 (ECPA): A law that regulates access, use, disclosure, interception, and privacy protections of electronic communications.

Errors in data: A privacy threat where there are inaccuracies in data.

Fair information practices (FIP) principles: Guidelines for how to deal with personal information, which include notice/awareness, choice/consent, access/participation, integrity/security, and enforcement/redress.

Family Educational Rights and Privacy Act (FERPA): A law that protects the privacy of student education records.

Federal Trade Commission (FTC): A government agency responsible for (among other things) ensuring that privacy policies are respected.

Gramm-Leach-Bliley Financial Services Modernization Act of 1999 (GLBA): A law that provides regulations to protect consumers' personal financial information held by financial institutions.

Health Insurance Portability and Accountability Act (HIPAA): A law that provides regulations to protect personal health information held by covered entities and gives patients an array of rights with respect to that information.

Identity theft: Using another person's personal information for fraudulent activities.

Improper access to data: A privacy threat where unauthorized individuals have access to one's private information.

Opt in: A privacy option where individuals state they agree that their data can be shared with others or used for other purposes, often to receive special deals or information from partner companies.

Opt out: A privacy option where individuals must state that they do not want their data to be shared with others or used for other purposes.

PAPA framework: A framework that identifies four major categories of concerns about the use of information: privacy, accuracy, property, and accessibility.

Personally identifiable information (PII): Also called sensitive personal information, is defined by U.S. law as any information that can be used to identify, contact, or locate an individual on its own or combined with other information.

Privacy: One's ability to control information about oneself.

Privacy policy: A statement that describes what the organization's practices are with respect to the privacy of its customers.

Privacy seal: A seal that a business can post on its website to show its commitment to privacy.

Property: Refers to who has ownership of the data.

Reputation seal: A seal that a business can post on its website to show its commitment to trustworthiness.

Seal program: A program offered by an organization that posts a set of rules that companies must follow to be a part of the seal program.

Security seal: A seal that a business can post on its website to show its commitment to security.

Self-regulation: An attempt by industry leaders to avoid government regulations by suggesting (rather than requiring) that companies have privacy policies—for example, with privacy seals and privacy policies.

Unauthorized secondary use of information: A privacy threat resulting from the use of data for purposes other than those for which they were originally collected.

SECTION III

Using Information

CHAPTER 10

Developing Information Systems

Learning Objectives

By reading and completing the activities in this chapter, you will be able to

- Explain the benefits of a software development methodology
- List and describe the phases in the traditional systems development life cycle
- Compare and contrast the traditional systems development life cycle with alternative methodologies
- Explain factors that influence the decision to build custom software or purchase commercial, off-the-shelf software
- Define open source software
- Describe major outsourcing models
- List the benefits and risks of outsourcing

Chapter Outline

Focusing Story: The $6 Billion Software Bug

Time, Cost, and Quality

Learning Activity 10.1: Determining Requirements

Software Development Methodologies

Traditional Systems Development Life Cycle

Learning Activity 10.2: Advantages and Disadvantages of the SDLC

Alternative Methodologies

Learning Activity 10.3: Comparing the Methods

Build or Buy Decision

Learning Activity 10.4: How Open Source Software Impacts Build versus Buy

In this chapter, you will gain a basic understanding of the software development process. In addition, the chapter will help you learn about alternatives to building software from scratch. Outsourcing information systems are also discussed.

FOCUSING STORY

The $6 Billion Software Bug

In August 2003, the largest power blackout in North American history hit the northeastern United States and southeastern Canada. More than 50 million people lost power, some for up to two days. At least 11 people died as a result of the blackout. Total cost: $6 billion. Investigators concluded that the initial problem started when a power line in Ohio sagged and hit an overgrown tree. Normally, this is an isolated incident. When such an incident occurs, alarm systems alert power systems operators of the problem so they can take appropriate steps to make sure that the problem remains isolated. Unfortunately, in this case, a software bug caused the alarm system to malfunction. This started a cascade of errors that led to more than 50 million people losing electrical power. The lack of power also led to water supply problems and the shutdown of major transportation systems, including railroads and airlines. Gas stations could not dispense fuel. Cell phone service was interrupted (although wired phones continued working).

While lack of proper maintenance was the root cause of the blackout, without the software bug, the impact would have been small and limited to relatively few people. With the software error, tens of millions of people were affected, and there were billions in economic costs.

There are many other examples of the serious consequences of faulty software:

- In 2017, Dodge Ram recalled 1.25 million Ram trucks due to a software glitch that caused the airbags and seatbelts to fail during a rollover accident.

- In 2017, a major software failure at British Airways caused a significant number of local flights to be canceled and several delays to international flights.

- In 2016, due to a software problem, the radar in the newly developed F-35 fighter jet would crash, leaving a pilot blind until a system reboot was performed.

- In 2013, the Patient Protection and Affordable Care Act (Obamacare) went live, and as millions of Americans accessed the newly created exchange websites, the websites crashed and became nonresponsive. As a result, millions of dollars had to be spent to get the websites working properly.

- In 2004, a software error disrupted communication at Los Angeles International Airport's air traffic control system; 800 flights were disrupted. Fortunately, there were no midair collisions, although there were several near misses.

FOCUSING QUESTIONS

1. Have you ever experienced software that did not operate correctly? What consequences did you experience?
2. What can be done to limit software errors?
3. Why is it important to catch software errors early in the development process?

Time, Cost, and Quality

Every software development project faces a tension among time, cost, and quality. This reality, which applies to all sorts of projects, is known by several names, including the *project triangle,* the *engineering triangle,* and the *design triangle.* The basic idea is that there are trade-offs among the three dimensions. The three constraints are as follows:

- *Time:* How long will the project take to complete?
- *Cost:* What resources are required to complete the project?
- *Quality:* How well does the completed project meet user requirements?

Some versions of the triangle substitute *scope* (what is done as part of the project) for quality. Scope and quality are closely related, especially when considering an overall project. Quality is related to user requirements, and increasing the scope of a software development project adds new requirements that need to be met. So increasing the scope of a project also makes it harder (more costly and/or longer in duration) to meet quality goals.

There is an old saying: "You want it fast, good, and cheap? Pick any two." Increase the speed with which a project is delivered and you will have to compromise on either quality or costs. Decreasing the cost requires a longer completion time or accepting lower quality. It is important to understand these trade-offs when making software development decisions. Typically, one of the three constraints is fixed (for example, you may have a strict budget or delivery date). As a result, the other two constraints must be managed against each other. For example, if you have a fixed budget, moving to an earlier delivery date requires changes in quality or scope. You can learn more about this in relation to project management in Appendices J and K on funding and managing projects.

LEARNING ACTIVITY 10.1

Determining Requirements

Determining system requirements is a major step in the software development process. One method for uncovering requirements is to interview the intended users of the software. Suppose that a club you belong to wants to create a system for keeping track of members. Get in pairs. One of you will act as the interviewer who is trying to discover requirements. The other will act as the user. Document at least 10 requirements for the system.

Software Development Methodologies

Developing software is a complex, time-consuming, and costly endeavor. Because of this, it is often useful to have a framework for planning, structuring, and controlling software development projects. Such frameworks are commonly called **software development methodologies**. These methodologies provide discipline to the software development process by defining processes, roles, and deliverables related to software development. Typically, the methodologies break down software development into phases, each of which has its own set of processes, roles, and deliverables. In some methodologies, the deliverables of one phase provide the inputs for the next phase.

Most large organizations have a standard software development methodology that is used across the organization, although many organizations may allow different methodologies for particular projects. For example, a Web-based system development project may follow a different methodology than a transaction processing system (TPS) development project.

The main reason to use a formal software development methodology is that it provides discipline by clearly defining how the project should proceed, what work should be done, how that work should be done, and what outputs should be produced. Having a standard methodology in an organization also allows individuals to more easily join a project in progress. The standardized roles, processes, documentation, and deliverables make it easier for a new team member to become familiar with what has been done on the project. It also makes it easier for the new member to find relevant information.

Traditional Systems Development Life Cycle

Traditionally, many systems development projects have followed a semisequential, phased approach, which is typically called the **systems development life cycle** (SDLC). The SDLC provides a disciplined approach to systems development. Projects follow a well-defined set of phases that have related objectives, processes, and deliverables. The traditional SDLC is sometimes called the *waterfall method*, since the results of one phase flow as inputs into the next phase. It is important to realize that there are many different versions of the "traditional" SDLC. The differences boil down to how the phases are divided; some versions have more phases than others. The versions with fewer phases collapse multiple phases from the more complex versions into a single phase. In this chapter, we present a relatively typical version with five phases, as shown in Figure 10.1. Note the dashed feedback lines on the left-hand side of the diagram. Sometimes you need to go back and refine an earlier phase based on new information that emerges.

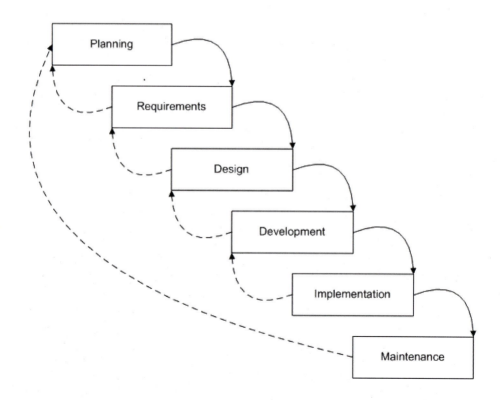

Figure 10.1 Traditional Systems Development Life Cycle

Planning Phase

The goal of the planning stage is to define the overall goal and scope of the system and determine the feasibility of the project. Essentially, you want to answer the question "Why build the system?" In addition, you need to establish whether the project is feasible. There are several different aspects to feasibility:

- *Technical feasibility* concerns whether the proposed system can be completed from a technical standpoint. It is important to consider whether the system fits with the existing technical infrastructure.

- *Economic feasibility* relates to whether the proposed system is affordable and worth the investment.

- *Organizational feasibility* concerns whether the project fits with the organization's existing strategies and practices. If the system does not fit with current ways of operating, the organization needs to determine what needs to be changed and whether these changes are feasible. Organizational feasibility should also consider whether the organization has access to the human resources necessary to complete the project.

- *Legal feasibility* concerns whether the proposed project violates any laws or regulations.

- *Ethical feasibility* considers whether the system fits within the ethical guidelines and practices of the organization and its industry.

The major deliverables of the planning phase are the feasibility analysis, project initiation document, and the project management plan. The project initiation document specifies the high-level goals of the system and describes the business case for the system. (A business case describes the system and why it is needed.) The feasibility analysis results are often included in the business case. The project management plan documents the scope of the project, identifies major tasks and resources, and describes any interrelationships with other projects.

Requirements Phase

The goal of the requirements phase is to uncover and document the functions that the system should provide and desired levels of performance. In other words, in the requirements phase, the task is to figure out and document what the system should do. There are two types of requirements: functional and nonfunctional. **Functional requirements** describe how the system should interact with users and other systems. An example of a functional requirement is "The system shall allow customers to look up the price of a product." **Nonfunctional requirements** are related to constraints on the system—for example, how well it should perform. An example of a nonfunctional requirement is "The system shall be available at least 23 hours per day."

Requirements elicitation involves gathering requirements from various stakeholders and is a primary task in the requirements phase. Gathering the requirements for a system is often a difficult, time-consuming, and error-prone process. To make things worse, requirements may change during the process. Despite the difficulties, it is very important to fully understand the system's requirements; they form the foundation for the rest of the development project.

The output of the requirements phase is a specification of the system's functional and nonfunctional requirements. Typically, this takes the form of a set of requirements statements (sometimes called *system shall* statements) or a set of use cases, in either text or diagram form. A *system shall* statement simply defines a requirement, such as "The system shall allow teachers to enter student grades." A **use case** describes a sequence of actions that results in an outcome for some actor. An actor can be a user or another external system. Figure 10.2 shows a use case diagram. (Use case diagrams are part of the Unified Modeling Language, which was developed as a standard way to specify models related to software systems.)

It is important to understand that requirements should specify *what* the system must do but not *how* the system should meet the requirements. This allows the system designers flexibility in the design of the system, which is covered in the next phase.

Design Phase

The main goal of the design phase is to describe in detail how the system will meet the requirements specified earlier. The requirements form the foundation of the

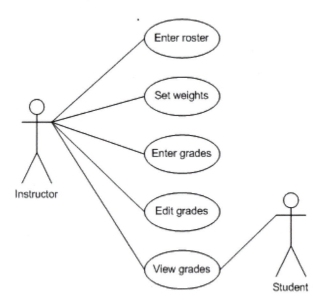

Figure 10.2 Use Case Diagram Example

system design. The focus here is on *how* the system will satisfy the requirements, although there are elements of the design phase that still deal with what the system is intended to do. These elements are known as the *logical system design,* which includes abstract models of what the system is intended to do. An example of such a model is the database diagram we saw in Chapter 5 (Figure 5.4). In addition to the database model, the user interface and business rules enforced by the system need to be designed. The design phase also specifies the plans for implementing and testing the system. The system design document is a major deliverable of the design phase. This document describes, in detail, the system requirements, operating environment, database design, user interface, and processing logic. Other deliverables include an implementation plan and a training plan.

Development Phase

During the development phase, the outputs of the design phase are converted into the actual information system. This is the phase in which the system is actually constructed. The software is written, databases are created, and any necessary hardware is installed. It is often necessary to integrate the new system with existing information systems; if needed, the integration occurs during the development phase. System testing is a critical part of the development phase. Testing occurs both during the development of the software and when the entire system is complete and integrated. Software testing is a complex, time-consuming, but critical aspect of systems development. It is necessary to thoroughly test the system prior to actual implementation. Errors are very expensive to correct when they are not discovered until after the system is implemented. The errors may also lead to business disruptions. The development phase's deliverables include the application software, data and files for testing, and documentation on how the software components interact with one another and external systems.

Implementation Phase

The goal of the implementation phase is to make the system operational in a production environment. One important implementation phase activity is to notify users of the rollout of the new system. This notification should include the implementation schedule, differences in work processes and responsibilities brought about by the new system, and the process for obtaining technical support for the new system. User training is also an important activity in this phase. Often, it is also necessary to convert data from the existing system into the new system. For example, a new product cataloging system might need to have data from the old system migrated into the new system. Finally, it is a good practice to have a postimplementation review that documents the project to date and makes recommendations for improvements for future projects. The main deliverable of the implementation phase is the system itself, installed and running correctly. The postimplementation review report is another deliverable from this phase.

There are four common approaches to system migration:

- *Direct changeover (also called immediate changeover):* At a specific point in time, the old system is no longer used and is replaced by the new system. While this has the advantage of being rapid, it is very risky. If the new system has problems, the functions available in the old system are also unavailable.

- *Parallel operation:* Both the old and new systems operate for some period of time. The parallel approach is less risky than direct changeover but also takes longer and is more expensive. The parallel approach is necessary for systems that cannot be taken out of service while changing from the old to the new system.

- *Phased implementation:* The new system is implemented in stages. This approach is an attractive compromise between direct and parallel approaches. However, it is best suited for systems that have clear modules that can be implemented in a phased manner. Systems with significant interdependencies between modules are not suitable for phased implementation.

- *Pilot operation:* The new system is implemented in a business unit (such as a store or department) or location (such as a state or country). The initial pilot is followed by other pilot changeovers or a full changeover to the new system. Each pilot changeover must use one of the other approaches.

Maintenance Phase

The final phase in the SDLC is the maintenance phase. This is usually the longest, most costly phase of the life cycle. It is not unusual for more than half of the total system cost to occur in the maintenance phase. The goal of this phase is ensuring that the system operates properly to meet current needs. This involves fixing any problems that are uncovered and may also involve modifying or adding to the programs to meet new needs. In addition, the system may be modified to improve performance or take advantage of new technologies. For example, an online ordering system may be modified to allow customers to order from their smartphones.

Although we presented the SDLC as a very linear process, where one phase follows the next in an orderly fashion, reality is rarely so neat. During the systems

---

LEARNING ACTIVITY 10.2

Advantages and Disadvantages of the SDLC

The traditional SDLC has been around for a long time (which is why it is called "traditional") and has been used successfully for many systems development projects. However, it is not without its drawbacks. With a partner, research the SDLC approach and develop a list of three advantages and three disadvantages to the traditional SDLC. Be prepared to share your list.

development process, it is often necessary to revisit an earlier phase when new needs arise or problems are discovered.

As you discovered in Learning Activity 10.2, there are advantages and disadvantages to the traditional SDLC. These drawbacks led to the development of alternative methodologies. In the next section, we describe several of these alternative approaches.

STATS BOX 10.1:
STANDISH CHAOS REPORT

Cancelled information technology (IT) projects and incorrect software cost the global economy billions of dollars each year. The Standish Group's CHAOS Report provides data on the failure rates of IT-related projects. Project outcomes are divided into three categories. Successful projects are delivered on time and on budget and meet requirements. Challenged projects are late, are over budget, and/or do not meet some requirements. Failed projects are cancelled before they are completed or are delivered but not used. For 2013, 16.2% of the IT projects studied were successful, while 52.7% were challenged, and 31.1% failed. For 2016, the success rate of projects had increased to 29%. This is a significant improvement over the first CHAOS Report, which found that only 16% of IT projects were successful, while 53% failed. However, even given the improved success of projects, there are still many causes for software failure. In some cases, the initial estimates of the costs, resources, and delivery date are unrealistic. Other causes include misunderstanding requirements, "feature creep" (expanding requirements), and inadequate testing. The costs of these failures are staggering. One estimate puts the global price tag of IT failure at more than $3 trillion (http://www.zdnet.com/article/worldwide-cost -of-it-failure-revisited-3-trillion/; https://speedandfunction.com/look-25-years -software-projects-can-learn/).

Alternative Methodologies

Prototyping

Prototyping is an approach to deal with aspects of a full methodology; it is not a complete, stand-alone methodology. In a prototyping approach to systems development, you begin with an initial investigation of the main requirements of the system. It is not necessary to have a full understanding of all requirements. After the initial investigation, a small-scale mock-up of the system (called the **prototype**) is built and reviewed by stakeholders. The stakeholders point out flaws, which reveals new or misunderstood requirements. The prototype is refined and reviewed. This cycle repeats until the stakeholders are satisfied that all requirements are met. Then the full system is implemented. Some prototypes are "throwaway" prototypes, which means that they are not intended to be part of the final system; their purpose is to uncover requirements and problems. Sometimes, however, prototypes become part of the final system. This is known as *evolutionary prototyping*.

Increased stakeholder involvement is a major benefit of the prototyping approach. The stakeholders know the particular business area addressed by a system much better than the systems developers, and having them involved throughout the development process can lead to systems that better meet their needs. In addition, stakeholder involvement may increase satisfaction with the final system. Prototyping is also potentially more effective for uncovering system requirements. This is especially important when requirements are unclear, ambiguous, or difficult to define. In some cases, a prototyping approach may be less expensive than a traditional SDLC approach.

There are also drawbacks to the prototyping approach. Prototyping can lead to poorly designed systems that do not perform well when scaled up for actual use. It is also difficult to estimate how many iterations are required, which makes it difficult to estimate costs and schedules. Usually, prototyping results in less-well-documented systems, which may cause problems later (for example, when the system needs to be revised or integrated with new systems). Finally, nonfunctional requirements (such as performance requirements) are difficult to establish using prototypes.

Prototyping is best for systems that require extensive user interaction and for which the analysts have some understanding of the business issues to be addressed, especially when functional requirements are not well understood. Prototyping is less well suited for systems that have well-defined requirements, when nonfunctional requirements are especially important, or when future scalability is important.

Rapid Application Development (RAD)

As the name implies, rapid application development (RAD) is intended to develop systems more quickly than traditional methods. It is an iterative method that uses rapid development of prototypes rather than engaging in extensive up-front planning. RAD typically breaks software development projects into smaller chunks in order to reduce overall project risk. This also facilitates making changes as the project's requirements emerge. The focus is usually on filling organizational needs rather than creating technically perfect systems.

Active user involvement is a key aspect of RAD. The idea is to work with users to determine high-level requirements and then build a prototype based on those requirements. Developers review the prototype with the users, who provide feedback. The prototype is refined based on the feedback. This process continues until the full system is developed. Interestingly, some of the same methods used in the traditional SDLC approach can also be applied in RAD. The RAD process is illustrated in Figure 10.3.

Development tools are integral parts of a RAD system. Computer-aided software engineering (CASE) tools, for example, automate many software design and development tasks. Tools for quickly developing graphical user interfaces are often included in a RAD environment. These tools allow developers to build user interfaces

Figure 10.3 Rapid Application Development (RAD) Cycle

by dragging and dropping interface elements onto a screen instead of having to write the software code.

In addition to delivering systems more quickly than the traditional SDLC, RAD often results in lower costs as well. Because user involvement is such an important aspect of RAD, systems developed using RAD often have greater buy-in from users. RAD also facilitates evolving requirements well. However, the speed of RAD may result in lower-quality software. Because users often want more and more features, "feature creep" may be more likely with RAD. Since there is less focus on nonfunctional requirements, systems may not perform well when scaled to more users or greater volumes of processing.

RAD is best suited for smaller-scale projects with well-focused organizational objectives and committed users. RAD does not work as well for very large projects or systems where performance and quality are critical. For example, you might not want to use RAD for a safety-critical system such as an air traffic control system.

Spiral Model

The spiral model, which is shown in Figure 10.4, is basically an iterative version of the standard "waterfall" SDLC. It is a risk-driven model, which focuses on reducing project risk by identifying risks and ways to reduce those risks throughout the

Figure 10.4 Spiral Model
Adapted from http://www.maxwideman.com/papers/linearity/spiral.htm

development process (Boehm 1988). Think of the development process as trips around the spiral. For each trip, you would perform the same steps:

- *Identify objectives, alternative approaches, and constraints:* Objectives correspond to the requirements we discussed earlier. They may include both functional and non-functional requirements. In addition, alternative means of achieving the objectives are identified. These might include different designs, purchasing the system, and so on. Constraints would include time, resources, costs, and the systems with which the new system must interact.

- *Evaluate the alternatives and identify and resolve risks:* Identifying potential risks is important. These risks are associated with project uncertainties. Developing effective methods for reducing these uncertainties is critical. For example, prototyping may help reduce risks related to misunderstanding functional requirements.

- *Develop and verify the deliverables from this iteration:* The prototype (or other deliverable) from the current iteration is developed and evaluated. Evaluation includes making sure that the prototype meets the current requirements. In early iterations, this may simply be a proof of concept. In later iterations, verification may include detailed testing.

- *Plan the next iteration:* Determine what should be accomplished in the next iteration. Also determine the resources needed.

The spiral model's focus on risk and risk reduction is a major advantage over other methods when developing critical systems. The approach also involves users throughout the process, which can build user commitment to the project. The spiral model allows developers to incorporate other approaches, such as the traditional SDLC and prototyping, when appropriate for individual iterations. Like RAD, the spiral model considers evolving requirements. Effectively using the spiral model requires highly skilled project managers. In addition, it is often difficult to know when to stop. Although originally intended to run for four cycles, there is a temptation to keep going to add more features.

The spiral model is most appropriate for critical systems, where there is a high priority on minimizing risk. It is less appropriate for projects where risk avoidance is not critical and when costs are especially important.

This is just a sampling of some of the more common systems development methodologies. There are many others. Several of these fall into the category of agile development methodologies. *Agile development* occurs in self-managed, cross-functional teams whose members include information systems professionals and user representatives. Rather than being process oriented, agile methods are people oriented. Agile methods emphasize multiple iterations and continuous feedback from user representatives. Many specific methodologies fall into the family of agile methods. These include extreme programming (XP), which uses frequent releases with short development cycles, and Scrum, which features work "sprints" of one to several weeks, at the end of which the development team meets with stakeholders to assess progress and plan what needs to be done next. As software and its uses continue to evolve, we expect that software development methodologies will do the same.

LEARNING ACTIVITY 10.3

Comparing the Methods

Pick one of the alternative software development methodologies described in the chapter. Compare it with the traditional SDLC. Find at least three ways in which they are similar and three ways in which they are different. Be prepared to share your answers.

As you can see, there are many different methods for developing systems; choosing the correct methodology depends on many factors. However, developing a system from scratch is not the only option available when an organization needs a new system. It may be preferable to buy rather than build the system. This choice is the topic of the next section.

App Developers Needed!

You may be aware of companies that only make apps and are very successful at doing so. As the vast majority of consumers own smartphones, the majority of their time is spent using apps specifically designed for their phones, as opposed to visiting sites through the mobile Web browser. This results in an increased demand by organizations for people to design apps for them. Unfortunately, there are not enough app developers available to meet this growing need. In fact, in a survey of 228 application development managers for enterprises, 85% reported that they had a backlog of between 1 and 20 mobile applications. Half of the managers reported that their backlog was between 10 and 20 applications. Furthermore, it can take up to a year to get an app into production. This has resulted in companies not being able to generate as much revenue as they otherwise would if they could create more apps for the marketplace and do so in a timely manner. In a 2017 survey, being a mobile app developer was ranked as the best job in America, with a median annual salary of $97,000 and a 10-year expected job growth of 19%.

Sources: http://techcrunch.com/2014/04/01/mobile-app-usage-increases-in-2014-as-mobile -web-surfing-declines/; http://www.zdnet.com/article/enterprises-we-need-more-mobile -app-developers/; https://www.outsystems.com/blog/2014/10/new-mobile-trend-statistics .html; http://money.cnn.com/gallery/pf/2017/01/05/best-jobs-2017/index.html.

Build or Buy Decision

When the need arises for a new software-based system, managers face a long-standing decision: whether to create the software or purchase existing commercial, off-the-shelf (COTS) software. This decision is complex and costly if you get it wrong. On the surface, it may seem like it is always preferable to purchase an existing system rather than going through the time, cost, and effort of creating a new system. However, the decision is not that easy. Often, the COTS software will need significant customization in order to meet business needs. In these cases, it may be more effective to build a new system. In between the extremes of custom and COTS software lie hybrid approaches. These hybrid approaches involve modifying COTS software to better fit organizational needs or combining COTS components to create the desired solution.

Custom-built software is software that is built from scratch using a few commercially obtained components. The main benefit of the custom approach is that the resulting system will likely be a better fit with business requirements. As a result, the custom system may be used to create a competitive advantage. In addition, the organization will have greater control over adding or modifying functions after the initial system is implemented. However, custom solutions usually take much longer and are more costly to develop than COTS or hybrid solutions. In addition, custom solutions are more prone to errors, which can further increase costs and time to delivery.

COTS software is a complete (or nearly complete) solution obtained from a third party. Examples range from office productivity systems to ERP systems. Often, COTS software is less expensive than custom or hybrid approaches. COTS software may also be higher quality, especially if it is a widely used system. Usually (although not always), COTS-based solutions can be provided in a much shorter time frame than custom or hybrid solutions. There are downsides to COTS software, however. First, COTS software often requires changing existing business practices to fit the COTS software. Second, companies are largely at the mercy of the vendor or consultants for support, including enhancements and fixes. In addition, a financially weak vendor may be unable to provide proper support or maintenance. In extreme cases, the vendor may go out of business.

Hybrid solutions may use components from different vendors to create the complete solution or may involve customizing COTS software by modifying programming code or adding small programs called *scripts*. In ideal cases, the hybrid solutions offer the best of custom and COTS approaches. The hybrid solutions usually better fit business requirements and existing processes but can be delivered less expensively and more quickly than custom solutions. However, hybrid solutions also suffer from some of the same drawbacks as custom-built systems and COTS solutions. In addition, it may be difficult to find the expertise necessary to modify or combine the COTS components. Figure 10.5 provides an overview of some of the characteristics of the three approaches.

When making the build versus buy decision, a number of questions must be addressed:

- *Is there COTS software that will meet the business's needs?* If the answer to this question is no, your choices are narrowed to custom development or a hybrid approach. If no COTS software can meet your organization's needs, you have to create the software or customize COTS software. In these cases, you may have the option of outsourcing the development or customization. (We discuss outsourcing later in this chapter.)

- *Will the software give your company a competitive advantage?* If COTS software is an option, the next question is to consider whether the system will give your company a competitive advantage. If so, the scale is tipped toward building custom software. If not, COTS software may be a better choice. To understand why, think about the example of a hotel chain. To such a company, a payroll system would not be likely to provide any competitive advantage. Payroll is a routine function, so it is a good candidate for COTS software. In contrast, having a custom system for analyzing the behaviors and preferences of frequent guests may give the company an advantage over its competitors and is therefore a better candidate for a custom-built system.

Figure 10.5 Comparing COTS and Custom Development
Source: Adapted from http://www.baselinemag.com/c/a/Application-Development/Buy-vs-Build
-Software-Applications-The-Eternal-Dilemma.

- *Does the COTS software fit with business processes?* COTS software will rarely
  match exactly with existing business processes. As a result, you will usually have
  to modify at least some business processes in order to use COTS software. Often,
  this is not a problem, but sometimes the changes necessary are so extensive that
  it may be better to build a custom system. The key issue is whether it is practical
  to alter existing processes in order to fit the way the COTS software operates.
- *Does the COTS software fit with existing IT architecture and staff?* To be successful,
  COTS software must fit with your organization's existing IT. Here is a simplistic example. Suppose that your organization used only Windows-based PCs.
  Macintosh-only COTS software would not be a good fit with your existing IT.
  It is also important that your IT staff be able to support any COTS software you
  use. If the existing staff cannot provide support, you will need to either contract
  with an outside company for support, train your existing staff, or hire new staff.
  All of these add to the cost and complexity of implementing the COTS software.
- *Do you have the capability to create the required system?* There are times when an
  organization simply does not have the capability to create a system that meets

requirements. In these cases, COTS software is often an attractive option. Outsourcing the development of the system is another option.

- *When is the system needed?* A COTS solution can almost always be implemented faster than a custom-built system. As a result, you should consider the "go-live" goal for the new system when making the build versus buy decision.

- *What is the total cost of ownership for each approach?* Finally, you should compare the total cost of ownership (TCO) for both approaches. The cost of purchasing or building the system is not the only cost you should consider. There are also support and maintenance costs, costs to integrate the system into the existing architecture, and costs related to enhancing the system in the future. One important point to keep in mind is that COTS systems usually are changed much more often than custom-built systems. When the vendor releases a new version of the software, you may incur additional costs related to deploying the new version. Of course, you could stay with the old version, but vendors often drop support for older versions, which may lead to problems.

LEARNING ACTIVITY 10.4

How Open Source Software Impacts Build versus Buy

Open source software is software that provides access to the program's code, which means that it can be freely modified. Often organizations must decide whether to build custom software or purchase a commercial software package. In pairs, discuss how open source software might impact the build versus buy decision. Prepare a bullet list of your findings.

Using Open Source Software in Business

Open source software is software that allows users to access the underlying source code for an application. Having the source code for a program allows users to modify the program's functions. The **source code** is the human-readable form of a software program. Typically, this source code is translated into computer instructions through a process called *compiling*. The compiled code is not in a form that is easily understood by a human. The licensing for open source software also allows users to modify the program, subject to some conditions. The Open Source Initiative provides a detailed definition for "open source" at http://www.opensource.org/docs/osd.

Open source software is usually available free of charge, although it is common for companies to distribute (for a fee) open source software along with support contracts or other enhancements. Open source software has been in existence for many years but has been largely unknown to the general population until recently. The rise of popular open source applications such as Mozilla Firefox (a Web browser), OpenOffice (a productivity suite), and operating and systems software such as the

Linux operating system and Apache Web server have increased the awareness of open source software.

More recently, Google's open source Android operating system has been credited with a rapid rise in the number of smartphones running Android. According to the Nielsen Company, in the second quarter of 2009, Android-based phones accounted for only 1% of the new smartphone purchases in the United States. By November 2010, they accounted for more than 40%. By the end of 2014, more than 75% of the smartphones in use were running the Android operating system (IDC 2014). Some believe that Android's openness is one reason for its rapid rise. The fact that Android was open allowed many smartphone manufacturers to implement Android on their handsets. The manufacturers were also able to modify Android to take advantage of their phone's specific features.

Businesses are adopting open source software for a variety of uses. For many years, the Apache Web server has held more than 50% of the U.S. Web server market. Most large organizations use Linux servers to some extent. According to the Linux Foundation, more than three-quarters of large organizations plan to add more Linux servers in the near future (Linux Foundation 2014). Open source is less popular for personal computer operating systems, with slightly more than 1% of personal computers using Linux. Open source for end users may be on the rise, however. The recent economic downturn has led some organizations to take another look at open source applications. In addition, many governments are actively promoting the use of open source alternatives to proprietary software among both governmental departments and citizens. Time will tell whether this trend continues.

Why would businesses use open source software? There is a variety of reasons. The most obvious is the potential cost savings. Most open source software can be acquired without charge. It is important to note that this does not mean that the software can be implemented without cost. There are ongoing costs associated with installation, support, and continuous training; these costs should not be ignored. Another reason businesses use open source software is to avoid being dependent on proprietary software vendors for ongoing development and support. For example, users of Microsoft Office are completely reliant on Microsoft for current developments (such as fixing errors or enhancing the software). With open source software, the larger community can carry out these functions. This means that continuous development and support are possible even if the creator of the software goes out of business. There is also some evidence that mature open source software is often more reliable than proprietary software. In addition, open source software is more likely to use open standards for things such as file formats. This reduces the reliance on any particular software vendor. Additional flexibility comes from the fact that users have the ability to modify the software as needed. This is not possible with proprietary software. (It should be noted that most users lack the technical skills necessary to modify software, which reduces the value of this benefit.)

One interesting aspect of open source software is that a community of volunteer programmers often does ongoing development. The structure of an open source development community is like an onion. Core developers are at the center, and passive users are at the outermost layer. The core developers do most of the programming for both the original creation and ongoing development. Core developers at outer layers report errors and request features and may also contribute fixes for the errors. Active users also report problems but do not contribute any programming code, and they often help less experienced users in community forums. Thus the community not only supports current users but also provides a platform for ongoing enhancements.

LEARNING ACTIVITY 10.5

What to Outsource

Outsourcing occurs when a company turns to an outside vendor to provide some service. While the definition of outsourcing is easy to understand, deciding what to outsource is much harder. For each of the following business scenarios, decide whether the system or operation should be outsourced. Explain your answer.

Organization	System/Function
1. Engineering company	Payroll and benefits management system
2. Regional beer brewery	Customer relationship management
3. University	Learning management system (e.g., Blackboard, Moodle)
4. Financial portfolio management company	Investment analysis software
5. Public radio station	Donor management system

Outsourcing Information Systems

Information technology **outsourcing** occurs when an organization goes to an outside company to provide IT services that were previously provided internally. (Outsourcing is not unique to IT. For example, some companies outsource the manufacturing of products that they sell.)

Outsourcing Models

There are many different outsourcing models. These differ in the degree of outsourcing and in what is outsourced. Some organizations contract with a service provider to provide all IT-related services. This is known as **full or complete outsourcing**. Full outsourcing allows an organization to focus on its core activities and may also reduce IT costs. Service providers may be able to provide services less expensively due to economies of scale.

In contrast, in **selective or partial outsourcing**, only certain aspects of IT are outsourced to a service provider. For example, AT&T recently outsourced the maintenance of its ERP system to Accenture. There are different approaches to deciding what to outsource. Under **process-based outsourcing**, an organization outsources a particular function or business process. Functions that are often outsourced include help desk support, payroll and benefits processing, and telecommunication services. Outsourcing specific functions is not new. For example, ADP has been providing payroll services to organizations for more than 50 years.

Personnel outsourcing is another form of outsourcing that has a long history. This form of outsourcing allows organizations to meet staffing needs without the long-term costs associated with hiring permanent workers. Bringing in temporary, contract-based workers may be effective when an organization needs specific expertise on a short-term basis or when the current workload is more than the internal IT staff can handle. In these cases, outsourcing can speed time to deployment for a system and avoid costs related to training the current staff.

Another approach is **project-based outsourcing**. As the name implies, this involves contracting with a vendor for a specific project. Since projects have specific start and end points, when the project is finished, the outsourcing engagement ends. Organizations outsource projects when they lack the internal resources necessary to complete the project. Earlier we mentioned outsourcing as an alternative for developing a custom system. This is an example of project-based outsourcing. When the system is developed and deployed, the outsourcing engagement ends. Interestingly, upgrades to the system may lead to future outsourcing engagements.

Application outsourcing involves a service provider handling activities related to a specific software application for a fee. There are different forms of application outsourcing. With application hosting, the client organization is responsible for operating the IT infrastructure associated with the application, but the client must purchase the software and pay any annual license or maintenance payments to the software publisher. Amazon's Web Services is an example of application hosting. Organizations can deploy applications on Amazon's systems. Amazon handles keeping the servers up and running but is not responsible for maintaining the application. This arrangement is often very cost effective, especially when there are demand spikes that may require additional server capacity. Software as a service (SaaS) provides on-demand Web-based access to an application on a per-use or per-user basis. Salesforce .com is a well-known provider of SaaS. Salesforce.com provides organizations with customer relationship management software for a monthly per-user fee. Different features lead to different fees. For example, a simple contact management currently costs $5 per user per month, while a full customer relationship management system costs $125 per user per month. The SaaS model provides a large degree of flexibility and can be cost effective. The client organization does not have to worry about maintaining the software or the servers. SaaS also provides very good scalability. However, there are security and privacy concerns with SaaS.

Benefits and Risks of Outsourcing

Outsourcing, when done well, can result in a variety of benefits. A major benefit of outsourcing is that it can give organizations access to specific expertise not available in-house. There can also be cost savings with outsourcing. These are normally associated with the vendor having lower cost structures, through either economies of scale or lower wage rates. Outsourcing also shifts employee-related fixed costs to variable costs. In addition, outsourcing may allow for more rapid delivery of projects through additional expertise and personnel and can be an effective means of managing capacity. It is generally easier to contract for additional capacity than to add it through other means. Selective outsourcing allows management to focus on core business activities. Finally, when outsourcing sites are spread across time zones, offshore outsourcing can lead to 24-hour productivity.

BUSINESS EXAMPLE BOX 10.2

Reversing the Outsourcing Decision

In 2005, Houston, Texas–based utility Reliant Energy outsourced some of its IT jobs to Accenture. As a result, Reliant cut approximately one-third of its 340 IT jobs. In 2009, Reliant reversed this decision and began hiring IT workers so it could bring the outsourced work back in house. Neither Reliant nor Accenture would comment on the reason for the reversal.

While still relatively rare, there are numerous other examples of "backsourcing" (bringing a previously outsourced function back in house). In 2004, JPMorgan Chase cancelled a multibillion-dollar outsourcing contract with IBM. IBM lost another contract when the UK Automobile Association canceled a £50 million outsourcing contract. In both cases, mergers were cited as the reason for the backsourcing. Poor performance can also cause backsourcing. In 2005, Sears Roebuck cancelled a $1.6 billion contract with Computer Sciences Corporation due to what Sears claimed was a failure to meet obligations. Another example of backsourcing comes from General Motors in 2012, which backsourced its IT from HP by hiring 3,000 HP workers who had been providing outsourced services to GM. This provided GM the ability to hire the expertise back into their company to provide the skills they lost when they chose to outsource their IT department.

Sources: http://www.computerweekly.com/blogs/outsourcing/2013/04/insourcing ---outsourcing-backsourcing.html; http://www.computerweekly.com/news/2240167895/ General-Motors-recruits-3000-HP-IT-workers; http://www.reuters.com/article/2010/ 01/30/urnidgns852573c400693880002576ba006e69d-idUS96268580820100130; http:// www.computerweekly.com/Articles/2007/09/24/226946/AA-cancels-16350m-IBM -outsourcing-contract.htm; http://www.smh.com.au/news/Breaking/Sears-cancels-big -outsourcing-contract/2005/05/20/1116533524145.html.

There are also risks associated with outsourcing. In some cases, outsourcing can lead to a loss of competencies within the organization. This is especially problematic when this loss is related to the core activities of the organization. There are also risks related to the outsourcing relationship. There is a risk of becoming dependent on the service provider, which can lower bargaining power in later negotiations. In addition, there is a danger that the vendor may behave opportunistically and take advantage of the organization's lack of expertise or inadequate monitoring. Risks from opportunism are especially high when the outsourcing contract is not well structured. Outsourcing may also hurt the morale of the remaining workforce. Finally, there are risks related to confidentiality. Outsourcing vendors must ensure that sensitive information is properly protected. This is both a technical and human problem. Even when the proper technical security measures are in place, the employees of the service provider can compromise confidentiality. The benefits and risks of outsourcing are summarized in Table 10.1.

Making the Outsourcing Decision

The decision of whether to outsource is very complex and depends greatly on the particular set of circumstances. However, there are some consistent factors that should be considered (Grover and Teng 1993):

- *How mature is the IT system in question?* Systems that have been around a long time are better candidates for outsourcing. There are several reasons for this. First, if the system is mature, organizations are less likely to be able to gain a competitive advantage from the system. Second, it is easier to find competent vendors for mature systems. This also means that organizations are more likely to have a choice of vendors, which is helpful during negotiations both initially and in the future.

- *How significant is the system to the organization's competitive advantage?* One common reason for outsourcing is to allow the organization to concentrate on core activities. Outsourcing is more suitable for systems that do not provide a

Table 10.1 Benefits and Risks of Outsourcing

Benefits of Outsourcing	Risks of Outsourcing
• Access to expertise not available in-house	• Loss of internal competencies
• Potential cost savings	• Dependence on service provider (lowers bargaining power)
• Shifting fixed costs to variable costs	• Opportunistic behavior by service provider
• Effective way to manage capacity	• Lower morale of remaining workers
• Focus on core activities	• Compromises to confidentiality
• Potential for 24-hour productivity	

competitive advantage. There is also a greater risk of loss of control when you outsource strategic systems; problems with strategic systems usually have serious consequences.

- *How does the organization's IT capability compare with that of its competitors?* In cases where an organization has relatively weak IT capabilities, it may be better to outsource. This is particularly true if the organization is weak in IT related to the system in question.

- *Are there cost advantages to outsourcing?* Of course, the question of costs is also important. Even if there are no savings through outsourcing, it may still be a good idea if outsourcing allows the organization to focus on critical areas or if the organization lacks the necessary capabilities.

Geographic Considerations

Where to outsource is an important aspect of outsourcing. (Note that choosing a vendor is also important, but here we focus on location.) **Offshore outsourcing** involves using a vendor that provides services from a location outside the client organization's region. A U.S. computer manufacturer outsourcing technical support to India is an example of offshore outsourcing. This is often done to reduce costs. Developing countries have much lower wages than developed countries, so offshore outsourcing can be very cost effective. However, there may be a backlash to offshore outsourcing. This can result from customers being upset about jobs sent overseas. Resistance can also come from poor language skills or cultural differences. Language and cultural differences, along with distance, can make offshore outsourcing arrangements difficult to manage.

Nearshore outsourcing is similar to offshore outsourcing. The difference is that nearshore outsourcing occurs close to the client's home location. If a U.S. company outsources to a Canadian firm, this would be a nearshore arrangement. The reduced travel times may make management easier. Cultural and language differences may be reduced, but this is not always the case. A U.S. company outsourcing to Mexico may still face considerable language and cultural barriers. A nearshore arrangement often results when a company wants to gain some of the cost savings of offshore outsourcing while reducing some of the management, language, and cultural difficulties.

Onshore outsourcing is outsourcing to a firm located in the same country. Onshore outsourcing may offer significant cost savings while eliminating the cultural and language barriers of offshore outsourcing. In addition, onshore outsourcing is less likely to bring about a customer backlash, since the jobs are staying in the country. Cost savings result from differences in wage rates for different areas of a country. Wages in rural areas are often considerably lower than in urban areas. As a result, rural onshore outsourcing saves significant money over urban areas and is only slightly more expensive than offshore outsourcing.

Chapter Summary

In this chapter, we discussed various approaches to developing information systems. We began by describing the time, cost, and quality trade-off. Then we talked about different software development methodologies, including the traditional systems development life cycle and its alternatives. We also discussed the build or buy decision and advantages and disadvantages of using open source software. The chapter concluded with a discussion of outsourcing. Here are the main points discussed in the chapter:

- Software development methodologies provide discipline to the development process by defining processes, roles, and deliverables.

- The traditional systems development life cycle (SDLC) is a semisequential, phased approach. There are different versions of the traditional SDLC.

- The SDLC described in this chapter consists of five phases: planning, requirements, development, implementation, and maintenance.

- Alternatives to the traditional SDLC include prototyping, rapid application development, and the spiral model.

- The decision of whether to build custom software or purchase commercial, off-the-shelf software is complex.

- Open source software allows users to access the underlying source code for the application, which allows users to modify the program.

- Open source software is usually free, although some companies charge a fee for ongoing support.

- Outsourcing occurs when an outside organization provides IT services that were previously provided internally.

- Outsourcing models include full (complete), process-based, personnel, project-based, and application outsourcing.

- There are both benefits and risks associated with outsourcing.

- Factors affecting the outsourcing decision include the maturity of the system, the system's significance to the organization's competitive advantage, the organization's IT capability, and cost.

- Offshore outsourcing occurs when an organization receives services from a company outside the organization's geographic region.

- Nearshore outsourcing occurs when an organization receives services from a company within the organization's geographic region but outside its home country.

- Onshore outsourcing occurs when an organization receives services from a company in the same country.

Review Questions

1. What is the major benefit of a software development methodology?
2. What aspects of software development does a methodology specify?
3. Name and briefly describe the phases of the systems development life cycle described in the chapter.
4. Name and briefly describe the aspects of feasibility described in the chapter.
5. Name and describe three alternatives to the traditional SDLC.
6. Name the advantages and disadvantages of each of the software development methodologies described in the chapter.
7. List the advantages and disadvantages of custom; commercial, off-the-shelf (COTS); and hybrid approaches to software.
8. List the main characteristics of custom-built and COTS software.
9. What are the main factors to consider when deciding whether to build or purchase software?
10. Define open source software.
11. What advantages does open source software offer to businesses?
12. List and briefly describe the outsourcing models presented in the chapter.
13. List the major benefits and risks of outsourcing.
14. What factors should organizations consider when deciding whether to outsource?
15. How do offshore, nearshore, and onshore outsourcing differ?

Reflection Questions

1. What is the most important thing you learned in this chapter? Why is it important?
2. What topics are unclear? What about them is unclear?
3. What relationships do you see between what you learned in this chapter and what you have learned in earlier chapters?
4. How is the traditional systems development life cycle related to systems theory? (Recall that you learned about systems theory in Chapter 2.)
5. What is the difference between functional and nonfunctional requirements? Why are they both important? Which do you think is harder to determine? Why?
6. Your organization needs to build a system to help users carry out a business process that is very unique to your organization.
   a. Should your organization build this system from scratch or use a COTS system? Why? What additional information would be helpful in making this decision?

b. Do you think this should be outsourced? Why? What additional information would be helpful in making this decision?

7. Commercial, off-the-shelf (COTS) software is often of higher quality than custom-built software. This is especially true if the COTS software is widely used.

   a. Why might COTS software be of higher quality?

   b. Why would this be more likely if the COTS software is widely used?

8. What ethical issues are related to the decision to outsource a function? Are these issues different for offshore, nearshore, and onshore outsourcing?

9. There have been several instances of software development companies making formerly proprietary software open source. (See http://en.wikipedia.org/wiki/List_of_formerly_proprietary_software for a partial list of proprietary software that has been shifted to open source.) Why would a software development company do this? What would the company potentially gain? What would it potentially lose?

Additional Learning Activities

10.A1. Form groups of two or three:

- One of you (the explainer) will answer the following question: What are the possible consequences of incorrect or poorly stated requirements?

- When the first person finishes, the other person (the questioner) will seek clarification and provides her or his own ideas.

- Record and be prepared to share your answer.

10.A2. You need to recommend a software development methodology for an upcoming project. From the methodologies presented in this chapter, choose a methodology for each of the following projects. Briefly provide the rationale for each choice.

   a. A system for monitoring electrical surges in an electrical power grid. The requirements for the system are well understood. Users will be required to use the system.

   b. A contact management system. The system's potential users are unsure of exactly what they want the system to do. Use of the system will be voluntary.

   c. A relatively small order-tracking system. The objectives of the system are well known, and potential users very much want such a system.

10.A3. For each of the following, recommend whether the organization should build or buy the system in question. Explain your recommendation.

a. A medium-sized company that sells roofing materials to contractors needs a system that will allow customers to check product inventory through a website.

b. A large (Fortune 500) retailer with a large, well-skilled IT department needs a system that will track the purchasing habits of its frequent customers.

c. A large (Fortune 500) defense contractor needs a system that will track payments to vendors.

10.A4. For each of the systems described in Learning Activity 10.A3, what additional information would be useful in making your recommendation? Explain why the information would help in the build versus buy decision.

10.A5. Locate open source alternatives for each of the following:

a. Microsoft Access database management system

b. Microsoft Outlook (email)

c. Adobe Photoshop

d. Salesforce.com customer relationship management system

e. iTunes media player

10.A6. Find two examples of backsourcing (bringing back in house previously outsourced functions or personnel) other than the examples described in the chapter. Provide a brief (one-paragraph) description of each. Include the reason for the backsourcing in your description.

10.A7. Find two examples of outsourcing (other than the examples from the chapter). Provide a brief (one-paragraph) description of the outsourcing arrangement. Include the reason for outsourcing in your description. Also indicate which outsourcing model best describes the example.

References

Boehm, B. 1988. "A Spiral Model of Software Development and Enhancement." *IEEE Computer* 21(5): 61–72.

Grover, V., and J. T. C. Teng. 1993. "The Decision to Outsource Information Systems Function." *Journal of Systems Management* 44(11): 34–38.

IDC. 2014. "Smartphone OS Market Share, Q4 2014." http://www.idc.com/prodserv/smartphone-os-market-share.jsp.

Linux Foundation. 2014. "The Linux Foundation Releases Report Detailing Linux User Trends among World's Largest Companies." http://www.linuxfoundation.org/news-media/announcements/2014/12/linux-foundation-releases-report-detailing-linux-user-trends-among.

Glossary

Application outsourcing: An outsourcing arrangement that involves a service provider handling activities related to a specific software application.

Full or complete outsourcing: Contracting with a service provider to provide all IT-related services.

Functional requirements: Describes how a system should interact with users and other systems.

Nearshore outsourcing: Using a vendor that provides services from a location close the client's location.

Nonfunctional requirements: Constraints on a system.

Offshore outsourcing: Using a vendor that provides services from a location outside the client organization's region.

Onshore outsourcing: Outsourcing to a firm located in the same country.

Open source software: Software that allows users to access the underlying source code for an application.

Outsourcing: An arrangement in which an organization contracts with a service provider to provide IT-related services.

Personnel outsourcing: An outsourcing arrangement in which a service provider places workers into an organization on a temporary contract basis.

Process-based outsourcing: An arrangement in which an organization outsources a particular function or business process.

Project-based outsourcing: An outsourcing arrangement that involves contracting with a service provider to complete a specific project.

Prototype: A small-scale mock-up of a system or a portion of a system.

Requirements elicitation: Gathering system requirements from various stakeholders.

Selective (partial) outsourcing: An outsourcing arrangement in which only certain aspects of IT are outsourced to a service provider.

Software development methodology: A framework for planning, structuring, and controlling software development projects.

Source code: Text-based computer programming language statements that can be read by humans.

Systems development life cycle (SDLC): A semisequential, phased approach to systems development.

Use case: Describes a series of actions that results in an outcome for an actor.

CHAPTER 11

Information-Based Business Processes

Learning Objectives

By reading and completing the activities in this chapter, you will be able to

- Explain what a business process is
- Perform business process modeling
- Discuss the impacts of technology on business processes
- Explain how business process improvement can be achieved with business process reengineering (BPR)

Chapter Outline

References

Further Readings

Glossary

FOCUSING STORY

Improving Processes Is for Everyone!

This book is about information, and many of our examples seem to showcase technology companies. However, when we talk about business processes, or the way things are done in organizations, everyone can benefit from improvements—even companies that are in basic manufacturing industries like the cement industry.

Cemex is a 100-year-old multinational cement corporation based in Monterrey, Mexico. For years, it functioned pretty much like every other cement company, with limited communication among its various plants, constant changes in order information (customers cannot pour concrete in bad weather), and difficulty confirming precise deliveries to customers due to weather, traffic, and labor problems. Needless to say, customer satisfaction is not always high in this industry.

When Lorenzo Zambrano, the grandson of Cemex's founder, was appointed CEO, he looked for ways to improve processes. To handle unpredictable demands and changing conditions, the company realized it needed better real-time communications. It therefore implemented a satellite communication system (which they called Cemexnet) to connect all its cement plants. It also linked all offices via satellite and the Internet and created a central office for coordination. This allowed plants to be constantly aware of fluctuating supply and demand. The second main aspect of the overhaul was to develop a new tracking, scheduling, and routing system (which the company called Dynamic Synchronization of Operations). This logistics application uses GPS transmitters in each delivery truck, allowing dispatchers to allocate trucks to the plants closest to where they are at a given time. With detailed information on traffic conditions, inventory, and the customers' location, trucks can be rerouted as needed. Finally, suppliers, distributors, and customers of Cemex can use an online application to check order status.

The results have been impressive for Cemex: decreased delivery time from 3 hours to 20 minutes (98% of the time), increased customer satisfaction, substantially increased net sales, decreased number of delivery trucks (35% decrease in the first year), and substantial cost savings overall (e.g., fuel, maintenance, and payroll).

FOCUSING QUESTIONS

Identify specific ways in which the new technologies at Cemex changed the following:

1. How customers do business with Cemex

2. How delivery truck drivers do their work

3. How office staff work at Cemex

4. How plant managers handle business at Cemex

Source: Kaplan, S. 2011. "Business Process Improvement at Concrete Co. Cemex." *CIO Magazine,* August 15. http://www.cio.com/article/2441369/process -improvement/business-process-improvement-at-concete-co--cemex.html.

LEARNING ACTIVITY 11.1

How Many Steps in This Process?

The organization you work for sells university-trademarked items to various consumers. It has traditionally sold goods through the bookstore but is now going to sell items (clothing, memorabilia, etc.) online. In this activity, your group represents a team of managers assembled to identify all the steps involved in managing the inventory for supporting the sale of goods online. Identify all the steps and substeps necessary for this to occur. Make a list of all the steps you think of.

What Is a Process?

A **process** is a series of steps or tasks required to achieve a specific goal. In organizations, everything that happens is based on a series of processes or key activities. They are often called *business processes,* but they could more precisely be labeled *organizational processes,* since processes exist not only in businesses but also in government agencies, charities, schools, and other noncommercial organizations. Figure 11.1 shows an example of a process: the process of acquiring materials needed for the production of an enterprise's main goods. It should be noted that while the process appears to be linear, it is not necessarily the case, since several activities can take place at the same time (concurrently).

Processes are not limited to one functional area of the organization. For example, in Figure 11.1, it is likely that a production department will request materials, while an accounting department will pay vendors. This is an important point: processes extend across many organizational boundaries and tend to involve several individuals. Another key characteristic of processes is the **all-or-nothing concept**. This implies that a process needs to be completed or not done at all. Looking again at Figure 11.1, requesting materials requires purchase orders, receiving materials, and so on. The process is not complete if there is no payment request or no payment made.

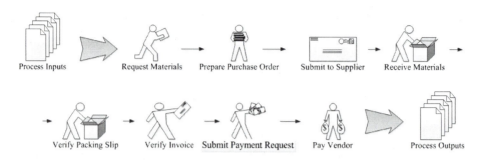

Figure 11.1 Example of a Process to Acquire Materials

Every business process can usually be decomposed into several tasks, also called **subprocesses**. This is because processes usually require several decisions and actions to be made along the way. In general, there can be several levels of subprocesses, all the way down to specific activities or tasks. For example, in the process shown in Figure 11.1, the subprocess of verifying the invoice involves viewing the invoice, viewing the ordering information, and comparing what was ordered with the charges. It can involve making sure that the proper discounts are given, which can require several steps (searching for discounts, comparing quantities, etc.). (See Figure 11.2 for some possible subprocesses.)

Mapping the processes and subprocesses is called *process modeling*, which we describe in more detail below. There are many examples of processes you are familiar with even if you do not realize they are considered processes. Think of course registration. What are the various steps involved? You need to identify the courses required for your program and the requirements for each course. You must then log into the registration system, enter your information, and make the requests. Next, you need to react to those requests that were denied. You can appeal them, try to force-add the course, or decide to take a different course. There are also processes for requesting transcripts, updating your personal information, or for instructors to enter grades, just to name a few.

Process Modeling

Process modeling is the mapping of processes and subprocesses used in an organization or division. Examine the process of acquiring materials needed for the production of an enterprise's main goods in Figure 11.1. Only the steps involved are identified. In process modeling, we need to expand the steps to identify when they are occurring and which decisions are involved. We must also recognize if there are any relationships between processes. The bottom line is that understanding which processes occur at different levels in the organization and how they interrelate is necessary to really understand how an organization works. Figure 11.3 shows a process model for customers acquiring goods from a firm.

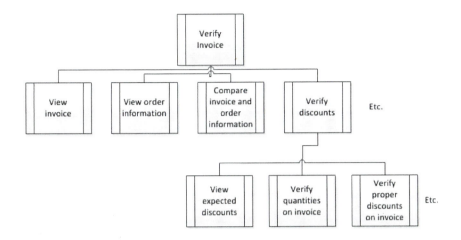

Figure 11.2 Examples of Subprocesses

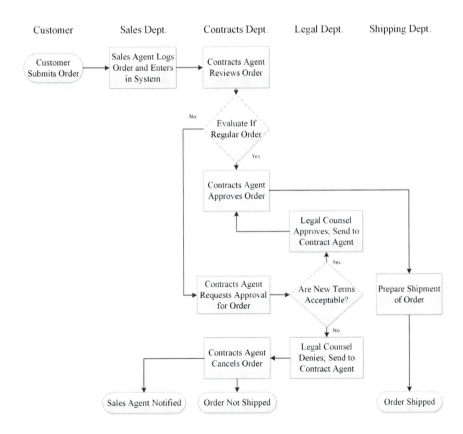

Figure 11.3 Process Model of a Process to Acquire Materials

A process model should clearly describe what happens as a process is performed. As analysts are modeling the processes, they should not analyze the process for improvements (yet); the goal is to describe the process as is. Process modeling can also be explanatory, in that the process modeling effort can identify the rationale for why processes are performed this way. Individual processes can be modeled, although organizations often model several processes simultaneously. Recall that processes are made of several subprocesses, which can also be modeled. As a result, process modeling usually results in "levels" of process models. Figure 11.4 shows a refinement of the order entry subprocess from the process shown in Figure 11.3.

LEARNING ACTIVITY 11.2

Model This!

Following up on Learning Activity 11.1, your group of managers must now model the steps you identified in the inventory management process for your company. Make your process model as complete as possible.

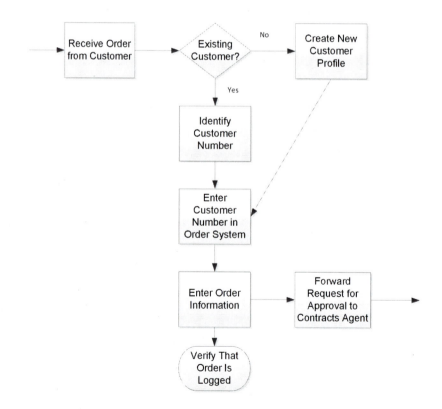

Figure 11.4 A Subprocess Model of Customer Goods Acquisition

Business Process Modeling Tools

There are many **process modeling tools** and software available to help analysts describe business processes and create business process models or diagrams. Mili et al. (2010) identify four types of such tools: traditional process modeling languages, object-oriented modeling languages, dynamic process modeling languages, and process integration languages. Table 11.1 describes these various categories and shows some examples of these languages.

Analysts can become well versed in some of the languages presented in Table 11.1, but to facilitate business process modeling, several companies have developed software specifically targeted at creating business process models. Table 11.2 shows a few of the popular process modeling companies and software.

Table 11.1   Examples of Business Process Modeling Tools

Category of Modeling Tool	Description	Sample Languages
Traditional process modeling languages	Software engineering and information systems modeling languages mostly used in business process engineering	• Event-Driven Process Chains (EPC) • Role Activity Diagrams (RAD) • Resource-Event-Agent (REA) • Architectural Modeling Box for Enterprise Redesign (AMBER)
Object-oriented modeling languages	Process modeling languages supporting the object-oriented approach to software development	• Object-Oriented Role Analysis Methodology (OORAM) • Enterprise Distributed Object Computing (EDOC) • Unified Modeling Language (UML) 1 and 2
Dynamic process modeling languages	Process modeling language standards proposed by various—mostly industrial—organizations	• Workflow Process Description Language (WPDL) • Business Process Modeling Language (BPML) • Web Services Business Process Execution Language (WS-BPEL) • Business Process Modeling Notation (BPMN) • Business Process Definition Metamodel (BPDM)
Process integration languages	Process modeling languages for the purpose of integrating the processes of two or more business partners in electronic business	• RosettaNet • Electronic Business Extensible Markup Language (ebXML) • Web Services Choreography Description Language (WS-CDL)

Source: Mili et al. (2010).

Table 11.2 Sample Business Process Modeling Companies and Software Products

Company	Product	Address
Corel Corporation	DESIGNER Technical Suite 2017	http://www.corel.com
CSG International	Business Support Systems	http://www.csgi.com/
Interfacing Technology	Enterprise Process Center	http://www.interfacing.com
KBSI, Knowledge Based Systems Inc.	Business Process Solutions (several)	http://www.kbsi.com/solutions -and-services/improve-business -processes
Microsoft Corporation	Visio Modeling Software	http://products.office.com/en-us/ visio/
OpenText	Business Process Management	https://www.opentext.com/ what-we-do/products/business -process-management
Oracle Corporation	Oracle Business Process Management	http://www.oracle.com/us/ technologies/bpm/overview/ index.html
Silverrun BPM	Silverrun Modeling Tools	http://www.silverrun.com
Software AG	ARIS Business Process Analysis	http://www.softwareag.com

Technology and Processes

Business processes have existed since organizations started to organize work activities into tasks. Today, however, information technologies play an ever-increasing role not only in how business processes are performed, since technology is embedded in most work environments, but also in how business processes are modified or improved. We discuss business process improvement in the next section. Before we discuss how things can be done better, however, it is important to realize that technology not only enables new business processes but can also be a barrier or constraint to business process improvement.

Think about how much the tasks individuals perform in organizations are dependent on how the technology they use functions. It might be more efficient to input data a certain way, but the system will not let you do it. It could be useful to create a new report, but the system does not allow the data to be collated appropriately. This is even more apparent when we talk about legacy systems. **Legacy systems** are often older, large applications that may be mission critical. They are hard to replace and can be somewhat inflexible. In addition, they are often still used to support key business processes. Even if an organization creates a new, graphically friendlier interface to access information, what can be done with the information can be highly dependent on the type of data warehouse or application performing the back-office processing.

Process Improvement

Once business processes are properly modeled, they can be analyzed for improvement. Business process improvement is an important goal for managers, and it is often labeled **business process reengineering (BPR).** BPR involves the redesign of business processes to improve how work is done, which of course means that BPR requires that business process modeling be done well first. It is important to realize that BPR often involves changing the way tasks are performed instead of just automating the tasks. It requires rethinking about what is done and how it is done (and even whether it should be done!). In one of their books on BPR, Michael Hammer and James Champy (2003) suggest that BPR involves the fundamental rethinking (really asking why an organization performs tasks in a certain way) and radical redesign of business processes (meaning that there is reinvention or re-creation, not just simple minor changes) in order to obtain dramatic improvements in performance (meaning that the goal is to achieve significant improvements for the organizations, whether in terms of cost, efficiency, satisfaction, or other important measures). There are usually four key areas for business process improvement: effectiveness, efficiency, internal control, and compliance. These goals are summarized in Table 11.3.

Summarizing our discussion so far, it is clear that BPR involves several phases, and just like our strategic planning process did in Chapter 4, it starts with a clear vision of the goal of the redesign. It follows with an understanding of what the current processes are, how they work, who performs them, and who uses their outcomes. At the same time, redesign involves rethinking business processes, so analysts should not end up limiting themselves by focusing too much on how things are done as opposed how they should be done. Finally, a very important part of the redesign process is ensuring that there are measurements to make certain that improvements are indeed being made. As you can expect, the BPR effort is an iterative process in which what is done or found in later stages may result in the need to revisit earlier stages. Figure 11.5 shows a sample BPR process.

Table 11.3 Typical Goals for Business Process Reengineering

Effectiveness	The extent to which the outputs of the process are obtained as expected
Efficiency	The average time it takes for the process to be completed
Internal control	The extent to which the information and data used in the performance of the process cannot be changed by error or illegally
Compliance	The extent to which the process follows the regulatory or statutory obligations of the organization

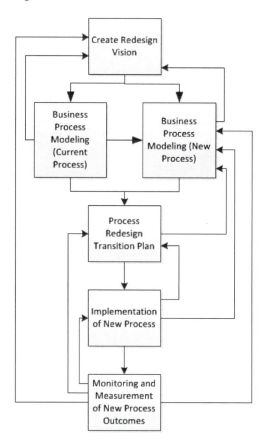

Figure 11.5 Business Process Redesign (Reengineering) Stages

Remember that, in the end, managers performing BPR need to ask themselves key questions such as the following:

- What are our key business processes?
- Do we have to execute each process?
- How can we use information technologies to perform these processes in better ways?
- What are the likely impacts of the business process redesign?

The result of a business process improvement effort should be a document that defines how the new business processes should or could be performed, indicating clear rules and guidelines that the processes must or should follow. For organizations, the results of a redesign of business processes are often streamlined ways of doing business. Figure 11.6 shows an example of the redesign of the business process from Figure 11.4 after the organization offers online ordering.

LEARNING ACTIVITY 11.3

Informal Business Processes

In an organization, there are two types of business processes: official business processes and informal businesses processes. An official business process is one that has been documented and defined, as discussed in this chapter. An informal business process is a process that the business relies on but has not been properly documented. Based on these definitions, one could claim that an official business process is not the same as an informal process. For this learning activity, think about these definitions as you answer the following questions. Have your responses ready for discussion in class.

1. Is it true that these two processes are not always the same?
2. Why is that?
3. Which one should you model? Why?

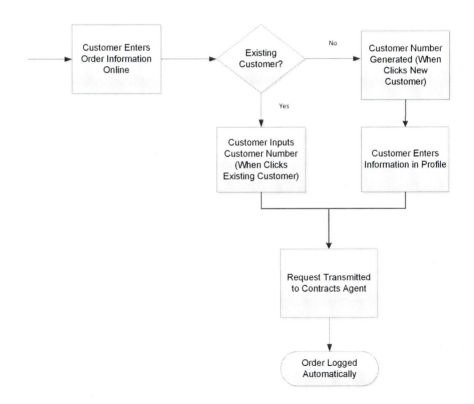

Figure 11.6 Online Ordering Redesign

Levels of Change

In Chapter 4, we introduced the idea that information technology can be implemented in organizations for strategic purposes—in other words, to create competitive advantages. When new information technology (IT) is implemented, it can have differing effects on organizations depending on the role it plays in changing or supporting business processes. One way to categorize these impacts is whether they represent

---

LEARNING ACTIVITY 11.4

Redesign This!

This activity builds on what you have accomplished in Learning Activity 11.3. Now that your team of managers has become more familiar with the inventory management system and has gained knowledge on business process improvement, your team should perform a redesign of the business process model you previously completed.

BUSINESS EXAMPLE BOX 11.1

Quicken Loans Rocket Mortgage: Moving the Mortgage Process Online

At some point many students will eventually purchase a home. In order to do so, they will likely take out a mortgage, as this is a very large purchase. The traditional way of completing this process has been very paperwork intensive: applicants need to provide mortgage lenders with two years or more of tax documentation, two months of bank statements, credit statements, paper applications, and more. Needless to say, this process is very time consuming.

To solve this situation, Quicken Loans created a product called Rocket Mortgage. They embraced the concept of financial technology (fintech) and moved this process online. While mortgage lenders still need the same information as they did before, Quicken realized that much of this could be provided seamlessly online. They claim that in only eight minutes, a person can apply for a loan using either the Rocket Mortgage app or their website. Getting the new loan may still take the same amount of time as a traditional mortgage given other processes that require in-person services like appraisals. However, the amount of time to refinance a mortgage is greatly decreased and applying for the mortgage is simpler. As technologies are increasingly looked at to improve processes, further improvements in the financial industry are also likely to occur.

Source: https://www.forbes.com/sites/markgreene/2016/02/14/will-rocket-mortgage -flameout/.

changes that automate, informate, or transform organizations (Dehning, Richardson, and Zmud 2003; Schein 1992).

- *Automate,* also called *first-order change,* involves using technology to perform a process more efficiently, often by replacing human labor with technology. It is usually fairly easy to justify because managers can quantify the benefits (e.g., reduced wages, reduced errors).

- *Informate,* also called *second-order change,* involves using technology to better inform people, which as a result can change how they perform business processes. Whenever people have to change how they perform business processes, it is more difficult to implement systems. Recall from our earlier discussions that people often resist technology implementations when they have to change their work habits.

- *Transform,* also called *third-order change,* requires a fundamental redefinition of the business processes, or how work is done. Obviously, since business process reengineering (BPR) involves the redesign of business processes, it is a third-order change. This is the most difficult level of change to deal with when implementing information systems.

Chapter Summary

In this chapter, we explained in greater depth what business processes are, how they can be modeled, and how organizations seek to improve business processes through business process reengineering (BPR). Here are the main points discussed in the chapter:

- A business process is a series of steps or tasks required to achieve a specific business goal of an organization.

- Business process modeling is the mapping of processes and subprocesses used in an organization or division. We demonstrated business process modeling with graphic models of a materials acquisition process and its subprocesses. Business process modeling helps us understand the various processes that occur at different levels in the organization and how they interrelate.

- Technology impacts business processes because it is embedded in how work is done in most work environments. Technology could be a constraint to business processes, especially when legacy systems are involved.

- Business process improvement can be achieved with business process reengineering (BPR), which involves the redesign of business processes to improve how work is done. BPR often involves changing the way tasks are performed instead of just automating the tasks. There are usually four key areas for business process improvement: effectiveness, efficiency, internal control, and compliance.

Review Questions

1. Explain what a business process is and give an example from your school environment.
2. Identify some of the important characteristics of processes.
3. What is business process modeling, and what is the purpose of business process modeling?
4. Identify some of the important characteristics of a process model.
5. What kinds of tools are available for business process modeling?
6. How does technology impact business processes?
7. What is business process reengineering (BPR), and what does it involve?
8. What are the four key areas for business process improvement?
9. Briefly explain the main steps involved in performing business process redesign.
10. What are some of the results expected from a business redesign effort?

Reflection Questions

1. What is the most important thing you learned in this chapter? Why is it important?
2. What topics are unclear? What about them is unclear?
3. Identify all the processes a student encounters during the first week of class as a freshman.
4. How does the business process-related material in this chapter relate to the security topics in Chapter 8?
5. How does the business process-related material in this chapter relate to the privacy topics in Chapter 9?
6. Can all business processes be redesigned? Why or why not?
7. What are the similarities and differences between process modeling as discussed in this chapter and data modeling as discussed in Chapter 5?
8. Should informal business processes (representing how things are really done, even if they do not follow recognized or documented procedures) be modeled or just formalized business processes (those documented by the organization)?
9. What is an example of technology being a barrier to redesign in a school setting?
10. Why do you think business process reengineering is an important concern for CIOs?

Additional Learning Activities

11.A1. This activity allows you to get some additional practice at business process redesign. First, you need to download the template of one of the business processes (your instructor will tell you which one) from Global 360: http://www.global360.com/process-templates/. In small groups, examine the template and then, with business process redesign in mind, modify the business process you downloaded to improve it.

11.A2. This activity requires you to complete a case analysis regarding business processes. The case may be accessed through your university website, the Ivey Business School business case website (https://www.iveycases.com), or the Harvard Business School cases website (http://cb.hbsp.harvard.edu/cbmp/pages/home), or it may be provided to you by your instructor.

Sousa, K. 2017. "BrightView Plumbing and Heating: A New Business Model." *Ivey School of Business,* August 17. Product number: 9B17D012.

11.A3. Examine Figure 11.2, identify one of the subprocesses of the order entry process, and model it, as was done in Figure 11.4 for the order entry part in the sales department.

11.A4. Select one of the key processes needed at your school and model it. You can select one from the following list or you can identify another important process and model it:

- Class registration
- Final grade assignment
- Student enrollment
- Tuition payment
- Requesting transcripts

11.A5. Use the process modeling tools in the Visio software to create your models in Learning Activities 11.A3 or 11.A4.

References

Dehning, B., V. J. Richardson, and R. W. Zmud. 2003, December. "The Value Relevance of Announcements of Transformational Information Technology Investments." *MIS Quarterly* 27(4): 637–56.

Hammer, M., and J. Champy. 2003. *Reengineering the Corporation: A Manifesto for Business Revolution.* New York: HarperCollins.

Mili, H., G. Tremblay, G. Bou Jaoude, É. Lefebvre, L. Elabed, and G. El Boussaidi. 2010, November. "Business Process Modeling Languages: Sorting through the Alphabet Soup." *ACM Computing Surveys* 43(1): 7–62.

Schein, E. H. 1992. "The Role of the CEO in the Management of Change: The Case of Information Technology." In *Transforming Organizations,* edited by T. A. Kochan and M. Useem, 325–45. Oxford: Oxford University Press.

Glossary

All-or-nothing concept: The idea that a process needs to be completed or not done at all.

Business process reengineering (BPR): The redesign of business processes to improve how work is done.

Compliance: A BPR goal that involves the extent to which the process follows the regulatory or statutory obligations of the organization.

Dynamic process modeling languages: Process modeling language standards proposed by various (mostly industrial) organizations.

Effectiveness: A BPR goal that involves the extent to which the expected outputs of the process are obtained as expected.

Efficiency: A BPR goal that looks at the average time it takes for the process to be completed.

Internal control: A BPR goal that involves the extent to which the information and data used in the performance of the process cannot be changed by error or illegally.

Legacy systems: Older, large applications that may be mission critical.

Object-oriented languages: Process modeling languages supporting the object-oriented approach to software development.

Process: A series of steps or tasks required to achieve a specific goal.

Process integration languages: Process modeling languages for the purpose of integrating the processes of two or more business partners in electronic business.

Process modeling: Mapping of processes and subprocesses used in an organization or division.

Process modeling tool: Tools and software available to help analysts describe business processes and create business process models or diagrams.

Subprocesses: Decomposition of business processes into several tasks.

Traditional process modeling languages: Software engineering and information systems modeling languages mostly used in business process engineering.

CHAPTER 12

Enterprise Information Systems

Learning Objectives

By reading and completing the activities in this chapter, you will be able to

- Identify the main characteristics and types of enterprise systems
- Discuss the purposes of enterprise resource planning (ERP) systems
- Explain the purposes and functioning of supply chain management (SCM) systems
- Identify the components of customer relationship management (CRM) systems
- Apply the customer life cycle concepts to CRM

Chapter Outline

Focusing Story: Supply Chain Innovations at Wal-Mart

Learning Activity 12.1: Finding the Components of an Enterprise System

Enterprise Systems

Enterprise Resource Planning (ERP)

Learning Activity 12.2: The Online Beer Game

Supply Chain Management Systems

Learning Activity 12.3: Blockchain and Supply Chain Management

Learning Activity 12.4: Customer Relationship Management

Customer Relationship Management Systems

Learning Activity 12.5: Self-Servicing

Customer-Managed Interactions (CMI)

Warehouse Automation and Robotics

Chapter Summary

Review Questions

Reflection Questions

Additional Learning Activities

References

Further Readings

Glossary

This chapter is about enterprise systems, which are systems that are used by a large number of individuals throughout an organization. We will discuss various ways enterprise systems are developed and explore several such systems. One of these enterprise applications is supply chain management (SCM), which is the topic of interest in the focusing study.

FOCUSING STORY

Supply Chain Innovations at Wal-Mart

You need a new pair of inexpensive jeans or maybe just a new set of travel speakers for your iPhone. Where would you go to buy these? Many students would turn to a local Wal-Mart store, since the company is well known throughout the world as a low-cost retailer of goods. What makes it possible for the company to offer prices that often seem to be well below what competitors can afford to offer? Of course, there are many answers to this, but one of the most important factors is how Wal-Mart manages the way it gets the products sold in its stores. This is the supply chain. Wal-Mart calls this the *productivity loop:* lower-cost products lead to lower prices for consumers, which lead to more sales, which increase profits, and then it repeats the loop as quickly as possible. However, there are many other benefits for Wal-Mart and its partners in the supply chain, as explained below.

Wal-Mart is well known for its innovative strategies regarding its supply chain and its tight management of its distribution channels. By 2010, Wal-Mart had established four very large global merchandising centers that are responsible for ordering goods and clothing products (also called *sourcing*) for the company's stores in 15 countries. It also uses direct purchasing of fresh fruits and vegetables from producers on a global basis, bypassing traditional suppliers.

Wal-Mart's supply chain strategies cover many aspects, but in a speech given at the Council of Supply Chain Management Professionals (CSCMP) annual conference in 2009, Gary Maxwell, then senior vice president of international supply at Wal-Mart, explained that effective inventory management may be the most critical element to master for an efficient supply chain.

To improve the effectiveness of its supply chain, Wal-Mart mandated in 2003 that its largest suppliers use **RFID (radio-frequency identification) tags**. This required suppliers to insert electronic tags into pallets of goods to be shipped to Wal-Mart. Using readers, both Wal-Mart and the supplier can then track the pallets as they move through the various distribution centers all the way to the store. Wal-Mart has been a leader in the development of the RFID technology. However, while it has successfully reduced out-of-stock items (8% worldwide) and improved its overall inventory data (it can resupply three times faster), the adoption of the technology was slower than expected. For many companies, the cost was quite high (from US$100,000 to US$300,000 for small companies to US$20 million for larger ones). In 2003, first-generation chips sold for US$1.25 each. In 2009, second-generation chips cost 7¢ to 10¢. By late 2008, 600 of Wal-Mart's 60,000 suppliers, plus 750 Sam's Club (owned by Wal-Mart) suppliers, deployed RFID to some degree. On Wal-Mart's end, RFID is deployed at about 1,000 of the roughly 4,000 Wal-Mart and Sam's Club stores in the United States.

Today, suppliers and Wal-Mart reap many other benefits from RFID, such as knowing in real time how long it takes for items in the promotional areas of stores to sell. They can even evaluate where in the store items sell better. This is a win-win situation for Wal-Mart and its suppliers. Some suppliers have even built the use of RFID tags into their whole information technology (IT) infrastructure, from acquisition to sales to replenishment.

Further innovations to Wal-Mart's supply chain have allowed them to compete better with Amazon.com in the e-commerce marketplace. These innovations include requiring suppliers to deliver orders to Wal-Mart within a one-day window as opposed to the prior four-day window. This allows Wal-Mart to carry less inventory and react quicker to the marketplace. However, in order to successfully work with their suppliers, Wal-Mart had to increase their ability to forecast demand and integrate this insight into their suppliers supply chain.

Wal-Mart continuously strives to innovate in its supply chain. Its most recent effort is convincing its suppliers that reducing gas emissions and becoming more "green" in their delivery of products to Wal-Mart can result in profitability and sustainability. Wal-Mart is asking some suppliers to report how much energy they use in manufacturing the products Wal-Mart buys from them and requires them to meet stricter quality and environmental standards.

FOCUSING QUESTIONS

1. What do you believe are the key success factors for the supply chain implementation at Wal-Mart? What would those factors be for other companies trying to imitate Wal-Mart's supply chain efforts?

2. What is your assessment of Wal-Mart's move into RFID technology as a leader? Could there be an issue being at the leading edge of technology?

3. How can technology be used to help Wal-Mart in its next endeavor—its green supply chain?

Sources: Compiled from Berman, J. October 2009. "Wal-Mart's Maxwell Cites Keys to Developing Best-in-Market Global Supply Chains." *Logistics Management*

48(10): 18; Birchall, J. 2010. "Wal-Mart Takes Aim at Supply Chain Cost." *Financial Times,* January 4: 1; Cassidy, W. B. 2010. "Wal-Mart Squeezes Costs from Supply Chain." *Journal of Commerce,* January 5; Lopez, E. 2017. "Behind the Scenes of Walmart's New On-Time, In-Full Policy." Supply Chain Dive. https://www.supplychaindive.com/news/Walmart-OTIF-inventory-flow-ecommerce-supply-chain/507301/; McCrea, B. 2010, March. "This Is Why 'Green' Equals Good Business." *Supply Chain Management Review* 14(2): 56; Webster, J. S. 2008. "Wal-Mart's RFID Revolution a Tough Sell." *Network World* 25(36): 34–36.

LEARNING ACTIVITY 12.1

Finding the Components of an Enterprise System

The supply chain management system at Wal-Mart represents only one type of enterprise system companies can use for running their businesses efficiently. One of the most popular enterprise systems in organizations is enterprise resource planning (ERP). We will discuss enterprise systems and ERP later, but for now, we want you to identify the components of an ERP system offered by the one of the larger companies, such as SAP, Oracle PeopleSoft, or Microsoft Dynamics.

Please prepare a short report for class that identifies the company that sells the ERP system, a brief background on the company, the components of the ERP system, and a brief description of each component. The report should be fewer than two pages long.

Enterprise Systems

Personal versus Enterprise Systems

There are many information system applications used by individuals and companies to perform tasks. For example, if you think of applications you use that are for individuals only, you might find that Quicken is used to manage your finances or that Microsoft Word is used to write your term papers. Those are considered **personal information systems.** Conversely, **enterprise systems** are information systems that serve the needs of the organization or parts of the organization. For example, the organization may use SAP's enterprise resource planning (ERP) applications to manage its finances, including paying bills, receiving invoices, and paying employees. In Learning Activity 12.1, you identified many other components of an ERP system. As you recall, many modules are available to perform functions needed across several departments in the organization.

Three perspectives on developing enterprise systems have emerged: the hierarchical perspective, the functional perspective, and the process perspective (Piccoli 2008).

In the **hierarchical perspective**, software developers build information systems to mirror the organization so that applications are built to meet the needs of individuals at a given level in the organization. The idea is that executives need strategic types of information they can use for decision making, whereas middle managers and front-line managers need tactical and operational information, respectively. Table 12.1 shows the type of information needed at each level and the characteristics of that information, which is also reproduced in Figure 12.1.

As a result, systems are built for operations, tactical, or strategic management, with sometimes limited interaction and consistency across these systems. Redundancy is also a problem, with different systems sometimes performing fairly similar functions.

In the **functional perspective,** information system applications are developed to meet the needs of individuals in a functional area, such as human resources or marketing. With this perspective, information system developers build a "financial" system, a "marketing" system, a "production" system, or a "human resources" system. The systems tend to serve the functional area well, as they are customized to the needs of the department. Again, when thinking about the various functional areas in an organization (often called *departments*), you can see that information system applications built this way could result in redundancy and inaccuracy of data. (Think of having to update customer information in five different departments.) This perspective also limits communication across functional areas.

Finally, in the **process perspective,** information systems applications are developed to support the task being done (or process) irrespective of the organizational level or functional area of the individual using the system. A *process* is a series of steps required to perform a task.

Integration and Enterprise Systems

The discussion of the three perspectives for the development of enterprise systems highlights some of the issues that arise when systems are not developed with the organization as a whole in mind. In particular, we discussed the issues of redundancy (identical data stored in multiple locations) and lack of communication across departments. To solve these problems, the process perspective focuses on integration. Integration is the unifying, or joining together, of resources and assets. This is clearly

Table 12.1 Types of Information Required by Hierarchical Level

Activity	Time Horizon	Hierarchical Level	Characteristics
Strategic	Long term	General management Functional management	• Externally focused • Highly unstructured
Tactical	Mid term	Middle management	• Semistructured • Recurrent
Operational	Short term	Operation management Employees	• Highly structured • Transaction focused

Source: Adapted from Piccoli (2008).

Figure 12.1 Hierarchical Information Systems

one of the primary advantages of enterprise systems, which are designed to integrate either across business processes or across information systems.

Business integration is the unification of business processes previously performed as separate activities in order to create cohesive and streamlined business processes. In other words, business integration refers to ensuring that processes are performed the best way they can be, without having barriers along the functional areas (departments) or hierarchical levels. This is accomplished by making sure the processes are performed at the best location and by allowing access to everyone who needs the information. This is also called **data integration**. Examples of enterprise systems that provide business integration include customer relationship management (CRM) and enterprise knowledge management. **Systems integration** is the unification of information systems and databases that were previously operating as separate systems. Systems integration focuses on the technological components of information systems. Examples of enterprise systems that are used for systems integration include enterprise resource planning (ERP), content management systems (CMSs), supply chain management (SCM), unified communications, and enterprise application integration. As you can see, most enterprise systems are designed to facilitate the flow of information among all business functions inside the boundaries of the organization and to manage connections to outside stakeholders. A brief description of some of these enterprise systems is provided in Table 12.2. The three most popular (ERP, SCM, and CRM) are further described in the chapter.

Characteristics of Enterprise Systems

The enterprise systems presented in Table 12.2 have some common characteristics. First, many of these systems are modular. This means that an organization can

Table 12.2 Examples of Enterprise Information Systems

Tool	Description
Customer relationship management (CRM)	An organization-wide strategy for managing an organization's multiple interactions with customers. It allows organizations to attract, retain, and manage customer relationships—for example, by offering personalized services and self-servicing tools. It also allows an organization to analyze customer data to find its most profitable products, services, and customers. It involves both technology and a philosophy of customer service.
Enterprise knowledge management (also called business intelligence [BI])	A set of tools used to analyze business data to find trends, issues, and opportunities. Companies have accumulated large amounts of data, such as sales, revenues, or expenses, to name a few, and BI tools show various views of these data to help decision makers. BI tools include a wide variety of analysis approaches, such as online analytical processing, business analytics, or data and text mining.
Enterprise resource planning (ERP)	ERP software allows organizations to manage resources throughout the organization, independently of which business function controls the resource. Typical modules in ERP software include financial management, order processing, or human resources management.
Content management systems (CMSs)	CMS applications allow companies to manage the vast amounts of information of various types (content) they have stored. This includes the capture, storing, preservation, and delivery of content. CMS refers to technologies, strategies, and approaches to managing content.
Unified communications (UC)	UC is a framework for the integration of the various modes of communication used by an organization, including email, voice mail, videoconferencing, instant messaging, texting, and voice over IP. For example, a customer may leave a voice mail that is automatically sent as an email to the account representative (based on preferences). Similarly, instead of sending an email, the voice mail can be transferred immediately to an instant message if the representative is currently online.
Enterprise application integration (EAI)	EAI is a set of tools and services (a framework instead of a single technology) to allow various enterprise systems (such as ERP or CRM) to share the data. It makes use of middleware (see Chapter 7) to perform this communication.
Supply chain management (SCM) systems	SCM software helps organizations manage the movement of materials or products from provision to production to consumption. SCM involves collaboration between partners both upstream and downstream from the focal organization. (Upstream and downstream flows are shown in Figure 12.3.)

Sources: Adapted from Pearlson and Saunders (2010); Piccoli (2008); Wikipedia.com.

implement the "pieces" it needs one at a time. By implementing modules as needed, the organization can limit its efforts and costs and limit disruptions for employees. However, because the modules are designed to be integrated with one another, they function more efficiently together. This concept, called **application integration,** works because an event that occurs in one module automatically triggers events in one or more of the other modules. In addition, because data are stored in one central database, by offering data integration, companies avoid the data redundancy and inaccuracy issues found in hierarchical or functional information systems.

Enterprise Resource Planning (ERP)

As previously discussed, an **enterprise resource planning (ERP)** system is a set of information systems tools that are used to manage an organization's resources and enable information to flow within and between processes (and departments). Before ERP, organizations developed different applications to manage the information processing and management needs of the different functional areas of the organization. With ERP, various modules offer integrated management of these resources. Typical modules in ERP systems include financials (accounts receivable, general ledger, accounts payable, etc.), distribution services, human resources, and product life cycle management (marketing). Some ERP systems also include other enterprise systems applications, such as customer relationship management (CRM), supply chain management (SCM), and warehouse management systems (WMS).

Like other enterprise systems, ERP applications are built on a centralized database, as shown in Figure 12.2, and offer system and business integration. The ERP system itself can reside on a centralized server, or it can be distributed across modular hardware and software units that are interconnected. Many vendors offer commercial ERP packages (such as SAP, Oracle PeopleSoft, and Microsoft Dynamics) that tend to include the collective experience of its consultants. As a result, such packages are said to include best practices from the industry. However, the biggest challenge with ERP systems is to customize them to the needs of the organization and to the computing platforms used within the organization.

Benefits and Disadvantages of ERP Systems

There are many benefits for organizations that successfully implement an ERP system. Efficiency is the most important of these, as it is quantifiable. Efficiency is achieved because ERP systems can reduce data redundancy (reduce direct costs of operation), improve communication (reduce indirect costs of operation through the streamlining of business processes), and in general allow complex systems to work together in an integrated fashion (also streamlining business operations and making sure tasks are performed in a standardized way). If properly implemented, ERP systems can also offer responsiveness to various stakeholders, including customers and suppliers, by providing more accurate information and more rapid responses

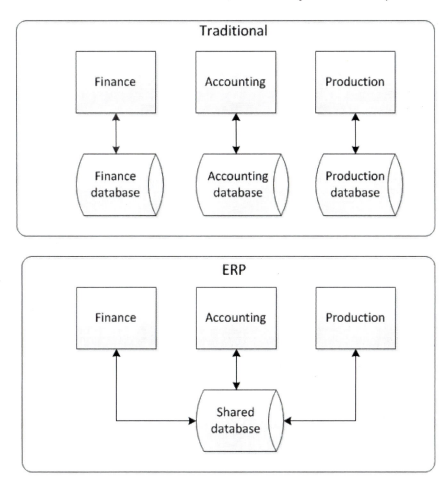

Figure 12.2 ERP Shared Database

to demands. ERP systems are also adaptable, since they can be configured to fit the organization's needs. However, when an ERP system becomes too customized, it can lose some of the advantages of integration and standardization offered by the standard packages. Finally, ERP systems benefit from the expertise of ERP software vendors and consultants who, through experience implementing many of these systems over the years, have embedded into their software packages the state-of-the-art processes used in an industry.

ERP systems also suffer from a number of significant disadvantages. First, they represent an enormous amount of work and very high costs. Because most organizations do not use directly "off-the-shelf" applications but instead customize them substantially, ERP implementations can take anywhere from six months (for a few modules) to six years (for a full implementation). There are even stories of implementations lasting up to 12 years. One study reveals that in recent implementations of ERP, 72% of organizations said the implementation took longer than expected (Panorama Consulting Group 2017). Costs of ERP implementations vary depending on the size of the implementation, from a few hundred thousand (US) dollars to many millions. One reason implementing an ERP system is not as simple as loading the software is that it involves changing the way business is done. Business processes that have been in place for a long time may need to be redesigned. Users accustomed to the old way of doing business may offer significant resistance to an ERP implementation. Departments that have to relinquish control of some data or applications may also be resistant to the implementation. The bottom line is that an ERP implementation is often risky and complex, but the benefits can be substantial and worth the effort.

A recent study confirms that the typical disadvantages of ERP implementations still exist. The study shows that ERP implementations take longer and cost more than expected and underdeliver business value. The study also reveals that organizations do not do a good job managing the organizational changes that result from an ERP implementation (Panorama Consulting Group 2017). Why is it that many ERP implementations are so difficult? Because, as we said, they often involve changes in processes and people's jobs; they therefore represent a third-order change (Chapter 11). In addition, they are often very large in scope and may require more customization than initially expected. Finally, ERP implementations require a strong champion, a person who believes enough in the implementation to see it through many obstacles and years of effort.

LEARNING ACTIVITY 12.2

The Online Beer Game

As seen in the focusing story, supply chain systems are very important enterprise systems for organizations that must receive raw materials or products needed for their manufacturing or resale operations. Before we discuss the concepts in greater depth, it is helpful to experience the issues surrounding proper management of supply chains. To do so, please connect to the Beer Game developed by MIT (Massachusetts Institute of Technology) professors, which can be found at https://beergameapp.firebaseapp.com/. Use the Web-based version of the Beer Game for this exercise. Select a new game and enter your name while leaving the default parameters box checked. Then choose one of the four positions and play the game.

After you have completed the game for the time allotted by your instructor, be prepared to discuss the following questions:

1. How does information impact your supply chain decisions?
2. How could information systems help with the information needs of managing a supply chain?

STATS BOX 12.1:
TOP FOUR SELECTED ERP VENDORS

In a 2017 survey of companies who have implemented an ERP system, Panorama Consulting identified the top four vendors that are most often selected (the percentage of time the company's software is selected from a short list of vendors) once they have made the short list of vendors: SAP (19%), Microsoft (16%), Oracle (13%), and Infor (13%).

Source: Panorama Consulting Group (2017).

BUSINESS EXAMPLE BOX 12.1

ERP Is Not Always a Horror Story: Cisco Implementation on Time and Budget

Enterprise resource planning (ERP) implementations make good horror stories for IT and business managers to talk about. As discussed in this chapter, they are often way over budget and delayed by months and sometimes years. However, there are also some good stories. For Cisco Systems, Inc., an ERP implementation went well and achieved its planned budget and time objectives.

Cisco, founded in 1984, produces telecommunications equipment. It quickly became a Fortune 500 company as a result of the growth of the Internet. To support its core business operations in the mid-1990s, Cisco used a UNIX-based software package that handled its core finance, manufacturing, and order entry functions. At the time, each functional area (business unit) used the system but made its own decisions regarding the future of its IT systems. As a result, the systems were often "upgraded" by each department for its own needs. When the CIO of Cisco at the time, Pete Solvik, decided to analyze the software applications, he found that the software package in use lacked the reliability, maintainability, and redundancy (backup) needed. A failure in the legacy system in 1994 that led to a two-day shutdown of operations resulted in the need for a new system.

As with many CIOs, Cisco's CIO was trying to avoid ERP because he was concerned that an ERP solution would involve implementation headaches and cost overruns. In particular, the independent department structure would not work well with an integrated ERP. However, the ERP did seem the best solution for the company's needs, so a consulting company was hired to help Cisco select a vendor and implement the ERP system. KPMG Consulting helped prepare the ERP request for proposal and then helped Cisco select Oracle as their ERP vendor. The agreement also involved Cisco helping Oracle market new releases to potential customers in exchange for a successful implementation within budget and on time.

The implementation team then prepared a budget and schedule, committing to top management that everything would be done within nine months for

$15 million. Using a rapid iterative prototyping to implement the ERP, 30 developers spent three months modifying the Oracle ERP system to support Cisco's business processes. After several phases of analysis, development, implementation, corrections, and training, the final implementation was done on time and below the $15 million budget. Meeting its goals, Cisco management offered the implementation team a bonus pool of more than $200,000.

Source: Datta, A. 2009, April–June. "Cisco Systems: Implementing 'Customized' ERP in Nine Months and within Budget." *Journal of Cases on Information Technology* 11(2): 56ff.

Supply Chain Management Systems

The focusing story at the beginning of the chapter introduced the concept of supply chain management (SCM) at Wal-Mart. We discussed how managing the flow of goods in its supplier and distribution channels helps the company tightly control its inventory and reduce its costs. Supply chain management, however, can also apply to services, financial products, knowledge, and relationships, as well as goods.

The typical **supply chain** involves the flow of goods from the manufacturer to the wholesaler to the retailer and to the consumer. A typical supply chain is shown in Figure 12.3. Firms that provide or supply an organization's products or services are considered upstream, while firms that distribute an organization's products or services are considered downstream.

As you can tell from your experience with the Beer Game (Learning Activity 12.2), everyone in the supply chain benefits from collaborating with other members of the supply chain. You have also discovered (depending on how you did) that

Figure 12.3 Traditional Supply Chain

a poorly managed flow of goods can result in a disaster for a company. Some of the worst supply chain disasters are presented in Table 12.3.

Enterprise systems are key to the management of the supply chain. A well-managed supply chain can result in a reduction in inventory costs, since products can be ordered as needed as opposed to being stored for long amounts of time. It can also reduce the amount of returned items through better inventory information. SCM can also improve a company's overall relationships with partners in the supply chain through more accurate and timely communication about the flow of products, information, and payments. These can be referred to, respectively, as the product flow (movement of goods), information flow (orders and delivery status), and financial flow (credit terms, payment schedules, and consignment and title ownership arrangements). A good SCM system also allows companies to offer just-in-time (JIT) inventory. This is when firms are able to maintain the lowest level of inventory while still being able to fulfill demand. Because SCM systems provide notices of inventory stock depletion in real time, personnel (or systems) are able to order new stock immediately.

The key to SCM's success rests in the sharing of information both upstream and downstream. Today, most companies use Web-based interfaces to access inventory, delivery, and other information from their SCM systems. The SCM systems also tend to be increasingly integrated with other enterprise systems, such as ERP and CRM systems.

STATS BOX 12.2:
SUPPLY CHAIN'S IMPACT ON COMPANY PERFORMANCE

Statistical evidence suggests that enhancements in their supply chain can help companies improve their performance. Here are some statistics that support this:

- The use of drones is making same-day delivery possible, especially in densely populated areas. Drones can travel at 50 miles per hour and carry up to five pounds; 86% of the items that Amazon.com sells are fewer than five pounds, which means there is a great potential for drone delivery.

- In 2014, 60% of organizations were automating their supply chains by pursuing increased mechanization. This is expected to increase to 83% by 2018.

- The Internet of Things has utilized RFID technologies in such a way that from 2012 to 2014, the value of the RFID market has increased from $6.96 billion to $8.89 billion. It is expected to reach $27.31 billion by 2024. The use of this technology enables smart devices in homes, cars, and elsewhere to seamlessly communicate with other devices over the Internet. This helps improve efficiencies in the supply chain.

Source: Cerasis, http://cerasis.com/2015/01/16/supply-chain-facts/.

Table 12.3 Supply Chain (and Other) Disaster Examples

Year	Company	What Happened?
Halloween 1999	Hershey	Due to new order management and shipping systems (implementing both ERP and SCM simultaneously), Hershey could not fulfill critical Halloween orders. $150 million in revenues were lost as stock dropped 30%.
Christmas 1999	ToysRUs.com	The online retail division could not make its Christmas delivery commitments to thousands. Infamous "We're sorry" emails were sent December 23; eventually, Amazon took over fulfillment.
2001	Cisco	A lack of demand and inventory visibility as the market slowed led to a $2.2 billion inventory write-off and stock prices cut in half.
2001	Nike	A new planning system caused inventory and order woes. This was blamed for $100 million in lost sales and depressed the stock price by 20%. It also triggered a flurry of class-action lawsuits.
2005	Loblaws	Plans for a significant logistics network makeover ran into poor execution problems. The company blamed two quarters of poor results on high costs and lost sales from the effort. The CEO apologized to shareholders. Even though the logistics issues largely stabilized by early 2006, the stock price never recovered from the hit.
2007−9	Boeing	Plans to radically overhaul the supply chain for the new *Dreamliner* 787 aircraft sound good, but massive problems with component deliveries led to a two-year delay in the aircraft's launch and some $2 billion in charges to fix supplier problems.
Christmas 2013	UPS	UPS did not have the capacity to supply deliveries for a spike in orders during Christmas 2013. In particular, on December 23, 2013, orders spiked by 63%. As a result, companies such as Toys R Us and Amazon.com had to inform customers that their products would not be delivered in time for Christmas.
April 2016	Toyota, Honda, and Sony	Two earthquakes hit Japan in April 2016. Due to suppliers being unable to deliver products and their own plants having sustained damage, all three companies slowed or temporarily stopped production.

Sources: Gilmore (2009); Reuters (2016); SCDigest (2014).

LEARNING ACTIVITY 12.3

Blockchain and Supply Chain Management

Blockchain is a recent technological solution that is finding its way into many business processes including supply chain management. Watch the video at the following link to see how IBM is using blockchain to help manage the supply chain and then answer the questions that follow: https://www.ibm.com/blockchain/supply-chain/.

1. How is IBM using blockchain to help with supply chain management?
2. What is the advantage that blockchain provides?
3. Can you think of other implementations of how blockchain could be used in business?

LEARNING ACTIVITY 12.4

Customer Relationship Management

An enterprise system that has gained importance in recent years is customer relationship management (CRM). Before we discuss the concept in greater depth, learn about CRM by visiting the following demonstration websites:

- Salesforce: https://www.youtube.com/watch?v=mbo8_VHaBWw
- Microsoft Dynamics CRM: http://www.microsoft.com/en-us/dynamics/crm.aspx

  Be prepared to discuss the following points in class:

1. What are the purposes of a CRM system?
2. What types of tasks can be accomplished with a CRM system?
3. Who benefits from a CRM system?
4. What are the benefits for each stakeholder?
5. What types of companies should have a CRM system? Why?

Customer Relationship Management Systems

Customer relationship management (CRM) refers to an organization-wide strategy for managing an organization's multiple interactions with customers. For example, when dealing with a company to buy a product, you might talk to a person via a toll-free phone number, send an email, chat in an instant messaging box with a customer representative, or simply perform your transaction online without "talking" with anyone. These are all channels of interaction.

CRM involves a set of activities (including a philosophy of customer service) and technologies (the CRM system) meant to help companies understand the needs of current and potential customers. The CRM system allows organizations to attract and retain customers and to manage customer relationships—for example, by offering personalized services and self-servicing tools. It also allows a company to analyze customer data to find its most profitable products, services, and customers.

Table 12.4 shows the three main goals for CRM (META Group 2001). First, CRM systems help organizations manage multiple channels of interaction with customers in ways that the customers prefer. The second goal of CRM systems is to provide an integrated picture of the customer across the various customer-facing parts of the organization. The third major goal of CRM systems is to enable the analysis of customer-related information. This information is gathered through interactions with customers, although external data (such as census data) may also be involved.

Customer Service Life Cycle

The **customer service life cycle (CSLC)** is a framework to help us understand the various tasks a CRM system can be useful for. The CSLC is a series of phases that customers pass through when interacting with an organization. There are a number of variations on the phases, but they are all similar. Our simplified CRM includes four phases: engage, transact, fulfill, and service. Table 12.5 summarizes the phases and shows some specific CRM-related applications that can be useful for each CSLC phase. The combined phases are referred to as a *cycle,* as shown in Figure 12.4, because completion of one round of the cycle often leads to another round. Note that in the following discussion, we refer to products, but similar statements could be made about services.

Components of CRM Systems

CRM systems have three main components: operational, collaborative, and analytical (Van Slyke and Bélanger 2003). Figure 12.5 shows how the components work together.

The **operational components of a CRM** system help an organization improve day-to-day interactions with customers. They are involved with the operations of the company, such as sales or repairs.

The **collaborative components of a CRM** system help the organization interact and collaborate with its customers. They include older applications, such as email and automated response systems, but also newer ones, such as interactive chat facilities for customer service, **interactive voice response (IVR)** systems, and voice over IP (VoIP), which allows a customer to talk to a "live" customer service representative while online.

The **analytical components of CRM** consist of technologies and processes organizations can use to analyze customer data. A critical analytical component in most CRM

Table 12.4 Goals of CRM

Manage multiple channels of interaction with the customer
Provide a unified view of the customer across the enterprise
Analyze information collected to improve campaigns, services, and products

Source: META Group (2001).

Table 12.5 Phases in the Customer Service Life Cycle

Phase	Description	Example of CRM System Use
Engage	Creating customer awareness of the product or service. The goal of the engage stage is to generate leads and then convert those leads into customers.	**Campaign management** Email marketing **Lead processing** **Sales force automation** Web-based catalogs
Transact	All activities associated with the purchase process. The goal of this phase is to efficiently and effectively complete the purchase process so that customers do not abandon the purchase process.	Order management Payment process and options **Product configuration** Product pricing
Fulfill	Delivery of the product or service to the customer.	Order tracking Supply chain integration
Service	Supporting the customer during the ownership of a product or service.	**Call center automation** **Customer issues management** Self-service

Source: Adapted from Van Slyke and Bélanger (2003).

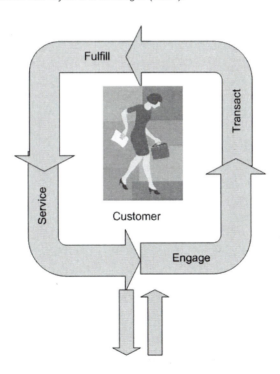

Figure 12.4 Customer Service Life Cycle
Source: Adapted from Van Slyke and Bélanger (2003).

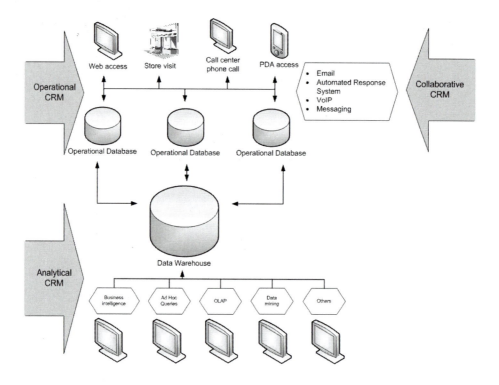

Figure 12.5 Sample CRM Architecture

systems is the data warehouse, which we discussed earlier. **Data mining** technologies and methods are often used to discover patterns and groups in the data stored in a data warehouse. Data mining involves using software that performs analyses of large data sets to find patterns that repeat themselves. For example, a grocery store might find that on college football weekends, certain items always seem to sell "together." The grocery store can then locate them together within the store. This is a very simple example, and data mining can find much more complex and detailed patterns. One analysis that many organizations find useful is customer segmentation (sometimes called *customer clustering*), which allows organizations to group customers that share certain characteristics. For example, Student Advantage, a company that provides college student–oriented marketing services, uses segmentation to place its student members into very small segments. This allows Student Advantage to provide extremely targeted marketing opportunities to a wide variety of clients. Data mining can also help in customer profiling. **Customer profiling** lets companies build a picture of a customer through data collected from their interactions with this customer. These profiles allow companies to better anticipate customer needs and better predict customer behavior.

LEARNING ACTIVITY 12.5

Self-Servicing

We discussed CRM applications as a way companies can gather information about their customers and as a way to manage their communications with them. An additional function of CRM applications is to permit **customer self-service,** allowing customers to take care of their service problems themselves. Before we discuss the pros and cons of doing this, you should try self-servicing.

1. *Scenario:* You ordered new noise-free headphones for taking on your multiple trips. You bought them on Amazon.com for $65. You opened the shipping package two months ago but never opened the actual package completely. (It has the original packaging.) You were busy with the start of classes, so you did not think about it again, but now your parents gave you the exact same item as a gift, so you want to return the package to Amazon.com.
2. Go to the Amazon website (http://www.amazon.com).
3. Figure out how much you are going to receive as a refund (not counting taxes, if any).
4. Estimate how long it is going to take for you to get your money once the headphones are shipped back to Amazon. Identify why this time is needed.
5. Figure out what you have to do to return the headphones.

Discussion Questions

1. How difficult was it to find the information needed?
2. How difficult do you think it would be to actually complete the return?
3. How likely are you to use this self-servicing application (Return Center) instead of calling someone at Amazon? Why?
4. What are the benefits to customers of self-servicing CRM applications?
5. What are the benefits to companies of self-servicing CRM applications?

STATS BOX 12.3:
CRM VENDORS

The CRM market has been growing, with revenues of $23.4 billion in 2014 and $26.3 billion in 2015. Research suggests that for 2015, the top vendors were Salesforce.com with about 20% of the CRM market, SAP with about a 10% share, and Oracle with about 6% of the market.

Source: http://www.crmsearch.com/crm-software-market-share.php.

CRM Implementation Options

Like most other enterprise systems, there are two main ways that CRM can be implemented: on premise or on demand. **On-premise CRM** implementation means that the CRM system is acquired, leased, or developed by the organization and installed on its local servers. This often has the advantage of providing a customized solution. However, the costs of development and maintenance could be substantial. **On-demand CRM**, also known as **software-as-a-service (SaaS) CRM**, refers to the remote use of a CRM provider's applications through the Internet. This offers advantages like up-to-date applications and no maintenance or implementation costs. Of course, the company has to use the standard functions, also known as *plain vanilla* software.

BUSINESS EXAMPLE BOX 12.2

DUFL Gains Competitive Advantage through Customer Service

DUFL is a company that strives to ease the burdens of traveling by shipping, storing, and cleaning their clients' business attire. Customers provide DUFL with their business attire, and DUFL stores the clothes. When it is time to travel, rather than pack their suitcases and take them to the airport with them, customers inform DUFL where they are staying, when they are arriving, and what clothes they want while they are there. DUFL then ensures that these clothes are at the hotel waiting for the clients. When the trip is over, the clothes are packed up and sent back to DUFL, where they are cleaned and stored for the next time they are needed.

A key aspect to DUFL's success is to provide a high level of customer service while keeping their costs low. In order to do so, DUFL relies on Salesforce to allow them to keep track of each customer's unique needs. Salesforce provides DUFL's customers and employees with a user-friendly interface that keeps track of every transaction and interaction. This results in consistent solutions when customers call back with similar requests. In addition to helping DUFL keep existing customers happy, the software also provides the ability to project future sales. All of this is done in a way that allows DUFL to focus on their core competencies of enhancing business travel and growing their business. The result has been 10% growth each month while maintaining a lean staff of 25 employees.

Sources: https://www.dufl.com/; https://www.salesforce.com/customer-success-stories/dufl/Benefits; and Limitations of CRM

There are many expected benefits from the use of CRM systems for organizations. First, CRM systems are expected to provide greater customer satisfaction because customers can receive personalized services and products, faster response time to their questions, and more streamlined interactions with the company. For companies, this results in improved customer relations, which should lead to repeat business (called *customer retention*). In addition, CRM systems can help an organization maximize its profits by reducing the costs for acquiring and servicing customers, and increasing overall revenues. Revenues can increase because of customer loyalty but also because of what is called *cross-selling*, or the selling of products to customers based on other products they acquired. For example, Amazon.com often sends its customers book recommendations based on books they have previously bought.

There are also some potential disadvantages to the use of CRM systems. First, the implementation of a CRM system requires more than simply installing the software application. In order to be successful in implementing a CRM system, an organization must look beyond purely technical issues and ensure that all customer-facing employees are customer minded. The company must also make sure that it identifies all channels of interactions with customers. The ability to achieve buy-in from various areas of the organization is key to a successful implementation. Of course, there are complicated technological issues that also must be addressed. First, the organization must ensure that its CRM architecture is scalable so that growth in customer demands is met without problems. Just like ERP systems, CRM systems can be customized to meet the specific needs of the organization. Overall, the ability to deal with both nontechnical and technical issues is a requirement for successfully implementing almost any enterprise system.

Customer-Managed Interactions (CMI)

One issue with CRM systems is that they are very firm centric in the sense that they focus on the existing transactional and behavioral data collected by the organization based on the prior and current interactions of the customer with the organization. While trends can be used to predict what customers might buy in the future, there are some acquisitions and customer activities that are unforeseeable unless the customer tells the company about it. For example, a customer might be interested in some products for a friend's upcoming wedding, but the company would not know of this need. To address this lack of information, some companies have turned their focus to customer-managed interactions (CMI).

Customer-managed interactions (CMI) involve letting customers store and manage data about themselves. Why would customers willingly tell companies of their buying intentions? For convenience, for money, or to obtain personalized service. Think of all your friends who create wish lists at some of the major online retailers like Amazon.com or Target.com. There is even a site dedicated to helping anyone create wish lists (WishList.com). Customers tell the company what they intend to buy; therefore, this information tends to be accurate. Once the company knows about intended purchases, it can perform targeted marketing, for example, by giving a specific discount, which may push the customer over into the buying phase of the customer service life cycle.

Warehouse Automation and Robotics

As organizations have focused on improving interactions with customers, they have also utilized advances in technologies to automate the operations of their warehouses. This has been made possible through the use of robotics. The way this often works is the robot completes jobs that are tedious and physically taxing, allowing the human workers to focus on less physically demanding aspects of warehouse operations. One downside to implementing the use of robotics is the loss of human jobs. However, at Amazon, the use of robotics has led to increased growth resulting in increased jobs. The fact that these robots can perform physically taxing tasks makes the jobs being hired for safer.

Chapter Summary

In this chapter, we discussed enterprise systems. We first presented the main components, characteristics, and types of enterprise systems. We then explored in greater depth three enterprise systems: enterprise resource planning (ERP) systems, supply chain management (SCM) systems, and customer relationship management (CRM) systems. Here are the main points discussed in the chapter:

- Enterprise systems are information systems that serve the needs of the organization or parts of the organization.
- Enterprise systems are modular; they are integrated with one another (offering application integration) and use a central database (offering data integration).
- The purpose of enterprise resource planning (ERP) systems is to manage an organization's resources and enable information flow within and between processes (and departments) via a set of integrated information systems tools.
- Supply chain management (SCM) systems help organizations manage the flow of goods in their supplier and distribution channels to better control inventory, reduce costs, and improve communication with their business partners.
- CRM systems have three main components: the operational component that helps an organization improve day-to-day interactions with customers; the collaborative component that helps the organization interact and collaborate with its customers; and the analytical component, which consists of technologies and processes organizations can use to analyze customer data.
- The customer life cycle is a series of phases that customers pass through when interacting with an organization, and it can be used to identify important CRM applications.

Review Questions

1. What is the difference between a personal and an enterprise information system?

2. How are applications developed using the functional perspective? The hierarchical perspective?

3. Define business integration and systems integration.

4. What is an enterprise resource planning (ERP) system, and how does it support systems integration?

5. What is the purpose of a supply chain management (SCM) system?

6. What is customer relationship management (CRM)?

7. What are the main components of a CRM system? Briefly describe each.

8. What are the main goals of a CRM system?

9. What is the difference between on-premise CRM systems and on-demand CRM systems?

10. What are customer-managed interactions? How do they differ from CRM?

Reflection Questions

1. What is the most important thing you learned in this chapter? Why is it important?

2. What topics are unclear? What about them is unclear?

3. How does the process perspective provide integration, and what types of integration are provided?

4. How does cloud computing relate to ERP and CRM applications?

5. How does the material in this chapter relate to the content of Chapter 4 on strategic information systems?

6. Explain how data integration is essential to the success of ERP, SCM, and CRM systems.

7. Which issues are similar for both the process and the hierarchical perspectives of developing enterprise systems? Why?

8. How can process modeling (Chapter 11) enable firms to successfully implement enterprise systems?

9. We discussed different types of integration in this chapter (system, business, and data). How do they relate to one another?

10. Can a very small business implement a CRM system? What would be the advantages and disadvantages of doing so?

Additional Learning Activities

12.A1. This activity requires you to complete a case analysis regarding an ERP acquisition. The case may be accessed through your university website, the Ivey Business School business case website (https://www.iveycases.com), or the Harvard Business School cases website (https://cb.hbsp.harvard .edu/cbmp/pages/home), or it may be provided to you by your instructor.

> Canniff, M. 2007. "Case: Enterprise Resource Planning Software— Ongoing Maintenance Cost Benefit Analysis." *Ivey School of Business,* September 9. Product Number: 906E12-PDF-ENG.

12.A2. Watch the following five-minute video:

- https://www.youtube.com/watch?v=xJfP_o_fANA

> The video discusses CRM but is focused more extensively on the use of the data available from CRM systems and the marketing that can be done with these data. Prepare a short report describing the main points of the video. Be sure to address the following questions:

> a. Who benefits from bigger and better data?

> b. How does one obtain better quality CRM data?

> c. How should strategy, process, and technology integrate to provide a better CRM system?

> d. What is data migration, and how does it improve data quality?

12.A3. Select a small organization you are familiar with. This could be your employer, a company where you parents or friends work, or just a company you know well. First, evaluate the company's need for a CRM system based on your knowledge from the readings, discussions, and activities you have done in this chapter. Prepare a short report including your recommended features, applications, and strategies for this small business.

12.A4. After completing Learning Activity 12.A3, watch the *Salesforce Marketing Cloud: Overview Demo* from Salesforce.com and include any changes to your report based on the information in the demo: https://www.youtube .com/watch?v=s5n4CJbGfi4.

12.A5. Compare and contrast in a table the advantages and disadvantages of each enterprise system perspective (hierarchical, functional, and process).

12.A6. Imagine that you are a new student at a university that requires each student to have a computer but does not provide guidelines beyond the fact that they have to be laptops, use wireless networks, and have the capability to use basic office applications and statistical analyses. The laptops have to be useful for three years. Develop a list of activities from the customer service life cycle that apply to this situation. Identify the CRM applications that can be used for each activity.

References

Gilmore, D. 2009. "The Top Supply Chain Disasters of All Time." *Supply Chain Digest*, May 7. http://www.scdigest.com/assets/FirstThoughts/09-05-07.php?cid=2451&ctype=content.

META Group. 2001. "META Group Report: Five CRM Trends for 2001–'02." May 18. http://www.cioupdate.com/reports/article.php/769091/META-Group-Report-Five-CRM-Trends-for-2001-02.htm.

Panorama Consulting Group. 2017. *2017 ERP REPORT.* https://www.panorama-consulting.com/resource-center/erp-industry-reports/2017-report-on-erp-systems-and-enterprise-software/.

Pearlson, K., and C. Saunders. 2010. *Managing and Using Information Systems.* 4th ed. Hoboken, NJ: Wiley.

Piccoli, G. 2008. *Information Systems for Managers.* Hoboken, NJ: Wiley.

Reuters. 2016. "Toyota, Other Major Japanese Firms Hit by Quake Damage, Supply Disruptions." April 17. http://fortune.com/2016/04/17/toyota-earthquake-disruptions/.

SCDigest Editorial Staff. 2014. "Supply Chain News: The Factors behind the UPS Failure to Deliver Christmas Goods." *SCDigest*, January 6. http://www.scdigest.com/ontarget/14-01-06-2.php?cid=7717

Van Slyke, C., and F. Bélanger. 2003. *Electronic Business Technologies.* New York: John Wiley & Sons.

Further Readings

SAP Information
- http://www.sap.com/pc/bp/erp.html
- http://go.sap.com/solution.html

Supply Chain Management Videos
- http://go.sap.com/product/scm.html
- http://www.youtube.com/watch?v=dDmGtPQAI24 (MS Dynamics)

CRM Videos
- http://www.youtube.com/watch?v=-_6c018ZI2g

Glossary

Analytical components of CRM: Technologies and processes organizations can use to analyze customer data.

Application integration: Applications where modules are designed to be integrated with one another.

Business integration: The unification of business processes previously performed as separate activities in order to create cohesive and streamlined business processes.

Business intelligence (BI): A set of applications, technologies, and processes for gathering, storing, analyzing, and accessing data to help users make better business decisions.

Business process reengineering (BPR): The redesign of business processes to improve how work is done.

Call center automation: Applications that support call centers, which are often the main contact point between an organization and its customers.

Campaign management: Applications that help organizations plan, carry out, and analyze the results of marketing campaigns.

Collaborative components of CRM: Technologies and processes that help organizations interact and collaborate with their customers.

Content management systems (CMSs): Applications that allow companies to manage the vast amounts of information of various types (content) they have stored. This includes the capture, storing, preservation, and delivery of content.

Customer issues management: Applications that help organizations with tasks such as scheduling, dispatching, and communicating with field service personnel.

Customer-managed interactions (CMI): Applications that let customers store and manage data about themselves.

Customer profiling: Applications that help organizations group customers according to demographic characteristics or behaviors.

Customer relationship management (CRM): An organization-wide strategy for managing an organization's multiple interactions with customers.

Customer self-service: Software that allows customers to find solutions to problems without interacting with a customer service representative.

Customer service life cycle (CSLC): A series of phases that customers pass through when interacting with an organization.

Data integration: Applications where data are stored in one central database.

Data mining: The process of analyzing data to identify trends, patterns, and other useful information to make predictions.

Enterprise application integration (EAI): A set of tools and services (a framework instead of a single technology) to allow various enterprise systems (such as ERP or CRM) to share data.

Enterprise resource planning (ERP): Software that allows organizations to manage resources throughout the organization, independently of which business function controls the resource.

Enterprise systems: Information systems that serve the needs of the organization or parts of the organization.

Functional perspective: Software development approach where information systems applications are developed to meet the needs of individuals in a functional area, such as human resources or marketing.

Hierarchical perspective: Software development approach where software developers build information systems to mirror the organization so that applications are built to meet the needs of individuals at a given level in the organization.

Interactive voice response (IVR): Applications that allow customers to use a telephone to navigate through various types of systems, such as product request systems or customer service systems.

Lead processing: Applications used to qualify, assign, and track sales leads to maximize the probability that the leads eventually turn into sales.

On-demand CRM: Remote use of a CRM provider's applications through the Internet.

On-premise CRM: CRM specifically developed for the organization and installed on its local servers.

Operational components of CRM: Technologies and processes that help improve day-to-day interactions with customers, such as sales, repairs, and so on.

Order tracking: Applications that allow customers to determine the status of their order.

Personal information systems: Information systems applications for individual use.

Process perspective: Software development approach where information systems applications are developed to support the task being done (or process) irrespective of the organizational level or functional area the individual using the system.

Product configuration: Applications used to properly configure or choose complex products.

Radio-frequency identification (RFID) tags: Electronic tags that can be tracked remotely using wireless networks.

Sales force automation: Applications that provide functions directed at making sales representatives more efficient and effective.

Software-as-a-service (SaaS) CRM: Remote use of a CRM provider's applications through the Internet.

Supply chain: Entities involved in the flow of goods from the manufacturer to the wholesaler to the retailer and to the consumer.

Supply chain management (SCM) systems: Software that helps organizations manage the movement of materials or products from provision to production to consumption.

Systems integration: The unification of information systems and databases that previously operated as separate systems.

Unified communications (UC): A framework for the integration of the various modes of communication used by an organization, including email, voice mail, videoconferencing, instant messaging, texting, and voice over IP.

CHAPTER 13

Information for Electronic Business

Learning Objectives

By reading and completing the activities in this chapter, you will be able to

- Describe the concept of e-business and various e-business models
- Identify the business-to-consumer (B2C) e-business models, enablers, and impacts
- Explain search engine optimization
- Discuss the main business-to-business (B2B) e-business models
- Identify the major trends related to e-business

Chapter Outline

Focusing Story: The iPod and the Music Industry
Learning Activity 13.1: Why Is E-Business Important?
Introduction to E-Business
E-Business Models
B2C E-Business Enablers
B2C E-Business Impacts
Learning Activity 13.2: Why Would I Trust Them or Buy from Them?
Design for B2C E-Business
Business-to-Business (B2B)
Learning Activity 13.3: B2C versus B2B
Search Engine Optimization
Learning Activity 13.4: Where Is My Web Page?
Trends in E-Business
Learning Activity 13.5: USA.gov

The growth of the Internet has changed our everyday lives, just as it has changed how businesses and governments interact and conduct transactions with consumers. These digital interactions have led to the phenomenon of e-business, also known as digital markets. In this chapter, we explore various ways that organizations and individuals interact online and the implications that digital interactions have for us all, as you will see in the focusing story on digital music.

FOCUSING STORY

The iPod and the Music Industry

Who would have thought that a small device like an iPod could dramatically change a well-established major industry? Yet that is what happened when Apple Inc. launched the iPod and electronic music downloads. Because of this new way of selling songs and albums, the music industry has been one of the most affected by e-business.

In the "old" music industry, artists recorded songs and albums through record companies, which were the major players in the industry. Companies could sell CDs (and before the 1980s, LPs) and make significant profits on each album customers bought, with some fees (rights) going to the artists and some commissions going to distributors and retailers. Eventually, the record companies decided not to release singles, only albums. That was not to the liking of music listeners. Then came the iPod, announced on October 23, 2001. It allowed users to download only the songs they wanted to a very portable device. The industry was never the same. The music industry faced two significant problems with the growing use of the Internet for access to digital music. The first is that digital music is easy to steal, and users started to download music illegally and share it with one another. In this scenario, everyone in the industry lost money. Even though illegal downloads had started years before, with Napster allowing illegal downloads for free between 1999 and 2001, the iPod made it easy to copy songs. At the same time, however, many users are happy to spend small amounts of money for legal downloads of the songs they really want. That is why Apple is said to have sold more than six billion songs on iTunes by the end of 2009.

A second phenomenon that occurred with the ability to download songs through the Internet was that some artists decided to sell their own music online. They were able to charge less to consumers because they only had to pay the e-business website for selling their music; they also made more profits this way. Apple keeps 30% of the profits from each song sold, with the rest going to the artist. So on a song that sells for $1.29, Apple receives about $0.39, and the label and artist receive about $0.90. When artists produce their own music, they get the full $0.90 that normally goes to the artist and label. Record companies changed their licensing approaches to embrace new online services in response to this major threat to the industry. However, they did not envision online streaming, the new online threat to the music industry. Online music streaming services allow listeners to play music on their computers or Internet-enabled devices instead of buying CDs or downloading music to their MP3 players (one of which is the iPod). These services, like Pandora (http://www.pandora.com), Last.fm (http://www.last.fm), Amazon Music Unlimited, Google Play Music, or Spotify (http://www.spotify.com), are free or relatively inexpensive. Some of these services allow you to download songs or playlists for offline listening. As users listen online instead of purchasing music, sales of music keep going down every year. The total music industry sales in 2000 were approximately US$14 billion but were down to US$10 billion by 2008. In 2014, revenue from streaming sources of music outpaced the revenue from CDs for the first time. By this time, sales of iPods had decreased dramatically due to the popularity of the iPhone and other smartphones. While today many of us listen to music on our phones rather than iPods, the impact of the iPod on the music industry remains.

FOCUSING QUESTIONS

1. Will the streaming audio approach change the music industry once more? How?

2. How can the streaming audio business model be successful?

3. What other ways could companies use to leverage digital music?

Sources: Woollaston, V. 2013. "15,000 Songs a MINUTE Downloaded on iTunes as Apple's Music Service Celebrates Its Tenth Birthday." *Daily Mail,* April 29. http://www.dailymail.co.uk/sciencetech/article-2316473/A-decade-iTunes -How-Apple-revolutionised-way-buy-music.html; MacMillan, D. 2009. "The Music Industry's New Internet Problem." *Bloomberg BusinessWeek,* March 6. http://www.bloomberg.com/bw/stories/2009-03-06/the-music-industrys-new -internet-problembusinessweek-business-news-stock-market-and-financial -advice; Mansfield, B. 2015. "Streaming Revenue Passes CDs for First Time." *USA Today,* March 19. http://www.usatoday.com/story/life/music/2015/03/19/ streaming-revenue-passes-cds-riaa-report/25023773/.

Why Is E-Business Important?

Most of you have already experienced **electronic business**, the topic of this chapter, when acquiring products electronically. E-business, however, is much broader than just buying something online. In this learning activity, we want you to think broadly about what e-business is and find two interesting, up-to-date statistics online about the size of electronic business. These can be for a subset (such as B2C or B2B), an industry, or a market segment. Make sure your statistics are current—say, within the last two years. Be careful about some of the older information available online. For example, you may find predictions from five years ago about expected e-business sales. It is much better to find out what current e-business sales are. Prepare a short report of your two statistics (make sure to include your citations!) and a brief discussion of why you think e-business is important today.

Introduction to E-Business

In Learning Activity 13.1, you found several statistics about e-business. What you found should have already convinced you of the importance of e-business in today's economy. However, the importance of e-business goes beyond any number you could find online. The reality is that e-business changed how most organizations interact with their customers and suppliers and even how they interact with the government. More important, complete industries have been transformed with the emergence of e-business applications. This is the case in the focusing story, which showed how e-business completely changed the music industry. What other industries have been changed by e-business? You may think of travel, publishing, and even education, just to name a few. Later in this chapter, we discuss specific impacts e-business has had on these industries.

What is e-business exactly? There are many definitions, but another way to look at it is as a digital market. Table 13.1 provides some terminology used when discussing e-business and digital markets. Note that **electronic funds transfer (EFT)** and electronic data interchange (EDI) provide tools for transferring documents or financial data between organizations, and we discussed them in Chapter 7. The other terms include variations on whether only the Web, other Internet tools, or any other electronic means are used for business transactions, such as collaboration software, kiosk technologies, and so on. For our purposes, we will use the term *e-business*, which is often recognized as the broader term that includes various electronic means of conducting business, as shown in Figure 13.1.

Table 13.1 E-Business Terminology

Term	Definition
Electronic funds transfer	Electronic means to conduct financial transactions such as payments and remittances
Electronic data interchange	Electronic means to transfer documents between organizations
Web commerce	Electronic means to conduct business transactions using the Web as an interface
Internet commerce	Electronic means to conduct business using the Internet (for example, email, the Web, or file transfers)
Electronic commerce	Electronic means to conduct business transactions, including the Internet, electronic data interchange, or private networks
Electronic government	Electronic means to interact or conduct transactions with government agencies
Electronic business	Electronic means to interact or conduct business with individuals, companies, or government agencies

Types of E-Businesses

In Table 13.1 and Figure 13.1, we differentiate between commerce and government. There are other ways to categorize the various types of e-business. Some of the most common categorizations are as follows:

- **Business-to-consumer (B2C)**: This is when interactions are taking place between a consumer and a business. For example, when you buy books on Amazon.com, you are conducting a B2C e-commerce transaction.

- **Business-to-business (B2B)**: This is when interactions are taking place between two businesses. For example, when Wal-Mart sends electronic requests for inventory to its suppliers, it is conducting a B2B e-commerce transaction.

- **Consumer-to-consumer (C2C)**: This is when interactions are taking place between two consumers. For example, when you buy goods from another individual on eBay.com, you are conducting a C2C e-commerce transaction.

- **Government-to-constituent (G2C)**: This is when interactions are taking place between a government agency and a constituent. Constituents could be citizens, businesses, or even other agencies. For example, when you pay your taxes online, you are having a G2C interaction with the government. This is most often referred to today as *electronic government*, or *e-government*.

There are many more types of e-business, although they tend to be variations of the definitions in Table 13.2; for example, consumer-to-business (C2B), business-to-employee (B2E), or government-to-government (G2G). The main ones outlined above, however, seem to be the most popular categories.

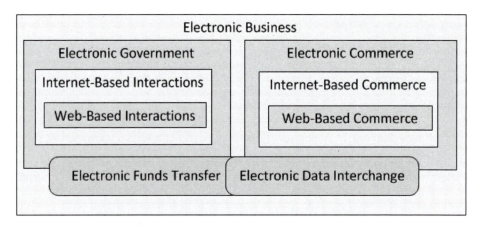

Figure 13.1 E-Business Terminology

There is another way to categorize commercial electronic business, and it refers to the online versus offline structure of the organization. There are three main categories used:

- **Bricks and mortar:** This category represents traditional organizations with physical locations. For example, large automobile manufacturers tend to have physical offices and operations.

- **Bricks and clicks:** This category represents traditional organizations with physical locations but that also operate an online business. There are many such companies today that have physical stores and online stores; for example, Wal-Mart has Walmart.com, BestBuy has BestBuy.com, and so on.

Table 13.2 Types of E-Businesses

E-Business Type	Acronym	Definitions	Parties Involved
Business-to-consumer	B2C	When interactions are taking place between a consumer and a business	• Consumers • Businesses
Business-to-business	B2B	When interactions are taking place between two businesses	• Businesses
Consumer-to-consumer	C2C	When interactions are taking place between two consumers	• Consumers
Government-to-constituent (e-government)	G2C	When interactions are taking place between a government agency and a constituent	• Citizens • Businesses • Government agencies

STATS BOX 13.1:
RETAIL E-COMMERCE IN THE UNITED STATES

As you might have found in Learning Activity 13.1, there are many statistics on e-business that are often not consistent with one another. One good source of statistics for the United States is the U.S. Census Bureau, which provides quarterly statistics on retail e-commerce. The following table shows the statistics available at the end of 2014. You can obtain the most recent statistics at the following site: http://www.census.gov/retail/#ecommerce/. Note that although the numbers are impressive, e-commerce still represents less than 8% of all retail sales in the country, as can be seen in the following figure.

Estimated Quarterly Total and E-Commerce U.S. Retail Sales, 2016–17

Quarter	Retail Sales Total	Retail Sales E-Commerce	E-Commerce as Percent of Total
3rd quarter 2017	1,268,877	115,345	9.1
2nd quarter 2017	1,254,819	111,369	8.9
1st quarter 2017	1,250,055	106,383	8.5
4th quarter 2016	1,236,638	101,606	8.2
3rd quarter 2016	1,217,100	99,875	8.2
2nd quarter 2016	1,206,395	96,014	8.0
1st quarter 2016	1,189,262	92,182	7.8

Estimated Quarterly U.S. Retail E-Commerce Sales as a Percent of Total Quarterly Retail Sales: 1st Quarter 2016–3rd Quarter 2017

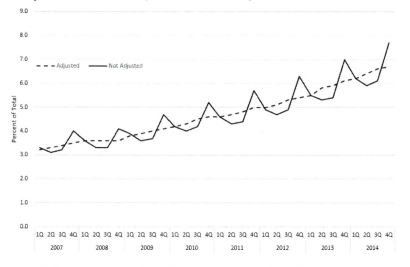

Source: U.S. Census Bureau, http://www.census.gov/retail/#ecommerce.

- **Pure play (or click only):** This category represents organizations with only an online business. For example, Amazon.com and eBay.com started as online companies only, where you could not go to a physical store to conduct a transaction. Many pure play companies, like Google, exist in the online world only, although they still have offices for people to work at.

E-Business Models

The various types of e-business previously discussed refer to who participates in the e-business interaction and whether this organization uses offline, online, or both business environments. Another important way to classify e-businesses is with respect to their business model.

What Is a Business Model?

A **business model** represents the way the organization functions and creates value. In other words, it is how an organization makes money. The business model often identifies the market that a business is in, the products or services that it offers, and the strategies and major activities it uses to seek competitive advantages in that market. Importantly, the business model should identify the organization's key business processes and organizational capabilities that allow the business to generate revenues and profits.

B2C E-Business Models

There are many different business models in the world of e-business, some more popular than others, and many that did not really exist before the increased use of the Internet for business. Table 13.3 shows a variety of B2C e-business models.

The e-business models presented in Table 13.3 continue to evolve as individuals find new ways to use the Internet and, increasingly, mobile technologies to create new approaches to generate revenue. In fact, the use of location-based services on mobile devices (knowing where you are based on your cell phone's location) allows marketing firms to offer targeted advertising and services that you may need at a specific moment based on where you are. Some of the business models would not exist without the Internet, like infrastructure companies such as PayPal.com or Squareup.com or social media websites like Facebook.com or Delphiforums.com. There are even some fairly unique business models in existence today, like the name-your-own-price model of Priceline.com (http://www.priceline.com).

It is necessary for business models to evolve with today's rapid changes in technology and the changes in the way individuals interact with one another. For example, as many students know, changes in your online profile on a social networking site result in changes in the types of ads you see when accessing the site. This change in the social media business model has occurred in the last few years. However, while keeping up with technological and social changes is important, the most important factor for success is to start with a proper business model. Back in the early days of e-business, many entrepreneurs jumped on the bandwagon of e-business without proper business models. Not surprisingly, many of them failed. This is one reason behind what is today called the *dot-com bust*, when many individuals and companies lost money in their attempts to take advantage of e-business. Today, there are too many e-business successes to even attempt to summarize them. Some are very innovative, while others simply follow solid business models.

BUSINESS EXAMPLE BOX 13.1

Adapting Its Business Model: Amazon.com

When the dot-com bust happened in the early 2000s, many e-businesses simply went out of business, unable to generate sufficient revenues to cover their costs. Others, however, were able to survive and thrive. One such company is Amazon .com. However, Amazon.com, which for most of its life span has existed only as a website, is now adapting to maintain its competitive advantage in the retail sector.

In 2015, Amazon.com opened its first retail store location on the campus of Purdue University. Students can place any orders that they want at the store but receive one-day shipping if they have it delivered to Amazon.com's on-campus location. Amazon.com plans to create more retail stores on other campuses in the future. Amazon expanded its physical stores to noncampus locations. As we are writing this, Amazon has stores in thirteen cities, including Chicago, New York, Seattle, Portland, Los Angeles, and San Diego, with three more locations "coming soon."

In 2017, Amazon.com surprised many by acquiring Whole Foods, a high-end chain of grocery stores. Almost immediately following the closing of the acquisition, Amazon lowered prices on many of Whole Food's best-selling items. Future plans include integrating Amazon Prime into Whole Food's information systems to allow Amazon Prime members to receive discounts and other in-store benefits.

Amazon is also in the process of testing and obtaining permission to utilize drones, or pilotless aircraft, to deliver packages. Doing so would allow Amazon .com to deliver products without requiring a human delivery driver to bring products to the customer's location.

Sources: "Amazon Opens Its First Store." 2015. *CNN Money,* February 4. http://money .cnn.com/2015/02/04/technology/amazon-purdue/; Lapowsky, I. 2015. "Amazon Can Now Test Its Delivery Drones in the U.S." *Wired,* April 10. http://www.wired.com/2015/ 04/amazon-drone-faa-green-light/; "Whole Foods Market @ Amazon." https://www .amazon.com/b?ie=UTF8&node=17235386011; "Why Amazon Is the World's Most Innovative Company of 2017." Fast Company, February 2. https://www.fastcompany.com/ 3067455/why-amazon-is-the-worlds-most-innovative-company-of-2017.

Table 13.3 B2C E-Business Models

E-Business Model	Description	Important Facts	Examples
Online retailing	Offers products or services for sale to consumers online. Some businesses acquire the products for resale, while others act as electronic intermediaries for selling products.	The ability to distribute products efficiently and effectively (fulfillment and logistics functions) is critical to success in this business model.	• LLBean.com • BestBuy.com, Staples.com
Infomediary	Offers specialized information to consumers via the Internet that aggregates or analyzes products or services from several providers. The term comes from **information intermediaries**.	These companies do not sell products or services directly, and they do not have any inventory. The ability to maintain up-to-date information is crucial in this business model.	• *Consumer goods:* MySimon.com • *Travel:* Kayak.com • *Automobiles:* Edmunds.com
Content providers	Offers consumers content or relevant information and receives money from vendors for ads or downloads or from consumers for subscriptions.	Content can be generated and published by the organization, or it can be user-generated content that the business publishes.	• *News:* Bloomberg Solutions (http://www.bloomberg.com) • *Entertainment:* Eonline.com • *Historical and reference:* Britannica.com • *Travel:* Tripadvisor.com
Exchanges	Offers a location (marketplace) for buyers and sellers to transact online. Revenues come from fees for sellers or buyers or commission on sales.	Generating a large number of buyers and sellers (a critical mass) is crucial for success in this business model.	• eBay.com • uBid.com
Online community or social media	Offers individuals with similar interests and/or goals an online meeting place to interact with one another. Many start as not-for-profit but end up charging for select services or information or allow ads to be posted on the community.	Online communities are virtual in the sense that the meeting place is online only.	• Facebook.com • Delphiforums.com

E-Business Model	Description	Important Facts	Examples
E-business infrastructure provider	Offers infrastructure hardware, software, or services to other organizations for e-business. Revenues come from fees paid for the services.	Online businesses can use these infrastructures through cloud computing (Chapter 7) or directly through the provider. This has substantially reduced the cost of starting online businesses.	• *Online payment service:* PayPal .com • *Credit card processing service:* Squareup .com • *Web and database hosting services:* Rackspace.com • *Domain name registration and Web and database hosting:* GoDaddy.com

B2C E-Business Enablers

The statistics previously presented and those that you found in Learning Activity 13.1 clearly show that B2C e-business continues to increase in value worldwide. What has made this growth possible? A combination of technological and social factors can help explain why B2C e-business has grown so much over the years.

Technological Enablers

There are several technological requirements that must be met for consumers to successfully acquire goods or services online. First, there must be an easy-to-navigate website. The graphical user interfaces of today's browsers and the search tools available on websites are examples of technological improvements that have enabled e-business to grow. In addition, e-business requires that consumers have sufficient network bandwidth to access e-businesses' websites. Think of how much time it takes sometimes to download images for goods you want to purchase. If it takes too long, you might end up going to a different site. The bandwidth required depends on the images and other features of the site, and the overall bandwidth is a function of the vendor's network bandwidth (and server processing capability) and the consumer's Internet access bandwidth. In recent years, the use of broadband networks for Internet access (see Chapter 7) has significantly improved the overall bandwidth availability and therefore the online shopping experience of consumers. However, there are still many rural locations that lack reliable high-speed Internet service.

A less visible but just as critical technological requirement is interoperability. We discussed **interoperability** in Chapter 7, where we defined it as the ability of heterogeneous systems to communicate with one another. Interoperability is key to e-business success because, by definition, e-business allows individuals using a wide variety of platforms (PCs, Macs, laptops, tablets, smartphones, etc.) to access businesses that also use a wide variety of platforms (with different operating systems, databases, Web servers, etc.).

Critical Mass

Beyond technological factors, one key social factor that has had a huge impact on the growth of e-business is the attainment of a critical mass of users. The impact of critical mass is best understood under the concept of network effects, which we define further below. In e-business, attaining **critical mass** means that there are sufficient buyers to sustain the business of vendors and sufficient vendors to attract buyers to the Internet.

Network effects or network economics can be used to discuss how value is created in a network. Recall from Chapter 4 that a firm can get competitive advantages when it owns a resource that is rare or unique. This is considered *value in scarcity.* In networks, however, there is also something completely opposite, which is *value in plentitude.* In a network (think of a group of people), the value of the network increases every time a new member is added to the network. Let us take the example of email. If only two of you use email, it makes one possible link. Eventually, you might find it limiting to only be able to send email to this one other person. Now if you add a third person to your group, you each have two potential people to send email to (or the existence of three links in the network). The addition of the third person adds value to your network. Now consider the networks in Figure 13.2. How many links are possible now?

Extend this concept to e-business, and you realize that the more vendors there are on the Internet, the more interesting it is for you to shop online. For vendors, the

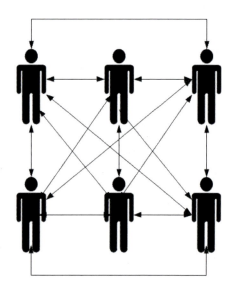

Figure 13.2 Networks of People

same is true: the more consumers there are shopping online, the more interesting it is to use the Internet to sell their goods or services. Today, as we saw in previous chapters, there are close to one billion hosts (servers) on the Internet and more than 30% of the world population has Internet access. We could say that the Internet and the Web have reached critical mass.

B2C E-Business Impacts

We discussed early in the chapter how e-business has changed industries. For some, these changes have been extremely positive (lower costs), while for others, the changes may be perceived as very negative (loss of profits or even disappearance of some businesses). There are two specific terms used to refer to two impacts of e-business: channel compression and channel expansion.

Channel Compression (Disintermediation)

Channel compression is an impact on the downstream portion of the supply chain. Recall from Chapter 12 that the supply chain consists of several distributors and retailers upstream and downstream of the focal firm. In the distribution channel, the distributors and retailers are called *intermediaries*. **Channel compression** refers to situations when the distribution chain is shortened by eliminating some or all of these intermediaries between the focal firm (product producer) and the end consumer. For this reason, channel compression is also called *disintermediation*. As previously discussed, this change in the distribution structure has led to some major restructuring in several industries, including the music, publishing, and travel industries. When organizations have to decide whether or not to eliminate members of their distribution channel, they are often faced with channel conflict, or when to eliminate distributors and when to work with them. For example, if the Dell company decides to offer products through Dell retailers but also to sell directly online, how can it price products so that its resellers can make a profit but its consumers still feel they are getting the best prices when they buy directly online?

Channel Expansion

While channel compression has resulted in fewer organizations involved in the supply chain for some industries, channel expansion offers the reverse impact. **Channel expansion** is the addition of intermediaries in an industry whose purpose is to aggregate and provide information or brokering functionalities. In other words, intermediaries facilitate bringing buyers and sellers together or bringing relevant information to buyers and sellers. Think of the role of Kayak.com. It does not offer its own flights but pulls information from different vendors (airlines) as well as other search engines (like Expedia.com or Priceline.com). These intermediaries can make money by receiving fees from vendors or by allowing ads on their sites. The larger the volume of users, the better they can sell ad placement (selling ads on their websites based on number of viewers). An overall important effect of these intermediaries is to reduce search costs and the information asymmetries that existed before the Internet and e-business. A good example is provided by real estate e-brokers. Figure 13.3 shows the most visited real estate websites in December 2014. How many of these companies existed before e-business?

LEARNING ACTIVITY 13.2

Why Would I Trust Them or Buy from Them?

In this activity, visit two retail websites and identify the factors that would make you more willing to trust the Web merchant and to buy and/or share information with the website. Select *two* of the following Web merchants:

- Dell: http://ww.dell.com
- Amazon: http://www.amazon.com
- BestBuy: http://www.bestbuy.com
- Sierra: http://www.sierratradingpost.com
- Road Runner: http://www.roadrunnersports.com
- Murad: http://www.murad.com

Create a table, as shown below, to list the specific features that would make you trust, buy, or share information:

	Trust	Intentions to Buy	Willingness to Share Information
Site A	Feature 1 Feature 2 (etc.)	Feature 1 Feature 2 (etc.)	Feature 1 Feature 2 (etc.)
Site B	Feature 1 Feature 2 (etc.)	Feature 1 Feature 2 (etc.)	Feature 1 Feature 2 (etc.)

Design for B2C E-Business

There are many important design features that can make e-business websites more or less successful. In Learning Activity 13.2, you identified several of them. For example, most of you will have identified the security of the website as a requirement for trusting the Web merchant and its privacy practices as a requirement for being willing to share information with the website. In Chapters 8 and 9, we discussed various features that increase (or reassure customers about) the security and privacy of information systems. In fact, many researchers have identified trust as one key determinant of individuals' intentions to buy from online merchants. Ease of use

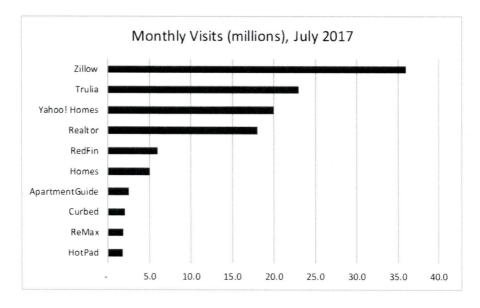

Figure 13.3 Top Real Estate Websites, July 2017

Source: https://www.statista.com/statistics/381468/most-popular-real-estate-websites-by
-monthly-visits-usa/.

of the system in terms of navigating, checking out, and accessing information are usually important design features as well. The overall look of the website is also a factor in online buying decisions. Sites that are overloaded with information can be distracting for some users, while sites that have features and graphics that are too simplistic may look unprofessional. There are also nontechnological features for website success, such as return policies, shipping policies, and communication tools. Research also suggests that websites that offer customer reviews see increased site traffic and overall conversion rate (http://www.eMarketer.com). The conversion rate is the rate at which consumers who are browsing the website end up buying from the website. Other features that are found to annoy customers on websites include pop-up ads, the need for extra software to view a site, dead links, confusing navigation, the need to log in to view content, slow-loading pages, and out-of-date content, to name a few (eMarketer.com 2015).

Business-to-Business (B2B)

Most of this chapter so far has discussed B2C e-business, mainly because you are more familiar with this type of e-business but also because many of the basic principles also apply to B2B e-business. However, there is a significant difference between B2C and B2B e-business beyond the type of players involved, and that is the size of the market involved. B2B e-business represents a significantly larger market than B2C.

B2C versus B2B

Every year, the U.S. Census Bureau collects data on e-commerce. Their studies reveal that the amount of money spent on e-commerce grows each year. For this learning activity, visit the following website and collect the amount of e-commerce sales over the last three years. While you are doing this, differentiate how many sales occur through B2C and B2B channels. Compare these numbers and write a short response as to what they tell you about these two markets:

http://www.census.gov/econ/estats/index.html

There are several other differences between B2B and B2C. Of course, B2B involves two or more organizations as opposed to individual consumers. In B2B, these organizations typically know their trading partners fairly well, and as a result, B2B is often relationship based, except for marketplaces that we will describe later.

B2B E-Business Models

B2B involves the sharing of electronic documents, funds, and/or information between organizations. There are many ways to implement this, which are summarized in Table 13.4. First, B2B e-business includes supply chain management (SCM), which we discussed in Chapter 12. In fact, when organizations share knowledge electronically across the supply chain to facilitate inventory control, reduce time delays in billing, and improve customer handling, they are conducting B2B e-business. Two other models of B2B e-business need further explanation: electronic data interchange and **e-marketplaces**.

Electronic data interchange (EDI) is the electronic exchange of information between two or more organizations using a standard format. The types of information exchanged are defined within the standards that are used and usually include business documents like bills, purchase orders, payment slips, invoices, and so on. EDI has been in existence for a very long time, allowing trading partners to lower transaction costs and improve profits through faster billing cycles, reduced errors, and improved customer responsiveness. Figure 13.4 shows a simplified sample set of EDI transactions.

An important characteristic of EDI is that organizations must use standardized formats for the documents they are exchanging. In fact, every organization has its own internal systems to handle purchase orders, invoices, and other business documents; therefore, each organization stores and handles data in different formats. An EDI transaction starts with the conversion of the documents and data from the format used by the internal system of the organization to an EDI format. This is called the **outbound transformation.** The EDI documents are then sent to the partner organization, where the company's systems must perform an **inbound transformation**, which involves the system converting the EDI documents into the format used by the

Table 13.4 B2B E-Business Models

Electronic data interchange (EDI)	Electronic exchange of information between two or more organizations using a standard format.
Supply chain management (SCM)	Allows organizations to manage the movement of materials or products from provision to production to consumption. SCM involves collaboration between partners both upstream and downstream from the focal organization.
E-marketplaces	Also known as an *exchange*. Allows vending companies and buying companies to "meet" electronically to conduct transactions.

internal systems of that organization. The most-used standardized formats for EDI are **ANSI X.12** and **EDIFACT**.

EDI used to be limited to one-to-one communications between two trading partners. Today, it has evolved into a multipartner environment, allowing transmission of documents across a variety of information systems, even if they are incompatible in terms of hardware and software, since EDI documents themselves have to be in a very strict format. The use of a strict format is both an advantage and a disadvantage

Figure 13.4 Electronic Data Interchange Example

of EDI systems; on the one hand, it allows for fast processing and support for the various platforms, but on the other hand, it limits the flexibility of transmission that organizations want. Today, organizations want to conduct more complex activities than simply trading documents with one another to support their business processes, and they want to use the Internet as opposed to proprietary networks for the transmissions. This is where **extensible markup language (XML)** becomes a popular way of conducting B2B transactions. XML is a markup language that allows organizations to give meaning to their data but inserts tags that describe the data within documents. A **markup language** (such as HTML or XML) is used to give "meaning" to information by placing a beginning and end tag around the information. For example, in HTML, we can use bold tags: this is bolded. This will appear as **this is bolded** on the Web page.

XML is very flexible, since organizations can define their own tags. Once documents are tagged with XML, a variety of systems can read and understand the documents, as long at the systems know the definitions of the tags. In conducting B2B, therefore, organizations have to agree on the meaning of the tags. For example, if one company decides to code its standardized documents in XML using the term *client* (<CLIENT> Mr. Jones </CLIENT>) but its trading partner uses the term *customer* (<CUSTOMER> Mr. Jones </CUSTOMER>), their respective systems could not read each other's data. Some industries are tackling this problem by developing industry-wide XML definitions or standards, such as **electronic business extensible markup language (ebXML) for e-business**.

Finally, B2B can also be conducted in marketplaces, also known as exchanges. An **exchange** allows vendors or sellers to meet electronically. When a limited number of buyers or sellers are allowed to use a marketplace, we refer to this as a *consortia marketplace* or even a *private market*. When a large number of buyers and sellers exist, it is considered a **neutral auction**. Sometimes many buyers bid on a seller's products (a **seller-oriented or forward auction**), or sometimes many sellers offer their products to a single buyer (a **buyer-oriented or reverse auction**). Over the years, many B2B marketplaces have come and gone, although some have succeeded. For example, Buyerzone.com allows small businesses to buy and sell products to one another. However, marketplaces are difficult to sustain because they need to have a sufficient number of buyers and sellers to ensure the growth of the marketplace.

Search Engine Optimization

Anyone involved in B2C e-business today would probably tell you that one of the most important factors for success online is being visible, which means showing up in searches. In fact, research has shown that if an organization's link is not in the top 30, it does not exist. Other research says that it is the first page of results that counts. In a study of which links individuals click on in the search results page, 42% of individuals clicked on the first organic link (explained below); 12% on the second; 8% on the

LEARNING ACTIVITY 13.4

Where Is My Web Page?

In this activity, you will select two different Internet search engines to find some specific items. Record your results in a word processing file.

1. First, search for "intellectual property rights." Identify the top three sponsored (if any) and the top three organic links found.
2. Use the same two search engines to find the following products: a Trek mountain bike and an iPad Air 2.

Indicate in your document the search engine used, the links you found, and your preferred search engine. Explain why you prefer a specific search engine.

third; and then 6%, 5%, and 4% on the following ones, with 3% for the remainder of the links on the first page of search results (http://www.redcardinal.ie/search-engine -optimisation/). Clearly, being at the top of the search results page is important for e-businesses. But how does an organization make sure it shows up toward the top of the search results? This is the role of **search engine optimization (SEO)**, which is the series of practices an organization can use to improve its visibility or optimize how its Web pages or website shows up on the search engine results pages. SEO uses a combination of how the Web page is designed, which keywords and language are used on the Web page, and which search engines are most used by specific audiences.

SEO is not a one-time effort, since search engines change their requirements often, people change their searching patterns, and competitors also try to optimize their own websites. In terms of design, one of the most important first steps for an organization is to clearly identify which keywords best represent what the organization's *intended audience* would use to find them. The key is to identify what the targeted audience thinks when they search online. It is also important to note that a keyword could actually be a keyword phrase, such as "mortgage lender" or "best place to eat." With this information, the Web designers can do several things to help the ranking of the Web page. They can include the main keywords more often on the page and in more prominent places (headings, for example). They can include key-words in meta tags, which is information included with the page but not seen on the Web. There are many other factors that impact the ranking, such as including in-links, or inbound links, where other sites link to the organization; the age of the website domain (the older the better); and the overall size of the website. The exact details of how a website is more highly ranked vary over time and across search engines. This is why many consultants have started to offer SEO services to small, medium, and even large e-businesses.

Another way to have an organization's website show up higher in the rankings is to pay for placement. These are considered **sponsored links,** as opposed to **organic**

links (ranked by design and SEO only). Some research suggests that most individuals prefer organic links, with 80% to 90% of the clicks being on organic links (http://www.redcardinal.ie/search-engine-optimisation/). Sponsored links show up separate from the search results and are based on the keywords entered in the search engines, as seen in Figure 13.5. The figure shows an example of Google AdWords, which is Google's sponsored link service.

Keyword bidding is another form of paying for a better ranking. It is also known as pay-per-click (PPC). The concept is that an organization pays the search engine owners only when someone clicks its link on the search results page. In most cases, companies bid for keywords, and the company that bids the highest will show up higher in the results when someone uses the keywords in a search. There is another type of PPC called *flat-rate PPC*, where the price of keywords is fixed. Nevertheless, you can easily see why PPC is an important source of revenues for companies like Google AdWords, Yahoo!, Search Marketing, or Bing Ads. Every time a user clicks on a link, the organization pays the search engine. In fact, many companies increased their paid search engine use for the holiday season in 2014 and saw revenue increase 50% on Thanksgiving Day due to online sales directly attributable to paid searches (Enright 2011). What does it cost to "buy" a keyword from a search engine? The cost varies substantially depending on the month of the year and what is going on at that time. In an earlier edition of this book, we reported that in May 2014, the most expensive keywords were "insurance" at $54.91 per click and "loans" at $44.28 per click. In December 2017, the list was substantially different; the most expensive keywords were "business services" at $58.64 per click, with "bail bonds" close behind at $58.48 per click. Table 13.5 shows some of the other expensive keywords as of December 2017. As you can see, keywords can be very expensive. Therefore, organizations are often told to find the best and most representative keywords for their businesses and to aim to be number two instead of number one in the search results.

Paid search engines are a huge business, and the main players in the United States are Google, Yahoo!, and Bing. However, when considering the global market, another player enters the scene: Baidu. As of mid-2015, Google owned about 66% of the market; Baidu, 13%; Yahoo!, 9%; and Bing, 9%. In China, the search engine Baidu owns the majority of the market share, helping it reach second place in the global rankings (https://www.netmarketshare.com/search-engine-market-share.aspx?qprid=4&qpcustomd=0).

Trends in E-Business

E-business has become mainstream, with individuals and organizations becoming increasingly comfortable transacting and interacting electronically. We discuss three major trends in e-business in the remainder of the chapter. Students, however, can go to the book's website for more interesting trends.

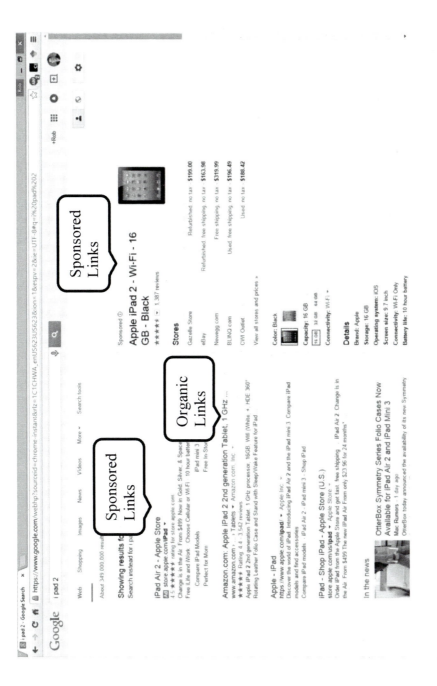

Figure 13.5 Search Results for Organic and Sponsored Links

Table 13.5 Most Expensive Keywords, December 2017

1. Business services	$58.64
2. Bail bonds	$58.48
3. Casino	$55.48
4. Lawyer	$54.86
5. Asset management	$49.86
6. Insurance	$48.41
7. Cash services and payday loans	$48.18
8. Cleanup and restoration services	$47.61
9. Degree	$47.36
10. Medical coding services	$46.84

Source: Based on data by WordStream, available at https://www.wordstream.com/blog/ws/2017/06/27/most-expensive-keywords.

Mobile Business

Today, many individuals use sophisticated Internet-enabled mobile technologies, such as cellular phones, smartphones, and tablets in their daily work and personal lives. This has enabled another form of e-business known as **mobile business (m-business)**, which is when individuals conduct commercial transactions and interactions using handheld mobile devices and wireless communication networks. With mobile devices, users have access to critical information anywhere and anytime, which allows them to seize business opportunities (such as enjoying the sale of the day on Woot! [http://www.woot.com]). While mobile business has become well established, some elements are still emerging in importance. For example, as discussed earlier, **location-based services (LBS)** make it possible to provide targeted advertisements to users, such as discounts based on their current location. Therefore, as the user walks in front of a certain restaurant at mealtime, a coupon appears on the user's mobile device.

Global E-Business

Another important trend for e-business is the global nature of the phenomenon. Usage of electronic means for business is growing everywhere in the world. In fact, the Internet is also becoming multilingual, facilitating e-business. By the end of 2013, there were 800.6 million users of English websites on the Internet (http://www.internetworldstats.com/stats7.htm). At the same time, 649.4 million used Chinese, 222.4 million used Spanish, and 135.6 million used Arabic websites. As you might have learned in Learning Activity 13.1, the growth of e-commerce sales corresponds with this growth in Internet usage. Stats Box 13.3 lists some global e-business facts published by eMarketer.com.

STATS BOX 13.2:
MOBILE PHONE STATISTICS

Mobile phones are being used by almost everyone today. In the following table, you can see the mobile technology usage of people in the United States.

Mobile Phone Ownership in the United States, November 2016

	Percentage of Population
Adults who own a smartphone	77
Adults who own a cell phone	95
Adults who own an e-reader	22
Adults who own a tablet	51
Smartphone is only access to the Internet	12

Source: http://www.pewinternet.org/fact-sheets/mobile-technology-fact-sheet/.

LEARNING ACTIVITY 13.5

USA.gov

Government websites are sometimes different than e-commerce websites. In this learning activity, you are to interact with the USA.gov website (http://www.usa.gov) or your local government's website. Identify five similarities and differences between this e-government site and the e-commerce sites used in Learning Activity 13.2.

E-Government

A final trend we discuss is e-government, which was introduced at the beginning of the chapter. **E-government** involves using information technologies to enable and improve the efficiency with which government services are provided to citizens, employees, businesses, and agencies. It can occur at various levels of government, such as municipalities, counties, districts, states, provinces, or countries. It has become popular not only for obtaining information from government agencies but also for conducting transactions such as paying taxes, renewing licenses, or downloading government forms. According to Smith (2010), 82% of Internet users search for government information or complete government transactions online. The most leading-edge applications in e-government include platforms for citizen feedback via blogs, Twitter, or social networking sites. The future of e-government is also likely to include some form of **Internet voting**, where citizens will be able to cast their votes

---

STATS BOX 13.3:
GLOBAL E-BUSINESS

E-business is a global phenomenon. eMarketer.com, a leading digital research firm, offers the following statistics:

- In 2012, B2C e-commerce sales topped $1 trillion for the first time.

- In 2017, B2C e-commerce reached $2.3 trillion worldwide. Estimates indicate that e-commerce sales will reach almost $4.5 trillion in 2021.

- B2B e-commerce is still much larger than B2C e-commerce. In 2017, B2B e-commerce reached $7.7 trillion, making B2B e-commerce more than three times the size of B2C e-commerce.

- In 2017, China was the largest e-commerce market in the world ($673 billion), followed by the United States ($340 billion), the United Kingdom ($99 billion), Japan ($79 billion), and Germany ($73 billion).

- Most online shoppers (57%) purchase from overseas retailers. For all continents, the majority of consumers' online purchases were made from overseas retailers.

Sources: "Ecommerce Sales Topped $1 Trillion for First Time in 2012," http://www.eMarketer.com/Article/Ecommerce-Sales-Topped-1-Trillion-First-Time-2012/1009649; "10 of the Largest Ecommerce Markets in the World by Country," https://www.business.com/articles/10-of-the-largest-ecommerce-markets-in-the-world-b/; "Global Ecommerce Statistics and 10 International Growth Trends You Need to Know," https://www.shopify.com/enterprise/global-ecommerce-statistics.

---

electronically via the Internet. In fact, some countries and states have already started to allow citizens to vote via the Internet.

Chapter Summary

In this chapter, we discussed e-business. We first presented various ways to categorize e-business and then explored specific business models in greater depth. More specifically, we explained how business-to-consumer (B2C) e-business is conducted and what its enablers and impacts are. We also discussed business-to-business (B2B) e-business models in depth. The chapter concluded with search engine optimization and a discussion of important trends related to e-business.

Here are the main points discussed in the chapter:

- E-business involves electronic means to interact or conduct business with individuals, companies, or government agencies. E-business can be classified according to type: business-to-consumer (B2C; interactions are taking place between a consumer and a business), business-to-business (B2B; interactions are taking place between two businesses), consumer-to-consumer (C2C; interactions are taking place between two consumers), and government-to-constituent (G2C; interactions are taking place between a government agency and a constituent). E-businesses can also be classified according to their online component: bricks and mortar are traditional organizations with physical locations, bricks and clicks are traditional organizations with physical locations but that also operate an online business, and pure plays are organizations with only an online business.

- Business-to-consumer (B2C) e-business models include online retailing (offering products or services for sale to consumers online), infomediaries (offering specialized information to consumers via the Internet that aggregates or analyzes products or services from several providers), content providers (offering consumers content or relevant information), exchanges (offering a location [marketplace] for buyers and sellers to transact online), online communities or social media (offering individuals with similar interests and/or goals an online meeting place to interact with each other), and e-business infrastructure providers (offering infrastructure hardware, software, or services to other organizations for e-business). Enablers of B2C e-business include technological enablers (ease of use, bandwidth, and interoperability) as well as a social enabler (critical mass). Finally, impacts of e-business include channel compression and channel expansion.

- Search engine optimization (SEO) is the series of practices an organization can use to improve its visibility, or optimize how its Web pages or website show up on the search engine results pages. SEO uses a combination of Web page design, keywords and languages used on the Web page, and listings on search engines most used by specific audiences. One way to optimize placement is through sponsored links, where companies pay for placement or use keyword bidding, which gives companies with the highest bids higher placement in search engine results.

- Business-to-business (B2B) e-business involves the sharing of electronic documents, funds, and/or information between organizations. B2B e-business models include supply chain management, electronic data interchange (EDI), and e-marketplaces. EDI is the electronic exchange of information between two or more organizations using a standard format. The most-used standardized formats for EDI are ANSI X.12 and EDIFACT, but organizations are increasingly using XML (extensible markup language) to conduct B2B transactions because it is much more flexible in terms of the types of information it allows organizations to exchange with one another. B2B marketplaces, or exchanges, allow vendors or sellers to "meet" electronically.

- Three major trends in e-business are mobile business, global e-business, and e-government. Mobile business, or m-business, occurs when individuals conduct commercial transactions and interactions using handheld mobile devices and wireless communications networks. Global e-business is occurring because usage of electronic means for business is growing everywhere in the world and the Internet is becoming increasingly multilingual. E-government involves using information technologies to enable and improve the efficiency with which government services are provided to citizens, employees, businesses, and agencies.

Review Questions

1. Define e-business and compare this to e-commerce, e-government, and Internet commerce. Is Internet commerce considered e-business?
2. Explain what a business model is and what it should include.
3. Describe the various ways to classify e-business models, including B2C and B2B models.
4. Identify the main technological factors that have enabled e-business growth and compare them to the technological enablers of m-business.
5. Explain the concept of network effects or network economics and its importance to e-business.
6. Explain how e-business has led to disintermediation and provide examples.
7. Explain how e-business has led to channel expansion, discuss its impacts, and provide examples.
8. Describe the goals of search engine optimization, the various ways in which it is performed, and other options organizations have for marketing their websites.
9. Compare and contrast B2B e-business to B2C e-business.
10. Describe how electronic data interchange (EDI) functions and how it is evolving today.

Reflection Questions

1. What is the most important thing you learned in this chapter? Why is it important?
2. What topics are unclear? What about them is unclear?
3. Is it important to distinguish among e-business, e-commerce, and Internet commerce? Why or why not?
4. How is the material in this chapter related to the material on transmitting information in Chapter 7?
5. What is the relationship between network effects and the material on competitive advantages in Chapter 4?
6. What is the role of security in e-business success?

7. What is the role of privacy in e-business success?

8. If both channel compression and channel expansion occur in an industry because of e-business, does that mean that e-business had limited impacts on that industry? Why or why not?

9. A businessperson the authors know said that search engine optimization is as much art as science. What does he mean?

10. Why is mobile commerce more popular in other areas of the world compared to the United States?

Additional Learning Activities

13.A1. This activity requires you to complete a case analysis regarding e-business. The case may be accessed through your university website or the Ivey Business School business case website (https://www.iveycases.com), or it may be provided to you by your instructor:

Su, N., P. Bansai, and P. Laugland. 2017. *Alibaba Group: Technology, Strategy, and Sustainability.* Ivey Publishing. Product Number: 9B16E036 (revised).

13.A2. E-business has become a global phenomenon. However, not all countries are equal when it comes to having infrastructures, laws, and business practices that support e-business. The Economist Intelligence Unit (EIU; http://www.eiu.com) ranks each country on its digital economy readiness (see http://country.eiu.com/AllCountries.aspx). In this learning activity, you will be assigned a country and will need to explore its e-business readiness. Your instructor will assign you a country to research. Bring a short report to class that includes the following:

• The country you are assigned

• The EIU ranking for digital economy readiness

• Any e-business statistics you can find about your assigned country

• Your research of potential explanations for the ranking of your country (You will have to make assumptions.)

13.A3. Conduct research on the Web to give examples of each type of e-business defined in Table 13.1.

13.A4. Extend the existing business models presented in Table 13.2 with the use of location-based services (LBS). Describe how mobile users could make use of these models.

13.A5. Identify the business models of the following websites: http://www.pandora.com, http://www.consumerreports.org, http://www.yahoo.com, and http://www.weightwatchers.com.

References

eMarketer. 2015. "Referrals Fuel Highest B2B Conversion Rates." *eMarketer.com*, February 10. http://www.eMarketer.com/Article/Referrals-Fuel-Highest-B2B -Conversion-Rates/1012000.

Enright, A. 2011. "Paid Search Pays Off over the Holidays: Budgets Were Up 52% during November and December, and Related Sales Rose 69%." *Internet Retailer*, January 13. http://www.internetretailer.com/2011/01/13/paid-search-paid-over -holidays.

Smith, A. 2010. "Government Online: The Internet Gives Citizens New Paths to Government Services and Information." *Pew Internet and American Life Project Report*. Retrieved January 26, 2011, from http://pewinternet.org/Reports/2010/ Government-Online.aspx/.

Glossary

ANSI X.12: One of the most-used standardized formats for EDI.

Bricks and clicks: Traditional organizations with physical locations as well as an online businesses.

Bricks and mortar: Traditional organizations with physical locations.

Business model: The way the organization functions and creates value.

Business-to-business (B2B): A type of e-business where interactions are taking place between two businesses.

Business-to-consumer (B2C): A type of e-business where interactions are taking place between a consumer and a business.

Buyer-oriented or reverse auction: Many sellers offer their products to a single buyer.

Channel compression (disintermediation): A situation in which the distribution chain is shortened by eliminating some or all of the intermediaries between the focal firm (product producer) and the end consumer.

Channel expansion: The addition of intermediaries in an industry whose purpose is to aggregate and provide information or brokering functionalities.

Consumer-to-consumer (C2C): A type of e-business where interactions are taking place between two consumers.

Content providers: An e-business model where companies offer consumers content or relevant information and receive money from vendors for ads or downloads or from consumers for subscriptions.

Critical mass: A point when there are sufficient buyers to sustain the business of vendors and sufficient vendors to attract buyers to the Internet.

E-business infrastructure provider: A company that offers infrastructure hardware, software, or services to other organizations for e-business.

EDIFACT: One of the most-used standardized formats for EDI.

Electronic business (e-business): An electronic means to interact or conduct business with individuals, companies, or government agencies.

Electronic business extensible markup language (ebXML) for e-business: An industry-wide set of XML definitions or standards for e-business.

Electronic commerce (e-commerce): An electronic means to conduct business transactions, including the Internet, EDI, or private networks.

Electronic data interchange (EDI): A B2B e-business model focusing on the electronic exchange of information between two or more organizations using a standard format.

Electronic funds transfer (EFT): An electronic means to conduct financial transactions such as payments and remittances.

Electronic government (e-government): An electronic means to interact or conduct transactions with government agencies.

E-marketplaces (exchanges): Allows vendors or sellers to "meet" electronically.

Exchange: An e-business model where companies offer a location (marketplace) for buyers and sellers to transact online.

Extensible markup language (XML): A markup language that allows organizations to give meaning to their data by inserting tags that describe the data within documents; a popular way of conducting B2B transactions.

Government-to-constituent (G2C): A type of e-business where interactions are taking place between a government agency and a constituent.

Inbound transformation: Converting the EDI documents into the format used by the internal systems of that organization.

Infomediaries: An e-business model where companies offer specialized information to consumers via the Internet that aggregates or analyzes products or services from several providers.

Internet commerce: An electronic means to conduct business using the Internet (for example, email, the Web, or file transfers).

Internet voting: When citizens are able to cast their votes electronically via the Internet.

Interoperability: The ability of heterogeneous systems to communicate with each other.

Keyword bidding (pay-per-click: PPC): When organizations pay the search engine owners when someone clicks their links on the search engine results page.

Location-based services (LBS): Services that make use of knowing where users are based on their cell phone location to offer targeted advertising or services at a specific moment.

Markup language (such as HTML or XML): Used to give "meaning" to information by placing a beginning and end tag around the information.

Mobile business (m-business): When individuals conduct commercial transactions and interactions using handheld mobile devices and wireless communications networks.

Network effects or network economics: Explains how value is attained in a network when critical mass, or plentitude of members, is achieved. The value of the network increases every time a new member is added to the network.

Neutral auction: A marketplace with a large number of buyers and sellers.

Online community or social media: An e-business model where organizations offer individuals with similar interests and/or goals an online meeting place to interact with one another.

Online retailing: An e-business model where companies offer products or services for sale to consumers online.

Organic links: Links on search engine results achieved by design and search engine optimization.

Outbound transformation: Conversion of the documents and data from the format used by the internal system of the organization to an EDI format.

Pure play (or click only): Organizations with only an online business.

Search engine optimization (SEO): A series of practices an organization can use to improve its visibility or optimize how its Web pages or website shows up on the search engine results pages.

Seller-oriented or forward auction: Many buyers bid on a seller's products.

Sponsored links: Links that show up higher in the search engine results because the organization has paid for placement.

Supply chain management (SCM): A B2B e-business model focusing on the electronic exchange of information along the supply chain.

Web commerce: An electronic means to conduct business transactions using the Web as an interface.

CHAPTER 14

Information and Knowledge for Business Decision Making

Learning Objectives

By reading and completing the activities in this chapter, you will be able to

- Explain why knowledge management is important to organizations
- Compare and contrast explicit and tacit knowledge
- Describe the main processes for knowledge management
- Compare and contrast major knowledge management technologies

Chapter Outline

Additional Learning Activities

References

Glossary

Ultimately, a business's ability to compete depends heavily on how its employees apply knowledge to make decisions and solve problems. Information systems and technologies can help organizations better manage knowledge. In addition, information systems and technologies can facilitate better decision making. In this chapter, we help you understand knowledge management and how technologies can help organizations manage knowledge. Knowledge is often applied to decision making. Because of this, we also discuss decision support systems. As organizations gather an increasing amount of data, being able to leverage these data for decision making and action is an increasingly important aspect of business. Business intelligence systems, which we also discuss in this chapter, help organizations make sense of this sea of data.

FOCUSING STORY

Managing Knowledge by Texting

Several years ago, I was teaching an onsite class to information technology (IT) professionals working at a major logistics company. While waiting for class to start one night, I overheard one of the students asking another if he had received a text message regarding a problem he was having with a computer program. This surprised me. At the time, such messaging was generally done more for personal than business reasons. So I asked the student who sent the text how frequently they exchanged such messages. The student replied, "All the time. Whenever one of us runs into a problem we haven't seen before, we send a message to the group. Usually someone has seen a similar problem, so they can help." Essentially, the group had informally created a "knowledge network" of shared expertise. By sending a simple text message, an individual worker can tap into the knowledge of the entire group. The result is hours of saved time and frustration.

More recently, people are using social networking sites such as LinkedIn and Facebook as a means of accessing the knowledge of others. For example, when I had to write a job description for an unusual faculty job, I turned to several LinkedIn groups for advice. Some individuals responded with helpful advice. When you are faced with a decision, it is often necessary to reach out to those who may have knowledge useful to the decision. This may be as simple as calling your car-loving brother when you are buying a new vehicle, or it may mean convening a meeting of experts to help a corporate board decide whether to pursue a merger. Regardless of the decision, the intent is the same. Additional knowledge can have great value to decision making. Whether you use text messaging to get help solve a computer problem or you fly in experts from around the world, you are still trying to leverage the knowledge of others to help you make a decision. Fortunately, information technologies can aid in the quest to use the knowledge of others to help make better decisions.

FOCUSING QUESTIONS

1. When have you used the knowledge of others to help you make a decision? Briefly describe the decision. Whom did you contact to help you? What knowledge were you trying to access?

2. How have you used information technologies to help you connect with others for the purpose of tapping their knowledge? Why did you use those technologies?

LEARNING ACTIVITY 14.1

How You Manage Knowledge

This chapter helps you understand organizational knowledge management, but individuals also manage their knowledge. The goal of knowledge management is to make sure the right knowledge is available in a useful form to the right people. Personal knowledge management is the process of determining what knowledge you need and how to find, organize, and use that knowledge. Prepare a one- to two-page paper on how you manage your personal knowledge. What tools do you use? How effective are they? Compare your response with another student's response.

Knowledge Management

In an earlier chapter, we introduced you to the concepts of data, information, and knowledge. You may recall that data are unconnected facts, information is data that have been processed so that they are useful, and knowledge is information that is applied to a decision or action. If you think about these differences, you may see that as we progress from data to information to knowledge, there is a greater level of human contribution and greater value.

However, as we move up the hierarchy toward knowledge, things get harder to manage, in part because of the increased level of human contribution. It is relatively easy to manage data, but managing knowledge is quite difficult. Table 14.1 shows some characteristics of data, information, and knowledge. As you can see from the table, knowledge is hard to structure, transfer, and capture, which leads to knowledge being much harder to manage than data or information.

Knowledge management is a process that allows organizations to generate value from their knowledge-based assets. Knowledge management involves capturing and documenting what employees and other stakeholders know and developing systems

Table 14.1 Characteristics of Data, Information, and Knowledge

Data	Information	Knowledge
Easily structured	Made up of processed data	Hard to structure
Easily captured	Requires unit of analysis	Difficult to capture
Easily transferred	Requires human involvement	Often tacit
Often quantified		Hard to transfer
Made up of mere facts		Information applied to some decision or action

Source: Adapted from Pearlson and Saunders (2006).

that make it easier to share and use that knowledge. Later in this chapter, we discuss the process of knowledge management. Before getting into that, however, we help you understand why knowledge management is important.

Why Managing Knowledge Is Important

Knowledge is among the most important resources of any organization. Recall that knowledge is information directed toward action and decision making. To be successful, organizations must not only effectively manage information, but they must also manage knowledge. Unfortunately, knowledge management is often messy and complex.

Organizations have always managed knowledge. More recently, however, organizations have begun using information and communication technologies to help manage knowledge. Organizations that manage knowledge well make better decisions, are generally more innovative, and tend to be more successful overall than those that do not.

Effective knowledge management can bring about big benefits, including the following:

- Better problem solving
- Improved customer service
- More effective product management
- Increased innovation
- More efficient and more effective processes
- Increased intellectual capital
- Better leveraging of intellectual assets

Types of Knowledge

Understanding more about knowledge will help you better understand important aspects of knowledge management systems. We can divide knowledge into two categories: explicit knowledge and tacit knowledge. **Explicit knowledge** can be expressed relatively easily. Examples include operations manuals, books and articles, scientific formulas, and statistical analysis. Because explicit knowledge can be easily expressed, it can be more easily shared, stored, and managed than our other category of knowledge, tacit knowledge. It may be helpful to think of explicit knowledge as "knowing that," while tacit knowledge is more about "knowing how."

Tacit knowledge is not easy to express or communicate. It is internalized and highly individualized. An individual's tacit knowledge is rooted in life experiences, values, and biases. Ask an artist how to create a beautiful piece of art. The chances are that he or she will have trouble expressing exactly how striking art is created. This is an example of tacit knowledge. The artist may be able to create such art but may not be able to easily communicate the process to you. In fact, sometimes the person who possesses the tacit knowledge may not even be aware that he or she has the knowledge.

Tacit knowledge also exists in more mundane contexts. A good salesperson knows when to close a sale and when to back off. A knowledgeable computer programmer can quickly diagnose an error message. There are examples of tacit knowledge in any organization and in any profession. One of the most interesting examples comes from the world of poultry. Determining the sex of a baby chick immediately after hatching is important for commercial egg producers. Egg producers prefer female chicks, since they will be able to lay eggs. Egg producers employ chicken sexers, who have the uncanny ability to discriminate between female and male chicks with a quick glance. What is interesting about this ability is that most expert chicken sexers cannot tell you how they make their decisions, yet they are very accurate. They have the tacit knowledge but are unable to easily convert this into explicit knowledge. Capturing tacit knowledge and codifying it so that it can be shared is one of the major challenges of knowledge management.

Types of Knowledge Resources

Knowledge is a critical resource for organizations, as we noted earlier. There are different types of knowledge resources in any organization. Understanding these will help you understand knowledge management, which we discuss later. Knowledge resources can be divided into four categories (Nonaka and Takeuchi 1995):

- **Experiential knowledge** resources consist of tacit knowledge that can be shared through common experiences and interpersonal communication. Examples include skills, know-how, and emotional knowledge.

- **Conceptual knowledge** resources are made up of explicit knowledge that is embodied in language, symbols, and images. Concepts for products, services, and designs are examples.

- **Systemic knowledge** resources consist of explicit knowledge that has been systemized and packaged. Knowledge assets in this category are the easiest to share and manage. Intellectual property, such as patents and licenses, documents, and databases are examples.

- **Routine knowledge** resources are made up of the tacit knowledge embedded in the organization's practices. Organizational routines for day-to-day activities and organizational culture are examples of routine knowledge.

Now that you understand more about knowledge and its characteristics, we can turn our attention to how to manage knowledge.

Main Processes for Knowledge Management

A complete knowledge management system should consist of knowledge creation, capture, codification, storage, retrieval, transfer, and application, as shown in Figure 14.1. Knowledge management processes form a cycle. Applying knowledge often leads to the creation of new knowledge, which restarts the cycle. While information technology is not required for any of these, as you will see, IT can facilitate each process in a knowledge management system. In this section, we discuss each of these processes.

Information technology is critical to modern knowledge management, but technology alone cannot ensure effective knowledge management. Effective knowledge management also requires social and structural mechanisms that support knowledge management. For example, a culture of trust can greatly enhance knowledge sharing within an organization. Poor organizational processes and culture can bring about knowledge management failure.

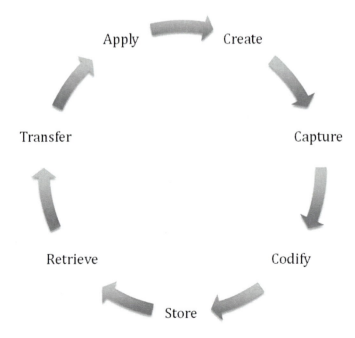

Figure 14.1 Knowledge Management Cycle

Creating Knowledge

While knowledge exists in individuals, organizational knowledge can also be created. Nonaka and Takeuchi (1995) proposed the SECI model of organizational knowledge creation. The model is shown in Figure 14.2. According to the model, knowledge creation is a continuous process consisting of interactions between implicit and explicit knowledge. There are four processes by which knowledge is created:

- *Socialization* involves sharing tacit knowledge through direct communication or shared experience. This is tacit-to-tacit communication.

- *Externalization* is tacit-to-explicit communication. Tacit knowledge is converted to explicit knowledge by developing specific concepts, models, and the like. This conversion allows the knowledge to be understood and interpreted by others. This also serves as a foundation for creating new knowledge.

- *Combination* is the process of combining the externalized explicit knowledge to form broader concepts, models, and theories.

- *Internalization* occurs when explicit knowledge transforms to tacit knowledge and becomes internalized by individuals within the organization. This can start a new cycle, beginning with the socialization of the new tacit knowledge.

These four processes form a cycle of increasing knowledge. Completing one cycle can start a new trip through the four processes, but with an ever-increasing amount of knowledge. This is represented by the spiral in Figure 14.2.

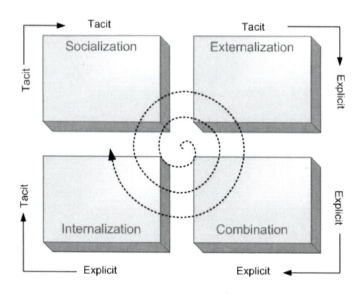

Figure 14.2 SECI Model of Organizational Knowledge Creation

Knowledge can also be "purchased" by hiring knowledgeable individuals as either consultants or employees. Knowledge can also be acquired by purchasing reports or even entire companies. An organization may acquire another company to gain access to the company's knowledge assets.

Capturing and Codifying Knowledge

Once knowledge is created or otherwise acquired, it needs to be captured and codified. There are many techniques for capturing knowledge, including interviewing experts, observing groups as they make decisions, forming focus groups, holding "lessons learned" debriefings, and performing task analysis.

Codifying knowledge means converting tacit and explicit knowledge into a form that organizational members can use. It is representing knowledge so that it can be reused. This also includes documenting knowledge that was previously undocumented. To codify knowledge, organizations should do the following (Davenport and Prusak 1998):

- Define the strategic intent. (How will the codified knowledge serve the organization?)
- Identify the knowledge necessary to achieve the intent.
- Evaluate the existing knowledge's usefulness and ability to be codified.
- Determine the best way to codify and distribute the knowledge.

Codifying knowledge is difficult, but there are tools that can help. Some of these are described below.

Cognitive maps represent the mental model of the expert's knowledge. Key concepts and the relationships among them are shown. Software such as Freemind, MindMeister, and Visio can help document the maps. Figure 14.3 illustrates a cognitive map of Web 2.0 concepts and tools.

Decision tables show a list of conditions and their values along with a list of conclusions or actions. The conditions necessary for each conclusion are indicated. Figure 14.4 shows a decision table for making MBA admission decisions. In each column, Y indicates that the condition was met, while N means that the condition was not met. The X entries indicate the appropriate action.

Decision trees show the alternate paths that impact decisions. The tree shows various paths that can lead to certain outcomes. Here the idea is to use decision trees as a way to document how a decision is made. Figure 14.5 shows a decision tree for making MBA admission decisions.

The purpose of these and other codification tools is to systematically document knowledge that is "stored" in the minds of experts. By working with the experts to create these diagrams and tables, knowledge modelers can help capture and document experts' knowledge. Documenting the knowledge allows us to store, organize, and share the knowledge so that others can use it.

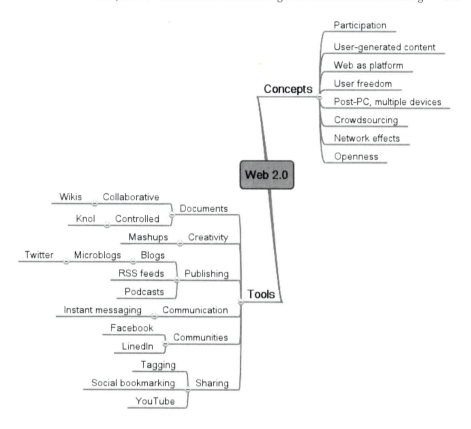

Figure 14.3 Cognitive Map of Web 2.0 Concepts and Tools

The Issue of Trust in Knowledge Management

Managers who want to have good knowledge management systems must work hard to create a culture that rewards rather than punishes knowledge sharing. Knowledge is a critical asset for any business professional. The more useful knowledge you possess, the more valuable you are to the organization. As is the case with any resource, the rarer the knowledge, the more valuable it is. In other words, if you have knowledge that few others have, you are more valuable to the business.

This simple fact can hinder knowledge management. Since sharing knowledge makes it more widespread (less rare), sharing decreases the value of possessing that knowledge. So if you share your knowledge, you become less valuable to the organization. Because of this, trust is important to knowledge management. Experts who possess knowledge must trust that their organization will not unfairly take advantage of the individual who shares the knowledge. If this trust does not exist, the expert may hoard the knowledge to maintain its value.

Condition Stub		Condition Entry						
		1	2	3	4	5	6	7
If (condition)	Applicant has undergraduate degree	Y	Y	Y	Y	Y	Y	N
	Applicant has > 2 years work experience	Y	Y	Y	Y	N	N	
	GMAT > 600	Y	Y	N	N	N	Y	
	Undergraduate GPA > 3.0	Y	N	Y	N	N	Y	
Then (action)	Admit	X						
	Conditionally admit		X		X			
	Advise to retake GMAT			X				
	Decline admission					X	X	X

Figure 14.4 Decision Table Example

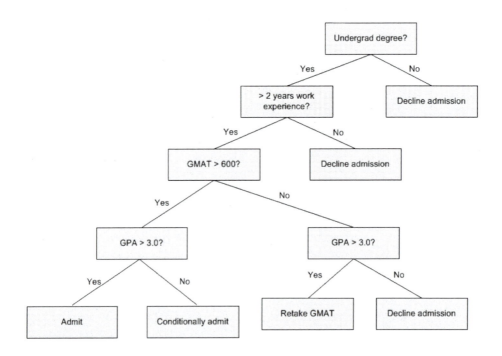

Figure 14.5 Decision Tree Example

Storing and Retrieving Knowledge

Organizing knowledge so that it can be easily accessed is challenging. One reason for this is that knowledge can exist and be documented in many different forms. As a result, there is no single knowledge base for an organization. Knowledge is stored in a variety of forms, including some that you might find surprising. For example, a well-organized corporate directory that lists areas of expertise can be thought of as a knowledge store. Such a directory effectively points to experts who are repositories of knowledge. Document storage systems are also examples of knowledge stores.

Knowledge storage and retrieval are closely interrelated. Even the most well-designed knowledge storage system is ineffective if knowledge consumers cannot retrieve the knowledge. Search technologies are important knowledge retrieval tools. Think about how many times you have used Google or some other search tool to locate knowledge. Accurate, fast search results are a boon to anyone seeking knowledge.

Transferring and Applying Knowledge

Knowledge needs to be applied to be useful, and application implies that knowledge is available to those who need it. Knowledge maps can facilitate knowledge transfer. Knowledge maps show the location of knowledge within the organization. A knowledge map can identify individual experts, networks of experts, or documents and databases.

To manage knowledge transfer, you must consider the sources of knowledge, the media used to transfer the knowledge, and the knowledge consumers. Sources of knowledge include experts, knowledge bases (databases for knowledge), and document repositories. Media may include computer networks and other communication media. Consumers are the individuals and groups that apply the knowledge.

You have engaged in knowledge transfer, even though you may not have realized it. Education is a form of knowledge transfer; your instructor is transferring some of her or his knowledge to you. Have you ever contacted a friend for help on an assignment or project? If so, you used your social network for transferring knowledge.

While humans have always used their social networks to access knowledge, the emergence of social networking technologies is increasing this sort of knowledge transfer. The use of instant messaging in the focusing story is an early example of using software to tap into others' knowledge. New social networking tools make this sort of knowledge transfer even more effective.

LEARNING ACTIVITY 14.2

Wikis for Managing Knowledge

A wiki is a website that allows individuals to jointly create and edit Web pages about a chosen topic using a simple Web-based interface. (You learned about wikis in Chapter 7. See the book's website for a link to a video explaining wikis.) Wikipedia, the online collaborative encyclopedia, is the most popular use of a wiki, but many other wikis exist. Prepare a one-page paper that discusses how a wiki can be used for knowledge management.

Knowledge Management Technologies

Information and communication technologies have helped with knowledge management for a long time. Even the telephone can be used to help individuals tap external knowledge. In this section, we discuss several knowledge management technologies.

Repositories

The goal of **knowledge repositories** is to make it easy to find and retrieve documents that contain knowledge. According to Pearlson and Saunders (2006), there are three main types of knowledge repositories:

- Externally focused knowledge
- Structured internal knowledge, such as research reports and marketing materials
- Informal internal knowledge, such as "lessons learned" reports and discussion databases and frequently-asked-questions collections

Communication-Based Tools

There are many communication-oriented tools for knowledge management. Email is an example. We often email colleagues when we need knowledge that we do not possess. For example, a sales representative may email another sales rep for advice on how to position a certain offering. While email can be effective, you need to know who has the knowledge you need. You also need access to that individual. Social networks can help overcome these limitations. **Communities of practice** that exist within networks are especially helpful. LinkedIn groups are an example. Some of these groups are effectively communities of practice. For example, the group "Technology-Using Professors" is a network of college faculty who are interested in how technology can enhance learning.

Collaboration tools combine elements of repositories and communication-based knowledge management tools. Systems such as Google Docs and Microsoft Share-Point allow for document sharing and coediting. (You may recall that we discussed Google Docs in Chapter 7.)

Some knowledge management experts see a trend from a content-focused view of knowledge management to one that is more connection focused. This means that rather than being centered around the ideas of collecting knowledge, the focus is shifting to tools that help you manage your connections to those who have helpful knowledge. The social networking tools we mentioned earlier are among the technologies that can help you with this form of knowledge management. For example, Stats Box 14.1 provides some statistics for groups in LinkedIn. These groups are good examples of how social networking tools can be used for connection-focused knowledge management.

Executive Information Systems and Dashboards

Executive information systems (EISs) help provide high-level managers with the information they need to monitor business activities and make decisions. EISs typically make heavy use of graphical displays of data. They also tend to have easy-to-use interfaces that let executives quickly access the information they need. Both prebuilt reports and tools for custom queries are important components of an EIS. EISs also give executives the ability to "drill down" into information to access more detailed data when necessary. EISs have evolved to make greater use of the dashboard concept. **Digital dashboards** provide graphical views of key data along with graphical warnings when data indicate areas that need attention. Table 14.2 lists a number of companies that create dashboard products. Visit these to view the various ways visuals are used to present data using dashboard software.

Expert Systems

Expert systems help users solve problems or answer questions in a way that mimics an expert's thought processes. An expert system typically has a narrow focus on a particular problem domain. For example, an insurance company can use an expert system to guide a salesperson through the process of selecting the most appropriate product for a customer. Many organizations use expert systems to guide nonexpert employees through complex decisions or problems such as technical troubleshooting. There

Table 14.2 Dashboard Products

Company	Link
BOARD	http://www.board.com/en/solutions-overview
ClicData	http://www.clicdata.com/dashboards/
Dash	https://www.thedash.com/
IBM	https://www.ibm.com/business-intelligence
iDashboards	https://www.idashboards.com/solutions/
Klipfolio	http://www.klipfolio.com/guide-to-business-dashboards
SAP	https://www.sap.com/products/analytics/business-intelligence-bi.html
Tableau	http://www.tableau.com/solutions/business-dashboards

are also systems for medical self-diagnosis, although these systems should be used with caution, as they do not make a true diagnosis but rather provide probabilities of underlying causes for symptoms.

To close this section, we want to make sure that you understand that all organizations need to manage knowledge, even if they do not have formal knowledge management systems. Managing the knowledge resources of an organization is a critically important aspect of organizational success. While knowledge management is seen by some as an esoteric concept favored only by academics, in our opinion, organizational leaders are well advised to pay more attention to how they manage knowledge.

LEARNING ACTIVITY 14.3

Using a Decision Support System

Pick one of the following decisions and use the associated decision support system (DSS) to help you analyze the decision. (Your instructor may give you a different decision and DSS.)

- What car can you afford? DSS: http://www.edmunds.com/calculators/affordability.html
- Should you trade your "gas guzzler" for a more fuel-efficient vehicle? DSS: http://www.edmunds.com/calculators/gas-guzzler.html
- Should you buy or rent a house? DSS: http://www.realtor.com/mortgage/tools/rent-or-buy-calculator/

Partner with another student and describe your experience using the DSS. Was it useful? Why or why not?

Knowledge is typically applied to some decisions; decision making requires knowledge. While knowledge management technologies are relatively immature, decision support technologies are much more mature in comparison. Decision support systems provide technology tools for helping decision makers deal with the data and information that are necessary for applying knowledge. The next section discusses these tools.

Decision Support Systems and Group Decision Support Systems

Decision support systems (DSSs) are computer-based systems that help decision makers use data and models to solve semistructured or unstructured problems. There are many different types of DSSs, so it is convenient to divide them into categories. Our categories are based on Alter's (1977) and Power's (2001) DSS frameworks (http://www.dssresources.com).

- A **data-driven DSS** focuses on the retrieval and manipulation of data that are stored in an organization's data stores. Data warehouses (which we discuss in the next section) are often important data-driven DSSs. While these DSSs are useful, they do little to guide the decision maker in making the decision. So if the decision maker does not use the data properly, a poor decision is likely. However, in the case of unstructured decisions, a data-driven DSS may be particularly useful because of the amount of data retrieval required.

- A **model-driven DSS** focuses on providing the decision maker with the ability to access and manipulate analytical models. These models are used to help the decision maker perform sophisticated analysis that would be difficult and time-consuming without the DSS. Model-driven DSSs are appropriate for semistructured decisions. Without some degree of structure, it is difficult to build an appropriate model. A model-driven DSS can be applied to decisions in a wide variety of domains, including logistics, portfolio management, demand forecasting, and optimization.

- A **document-driven DSS** focuses on managing and retrieving documents that may help with decision making. The term *documents* should be taken broadly to include chat session transcripts, graphics, and even video and audio files. Document-driven DSSs are particularly useful for less structured decisions. Because there is no analytical aspect of document-driven DSSs, they draw heavily on the decision maker's analytical ability and cognitive models.

- A **communication-driven DSS** facilitates collaboration and group-based decision making. According to Power (2001), communication-driven DSSs support one or more of the following: communication, information sharing, collaboration, and/or group-based decision making. Groupware, which we discuss next, is one type of communication-driven DSS. Email, document sharing, coediting systems (such as Google Docs), and remote meeting systems are other examples.

Groupware is a network-based system that helps workgroups communicate and collaborate. Time and place are often used to categorize groupware. *Synchronous* and *asynchronous* describe whether the users collaborate at the same time (synchronous) or at different times (asynchronous). When group members are in the same physical location, they are colocated. Figure 14.6 uses the dimensions of time and place to categorize common groupware applications, which are described following the figure.

- *Group decision support systems:* Group decision support systems (GDSSs) facilitate group-based decision-making tasks. GDSSs often include applications for brainstorming, anonymous commenting, and voting. The goal of GDSSs is to make group decision making more rational by supporting established group methods that encourage equal participation. Some organizations have "decision rooms," which consist of individual computers that access GDSS software, along with shared devices, such as projection systems. GDSSs can also be used remotely.

	Same time (synchronous)	Different time (asynchronous)
Same place (colocated)	Group decision support systems (decision room), presentation support	
Different place (distant)	Group decision support systems (remote), videoconferencing, chat, remote presentation, shared whiteboards	Discussion databases, email, email lists, workflow, document coediting

Figure 14.6 Groupware Examples

- *Shared whiteboards:* Whiteboards have long been used to help workgroups communicate. You have probably used one yourself. Shared whiteboard systems allow users who are not colocated to share drawings or notes in the same way. Often, shared whiteboard systems assign different colors to each user so that you can tell who is drawing each element.

- *Videoconferencing:* Videoconferencing allows individuals to communicate using both voice and video. Videoconferencing systems range from free services such as Skype that you can access through your personal computer to dedicated rooms that have special equipment and software installed. Capability and quality vary widely from the simple desktop systems to the dedicated videoconferencing rooms.

- *Chat systems:* Online chat systems allow users to write real-time messages in a public space. (Note that we are specifically referring to group-oriented chat systems.) Some systems allow for a moderator to lead the interaction. Many chat systems capture a transcript of a session, which can be useful for documentation purposes.

- *Remote presentation:* Remote presentation software allows noncolocated groups to view a presentation remotely. These systems often have a chat window that allows the presenter and remote audience to interact.

- *Email and email lists:* Email is one of the simplest groupware applications. Most of us have used email to distribute documents or ideas to a group. Email lists facilitate group communication by making broadcasting emails to the group easier. Some systems allow you to subscribe to an email list. These often let you choose whether you want to see each individual message or periodically receive digests of messages that show all messages sent to the group in a single email message.

- *Discussion databases:* Similar to discussion forums, discussion databases store threaded, online, asynchronous discussions in a way that allows users to search and retrieve relevant information. These are different from chat session transcripts in that discussion databases are oriented toward asynchronous discussions.

Discussion databases are particularly useful for new group members who need to come up to speed on the group's discussions.

- *Workflow systems:* Workflow systems route documents through a group in a relatively predetermined manner. Workflow systems ensure that documents are routed properly so that the relevant group members are provided with documents in a timely manner. These systems also make sure that the proper authorities within the group review the documents.

- *Document coediting:* Document coediting systems, which we discussed earlier, help groups with their work by allowing group members to work on documents synchronously rather than having to email documents back and forth (or otherwise share them). These systems also help with versioning by having all members work on the same version of a document. (If you have ever spent time editing the wrong version of a document, you will appreciate the importance of versioning.) While we list document coediting in the "asynchronous" column of Figure 14.6, most systems allow for simultaneous coediting.

It is important to understand that DSSs support decision making. The decision maker's knowledge is still critical to the decision-making process. The DSS provides tools that help the decision maker operate more efficiently and effectively, but the DSS does not replace the decision maker.

Business Intelligence

Organizations are drowning in a sea of information. A major goal of this book is to help you understand how organizations are trying to cope with the ever-increasing amount of information. Managers know that this information potentially represents a gold mine of value but are often unsure how to transform the raw material into an information treasure. Business intelligence (BI) systems may hold the key to unearthing the value of the information.

Business intelligence is set of applications, technologies, and processes for gathering, storing, analyzing, and accessing data to help users make better business decisions. Often, BI combines two sets of technologies, data warehousing and data mining, to help managers leverage the organization's data resources for better decision making. Figure 14.7 illustrates how data warehousing and data mining combine with transactional systems to enable BI.

The goal of BI is to help managers make sense of data. To get to that level, the data first must be generated. Transactional databases "create" the data. (Data may also come from other sources, such as external systems and databases, but most will come from the organization's internal transactional systems.) The data from the transactional databases are put into the data warehouse by a process called extract, transform, and load (E/T/L), which we discuss later. The data warehouse stores and organizes the data in a way that is better suited for supporting decision making.

Figure 14.7 Business Intelligence Framework

Analysts and managers use data mining tools make sense of the data stored in the data warehouse.

Business intelligence tools help many different types of organizations reduce spending and increase sales. BI software helped eHarmony evaluate the effectiveness of their marketing program, causing them to save $5 million by eliminating an affiliate program that only provided low-quality traffic. Toyota used BI tools to save more than $800,000 by eliminating double payments to shippers. American Airlines used BI to save $5 million by detecting fraudulent ticket sales. There are many similar examples (http://www.cio.com/article/2845557/mobile-application -management/business-intelligence-meets-mobility-at-eharmony.html; http:// www.thebusinessintelligenceguide.com/industry_solutions/airline/Amercian _Airlines.php; http://smallbusiness.chron.com/advantages-business-intelligence -24548.html).

Data Warehousing

Data warehouses support decision making. Understanding this is a key to understanding the purpose of data warehousing. Supporting transactions requires that databases perform many data additions, deletions, and updates. Decision support, in contrast, is more about data retrieval. Unfortunately, a database that is very efficient for data updates usually does not perform as well for data retrieval. There is another problem: decision making often requires getting data from multiple transaction databases.

Finally, transaction databases usually store data at a very detailed level. Aggregated data are often better for decision making. So gathering all the data necessary for decision making can be time consuming and inefficient. Data warehousing addresses these issues. Data warehousing is a process, the goal of which is to gain value from an organization's information through the use of data warehouses. A **data warehouse** is a copy of transactional data (and other data) that is formatted so that it is useful for decision support.

Data warehouses have several characteristics that set them apart from transactional databases:

- Data warehouses are subject oriented. They are organized around particular subjects such as marketing, human resources, sales, or production.

- Data in data warehouses are integrated from a variety of internal and external sources.

- Data in data warehouses are typically transformed from their original format. Detailed data are often aggregated. For example, a data warehouse for a restaurant chain would aggregate individual sales into total sales from some time period (such as per hour).

- Data in data warehouses typically are nonvolatile, which means that the data do not change. Once data are in the warehouse, they stay in the warehouse and are not changed. (Data that are no longer of value may be deleted from the warehouse.)

Data from various sources are gathered together, prepared, and loaded into the data warehouse through the extract, transform, load (E/T/L) process, as mentioned earlier. The E/T/L process is easy to understand conceptually but is often very complex and time consuming to perform in practice. Each element is described below.

- *Extract:* Data are pulled from the source systems (such as the transactional databases). Deciding exactly what data to extract is important.

- *Transform:* Data must be changed into a form that is suitable for decision support. Often this involves aggregating detailed data. Data cleansing is also an important part of the transform process. Data in transactional databases are often messy. This problem gets worse when data are extracted from multiple systems. These messy data must be cleaned up before being loaded into the warehouse. Think about all the ways a company such as AT&T could be represented in different databases: AT&T, ATT, American Telephone and Telegraph, American Tel and Tel, AT and T, and so on. All these need to be recognized as the same company; otherwise, you could make decisions based on faulty data. Data cleansing is often complicated and expensive.

- *Load:* The cleaned data needs to be put into the data warehouse. This must be repeated periodically. Figuring out how often data should be loaded can be difficult. It primarily depends on how up to date the data need to be in order to support good decision making. The more time-critical the data, the more frequent the loads.

Once you have the data in the data warehouse, you need to be able to retrieve and analyze in order to gain value from the information. Data mining can help with this.

Data Mining
Data mining is the process of analyzing data to identify trends, patterns, and other useful information. Data mining typically involves applying statistical techniques to identify trends and patterns. Some people consider querying and visualization to be related to data mining. Since we covered those topics in earlier chapters, the focus here is on statistical data mining.

Wouldn't it be nice to be able to predict the future? That is a goal of data mining. Data mining techniques seek to take large amounts of data and form predictions based on the data. There are wide applications of data mining in areas ranging from business to picking players in a pro sports draft. The basic process of data mining is shown in Figure 14.8. Existing data are analyzed using the appropriate data mining

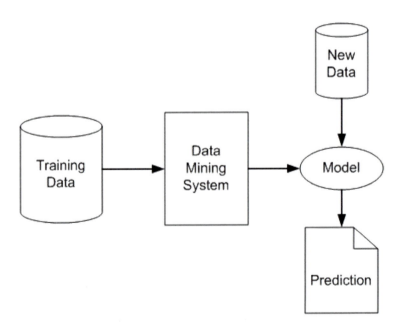

Figure 14.8 High-Level View of Data Mining
Source: Adapted from http://www.thearling.com/dmintro/dmintro_2.htm/.

technique to build a predictive model. The new model is then applied to new data to make a prediction.

While data mining uses many statistical techniques, it is important to understand the difference between traditional statistical analysis and data mining. In most traditional statistical analyses, you create a model (such as a regression equation) and then test that model using data. Essentially, you have a hypothesis and then use data and statistical analysis to test that hypothesis. While this is often effective, it is limited by your knowledge and creativity. You can only test what you can hypothesize. Data mining can help overcome these limitations. In data mining, the emphasis is on discovering the model and then testing the validity of the model. Statistical techniques are used to uncover the relationships in the data that lead to the model. Table 14.3 shows common data mining techniques with descriptions and examples.

Data mining has many applications in business. You may have talked about customer segmentation in a marketing class. Customer groups (segments) can be built through cluster analysis. Cluster analysis divides information into mutually exclusive groups. (Each member can be in at most one group.) The goal is to build the groups so that each member in a group is as close as possible to every other member of the group and the different groups are as different as possible. For example, a hotel chain might use cluster analysis to segment customers into different groups, such as short-stay business customers, vacationers, and long-stay business customers. Advertisements could then be tailored to each of these customers, which should increase the ads' effectiveness. CRM systems can use cluster analysis to customize product or service offerings.

Table 14.3 Common Data Mining Techniques

Technique	Description	Example
Association detection	Discovering patterns in which multiple events are connected	Customers tend to purchase eggs and butter together.
Sequence analysis	Discovering when one event leads to another event	A student graduates from college and then buys a new car.
Classification	Dividing data into mutually exclusive groups based on the variable you want to predict	Students are classified according to whether they are likely to drop out.
Clustering	Dividing data into mutually exclusive groups using all available data (not just the variable you want to predict)	Hotel guests are grouped according to various preferences.
Forecasting	Making predictions using discovered patterns	Past repayment and employment histories predict whether a mortgage applicant will default.

Market basket analysis identifies affinities among customers' product or service offerings. Retailers often use checkout scanner data to identify products that customers tend to buy together. For example, a restaurant might determine that customers who order wine typically buy dessert, while beer drinkers usually buy appetizers. The restaurant could develop special offerings based on this information. Market basket analysis is an example of association detection. Association examines the degree to which variables in a data set are related by considering the frequency with which the variables occur together.

Have you ever played the 20-questions game? If so, you have some familiarity with the concept of decision trees, which are a classification technique. A decision tree makes a prediction based on a series of questions. The next question in the series depends on the answer to the current question. You might have concluded that decision trees are useful devices, since we have discussed them twice in this chapter. Earlier, we discussed decision trees as a method for knowledge capture. Here the focus is on prediction rather than knowledge capture.

There are many other data mining techniques, including statistical methods such as regression analysis, time series analysis, neural networks, and text analysis. As we mentioned earlier, statistical analysis emphasizes testing preexisting models, while data mining tries to discover the models. Many of the same statistical techniques can be applied to both.

Reporting and data visualization tools (discussed in Chapter 6) are also considered by some to be data mining tools. (There is some debate about this.) These tools help you quickly build different views of your data. In some cases, these views are in the form of visualizations, while in other cases, they are built around numbers and text. Spreadsheet pivot tables are an example. Pivot tables allow you to see multidimensional views of a data set. For example, Figure 14.9 shows sales data from a small retail clothing chain. The data in this figure show the total revenue for each store, broken down by state and quarter.

You can quickly modify the dimensions by which you view the data. Suppose you want to add product categories to the analysis. In a matter of seconds, you can modify the pivot table to include the new dimension, as shown in Figure 14.10. (Note that only a portion of the table is shown in the figure.) The flexibility of pivot tables makes them ideal reporting and analysis tools for many common business decisions. You can learn how to build pivot tables in Appendix G.

One important point to keep in mind is that you should always assess whether your model and its predictions are reasonable. Many data mining techniques are based on mathematics; they are all about the numbers. The mathematics does not consider whether the underlying associations have any real meaning. That is where human interpretation and judgment come in.

Sum of Sales revenue	Column Labels				
Row Labels	Q1	Q2	Q3	Q4	Grand Total
⊟ California	1,899,680.30	1,760,147.80	1,930,516.50	1,889,224.70	7,479,569.30
e-Fashion San Francisco	770,502.70	779,742.50	822,383.60	886,011.70	3,258,640.50
e-Fashion San Diego	1,129,177.60	980,405.30	1,108,132.90	1,003,213.00	4,220,928.80
⊟ Colorado	525,682.20	500,076.00	510,776.90	523,740.10	2,060,275.20
e-Fashion Dillion	525,682.20	500,076.00	510,776.90	523,740.10	2,060,275.20
⊟ DC	766,821.70	706,446.60	692,258.20	796,423.40	2,961,949.90
e-Fashion Washington Midtown	766,821.70	706,446.60	692,258.20	796,423.40	2,961,949.90
⊟ Florida	515,687.70	489,997.80	387,809.70	485,663.30	1,879,158.50
e-Fashion Miami Beach	515,687.70	489,997.80	387,809.70	485,663.30	1,879,158.50
⊟ Illinois	846,408.40	850,595.00	610,765.20	714,889.80	3,022,658.40
e-Fashion Chicago Loop	846,408.40	850,595.00	610,765.20	714,889.80	3,022,658.40
⊟ Massachusetts	312,896.40	291,431.00	249,529.00	429,850.20	1,283,706.60
e-Fashion Boston Newbury	312,896.40	291,431.00	249,529.00	429,850.20	1,283,706.60
⊟ New York	1,987,114.70	2,028,090.70	1,672,580.70	1,894,434.50	7,582,220.60
e-Fashion New York 5th	804,084.40	795,193.60	637,277.10	723,811.40	2,960,366.50
e-Fashion New York Midtown	1,183,030.30	1,232,897.10	1,035,303.60	1,170,623.10	4,621,854.10
⊟ Texas	2,875,569.20	2,499,276.80	2,146,302.80	2,596,515.50	10,117,664.30
e-Fashion Dallas	555,458.70	450,588.30	467,925.90	496,061.30	1,970,034.20
e-Fashion Houston	614,284.60	560,650.20	465,677.10	662,570.90	2,303,182.80
e-Fashion DFW	775,482.70	667,850.30	581,470.40	674,869.80	2,699,673.20
e-Fashion Houston Downtown	930,343.20	820,188.00	631,229.40	763,013.50	3,144,774.10
Grand Total	9,729,860.60	9,126,061.70	8,200,539.00	9,330,741.50	36,387,202.80

Figure 14.9 Pivot Table Example

Sum of Sales revenue	Column Labels				
Row Labels	Q1	Q2	Q3	Q4	Grand Total
⊟ California	1,899,680.30	1,760,147.80	1,930,516.50	1,889,224.70	7,479,569.30
⊟ e-Fashion San Francisco	770,502.70	779,742.50	822,383.60	886,011.70	3,258,640.50
2 Pocket shirts	27,876.20	33,324.60	30,122.00	31,773.80	123,096.60
Belts,bags,wallets	49,517.90	40,896.40	17,621.40	29,908.20	137,943.90
Bermudas	994.90		340.30	4,883.40	6,218.60
Boatwear	11,091.60	2,065.60	2,040.30	8,949.70	24,147.20
Cardigan	36,084.10	22,446.50	14,003.60	1,176.40	73,710.60
Casual dresses	4,293.20	4,458.50	12,908.10	5,014.70	26,674.50
Day wear	4,344.90	28,676.30	29,980.00		63,001.20
Dry wear	1,396.10		6,236.20	10,935.60	18,567.90
Evening wear	26,296.00	4,699.80	32,976.70	101,981.50	165,954.00
Fancy fabric	4,758.00	3,607.60	3,646.70	4,964.70	16,977.00
Full length	1,935.50		4,459.90	15,833.50	22,228.90
Hair accessories	4,852.80		3,388.10	7,065.60	15,306.50
Hats,gloves,scarves	66,386.40	24,783.20	19,091.00	3,175.00	113,435.60
Jackets			6,570.00	381.30	6,951.30
Jeans	4,238.70	1,711.80	5,678.80	10,353.60	21,982.90
Jewelry	185,083.10	209,951.90	43,683.00	1,815.20	440,533.20
Long lounge pants	970.80	424.60	5,234.90	7,961.90	14,592.20
Long sleeve	17,300.00	10,490.60	40,848.40	61,425.20	130,064.20
Lounge wear	6,423.70	16,771.60	16,017.80	5,639.40	44,852.50
Mini city	818.00	3,445.20	5,697.80	1,098.40	11,059.40
Night wear			1,837.80	2,846.00	4,683.80
Outdoor	3,151.00	3,503.40	7,544.60	6,310.50	20,509.50
Pants	572.90		1,831.60	946.20	3,350.70
Party pants	8,416.00	14,143.80	59,198.40	4,208.90	85,967.10
Samples	1,022.80	10,618.70	12,960.80	7,878.90	32,481.20

Sheet1 / Report 1

Figure 14.10 Pivot Table with Additional Dimension

Chapter Summary

In this chapter, we discussed knowledge and the processes and tools that help organizations manage knowledge. We also helped you understand technologies that support decision making and that help organizations gain more value from their information resources. Here are the main points discussed in the chapter:

- Knowledge management is a process that allows organizations to generate value from their knowledge-based assets.
- Managing knowledge is important because knowledge is among the most important resources of any organization.
- Explicit knowledge can be easily expressed. Tacit knowledge is difficult to express and communicate.
- The main processes for knowledge management are create, capture, codify, store, retrieve, transfer, and apply.
- Information and communication technologies that facilitate knowledge management include knowledge repositories, communication and collaboration tools, executive information systems, dashboards, and expert systems.
- Decision support systems are computer-based systems that help decision makers use data and models to solve semistructured or unstructured problems.
- Business intelligence is a set of applications, technologies, and processes for gathering, storing, analyzing, and accessing data to help decision makers.
- Data warehouses and data mining systems are important business intelligence components.
- Data warehouses store and organize data for decision support.
- Data mining is the process of analyzing data to identify trends, patterns, and other useful information.

Review Questions

1. Briefly explain how knowledge and information differ in the terms of ease of management and the level of human contribution.
2. Why is managing knowledge important to organizations?
3. State five benefits of effective knowledge management.
4. Contrast explicit and tacit knowledge.
5. Give an example of tacit knowledge.
6. Name and briefly describe the four types of knowledge resources described in the chapter.
7. Name the processes in the knowledge management cycle.

8. Briefly describe the four knowledge creation processes in the SECI model.

9. What is knowledge codification? Why is it important to knowledge management?

10. Compare and contrast decision tables and decision trees.

11. Explain why search technologies are important to knowledge management.

12. Give an example of each of the following: a knowledge repository and a communication-based knowledge management tool.

13. What is a digital dashboard?

14. Name and briefly describe the DSS categories described in the chapter.

15. Compare and contrast synchronous and asynchronous groupware.

16. Name and briefly describe the groupware examples discussed in the chapter.

17. What are the two main components of a business intelligence system? Briefly describe each component.

18. Describe the E/T/L process.

19. What is the purpose of data mining?

20. Name three data mining techniques.

Reflection Questions

1. What is the most important thing you learned in this chapter? Why is it important?

2. What topics are unclear? What about them is unclear?

3. What relationships do you see between what you learned in this chapter and what you have learned in earlier chapters?

4. The chapter focused on organizational knowledge management, but knowledge management is also important to individuals. (This is called personal knowledge management.) Why is knowledge management important to your personal and professional development?

5. Have you ever tried to explain to someone how you are able to do something (hit a golf ball, draw, study, etc.)? Was it easy or hard to explain? What about the knowledge you were trying to transfer determined whether it was easy or hard to explain?

6. In Chapter 7, you learned about cloud computing. How can cloud computing facilitate knowledge management?

7. How does data warehousing facilitate data mining?

8. What is the relationship between business intelligence and knowledge management?

9. How is the need for quick decisions related to the need to make ethical decisions?

Additional Learning Activities

14.A1. Describe a situation in which you used technology to access knowledge. Address the following in your description: What knowledge were you seeking? How did you go about finding the knowledge? What technologies did you use? How effective were they?

14.A2. Form groups of two or three.

　　 a. One of you (the explainer) will answer the following question: Why is knowledge management important to organizational success?

　　 b. When the first person finishes, the other person (the questioner) will seek clarification and provide her or his own ideas.

　　 Record and be prepared to share your answers.

14.A3. Some music services, including Pandora and iTunes, can build smart playlists that use the songs in your library (or playlists) to build playlists that you will like. Research how these services work and prepare a one-page paper on how these services relate to the data mining tools you read about in this chapter.

14.A4. Create a decision table or decision tree to document how you go about making the following decisions:

　　 a. Deciding whether to take a class

　　 b. Deciding which section of a class to take

　　 c. Deciding on a major

　　 d. Deciding whether to join a club

14.A5. Partner with two other students. Create a wiki on how to choose which section of a multisection class to take. You can use Wikispaces (http://www.wikispaces.com), PK Works (http://pbworks.com), or any other wiki service to create your wiki. Be prepared to share your wiki with the class.

14.A6. Research how companies are using data mining. Pick one example and prepare a one- to two-page report on how the company used data mining.

References

Alter, S. 1977. "Why Is Man-Computer Interaction Important for Decision Support Systems?" *Interfaces* 7(2): 109–15.

Davenport, T., and L. Prusak. 1998. *Working Knowledge: How Organizations Manage What They Know.* Boston, MA: Harvard Business School Press.

Nonaka, I., and H. Takeuchi. 1995. *The Knowledge Creating Company.* New York: Oxford University Press.

Pearlson, K., and C. Saunders. 2006. *Managing and Using Information Systems.* 3rd ed. Hoboken, NJ: John Wiley & Sons.

Power, D. 2001. "Supporting Decision-Makers: An Expanded Framework." In *E-Proceedings of the Informing Science Conference,* Krakow, Poland, edited by A. Harriger, June 19–22: 431–36.

Glossary

Business intelligence (BI): A set of applications, technologies, and processes for gathering, storing, analyzing, and accessing data to help users make better business decisions.

Codifying knowledge: Converting tacit and explicit knowledge into a form that organizational members can use.

Cognitive map: A graphical representation of a mental model of an expert's knowledge.

Communication-driven decision support system: A DSS that facilitates collaboration and group-based decision making.

Community of practice: A group of people who share a common interest, usually in a craft or profession, and who interact to share knowledge.

Conceptual knowledge: Explicit knowledge that is embodied in language, symbols, and images.

Data-driven decision support system: A DSS that focuses on the retrieval and manipulation of data that is stored in an organization's data stores.

Data mining: The process of analyzing data to identify trends, patterns, and other useful information to make predictions.

Data warehouse: A copy of transactional data (and other data) that is formatted so that it is useful for decision support.

Decision support systems (DSS): Computer-based systems that help decision makers use data and models to solve semistructured or unstructured problems.

Decision table: A list of conditions and their values along with a list of conclusions or actions.

Decision tree: A diagram that shows alternate paths that impact decisions.

Digital dashboards: Computer-based systems that provide graphical views of key data along with graphical warnings when data indicate areas that need attention.

Document-driven decision support system: A DSS that facilitates the management and retrieval of documents that may help with decision making.

Executive information systems (EISs): Information systems that help provide high-level managers with the information they need to monitor business activities and make decisions.

Experiential knowledge: Tacit knowledge that can be shared through common experiences and interpersonal communication.

Expert systems: Systems that help users solve problems or answer questions in a way that mimics an expert's thought processes.

Explicit knowledge: Knowledge that can be expressed relatively easily.

Groupware: A network-based system that helps workgroups communicate and collaborate.

Knowledge management: The process by which organizations create, capture, store, apply, and protect knowledge to achieve organizational objectives.

Knowledge repositories: Tools that make it easy to find and retrieve documents that contain knowledge.

Model-driven decision support system: A DSS that provides the decision maker with the ability to access and manipulate analytical models.

Routine knowledge: Tacit knowledge that is embedded in the organization's practices.

Systemic knowledge: Explicit knowledge that has been systemized and packaged.

Tacit knowledge: Internalized and highly individualized knowledge that is difficult to express or communicate.

Index

Page numbers followed by *f* and *t* refer to figures and tables, respectively.